EDUCATION OF THE SPANISH-SPEAKING URBAN CHILD

A Book of Readings

By

EARL J. OGLETREE

Associate Professor of Education
Chicago State University
Chicago, Illinois

and

DAVID GARCIA

Coordinator, Career Opportunities Program
Chicago Board of Education
Chicago, Illinois

CHARLES C THOMAS · PUBLISHER
Springfield · Illinois · USA

Published and Distributed Throughout the World by
CHARLES C THOMAS • PUBLISHER
Bannerstone House
301-327 East Lawrence Avenue, Springfield, Illinois, U.S.A.

© 1975, by CHARLES C THOMAS • PUBLISHER
ISBN 0-398-03335-8
Library of Congress Catalog Card Number: 74-19419

With THOMAS BOOKS careful attention is given to all details of
manufacturing and design. It is the Publisher's desire to present books that are
satisfactory as to their physical qualities and artistic possibilities and
appropriate for their particular use. THOMAS BOOKS will be true to those
laws of quality that assure a good name and good will.

Printed in the United States of America
C-1

Library of Congress Cataloging in Publication Data

Ogletree, Earl J.   comp.
Education of the Spanish-speaking urban child.

Bibliography: p.
1. Spanish Americans in the United States—Education.
I. Garcia, David, 1932-   joint comp. II. Title.
LC2669.035   371.9'7'68073   74-19419
ISBN 0-398-03335-8

CONTRIBUTORS

Patricia G. Adkins, Director, Education Professions Development, Region XIX Education Service Center, El Paso, Texas.

Samuel Betances, Publisher of *The Rican* and Professor of Sociology, Northeastern University, Chicago.

Peter Born, Editor, reporter and writer for *The Chicago Tribune.*

Nelson Brooks, Associate Professor of French, Yale University.

Thomas P. Carter, Dean, College of Education, Sacramento State College, Sacramento, California.

Edward Casavantes, Psychologist and Deputy Chief of the Mexican American Studies Division of the U. S. Commission on Civil Rights.

Frances Castan, Assistant Editor of *Scholastic Teacher.*

Francesco Cordasco, Professor of Education, Montclair State College and Educational Consultant, Migration Division, Commonwealth of Puerto Rico.

Juan Cruz, Department of Human Relations, Chicago Board of Education.

J. Michael Davis, Assistant Director, Cuban Teacher Program, School of Education, University of Miami.

Marion L. Dobbert, Instructor, Aurora College, Aurora, Illinois.

Diane M. Drake, Assistant Professor of Child Development, University of Wisconsin, Madison, Wisconsin.

H. John Van Duyne, Assistant Professor of Educational Psychology, Northern Illinois University.

Jack Forbes, Associate Professor of History, University of Nevada, Reno, Nevada.

v

Minerva Mendoza-Friedman, Teacher and School Psychologist, San Francisco Public Schools.

Bruce A. Gaarder, U. S. Office of Education.

Ray Gurule, Chairwoman, Textbook Task Force, Mexican-American Education Commission, Los Angeles, California.

Glenn L. Hendricks, Assistant Professor of Anthropology and Director, Student Life Studies, University of Minnesota.

Neal Justin, Assistant Professor of Education, College of Education, Florida Atlantic University.

Jeffrey W. Kobrick, Attorney at the Harvard Center for Law and Education.

Guy J. Manaster, Professor of Education, University of Texas.

Ruth H. Mattila, Professor of Education, New Mexico Highlands University.

Luiz F. S. Natalicio, Professor of Psychology, Dept. of Educational Psychology, University of Texas.

Henry M. Ramirez, Chairman of the Cabinet Committee on Opportunities for Spanish-Speaking People.

Diego Rangel, Administrator for the Chicago Board of Education.

Jerome R. Reich, Professor of History, Chicago State University.

George R. Ricks, Director, Department of Human Relations, Chicago Board of Education.

Harry Rivlin, Professor of Education, School of Education at Lincoln Center, Fordham University.

Ron Rodgers, Education writer for the Lerner Newspapers, Chicago.

Armando Rodriguez, Chief, Office for the Spanish-Speaking, U. S. Office of Education.

Muriel R. Saville, Assistant Professor of Curriculum and Instruction, University of Texas, Austin, Texas.

Ozzie G. Simmons, Professor and Director of Behavioral Sciences, University of Colorado.

Richard L. Tobin, Managing Editor of *Saturday Review*.

Lawrence Wright, free lance and staff writer for the *Race Relations Reporter*.

Perry Alan Zirkel, Assistant Professor of Education, University of Hartford.

INTRODUCTION

THE SCHOOLS AND THE SPANISH-SPEAKING
URBAN CHILD

THE EDUCATIONAL PROBLEMS confronting the Spanish-speaking urban child have reached the critical level of the black inner-city child. in the 1960's. The inequalities that both minority groups endure are similar. For example:

The 1973 *Manpower Report of the President* shows that the typical Spanish adult has 9.6 years of schooling, compared to 9.8 for blacks and 12.1 for the total adult population. The median annual income of Spanish families is $7,500 as compared to $6,400 for blacks and $10,700 for Anglos. However, much of the literature on the minority child assumes that the problems of the black and Spanish-speaking have equal solutions. In some instances this is true. The Spanish-speaking, however, have different and unique problems which call for unique solutions. One could also state that it is not the Spanish-speaking who have the problem, but the Spanish-speaking have problems caused by the anglo-society.

It is, however, a misnomer to classify Spanish-speaking in one stereotyped, single group just as it is to classify blacks and whites in a single category. Just as whites have their origin in different nationalities, ethnic groups and cultures, so do the Spanish-speaking. Manaster indicates there are five or six different basic Spanish-speaking groups:

> I come to five or six groups. The Cubans as one, the Puerto Ricans— permanent and temporary, as they consider themselves, and the Mexicans into two, three or four groups—those of Texas, particularly the valley, the New Mexico-Arizona group, the California group and the Mexican-Americans in the North. And this does not regard migrant laborers and families as a separate group.[2]

Country of origin, time and location in the United States, goals and intentions are fairly critical factors describing the Spanish-speaking as a minority group.

Nevertheless, the basic problems common to many black and Spanish-speaking groups are poor housing, poor jobs, poor food, poor education, poor governmental representation and defacto segregation. The Spanish-speaking have the additional problems of English language deficiencies and cultural differences.

Historically the school has been relied upon as the major formal socialization agency for the social mobility of immigrants and the poor. The role of the school as a "melting pot" and social class equalizer has been a myth. It is ancient history that the public schools have not been able to educate the poor or culturally different. The high school dropout rate has not changed appreciably over the past fifty years.[3] The great public school legend has not lived up to its tradition of equal opportunity for all children.

One major factor is the schools are middle-class institutions, charged to teach a common language, work habits, political faith, national faith and the values of the dominant culture. Increased industrialization and the manifold technological advances have made the schools a formal socialization agency of society. At one time the extended family was able to train (educate) their offspring for occupations. With industrialization came economic demands not met by the family process; the result was a destruction of the extended family, increased population shifts to the cities and changing social and work values. The school became the place where one had to learn new social and economic values. Educational institutions began teaching work relations, ethics, and the morality of working for rewards. In short, the schools began serving specific aspects of society, basically industry. For example, the school leaving age was not increased wholly for academic reasons but for economic expediency. As the unskilled job market decreased, the school leaving age increased. In 1917 the school leaving age was raised from twelve to fourteen years and in 1925 from fourteen to sixteen years to keep the young jobless off the job market. The schools were expected to fill the gap between the number of potential workers and the number of available jobs. The school facilities were overcrowded and the curriculum was "stretched." As a result, both the quality and quantity of the academic work required was reduced considerably.

Even today we add layers of education stretching from grammar school to college, piling more on top of what we already have. As Greer states: "When we reevaluate we change a few things to keep the rest pretty much the same. . . . Every time we add a new level we contribute to the mistaken belief that schooling beneath that (added) level must be working well since, after all, it seems to be successfully preparing students for more advanced work (or levels)."[4] Often the new layer means stretching . . . "out the process of failure."

Historically, the role of the schools was thought to be the most important socializing agency in terms of socio-economic mobility. Gans writes in the preface of Colin Greer's recent book, *The Great School Legend:* "The legend has it, that once upon a time the public school was an effective antipoverty agency, that took poor immigrant children and taught them so well that eventually they became affluent Americans."[5] Colin Greer sets out to show that the legend does not coincide with reality. In fact the reverse was true; large numbers of poor children failed and were forced out of school early in their academic career. This was true of all ethnic groups—Jews, Polish, Greeks, Italians and so forth. Greer so aptly emphasizes that if the great school legend and the public schools were as effective an agency for social regeneration as they are believed to be, why aren't the following factors observable in the wider society:

1) Why aren't the blacks and other minority groups, after a number of generations assimilated into the middle class culture?

2) Why aren't Puerto Ricans and blacks, the new migrants moving wholesale across the cities they live in and out into the suburbs?

3) Why aren't the schools providing equal opportunities and treatment in terms of children's socioeconomic, ethnic and cultural background in a broad sense?[6]

Greer maintains that in the past, poor people did not succeed socially or economically through the schools, but, on the contrary, they first succeed economically outside of the educational institutions. Then the new middle-class parents exerted pressure on their children, the teachers and the schools to make sure their children would succeed in school. In other words, as also implied in the Coleman report, economic success preceded academic success. The Jews, Scandanavians and Greeks each developed a middle-class economic base in their ethnic community. Then they established themselves in the dominant middle-class culture.

Greer's theory is supported by the fact that those children, whose familial socioeconomic background and experiences are most like those that the schools embrace, succeed in the educational process. It is well known that:

> 1) School achievement is positively related to social class and cultural status.
>
> 2) Parents with more education, income and higher status jobs produce children who perform better in school.
>
> 3) The more the child is like what the school expects, the better he will achieve.

These statements probably hold true for the Spanish-speaking as well. The higher the social status of the Mexican, Puerto Rican or Cuban the faster he becomes acculturized and Americanized and the better his children will do in school as compared to children whose families have not been Americanized to the same degree. This includes the learning and acceptance of Anglo middle-class standards and mores, which does not preclude such factors as parental aspirations and the language spoken at home. Greer's viewpoint on the effectiveness of the schools may be somewhat extreme. There are many factors that influence the achievement of children, the least of which is the school. The four major influences are: 1) the person's biological equipment, aspirations and expectations, 2) the socioeconomic and educational level of the family, 3) the geographic location, socioeconomic and ethnic composition of the community and, 4) the quality of the school. The first three factors are the most influential being the primary socializing agency and milieu. The school has the least influence being a secondary socializing agency. While it is true that the schools have not been able to bring the achievement average of poor children up to the national average, nevertheless some children of the poor have done well in the schools.

The "reflective or mirror theory" of the schools to society has given birth to the "cultural deprivation" theory. Explicit in this theory is that some children are culturally or socially deprived because their culture (racial, ethnicity, social class, etc.) groups do not provide the necessary familial, social and educational experiences to succeed in school or to take their place in the majority culture, the middle class. Like other minority groups, the Latino community has an uphill struggle to overcome ignorance of and prejudice against their culture. It is out of this ignorance that the anglo-society has developed a clearly preconceived but erroneous stereotype of the Latino and misconceived ideas of the group personality. Ignorance, prejudice and lack of mobility has led to educational segregation. The urban mileau has intensified economic, social and racial segregation of the population. Schools are ethnically and socially out of balance in urban areas because housing patterns continue to influence the placement of new schools and boundaries within which children must live to attend them, hence compounding the problem.

Greer views the problem of low achievement of poor children as related to segregation: "One major result in schools is the segregation of lower-class boys and girls into elementary and secondary schools where they are exposed only to other children of similar socioeconomic status (and cultural origin)."[7] The Coleman Report implied that integration influenced school achievement. Carter, on the other hand, points out:

> American educators, pressed to explain the failure in school of low-status and minority-group children, rely heavily on the theory of "cultural deprivation." The fault is seen to lie in the socialization afforded by the home and neighborhood, and it is assumed that the child must be changed, not society or its educational institutions.[8]

It has been observed that in case after case, the public school officials pretend, despite statistical evidence on the schools' failure with the disadvantaged, that it was individual children, not schools, that failed. Carter states that what is needed is a "radical modification of the school to eliminate factors discouraging the success of minority-group children. . . ."[9] The schools must adapt their programs and methods to the child rather than attempting to "fit the child" into a strait-laced curriculum. It is the duty of the schools to recognize the influences of culture on personality and development; teachers and administrators should have a good understanding of the cultures of the Spanish-speaking; and understand the function of the school as it relates to the culturally-different community.

It is recognized that cultural as well as social class differences give birth to patterns and content of thought. Whorf claims that one's language determines one's cognitive style and knowledge.[10] That is to say, the world is seen and understood differently according to the different languages spoken. Since one's experiences are affected by the languages, the cognitive styles may differ between different ethnic groups. For example, Lesser studied the cognitive abilities of Chinese, Jewish, Puerto Rican and Negro children.[11] He found that Jewish children scored highest in verbal skills, and Negroes and Puerto Ricans scored lower than Jewish and Chinese children in the four areas of verbal, reasoning, number and spatial. In the case of Puerto Rican children, their best ability was verbal, spatial was second, and number and reasoning in that order. Lesser's study also showed that middle-class children in each ethnic group scored higher than their lower-class peers. As to why there is a difference in abilities and ethnic group must adapt to an environment which is in some respects unique and distinct and, therefore, requires a unique pattern of mental abilities. Or as Whorf indicates, the difference in cognitive style is the result of language difference. Does the difference really matter? Ginsberg doesn't think so:

> It will benefit us little to simply tabulate the number of problems on which middle and lower class (and different group), children are correct or incorrect. We should save wasted effort by attempting to measure instead the types of reasoning that both kinds of children employ . . . much theory concerning poor children's thinking is often misleading and incorrect.[12]

Ginsberg's theory may be correct for English-speaking disadvantaged children, but the Spanish-speaking child has a compounded problem, a foreign language. Perez states: "Our children continue to be tested in English and are classified as stupid because they can't understand the test itself. To compound the problem, testing itself is often delayed years."[13] This leads to stereotyping Spanish-speaking children as low intelligence and poor school performers. The use of cultural-biased tests, overdependency on the IQ score, and the placement of a disproportionate percentage of Latinos in slow or special education classes simply perpetuates the "self-fulfilling prophecy."

Other educators view the problem as more basic than specific educational paraphernalia. Greer feels that the problem does not rest with the tests, but in the rigidity of the schools:

> The schools are more culture-bound than any of our most vociferously denounced tests, culture-bound in the sense that they present a different and more threatening set of cultural norms than those many of the children have experienced, but in the sense that the schools project and impose deadening conventions.[14]

The public schools are unable to adopt to their curriculum methods even on a broad scale, let alone to a specific community or group.

For the Spanish-speaking the problem of bilingualism is a crucial issue as much as it relates to school achievement. Only about three out of four adults of Spanish origin can speak English, whereas it is nine out of ten for children and adolescents.[15] When you calculate that there are at least ten million people of Spanish-speaking backgrounds in the United States it constitutes at least several million who do not speak English. However, these statistics say nothing of the quality or level of understanding of the English language. In 1970 in New York City alone, there were 105,482 Spanish-speaking children who were classified as having a language difficulty.[16] In addition there are 150,000 Puerto Rican students who qualify as English-speaking although their knowledge of English is only functional. "Most of these have difficulty with the English language, but they are put into regular classrooms—where too often their English language problems are not responded to, and their use of Spanish is discouraged and eventually forgotten."[17] In Chicago there are approximately 67,952 (1974 figures) Latino school children whose primary language is Spanish.[18]

On the other hand, there is the linguistic problem of monolingualism vs. bilingualism. The majority of educators believe that bilingualism as compared to monolingualism interferes with school learning. Although there are more studies indicating learning being hampered by bilingualism, nevertheless there are a smaller number, but significant, research studies demonstrating no adverse effects of bilingualism on school learning. Another problem in language development is that many poor Latino children are alingual, possessing neither the language ability in Spanish nor English to succeed in school. They possess a "restricted" as opposed to a "standard" language development. However, there is some question as to whether the lower socioeconomic, restricted language (English or Spanish) is really so different from standard language to affect school performance. It goes without saying that the inability to communicate in English will have a deleterious effect on school achievement and grade promotion. Consequently, educators are learning that it may be easier and more effective in the long run to change the school's language instead of the child's. Research studies and educational programs have shown that children learn better when taught in their native language. Special classes in English have, in the main, been a failure because the child is soon returned to the regular classroom knowing only a smattering of English. He knows enough to get by sometimes but nowhere near enough to deal intelligently with the regular curriculum. His Spanish is inhibited and his English is sketchy. He becomes illiterate in two languages.[19] A study done in the Philippines suggested that teaching school subjects in the native language or through a bilingual approach was more effective than teaching school content in a foreign language—English: ". . . initial instruction in the child's vernacular during the first school year with a gradual shift to English during the second school year does not retard the later learning of English and does contribute to a better adjustment of the pupil."[20]

Title VII of the Elementary and Secondary Education Act has provided for Bilingual Education Programs. During 1972, the U. S. Office of Education funded 217 bilingual demonstration

---

NOTE: There are approximately 360 Bilingual Projects funded under Title VII of the ESEA serving 246,000 children, costing $68.22 million to $100 million.

programs, located in 34 states, serving approximately 100,000 children.[21] Some of the programs are bicultural as well as bilingual. Although the bilingual programs are not a panacea, they do appear to eliminate some of the problems related to school learning. Margolis reports some recent findings on the effectiveness of the programs. At a demonstration school in Hoboken, N. J., Latino first graders ". . . are learning at a faster rate than comparable children in English classrooms."[22] The bilingual programs appear to be effective at the junior high school level as well:

> In a three year study of Spanish-speaking junior high school students . . . it was found that those who were taught in Spanish performed better than those who were taught science in English. The first group also scored higher on a city-wide (New York), reading test and displayed a more positive attitude toward self and background culture.[23]

In spite of the 360 bilingual programs, bilingual education is underfinanced and understaffed. Even with additional funding, the shortage of qualified bilingual teachers is, in many ways, a more critical problem. In Chicago, for example, 20,425 of a total of 67,952 Spanish-speaking students are getting bilingual training and 636 bilingual teachers and coordinators are available to service the students (according to 1974 data).[24] One solution to the bilingual teacher shortage is to change the Board of Education certification requirements to certify bilingual teachers certified in Latin countries to teach in American urban schools.

Those close to the problems of the education of the Spanish-speaking urban child feel that it is imperative that the school system respond to this crisis with greater effort than heretofore has been the case. It goes without saying that present programs are inadequate and fail to meet the increasing exigencies of the Spanish-speaking child.

Alloway and Cordasco consider education as the root cause of unemployment and unwholesome environment. "Until educational deficiencies are relieved, the problem of inadequate employment and unwholesome environment will continue to defy solution."[25] However, Greer sees the solution as one of economics first, environment second and education last. Only when poverty is eliminated through the creation of decent, secure, and well-paying jobs for the unemployed and underemployed, thus creating a "generation of economically secure graduates from poverty, will it be possible for the public schools to do the job intended. Perhaps there is a middle-road in which the three E's (education, employment and environment) can be reviewed, rehabilitated and realigned simultaneously.

Perhaps a partial solution is to allow "culture inclusion," the integration of the history, culture and language associated with the Latino child's heritage into the school. This means the abolishment of the "no Spanish rule" and the inflexibility in the curriculum and employment of teachers, who are not only interested in the Latino Community, but have knowledge of and experience with the culture and history of the Spanish-speaking. In this way educators will have an appreciation and understanding of the effects of the Mexican, Puerto Rican and Cuban cultures on the personality and behavior of Spanish-speaking children. They will better understand the role of the school vis-à-vis the particular Latino Community and, perhaps, effect a positive change in the education and life of Spanish-speaking students. It could perhaps bring about a much needed marriage between the school and the community.

This volume explores the unique educational problems confronting the Spanish-speaking urban child. The volume is divided into nine sections: Section I, "Cultural Heritage, Immigration and Migration: A Profile," includes a selection of articles that reflect the unique cultural and heritage backgrounds of the Mexican-American, Cuban and Puerto Rican population. The readings explicate how their divergent values, mores and attitudes, are both congruent and incongruent with the anglo-American culture. This section also discusses the plight of the Mexican-American migrant farm workers and the socioeconomic inequalities they confront as less than "second-class citizens." The problems rooted in prejudice and discrimination are also those of the Puerto Rican and Cuban population as they struggle for equality and opportunity in housing, employment and education.

Section II, "Problems of Segregation and Integration," is concerned with the effects of race and color on integration and culture assimilation. Race and color, fostered by the Anglo's bias of the inferiority of darker skinned persons, is as a pervading factor in discrimination as social class and language. Questions of racial and cultural pluralism are raised concerning social isolation, "tribalization" and ethnic tensions between the Spanish-speaking groups. Does emphasis on cultural and ethnic differences facilitate or retard the process of dominant culture assimilation?

Section III, "Expectation and Self-Concept: A Profile," examines the problems of self-identity of Latino children in the anglo-culture dominated urban schools. The Latino child, stereotyped with the "culture deprivation" label, the "folk-culture" concept and "second class citizenship" has an up-hill battle to sustain and, in some cases, to rebuild his self-image.

Section IV, "The Schools and the Spanish Speaking," deals with the problems of the effectiveness and meaning of schools for the poor and the culturally different. Cordasco in "The Challenge of the Non-English Speaking Child in American Schools," contends that the Spanish-speaking child is not unlike the child of poverty of past eras. Therefore it is necessary for the schools to build on the cultural strengths which the child brings to the classroom; "to cultivate in him ancestrial pride." The additional articles discuss program development and recommendations, which include bilingual-bicultural programs, community and school adjustment, curriculum changes, differential staffing and teacher retraining programs.

Section V, "Problems of Language and Learning: A Challenge," explores the effects of language on school achievement. The articles explore factors influencing English language acquisition and development. Saville in "Interference Phenomena in English Teaching," categorizes three levels of interference phenomena—linguistic, psychological and educational. Duyne and Gutierrez in "The Regulatory Function of Language in Bilingual Children," found that bilingual children, five to seven years of age, acquired linguistic understanding and stability in Spanish before they do in English, indicating a regulatory, sequential function of two languages in bilingual children. Rodgers and Rangel in "Learning for Two Worlds," discuss a successful bilingual program for Puerto Ricans in Chicago.

Section VI, "Achievement and Intelligence: Cultural Influences," examines the controversial issue leading to the stereotyping of Spanish-speaking children as low intelligence and poor performers. The use of cultural-biased tests, overdependence on the IQ score, and the placement of a disproportionate percentage of Latinos in slow or special education classes perpetuate the "self-fulfilling prophecy."

Section VII, "Bilingual-Bicultural Education: A Necessity," defines bilingualism and explores the pros and cons and the future of bilingual programs. Reich and Reich in "On Bilingual Education," suggest six models for teaching non-English speaking children academic subjects. Dobbert in "Bilingual Education—No! Bicultural Education—Yes!," analyzes the limitations of bilingual programs. She rationalizes that bicultural programs deal with more than just language differences, but include their cultural heritage and differences and life style. Bilingual programs are only a partial solution, whereas bicultural programs teach the whole child.

Section VIII, "Reshaping Teacher Education for the Spanish-Speaking Child," is concerned with the preparation of teachers and the modification of inservice programs. Any teacher training program designed to work with the Spanish-speaking should deal with effects of culture on personality, behavior, the historical and cultural background of the Spanish-speaking, and the role of school vis-à-vis the Latino community.

Section IX, "Educational and Social Issues," examines a variety of topics such as the continual struggle for socioeconomic and educational equalities in an anglo-dominated culture, the cultural and linguistic dissonance in the public schools, the biased-nature of and historical distortions in textbooks.

This text will be particularly useful in foundation, sociology of education, urban education, urban child and teacher preparation courses at the undergraduate and graduate level. Perhaps more important it is hoped that this book will find its way into the hands of administrators and teachers, who are responsible for the education of Spanish-speaking children.

One of the editors (Ogletree) would especially like to thank the following teachers and graduate students for their inspiration to develop this volume and for their contributions and evaluations of a number of articles that have and have not been included in this volume: Lucia Barba, Bethsaida Colm, Carmen Diaz, Anselma Fuentas, Vilma Guzman, John Marquez, Aedo Molina, Josefina Mounts, Margarita O'Ferral, Carmen Rivera, Felix Rodriguez, Juanita Rodriguez, Carlos Rosa and Elba Vazquez.

EJO

DG

We particularly extend our appreciation to the authors and publishers who gave us permission to include their articles in this volume.

REFERENCES

1. *1972 Manpower Report of the President,* Washington, D. C.: U. S. Government Printing Office.
2. Manaster, Guy J.: *Letter,* December 12, 1973.
3. Greer, Colin: Public schools: the myth of the melting pot, *Saturday Review,* November 15, 1969, p. 86.
4. ———: *The Great School Legend,* New York, Viking Press, 1973, p. 5.
5. ———: *The Great School Legend,* New York, Viking Press, 1973, p. vii.
6. ———: *The Great School Legend,* New York, Viking Press, 1973, pp. 23-24.
7. ———: *The Great School Legend,* New York, Viking Press, 1973, p. 28.
8. Carter, Thomas: Mexican Americans in School: *A History of Educational Neglect,* New York, College Entrance Examination Board, 1970, p. 60.
9. ———: Mexican Americans in School: *A History of Educational Neglect,* New York, College Entrance Examination Board, 1970, p. 60.
10. Whorf, B. L.: A linguistic consideration of thinking in primitive communities, *Language, Thought and Reality,* ed. J. B. Carroll, Mass., MIT Press, 1968, pp. 25-72.
11. Lesser, G. S., Fifer, G., and Clark, D. H.: Mental abilities of children from different social-class and cultural groups, *Monograph of the Society for Research in Child Development,* 1965, 30 (Series No. 102).
12. Ginsberg, Herbert: *The Myth of the Deprived Child,* Englewood Cliffs, Prentice-Hall, Inc., 1972, p. 122.
13. Perez, Patricia: A program for Latin educators, *United Teachers of Chicago,* May 1973, p. 4.
14. Greer, Colin: *The Great School Legend,* New York, Viking Press, 1973, p. 5.
15. *1972 Manpower Report of the President,* Washington, D. C., U. S. Government Printing Office.
16. *Survey of Pupils Who Have Difficulties with English Language,* New York,

New York City Board of Education, Publication No. 334 (P.N.S. 408), 1970.

17. *The Puerto Rican Child in the New York City School System,* New York, New York City Board of Education, 1972, p. 23.

18. *Report Race Relations Survey: Student.* Bureau of Administrative Research, Chicago Board of Education, December 1974, pp. 1-2.

19. Margolis, Richard: *The Losers: A Report on Puerto Ricans and the Public Schools,* Chicago, Aspira, Inc. (monograph), May 1968, p. 9.

20. *The Puerto Rican Study,* 1953-1957, New York: New York City Board of Education, 1958, p. 1001.

21. Demonstration projects in bilingual education, *American Education, 9 (6):*32, July 1973.

22. Margolia, Richard: *The Losers: A Report on Puerto Ricans and the Public Schools,* Chicago, Aspira, Inc. (monograph), May 1968, p. 9.

23. ———: *The Losers: A Report on Puerto Ricans and the Public Schools,* Chicago, Aspira, Inc. (monograph), May 1968, p. 9.

24. Data obtained from the Chicago Board of Education, Bureau of Administrative Research, November 1974.

25. Alloway, David N., and Cordasco, Francesco: *Minorities and the American City,* New York, David McKay Company, Inc., 1970, p. 65.

CONTENTS

PART IV

The Schools and the Spanish-Speaking

PART V

Problems of Language and Learning: A Challenge

PART VI

Achievement and Intelligence: Cultural Influences

PART VII

Bilingual-Bicultural Education: A Necessity

PART VIII

Reshaping Teacher Education for the Spanish-Speaking Child

PART IX

Educational and Social Issues

EDUCATION OF THE
SPANISH-SPEAKING
URBAN CHILD

PART I

CULTURAL HERITAGE, IMMIGRATION AND MIGRATION: A PROFILE

CHAPTER 1

HERITAGE
THE ROOTS LIE IN THE
MOTHER COUNTRY

PETER BORN

Oh, land of the sun,
I sigh for your sight—
Now I am so distant
I go without love—
—AN OLD MIGRANT FOLK BALLAD

L ATINS OF MEXICAN EXTRACTION talk of how the old Mexican
civilizations created great architecture, huge pyramids rival-
ing those of Egypt. They are justifiably proud of the ancestors
who developed advanced philosophies and educational systems
and who pioneered an early version of astronomy.

While the ancient Greeks and Romans worshipped a multitude
of gods, the philosopher-king of Mexico, Nezahualcoyotl, put
forth the view that there was only one god-creator. The scientists
of the Mayan tribes (1500 B.C. to A.D. 1697) developed a calendar more accurate than the one we use today. Political science,
as well as other disciplines, flourished in ancient universities with
the aid of well-illustrated textbooks.

Knowledge mastered by these scholars spread northward toward what is now the southwestern United States by way of wan-
dering Indian tribes. The Pueblo Indians, for example, developed clusters of adobe high-rise buildings in the New Mexican
deserts around A.D. 500.

Another famous Mexican civilization was established by the
Aztecs. Legend says the forerunners of the Aztecs set out on a
pilgrimage from the southwest deserts around 1168 because of
a prophecy from Huitzilopochtli, their god of sun and war.

Born, Peter, "The Roots Lie in the Mother Country," *The Latins*, A background
report prepared by the Chicago Tribune Educational Service Department, 1972,
pp. 3-8.

5

Huitzilopochtli told them that they would found a mighty kingdom in the south at the spot where they saw an eagle devouring a serpent by a lake.

The Aztecs supposedly witnessed that sight on a marshy island in an area now occupied by Mexico City. There, in 1325, they built their capital, Tenochtitlan.

By continually waging war on the surrounding tribal states, the Aztecs became one of the most powerful groups in Mexico but unwittingly weakened themselves for conquest by the invading Spaniards in 1519. Despite a noble defense mounted by Cuauhtemoc (the present-day national hero of Mexico), the Spanish conquistadors led by Hernando Cortes conquered most of the country within two years.

Cortes was aided by an Aztec prophecy that the white son of a god would one day arrive from the sea. The Spaniards made wicked use of the legend and within four years all the Aztec leaders, including the last ruler, Montezuma II, had been murdered.

The invaders developed an empire called New Spain that spread northward, embracing New Mexico, Texas, Arizona, parts of Colorado, and all of California. The new territory was sparsely settled under the dual guidance of the king and the church of Spain.

The Church, which proceeded to convert the Indians to Catholicism, established a string of mission colonies. Meanwhile, the crown was only slightly interested in the word of God and even less dedicated to economic and social development within the empire. Instead, Spanish noblemen were sent on treasure hunts to fill the king's treasury.

Even though there was little of gold and silver available for picking off the ground, fortune-hunters were rewarded with fat land grants. After settling down with Indian wives, the Spanish soldiers and officials established a network of pueblo settlements across the Southwest.

Under an urban plan that was also used in Puerto Rico and Cuba, each pueblo had a church facing a central square intended for use during the celebration of holy days. To be a member of the pueblo, and therefore have access to the commonly shared land, a man had to be a member of the church.

Cattle and sheep were raised on the private estates by the labor of the poorer colonists and Indians who were coerced into a system of voluntary servitude called peonage. In return for any money or favors given by the owner, a peasant and his family were bound to the master.

This institution of quasi-slavery was described by James Josiah Webb, a Santa Fe trader, in 1844. He said the heartlessness of the landlords was matched only by the greed of the church.

"The wages of the laborers were only from three dollars to six dollars a month, and a ration of food feeds the worker only," Webb wrote. "From this he would have to support his family and pay the dues to a priest for marrying, baptizing, and burial of seven dollars and upward, depending on the ability and ambition of the individuals desiring the services. An inflexible rule with the priests was no money, no marrying; no money, no baptizing; no money, no burying."

"As a consequence, the poor were extremely so, and without hope of bettering their condition. The priesthood [was] corrupt, vicious, and improvident."

The oppressed peons became ripe for revolution as the king and church quarreled over who should control the colonies. In 1810, a priest named Hidalgo y Costilla led a revolt that ultimately failed, but later uprisings ended in the creation of the Mexican republic thirteen years later.

The assumption of dictatorial powers by President Santa Anna in 1834 foreshadowed doom for the northern part of the republic. Anxious to populate Texas and New Mexico, the president encouraged settlers from foreign countries, notably from the United States. As the Anglos homesteaded by the thousands, tensions developed between the Mexicans and the foreigners.

The older inhabitants whose families had been established there for centuries were dismayed by the Americans who tried to transplant their Protestant, Yankee attitudes from "back East" rather than adopting the Mexican methods of doing things. Added to this was the fact that a good number of the "homesteaders" were desperadoes escaping the reach of the U. S. courts in the newly purchased Louisiana Territory.

And the Americans were not pleased with the Mexicans. Not only were their ways and language foreign, but their bloodline was predominantly Indian, a race for which the frontiersmen had no love. (Today 95 percent of the Mexicans are part Indian and 40 percent of those have full Indian blood.)

Besides viewing their neighbors with ethnic and racial contempt, the Americans wanted to introduce slavery, which was outlawed in Mexico.

Anglo dissatisfaction led to the Texan Revolution of 1835 and the territory's subsequent declaration of independence the following year. It became an independent republic and remained under its Lone Star flag for nearly ten years.

A strong movement for annexation to the U. S. had existed ever since American settlement of the territory. When the republic sank into poverty, negotiations toward annexation began. The result of annexation in 1845 was the Mexican-American War of 1846 to 1848.

This chapter in American history has been severely criticized. Ulysses S. Grant, Union commander during the Civil War and later President, described the Mexican-American War as "the most unjust war ever waged by a stronger nation against a weaker nation."

General Winfield Scott, the American army commander, said his troops committed atrocities on Mexican civilians "to make heaven weep and every American of Christian morals blush for his country."

The fighting ended with the Treaty of Guadalupe-Hidalgo, after which the United States paid 15 million dollars for Texas, New Mexico, Arizona, California, Utah, Nevada, and part of Colorado. Now the long-established Mexican families found themselves on foreign soil.

Their position was particularly delicate in the midst of the American takeover because their way of life was obsolete. They had preserved the ways of Old Spain and many of the ways of the Indians. But they had not advanced. Their culture was rooted in the past, in traditions, usages, and social attitudes that had become archaic. They had no manufacturing—Spain had made sure of that with her mercantilistic policies. The closest thing to industry was the craftsmanship of the local wood and metal workers, but they did not devise new techniques, only new styles.

Agriculture, the mainstay of the region, was also tied to the practices of past centuries. Their concept of land ownership was obsolete. A blending of property-use theories handed down from Spanish kings and Pueblo Indians resulted in enormous tracts of land being deeded either to one family or groups of families. The large size of these land parcels stemmed partly from the fact that with antiquated farming methods, it took vast spaces to grow more than a meager crop.

But an equally strong factor was the concept of communal sharing. The Indians, and later the Mexicans, viewed the earth as the creative source of all nourishment. Farm land was an almost mystic entity that was indivisible; it could not be chopped up like a piece of cloth and marketed. It belonged to everyone in the community.

To the landless American settlers, many of whom were poor and uneducated, such concepts were incomprehensible. When the Anglos arrived in New Mexico and California, they found most of the usable land locked up by a few thousand old Spanish or Mexican land grants. They found it intolerable to see millions of acres unused and begging to be tilled, and then be told that all this land was off limits.

Mexican-American critics have called the forty-year period following the Mexican War the worst land grab in United States history other than the uprooting of American Indians. Even though the Treaty of Guadalupe-Hidalgo guaranteed the full rights of existing Mexican land ownership, four fifths of the old deeds had been nullified or ignored outright by the turn of the 20th Century.

After the war, the Mexicans of the Southwest were given an opportunity to become American citizens. But they refused the citizenship, leaving the power to elect judges and other officials in the hands of the new settlers.

Many of the old land grants were stricken in the courts, and other pieces of property were simply taken outright. Legal tricks were employed in yanking thousands of acres out from under unsuspecting and ignorant villagers.

In 1863 the *Rio Abajo Weekly Press* of Albuquerque made this observation: "He who steals a million [acres] is a financier. He who steals half a million is only a defaulter. He who steals a quarter of a million is a swindler. He who steals fifty thousand is a knave. But he who steals a pair of boots or a loaf of bread is a scoundrel and deserves hanging."

Anyone who resisted the new age of progress was treated with less than understanding. It is estimated by some historians that more Mexicans were lynched in the Southwest between 1865 and 1920 than blacks were hanged in the Southeast during the same period.

The dean of Texas historians, Walter Prescott Webb, estimated that 500 to 5,000 Mexicans—men, women, and children—were murdered by Texans in the Rio Grande Valley between 1908 and 1925. Mexican President Venustiano Carranza offered evidence to U. S. government that 114 Mexican citizens were "mistakenly" hanged by Texas Rangers. In Langtry, Texas, Judge Roy Bean (who called himself "The Law West of the Pecos") used to dispense justice from his back porch. Reportedly he considered one case in which a Texan was accused of killing a Mexican. Judge Bean said he could find "no law in his books against killing a Mexican."

But regardless of the injustices encountered north of the Rio Grande River, the United States looked more inviting then native Mexico. Under the reform dictatorship of Porforio Diaz 90 percent of the peasants lost their land. A prolonged drought and bloody revolution between 1910 and 1920 drove thousands of Mexicans into the Southwest.

Mexican nationals and Mexican-Americans became an invaluable source of cheap labor in the Southwest.

By 1907, they constituted 80 percent of the agricultural labor force, 90 percent of the railroad workers, and 60 percent of the mine workers.

A rural people, their first impulse was to farm; but as a middle class developed in the 1920s, many became urban. Bank foreclosures during the Depression drove farmers who had lost their land into the cities in search of work. By 1960, 80 percent of the Mexican-Americans lived in urban areas.

Even more urbanized are the Puerto Ricans, many of whom have come from the mountain villages of their native island. Close to 95 percent live in cities, including 1.3 million in New York City, making it the largest Puerto Rican community in the world—one-third larger than San Juan.

The rest of the Puerto Rican population is scattered mainly thru communities in Connecticut, New Jersey, and Illinois. Chicago's Puerto Rican population was estimated at 125,000 in 1969.

While their self-image of being a "conquered people" is not as strong as that of the Southwestern Mexican-Americans, the Puerto Rican identity lacks an ancient heritage. The Spaniards destroyed every trace of the native Indians in the 16th Century, replacing the unwilling natives with chattel labor from Africa.

Columbus visited the island on his second voyage in 1493. He was followed in 1508 by Ponce de Leon who named the harbor on the northern coast Puerto Rico (meaning "rich port").

The United States inherited the island thru the Spanish-American War in 1898. The Foraker Act of 1900 gave the United States' President the power to appoint a governor and executive council, but the disappointed islanders lobbied for more autonomy.

The Jones Act of 1917 made all Puerto Ricans United States citizens (and subject to the military draft) and gave them the power to elect both houses of their legislature plus a resident commissioner who represented the island as a nonvoting member of the United States Congress. The law was widened in 1947 to allow for the popular election of a governor who had the power to appoint all government officials except the government auditor and members of the island's Supreme Court.

At that time, the island was torn politically between two ideologies. The Independence Party pushed for complete separation from the United States, while the conservative statehood group wanted the island to have total equality with the states on the mainland.

Neither side won, and Puerto Rico became a Free Associated State (or commonwealth) of the U. S. in 1952 under its first full governor, Munoz Marin. For over a decade he led efforts to accelerate industrial growth in Puerto Rico. That program, known as Operation Bootstrap, turned the island into the "Japan of the Caribbean." Attracted by generous tax incentives and a cheap labor market, international industries jammed Puerto Rico with garment and textile factories.

The pre-World War II agricultural economy surged ahead faster than any national growth rate in the Western hemisphere. By 1964 there were 1,000 industrial plants employing 100,000 workers.

Between 1940 and 1960 the life expectancy increased from about 46 to 70 years. Reflecting the modernization, heart disease and cancer replaced tuberculosis and pneumonia as the main killing diseases.

Between 1940 and 1963 the average per capita income had multiplied by a factor of six, rising from 120 dollars a year to 740 dollars, about twice the average for Latin-American countries.

But Puerto Rico is tied to the U. S. mainland economy, not those of neighboring countries; and while it has made unbelievable progress, the island is still twice as poor as Mississippi.

The poorest of the poor are desperately impoverished. Modernization cut the death rate but could not reduce the birth level on the predominantly Catholic island. The population soared in the 1950s and, as it now approaches 3 million, is expected to double in the next thirty years.

The explosion of prosperity could not match the mushrooming throngs of the needy. The current unemployment rate is listed at 12.2 percent, but "in realistic terms, it reaches 25 to 30 percent when you consider those who have become so discouraged that they are no longer seeking work," said United States Representative Herman Badillo of New York, the only Puerto Rican in the House.

The hopeless struggle for survival has driven islanders by the hundreds of thousands out of the rotting barrios, or neighborhoods, of San Juan and into the sleek jets destined for New York's air terminals. The heavy migration—446,800 in the last decade—made air travel inexpensive and the trip could be made with ease. A Puerto Rican can travel from San Juan to John F.

Kennedy Airport in less time than a New Yorker can go from Coney Island to Times Square. The Puerto Ricans became the first immigrants of the American jet age.

They found this distinction less than a blessing. Other immigrant groups of the past who had arrived in pre-technology-laden America needed only a strong back for survival. The Puerto Rican and recent Mexican immigrants discovered that the best of unskilled jobs had vanished. In the words of one New York City reporter, they became the "busboys of paradise," toiling in the hotel, restaurant, and garment industries.

Unable to feed their large families, the unluckiest Puerto Ricans ended up on relief. The Spanish-speaking now comprise 40 percent of New York City's welfare cases, mostly in the aid to dependent children category. This has startled many in the Latin community because the Puerto Ricans make up only 14 percent of New York's population.

The city's welfare rolls have lengthened just as those of Puerto Rico have shrunk. The island's welfare load decreased by a few thousand cases in the last ten years, while the commitments of New York have gone up 243 percent.

New York State Assemblyman Andrew Stein blamed federal regulations for the lopsided increases. He said the rule not allowing aid to dependent children to be given while the father is present encourages men to abandon their families because government benefits outweigh the size of paychecks.

Stein also attacked Washington for putting Puerto Rico on a fixed welfare budget instead of reimbursing the commonwealth for whatever costs are incurred. In comparison, the federal government picked up the tab for 81 percent of Alabama's costs in 1970 and 83 percent of Mississippi's.

The principal beneficiaries of these current welfare policies are American corporations with plants in Puerto Rico, which are able to capitalize on cheap Puerto Rican labor and gain special tax exemptions, and New York City sweatshop operators who pay substandard wages," Stein said. "The principal victims are the Puerto Rican migrants and New York City taxpayers."

The income level of both the Puerto Rican and Mexican communities in America are kept low by the closeness of the mother countries, even though that proximity has been a source of psychological strength.

When the hordes of immigrants left Eastern Europe for America in the 19th Century, they knew that only failure or quick success would bring them back. They felt driven to assimilate and succeed in the newly adopted country. Europe was very far away. Many of the Puerto Ricans and Mexicans can commute rather than migrate. The net annual levels of the Puerto Rican influx in the past three years have diminished from 40,000 to 12,600 to 3,000. Almost as many people are going from New York to San Juan as the other way around. And for Mexican-Americans living in Los Angeles or south Texas, returning to the land of your roots is easier than shuttling between Connecticut and Manhattan.

Many Puerto Ricans who attain professional status on the mainland return much richer to the island of their birth, but they are replaced in the barrios of New York by poor immigrants from San Juan, thus keeping the professional level of the New York colony lower than it should be.

The Mexican-Americans have the same problem compounded by the barrier of obtaining United States citizenship. It takes a minimum of fourteen months for a Mexican national to obtain legal entry papers. So thousands of them simply slip across the border. Since 1965, immigration and naturalization agents have arrested 2,500 illegal aliens in Chicago alone.

Compared to a U. S. citizen or alien working legally, an "illegal" will work for starvation level wages because he is terrified of being shipped back to the depressed economy of Mexico.

"The illegals are so vulnerable" said Robert Germain, investigations chief of the Chicago Bureau of Immigration and Naturalization. "An illegal can't complain about making less than the minimum wage. He's afraid his boss will turn him in. And he can't complain about other abuses either—like shakedowns, poor living conditions, or ill health."

There have been cases of policemen (or people posing as officers) shaking down Mexican nationals for 50 dollar bribes, smugglers transporting aliens across the border for 250 dollars a head

and then abandoning their human contraband on lonely highways instead of finding them jobs as promised. In even more elaborate schemes illegals are offered an American wife in name only for 1,000 to 2,000 dollars.

Not only is life made hard for the alien, but their presence in the labor force retards the upward mobility of the legal Latins. Not surprisingly, much of the information leading to the deportation of illegals comes from Mexican-Americans.

CHAPTER 2

ONE MILLION MIGRANTS

RICHARD L. TOBIN

J OE COLISEMA IS A HARD MAN to be around these days. Joe owns
a 110-acre truck farm in southern New Jersey, and last April
his part of the world was at its loveliest in years, but not for Joe.
The forsythia and tulips came out early; weather was great for
picking up a quick post-winter tan; spring tourists loved the early
country sun; but Joe's snap beans got too much of a start in the
prolonged premature warmth and so did his lettuce. Everything
on Joe's truck farm went disastrously ahead of its anticipated
schedule, so when Joe's lettuce went to the early market, the
Carolina lettuce crop was still at its peak and Joe couldn't sell
some of the best heads he had ever grown at anything like a decent price. In fact, the vegetable brokers Joe deals with regularly
have wanted no part of his produce so far in 1968 because the
timing has been two weeks off all along the line.

But if the lot of a Jersey truck farmer is an unhappy one this
hot, humid summer of 1968, it has not been much better for the
migratory workers who come up each year from DeKalb County,
Mississippi, to help Joe Colisema harvest his crops. Through bitter experience the migratory worker knows that even in good
times things are bad for stoop labor, though by no means as bad
as they used to be. Nimble-fingered families from the deep South
still ride the rickety bus, eat questionable meals, live in unhygien-
ic work camps, and are often forced to neglect their children's
education and upbringing. Now, at long last, things are beginning to change. Including their families, 1,000,000 migrants make
the annual pilgrimage across state and county lines as the harvests
peak, and their trek is still one of the saddest and most perplex-

ing of all America's social woes. Two million more individuals work in their local farm areas, and while their environment is better, their condition of work is often comparable, and so are the problems.

Not the least of these problems has been and continues to be exploitation. State and federal laws have alleviated some of the conditions migrants faced in *The Grapes of Wrath,* including federal minimum wage coverage of some farm workers. As a result chiefly of the amazing accomplishments of a lone man, Cesar Chavez, and his infant United Farm Workers Organizing Committee, Congress has been pushed toward giving certain farm labor the right to organize, a minimum wage, the benefits of the collective bargaining process, and other advances in industrial democracy that began with Franklin D. Roosevelt. Like the auto industry in the 1930s, the battle between farm owner and farm worker has now been joined for keeps, and the bloodiest and fiercest fighting lies in the months just ahead.

Three years ago the UFWOC (AFL-CIO) sought union recognition from the grape growers of Delano, California. Although the union apparently represented a majority of field hands, the growers refused. In September 1965, the union struck the Delano growers and since then, mainly because of sympathetic consumer boycotts, the union has won several contracts in California grape country. By far the largest grape grower is Giumarra, and when Giumarra, through strike-crippling injunctions and imported labor, kept on producing, a nationwide boycott evolved. Since New York is Giumarra's largest market and trading center, that city was picked as the first point of concentration. In January 1968, fifty farm workers traveled 3,000 miles in an unheated school bus to the doors of Paul Hall's Seafarers Union, which gave them a royal welcome and has taken care of all their organizational and material needs. Farm worker pickets set up their lines at Hunt's Point Terminal in the Bronx and immediately ran into trouble. They were harassed, threatened, and insulted. Early in February, twenty-two pickets and a six-year-old child were arrested on a mass-picketing charge filed by Kleiman & Hochberg, head of the Hunt's Point Produce Association. Later the charges were dropped, and the California grape boycott continued. (The grape growers are now suing the boycotters.) Early this summer New York City's government joined the national boycott of California-grown grapes. Since one-fifth of all Californias are sold in New York, the great metropolis has become a center of pro-union, anti-grower activity. Out in California, of course, the central figure is Cesar Chavez, the Reuther of the farm industry, the Bolívar of the migratory worker.

As recently as 1956, as many as 460,000 foreign workers—most of them Mexican nationals—were allowed into the United States during the peak harvest seasons in California, Michigan, Texas, Florida, New Jersey, and other major vegetable-fruit producing states. Under Public Law 78 the Mexican farm workers worked with domestic migrants from one crop peak to another. But by 1965, pushed for years by union labor lobbies in the United States, Congress had finally refused to renew P.L. 78, and Mexican labor declined as a factor in the American agricultural equation.

Migratory workers travel by three major routes northward from states along the southern border of the United States. The main stream flows west and north from Texas starting in the early spring; the crops involved are cotton, sugar beets, vegetables, and fruits. Many workers in this particular migratory stream are Americans of Mexican descent, and they usually take their families with them. As summer comes to the Middle West and Atlantic Coast states, migrants work northward, with Negroes constituting a large proportion of the East Coast work force. Because they take their families with them, of necessity, the problems of poor housing, malnutrition, low wages, inadequate medical care, disease, dangerous transportation, and callous brutality are part of the daily routine. About one third of the migrants actually work in the fields and vineyards.

Because migratory farm workers have been partly excluded from a number of routine benefits, such as unemployment insurance, workmen's compensation, social security, welfare assistance, child labor protection, even minimum wage standards, the plight of the migrant is geometrically intensified. One characteristic applies to all migratory farm workers: they travel in groups, usually family groups, with several members of each family working together in field or vineyard. However, if weather aberrations postpone or prematurely ripen by even a few days one harvest schedule or another, it is the migrant family that suffers most, living as it does from hand to mouth with little legal protection in its shabby home away from home. In 1966, annual income averaged $1,600 per worker, and it is little more today. That of nonmigrant seasonal workers is even less. The average migratory worker quit school early, and he has no skills other than agricultural field experience, which does not include handling sophisticated machinery.

Almost without exception the migratory workers endure the degrading environment of poverty where they live and where they travel to work. At home they are not accepted by their community, even less so on migration. The chief handicap is a subtle one: Being migrant they belong to no one and don't consider themselves as "belonging" even when they are home. Not being commuters they must make substantial living arrangements away from home, the most expensive way to live.

Farm work has always been done where little or no handy water supplies or toilet facilities are available. It almost always involves long hours plus exposure to heat, cold, dust, wind, chemicals, mechanical hazards, and bad hygiene. Since migrants' quarters frequently lack facilities for food storage, bathing, or laundry, disease is with them always. So are rats and insects, sewage and the burdens of ignorance. The migrant is at the mercy of every ill man can endure and a few most men could never possibly imagine.

Besides the heat of summer sun, at its brutal height during harvest time, the average farm laborer is up against a host of other enemies, some of them natural, some man-made, some obvious, others indistinct. The company store, the sprays used in agriculture but not meant for contact with human skin or lungs, accidents caused by farm machinery, rickety transportation between jobs—these are some of the obvious drawbacks, along with low pay. Some not so obvious include local prejudice and the impressment of child labor on grounds that the ripe harvest must be brought in. Doctors? Schooling? Legal recourse? Little of this is available to the average migratory worker.

The lot of migrant children everywhere is to live in ugly, barren, crowded surroundings, to work or wait in incredible heat from early morning until late evening, to lack parental companionship and supervision, to be fed poorly and irregularly, and, in general, to shift for themselves or be burdened with the care of babies and children smaller than themselves. Unless this vicious cycle is broken, the children are doomed to live the hopeless and uncertain lives of their ancestors, and they too will drop out of school—though, intelligence tests prove, not from lack of potential. Limited and inferior schooling combine with extreme deprivation to plague the children of migrant families.

Many states where migrant labor is essential have developed programs in recent years for the children of migrant families. Twenty-odd years ago New Jersey began to set up summer school and playgrounds for children of migrants and more than 1,000 children are now enrolled in a single season. Public health nurses, dentists, doctors, and professional playground supervisors assist the regular teaching personnel in a dozen summer schools. Practically every child in these schools gains weight and almost all seem to prefer the summer school program to what they know at home or other migratory farm sites. There is no problem in getting the children to wash—many youngsters clutch their bar of soap as if it were a precious toy or something to eat. One youngster carried his soap all the way through his regular classroom activities, refusing to put it down lest he lose it. He had never seen soap before.

Michael T. is a typical child who is typically happy in a New Jersey migrant farm school. Michael and his mother and sister came from South Philadelphia to New Jersey to pick blueberries. In the wintertime, Michael's fatherless family is "on the welfare." Coming to pick blueberries in New Jersey was a chance to earn some money and get the children out of the tenement. Michael's mother and sister went to work in the fields at once, but Michael came to school every day, though he was old enough to earn stoop money. Michael was a bag of bones, nowhere near the equal of his peers in strength, physique, or endurance. Though in his midteens, Michael was stunted in height and weighed less than 60 pounds. At school Michael ate as if there were no tomorrow. And the emptiness of his insides was matched by other emptinesses, evidence of what Michael had to live through in South Philadelphia. In a single morning one correspondent counted seven different occasions on which Michael ran to the teacher, a person of understanding and warmth, for a quick hug or other indications of affection. Michael's emotional hunger had gone unfed as long as had his emaciated body.

School during summertime in New Jersey migrant camps is entirely voluntary. Some of the twelve-year-olds-and-over look forward to rainy days when they can come to school, and it is obvious that children take turns staying home to care for the babies. It is better to come every other day than not to come at all. Music is a universal language—and most children in New Jersey's migrant summer school programs are instinctively musical. One fearful little boy who spoke so softly he could scarcely be heard came to school one morning after several days of musical participation and sang a greeting to all at the top of his lungs, "Hello, everybody. Yes, indeed! Yes, indeed!" A near-catatonic, Christopher hadn't smiled or voluntarily taken part in anything during the first two weeks. Two mornings before, the teacher had put a bongo drum in his lap. Perhaps because this was the most coveted of the rhythm instruments, or perhaps because of the faith expressed in him, Christopher for the first time laughed out loud and began to take part.

New Jersey is a highly agricultural state, particularly the central and southern sections. New Jersey labor law permits farms to employ children under the following conditions: 1) that they are twelve years of age; 2) that they work no more than sixty hours a week nor more than ten hours a day or six days in a row; 3) that they are allowed a thirty-minute meal or rest period after five consecutive hours of work. Any child twelve to sixteen in New Jersey may use any of the standard stationary machines associated with farm activities: egg graders, egg cleaners, egg washers, poultry feeders, and milking machines. As soon as a child has reached the ripe age of sixteen he or she may drive tractors and operate all except highly dangerous machinery. A boy of eighteen is free to do any work at all; he may handle acids and dyes, toxic and noxious dust, benzol compounds which penetrate the skin, explosive and highly flammable substances, grinding abrasive and buffing machinery, guillotine-action cutting machinery, power-field choppers, and corn pickers.

New Jersey's piece rates for stoop labor are better than most, but even they give one pause. Blueberries are paid at 8 cents per pint (did you ever pick a whole pint of blueberries?), strawberries at 10 cents per quart. Snap beans pay 90 cents per bushel, carrots 13 cents per bushel. Onions pay 13 cents per bushel, and potatoes and peppers up to $1.35 per hour. Tomatoes draw about 20 cents for a full basket. While no one would get rich at these prices, they are above scales paid in depressed areas to independents without a spokesman, and they are well above piecework schedules of a decade ago.

The United States Department of Agriculture recently described the personal and economic characteristics of domestic migratory farm workers. Essentially it is a young labor force: half of the migratory workers are less than twenty-five years of age. More than 70 percent are male and 80 percent are white. Migratory workers also share a relatively loose attachment to the labor force. More than half are out of the labor market most of the year attending school, keeping house, or doing other seasonal jobs. Fewer than half are heads of households. Those who have some high school education are likely to do some nonfarm work in the off-season, working where wage rates are higher than they are in the fields.

The average farm wage rate paid migratory workers in 1966 was $10.80 per day, but since many were away from home for weeks, even months at a time, and had to take care of their own living expenses out of this meager income, not much of the money from their stooping and picking went home with them. In eight out of ten households no children under fourteen accompanied them during migrancy. The remaining 20 percent reported 140,000 children under fourteen on the migration and back, and of these approximately 50,000 were on the road at some time between October and May when most other children their age were either in school or a permanent residence at or near the place their fathers worked.

Federal minimum wages apply to only a fraction of migrant labor. But since every state has a farm placement/employment service working with the federal government, and since practically everything grown and harvested is in interstate commerce, Uncle Sam is constantly looking over the shoulder of America's growers and producers. Before a crew leader is able to move a single busload of migratory help across a single state line, he will have to face up to federal vehicle registration, vehicle inspection, and registration contracts, and must comply with regulations involving the health, welfare, wages, housing conditions, education, and hygienic facilities on the road north.

The crew leader gets a cut of a penny or two from each hamper of fruit picked or from each hour of work by his crew members. Payment is usually made to the crew contractor who in turn pays the laborers, many of whom are in debt to him for transportation and expenses. State labor agencies specializing in migrant help make frequent visits to farm labor camps to be certain that contractor's rates are posted, that no improper deductions from pay have been taken out of the laborers' due, and that living conditions comply with minimum legal standards, which is to say pretty dreadful in some areas. But there simply are not enough inspectors to catch all the violations.

By and large, conditions have changed rapidly in recent years for both harvest labor market and grower. Although the refusal by Congress to renew P.L. 78 drastically reduced the number of foreign workers allowed into the United States during the peak harvest times, the Department of Labor has granted specific exceptions for short harvest jobs under stringent conditions. Most of these foreign permits have been issued to task force groups of Mexicans who by law are paid at the same rates as domestic farm labor. Since 1964, however, most of the foreign workers admitted to the United States for temporary farm employment have been British West Indians, not Mexicans. Also admitted are "green card" holders—foreign nationals who enter this country as legal immigrants (although they may reside outside the United States) and who are therefore permitted to "travel" anywhere in the country for an unlimited time. A great many Mexicans have obtained these green cards over the years and some move immediately to peak harvest areas where they are gobbled up by eager employers. Nonetheless, the Department of Labor has set up criteria under P.L. 414 to make certain that the working conditions, hours, and wages of foreign agricultural help match those of domestic workers. These criteria have created a sort of minimum wage, or piece rates that enable a worker to earn approximately that much or more.

Partly as a result of the sudden demise of P.L. 78, the mechanization of the harvest of fruits and vegetables has grown at an increasing rate, and that, in the long run, will probably be the most important development of all. Some 80 percent of California's huge tomato crop and 90 percent of the large Long Island potato crop are now harvested by machine. Mechanization of harvest equipment has been so dramatic in the past ten years that New York State alone has noted a 50 percent drop in migrant workers. Though there will always be a need for hand-pickers to satisfy the store and fruit stand and the consumer who wants unbruised and undamaged fruit, mechanized harvesting is now expanding so rapidly that the seed and plant producers have fallen far behind in providing character changes essential to the use of mechanical harvesting, particularly of fruits and vegetables.

Sugar beets are now almost completely a mechanical crop; mechanization of the harvesting of snap beans alone will end 10,000 stoop labor jobs in the next few years. There is now a mechanical lettuce harvester that can tell whether the lettuce head is firm enough to pick. Similarly, certain apple crops can be brought in by mechanization with less damage to the fruit than if the crop were hand-picked. Twenty years ago, no one envisaged harvesting beans or tomatoes by machine; today the majority of these crops are brought to the edge of the field without a hand laid on them, though many hands run the machinery and try to keep up with the filled baskets, carts, boxes, and hampers—sorting and separating and grading, much as it has always been done.

Undoubtedly, there will be fewer stoop labor jobs, but some of these jobs will be replaced by others. The machines will require operators who know something about farms and harvesting. Who better than the man or woman who once picked it all by hand? Will mechanization reduce the total number of workers needed to bring in America's harvests? The answer goes in two distinct directions, for mechanization is by no means uniform. In the case of fruit and vegetables sold as fresh produce and therefore requiring a pleasing appearance, harvesting by machine is generally not practical. Moreover, selective harvesting with machines—that is to say, choosing the ripe and leaving the unripe for later—is often prohibitively expensive. At the other extreme, about nine tenths of the cotton harvested in the United States in 1967 was brought in by machine. Moreover, the number of hoe hands needed for cotton chopping declines each year as chemicals to control weed and grass growth become cheaper and more reliable. Mechanization has made little progress and offers few prospects in tobacco, a crop using 200,000 workers.

It is no coincidence that the drive to unionize American migratory labor, indeed farm labor of all kinds, began to make real headway by 1966, a year after P.L. 78 expired. Cesar Chavez was there from the start. In many ways his story is the most dramatic in the whole unsavory mosaic of stoop labor.

Short (five feet, six inches), chunky, with broad hands and a smoothed-down shock of black hair, an easy smile, and dark, glowing eyes, Cesar Chavez is one of the most loved and hated men in California. "The revolution is not coming," he says. "It is here." As director of the UFWOC he has undertaken to lead it. Chavez, his wife, Helen, and their eight children live in a weather-worn, two-bedroom frame house in Delano. It is hard to gauge their housekeeping costs since the Chavez family, like the families of all the grape strikers, survive on public contributions. The figure, however, has been estimated at $300 a month. Born March 31, 1927, on his grandfather's farm near Yuma, Arizona, Chavez was one of six children. The farm was foreclosed during the Depression, and the family came to California as migrant workers. Depending on the harvest, they drifted back and forth between the Imperial Valley and the San Joaquin Valley. Chavez finished eighth grade, attending a total of thirty-seven schools— "I went to some of them, of course, for only two or three days."

Chavez is surprised when asked the lowest wage he ever earned during the family's migrations, but answers enthusiastically: "Why, it was 12½ cents an hour. We were thinning cantaloupes in the Imperial Valley. That was in 1941." The family eventually settled in a slum near San Jose called, by its inhabitants, "Sal Si Puedes" (Get out if you can). In 1951, having already committed himself to improving the lot of the farm worker, with the hope some day of establishing a union, he was recruited by Saul Alinsky's Community Service Organization. (Supported by donations, the organization operates in California and Arizona, offering Mexican-Americans legal assistance and advice on matters of citizenship.) Chavez worked first as an organizer of local programs and in 1958 became the executive director of the organization's headquarters in Los Angeles. He resigned in 1961 and returned to Delano, his wife's birthplace and the winter base of his own family for many years. Why?

"It is hard to answer that question without sounding presumptuous. I had seen so much injustice. I knew that organization is the key to change. Someone simply had to do the organizing." He has also said: "For many years I was a farm worker, a migratory worker, and well, personally, and I'm being very frank, maybe it's just a matter of trying to even the score, you know." He began organizing on April 10, 1962—"A day I shall never forget." He worked in the fields by day and organized by night, refusing offers of financial aid which would free him from the field. "I knew that in order to be successful, we had to have our beginnings from the people. If the farm workers themselves did not pay for such an organization, there was no use building it. We started organizing almost three years before anyone knew we were around. We kept our names out of the papers. That was part of our plan. Many people thought we were just another community group."

Chavez's organization was called the National Farm Workers Association (independent). During the summer of 1965 this group and another—the Agricultural Workers Organizing Committee (AFL-CIO)—were organizing the grape pickers around Delano. The prevailing hourly wage was $1.15, and on September 8, AWOC struck demanding a raise. Two weeks later, Chavez's union joined the strike, insisting then as it does now that recognition of farm unions is the principal issue. Later, in August 1966, the two groups merged and became the United Farm Workers Organizing Committee, AFL-CIO. Chavez was named director.

Twenty-four growers were struck in the Delano area during September 1965, and Chavez could no longer keep his name out of the papers. He began to make speaking appearances, gathering public support for the grape pickers. The Delano strike, in its infancy, was freighted with bitterness. Four attempts were made to burn the union office in Delano. A cooperative gas station owned by the farm laborers was bombed. One grower sued Chavez for libel, seeking $6,000,000 in damages, but later dropped the suit when the union settled its dispute with the company. In June 1966, he was arrested for trespassing on a Di Giorgio Corporation farm and fined $276. Later, the union and Di Giorgio signed a contract.

Throughout the strike, Chavez has called for peace and reason; violence is his bugbear. "Our greatest accomplishment has been to keep the farm movement nonviolent. We don't sit around and hope for it. We go out and see that it stays that way." Bloodshed has been prevented in strike areas "because we did not respond to the attacks on us." He has also said repeatedly: "No union movement is worth the life a single grower or his child, or the life of a single worker and his child."

To pursue the most intransigent of his rivals, Chavez organized a boycott of certain California wines and liquors. As the strike gathered momentum, so did the boycott. Eventually it was waged against the "fresh" (table) grape industry and is now about to assume international proportions. "We are taking on the whole fresh grape industry, except for the Di Giorgio Corporation," Chavez said. "We are going to extend the boycott into Canada and into Europe. We are friendly with several foreign labor unions, and they will help us in the Common Market countries."

What has been the effect of the boycott? "Of course, we don't have the growers' figures at hand, but we know we are affecting their market. Some of them have begun to advertise their table grapes in newspapers—they didn't do that before—and now coupons are being printed, offering 7 cents off. Generally, the boycott is getting better. We are learning every day how to have a more effective one. . . . I don't think we're going to have any more trouble from the wine industry. I think they're going to respect the wishes of the workers."

What gains has the strike yielded, and what is to be expected? Now nearly thirty-five months old, the Delano dispute has produced twelve contracts with growers, affecting between 6,000 and 8,000 workers. "It has increased wages at the most by 80 percent— and usually by 60 percent—and it has given workers the right to unemployment compensation," Chavez said. "We have won a modest health and welfare plan and a few paid holidays. We have secured some safety measures for machinery and farm chemicals. That is one of the most important things—the handling of pesticides."

Today, the union claims 17,000 dues-paying members, but not all of them are covered by contracts. "We are confident that by the end of this summer the number will increase by several thousand," Chavez reported. "The membership increases, whether or not we win more contracts, because of the momentum. It is more difficult now to organize than it was in the past because of the restrictions placed on us by law. The green-carders are our biggest problem, and because of them the Justice Department is breaking its own law."

Chavez's most persistent grievance with the federal government has been the refusal by Congress to extend union recognition and collective bargaining rights to farm workers. Hearings are now being held by the Senate Committee on Labor and Public Welfare, and Chavez, who has been to Washington three times to testify, expects that the law will be changed. "It's hard to predict when," he said, "but we know it's coming. It's just impossible to keep us out of it any more. We've been waiting for so many years that when it does come it's probably going to seem like a miracle."

Is the union concerned about mechanization? "Yes, it's a concern. But right now it's like putting the cart before the horse. We can't do anything about it unless the union is organized. We're not against modernization and new methods. We feel it's the responsibility of both the union and the employer if workers are replaced by machines. We are against crucifying jobs—ones that dehumanize workers—such as topping sugar beets and picking cotton. We'd like to see machines take over that kind of work."

As the grape strike spreads this summer to the hot, dry Coachella Valley in Riverside County (it began there on June 20), will Chavez's vital public support continue? "Yes, this is really a great country, and our support, I am happy to say, is actually increasing after thirty-four months of struggle," he explained. "We are now getting very good support from minority groups that we didn't have in the beginning. It is all part of a larger movement. The poor for the first time in the history of this country are going to get their just due. The revolution is not coming, it is here. For many years the liberals led them; now the liberals have taken a place on the sidelines, and the poor are doing it themselves."

Why has Chavez been successful when others have failed? As usual, he is modest: "It looks a lot more successful on the outside than it does on the inside. This time, however, the workers have made up their minds that they want a union enough to fight for it. I sort of stumbled into it at the right time. The workers deserve the credit. We have it rough now, but we will never have it as rough as they did thirty years ago. One reason is that there are more American farm workers—Negro, Mexican-American, and Filipino—than there ever were before. This makes a big difference in organizing a union."

Despite the gains, the threat of violence constantly nettles Chavez. He is a devout Roman Catholic and his movement has always had strong religious overtones. Some say it is not a union at all, but a group held together by racial and religious ties. Chavez fasted for twenty-five days this winter because he wanted to disabuse Mexican-Americans of the traditional belief in *machismo*—the test of manliness through violence. During the fast he lived in an unopened gas station and read two books—the Bible and a biography of Mahatma Gandhi. He lost 35 pounds, but has gained 11 of them back and now weighs 150. "The test we believe in now," he said as he broke the fast, "is how much a man is willing to sacrifice and how much he is willing to give to secure a better life for himself and his children."

CHAPTER 3

THE PREJUDICE OF HAVING NO PREJUDICE IN PUERTO RICO

SAMUEL BETANCES

The issue of identity as it relates to race and color in Puerto Rican life is very important. This article will focus on race prejudice in Puerto Rico. The myth that Puerto Rico is a kind of human relations paradise where racism is nonexistent has to be exploded. Wherever exploitation exists, racism also exists. Race prejudice is a tool of those who would exploit in order to justify and blame the victims for their condition.

To suggest that Puerto Rico is free of race prejudice is to ignore reality. To insist that one should not tell the awful truth found in Puerto Rican culture is to want unity at any cost—perhaps influenced by the notion of "my country right or wrong." Unity based on error is not lasting. Truth must be made available to the masses of people.

To suggest that it is irresponsible to debate with other Puerto Ricans, at the risk of racist Americans eavesdropping, the truth about our own hang-ups, is to take an elitist posture not conducive to trusting the will of those who depend upon us for information on which our community must decide a common fate.

A S WITH ALL OF THE ISLANDS in the Caribbean, Puerto Rico has a history of slavery, discrimination, and race prejudice all its own. The purpose of this article is to put into perspective why it is often believed, by Americans* and by Puerto Ricans them-

Samuel Betances, lecturer, consultant, founder of "La Orzanización" at Harvard University where he also obtained the Educational Masters (Ed.M.) and C.A.S. degrees. Presently a doctoral candidate at the Harvard Graduate School of Education, while working as special assistant in experimental programs with the U. S. Office of Education. Samuel Betances is publisher of *The Rican*.

* The term "American," for the purposes of this paper, designates the citizens of the United States mainland of non-Puerto Rican extraction, who for the most part identify themselves as "white" in terms of race and color.

Betances, Samuel, "The Prejudice of Having No Prejudices in Puerto Rico," *The Rican*, Winter 1972, no. 2, pp. 41-54.

selves, that there is an absence of race prejudice in Puerto Rico. (The view that Puerto Rico does not have race prejudice has been held by many students of the Island to the *detriment* of solving real and growing problems in Puerto Rican life.) A review of the relevant literature on the subject will reveal race prejudice in the context of the Puerto Rican sociocultural experience.

Several factors account for the mistaken attitude that no race prejudice or discrimination exists in the Island: (1) the notion that Iberian slave laws were more liberal and humane than slave laws of other nations, thus influencing the Latin Caribbean Islands to be more humane and liberal in matters of race relations to this date; (2) the belief that the absence of excessive violence and cruelty in the history of Puerto Rican race relations also indicates an absence of racism in Puerto Rico; (3) the belief that racial factors are not significant in determining social and class patterns of discrimination; (4) the belief that prejudice and race tolerance cannot exist simultaneously in the same family or culture—thus, the citing of mixed marriages in Puerto Rico as evidence of an absence of race prejudice; (5) the lack of analysis by Puerto Rican writers who for reasons all their own want to believe that a problem of race prejudice does not exist in Borinquen; (6) the effort of American writers to find in Puerto Rico an example of a place where problems between the races have been solved; (7) the fact that constant comparison by sociological writers of race relations in Puerto Rico with race relations in the United States leads to faulty conclusions.

Each of these allegations will be considered separately to explain how they have supported the myth for the absence of race prejudice in Puerto Rico.

LIBERAL SLAVE LAWS

George Flinter, an early student of the slave experience in Puerto Rico (1832) did a lot to spread the belief that the liberality of slave laws in Puerto Rico was responsible for the peaceful way in which slave and nonslave residents lived in Puerto Rico. His books, one in English, the other in Spanish,[1] developed a theme which would later be incorporated into what is known to students of slavery in the Western Hemisphere as "Tannenbaum's theory." Tannenbaum believed that "the degree of liberality or cruelty in systems of slavery is determined mainly by favorable or unfavorable influence of laws in a society.[2]

Unlike the slave laws of non-Iberians, it was believed by Flinter and made popular by Tannenbaum that the slave system of the Spaniards protected the "moral and legal dignity of the slave."[3] If and when "kindness, affection, and understanding between master and slave"[4] occurred in the southern United States, for example, Tannenbaum explained that such expressions were "personal and with no standing in the law. Legally, there were no effective remedies against abuse and no channels to freedom."[5]

Spanish slave laws were, in a sense, more liberal than non-Iberian slave laws. Perhaps of greater significance is the perspective offered by Maxine Gordon when she says, "We do not contest the claim for greater liberality in the Spanish colonial laws *as written* but we do not think any colonization program *in practice,* whether recent or early, has been marked by notorious leniency on matters of race."[6] Hoetink also notes, "the social reality of the application of those protective laws is far more significant than the laws as such."[7] Charles C. Rogler's study, "The Morality of Race Mixing in Puerto Rico," points out that while the Spanish had direct experience with enslaving black Africans for a period of seventy-five years more than other Western nations, such experience was not as extensive as some would make it; and it was probably important for economic reasons "to create at least a mild definition for it."[8]

While Puerto Rico has a common heritage of slavery with the Latin Caribbean, the fact is that Puerto Rico's "economic development during the slavery period took divergent lines."[9] As Eric Williams explains, Puerto Rico became a "white colony, a garrison rather than a plantation."[10] The regions which developed a plantation economy, which to some degree included Cuba . . . were "notoriously harsher on the slaves."[11] The economy of Puerto Rico was never based in any large degree to slave labor. Tomás Blanco, a Puerto Rican historian, summarizes the economic patterns of Puerto Rico in which he concludes "our modest welfare never reached a point of exclusive dependence on slavery."[12] The sugar industry came late to Puerto Rico (on the eve of the suppression of the slave trade) and even though slavery grew during this period, slaves still remained "proportionally and comparatively few in number."[13] Puerto Rico's black slave population, except for a brief period, never exceeded more than 14 percent of the total population.

The nonplantation economic life of the Island caused the system of slavery to become much more expansive than the employment of free laborers.[14] Economic realities were responsible for the "channels of freedom" explained by some to be founded in liberal laws. *The People of Puerto Rico*, edited by J. H. Steward, states:

> Manumission of slaves appears to have been common during this period [16th Century]. First, the irregular character of commercial enterprises means that the maintenance of a large number of slaves was a financial risk and burden.[15]

This economic influence operated also in the Southern United States where:

> Laws encouraging manumission in the Southern states . . . were revoked in the course of the eighteenth and nineteenth centuries, or amended in a spirit contrary to that law. It may be surmised that this tendency was attributed to the increasing importance of the cotton-plantation economy in the deep south.[16]

Liberal slave legislation in Puerto Rico did not keep the Negro slave in the Island from experiencing a miserable existence. Documents of the slave experience in Puerto Rico repeatedly point to the blatant disregard for laws designed to protect the "morals and dignity" of the slave whenever it suited the needs of the slave owner. Luis Díaz Soler and other students of slavery in Puerto Rico document the existence of "haciendas" which gained a reputation for the "taming" of rebellious slaves. Gordon reports "slaves were branded, beaten, burned, ravished, hung, shot or had their hands, arms, ears, or legs cut off, depending upon the offense and the punisher."[17] The author of the basic work concerning the slave experience in Puerto Rico indicates "some masters forced their slaves to eat human excrement."[18]

The role of the Catholic Church in relation to the hypothesis that Spanish laws were liberal must be briefly considered also. According to law, the clergy had the responsibility of attending to the spiritual and educational needs of the slaves in Puerto Rico.

In both of these responsibilities the record indicates that the church was derelict, except as an agent of the slave system. "Conversion of the Negro to the faith of the Spaniards was a necessity in order to establish a formula which would create a feeling of obedience, conformity, humility and sacrifice, which was to contribute in making slave life tolerable."[19]

Not only was the education of the slaves "abandoned by the 'eclesiásticos,' "[20] but the Catholic Church became a slave owner in Puerto Rico.[21] The leadership of the Church took initiative with civil authorities and other slave owners in causing Negro slaves to "marry" in efforts to "increase the slave population without having to pay the cost of importing slaves from Africa and Europe."[22]

In the area of race relations, the Church in Puerto Rico maintained separate baptismal records, segregated on the basis of "black" and "white"; the clergy issued certificates of the "purity of the blood" giving assurances that in the veins of a citizen flowed no Black or Indian blood.[23] The Spaniards, noted a British critic, related to slavery in their possessions so as not to let "their spiritual aims . . . interfere (with) their secular enterprises."[24]

Some have argued that Spaniards had extensive experience with slavery prior to the New World experience so as to have developed a "moral" philosophy which in turn carried benefits to the slaves. However, the history of the Puerto Rican slave experience found that "the introduction of Africans in the discovered lands found an absence of legislation as to punitive or corrective methods which in turn authorized slave masters and slave caretakers (mayorales) to make their own laws, causing in instances brutal and extremely inhuman punishment."[25]

It becomes clear, then, that (1) Spanish slave laws and codes in Puerto Rico were ignored or enforced with the welfare of the slave master as a point of departure; (2) the "channels of freedom" were more directly connected to the economic situation of Puerto Rico than to liberal laws. Under pressure from the abolition movement in Puerto Rico, a lot of liberal codes and regulations were put in the law books of the Island for "public consumption" as "propaganda," but in actuality established the myth that liberal laws meant humane treatment of slaves.[26]

ABSENCE OF EXCESSIVE VIOLENCE

While Puerto Rico has not experienced segregated neighborhoods, racial lynchings, race riots, church bombings, police brutality in the form of race beatings or other forms of interracial violence as one finds record of in the United States, the conclusion that one might reach concerning the absence of race prejudice in the Island might be misleading.

Any discussion of race prejudice must address itself to the context in which the term "race" is used. One type of race problem involves *sociological* factors exclusively; the other important aspect of race is definitely *biological*. In an exploitative situation [social]—a slavemaster, colonizer-colonized type of setting—"obvious advantages inhere in the fact of racial [biological] differences."[27] Exploitation is easier "in proportion as race or other differences makes possible exclusion of the slave from the human category."[28] By placing a negative value, a social act, on a biological difference, the oppressor is able to exploit his victim with a clearer conscience:

> Explicitly or implicitly, the assigning of values is intended to prove two things: the inferiority of the victim *and* the superiority of the racist. Better still, it proves the one by the other; inferiority of the black race automatically means superiority of white. Inferiority of the colonized vividly demonstrates the superiority of the colonizer.[29]

Henry Wells claims that it is impossible (for Americans) to know who is white, black or mulatto in Puerto Rico—"the numbers of contemporary Puerto Ricans in each of these categories is unknown and indeed unknowable."[30]

While pointing out that figures in the 1960 census *lacked* a breakdown on color or race categories in Puerto Rico he does mention a breakdown of racial categories in the 1950 census which indicated that 80 percent of the Puerto Rican population was white and 20 percent black. He has difficulty accepting such figures as fact. He cautions:

But these proportions must be taken as only rough estimates. Whether based on information given the census takers by the persons counted or on the census taker's own appraisal of the racial category to which the persons counted belong, the data reflect subjective judgment and social rather than biological definitions of racial types.[31]

Professor Wells would have his readers believe that the U. S. Bureau of the Census' categorization of racial types in the mainland is a more exacting science than in Puerto Rico. He believes that census takers in the United States count and categorize people by racial types as defined by biology. He also asserts that Americans in the privacy of their own homes, simply fill out their census forms and define themselves into racial types, using "biological" rather than "social" definitions for what constitutes a white or a black person. The following is a statement of the U. S. Bureau of the Census as to what constitutes racial and color types in their data:

> The concept of race as used by the Bureau of the Census is derived from that which is commonly accepted by the general public. It does not, therefore, reflect clear-cut definitions of biological stock, and several categories refer to nationality. "Color" divides the population into two groups, white and nonwhite. The nonwhite population consists of Negroes, American Indians, Japanese, Chinese, Filipino, and all others not classified as white. Persons of Mexican birth or ancestry who are definitely Indian or of other nonwhite stock are counted as white. Persons of mixed parentage are classified by the race of color of the nonwhite parent.[32]

If Americans in the mainland can define themselves into racial categories "derived from that which is commonly accepted by the general public," why can't Puerto Ricans *in* Puerto Rico do the same thing? Why does Wells assume that Puerto Ricans are not to be trusted either as census takers or as people filling out census forms when it comes to matters of race and color? Why should he demand "racial purity" in Puerto Rico when it does not exist in the United States?† Could it be that one of the built-in privi-

---

† Raymond Mack writes: "Many Negroes in the United States have more Caucasoid ancestry than Negroid, but they are still considered Negro if they are known to have Negro ancestors. This is pure social definition and pure biological nonsense. In no other area of biology would we reason similarly." *Race, Class and Power,* ed. (New York: American Book Co., 1968), p. 103.

leges of the colonizer in dealing with a colony is to ultimately define and categorize the colonized as he sees fit?

Historical evidence, past and present, indicates the presence of violence and race prejudice in Puerto Rico. Exploitation has been the social reality in Puerto Rico and "race" the tool which makes human beings "inferior" and thus "justly" exploitable. The Negro as slave suffered much in Puerto Rico, as has been indicated above. He continues to suffer in Puerto Rico, joined by other exploited poor ("low class" and "nonwhite"). But his badge of "inferiority" keeps the lowest rung in the social ladder for himself.[33]

Eduardo Seda makes a notable analysis of race prejudice in Puerto Rico when he calls attention to the "social hypocrisy which has come to drown in a conspiracy of silence the possibility of a frank and healthy discussion of the problem."[34] A barrier to "frank" and "healthy" discussion of the problem has been the belief that a lack of American-style, racial violence indicates an absence of race prejudice in Puerto Rico. Seda maintains that Puerto Ricans have a "head-in-the-sand" attitude toward the race problem which in the final analysis is "childish" and mitigates against efforts to resolve the problem.[35]

While there might be some truth to the assertion that violence of the kind, or perhaps in some instances to the degree found in the United States, is not as rampant in Puerto Rico, violence inspired by racism *is* present in the Island.

One type of race-violence has special psychological implications for Puerto Ricans. It is defined by Renzo Sereno as "crypto-melanism."[36] He defines the concept as it relates to the mental turmoil that some Puerto Ricans go through as they make "constant efforts to hide the existence of the color problem within the self."[37] There exists in the Island "color insecurity," a drive to be non-Negro or completely white:

> The hostile drives deriving from such insecurity are not externalized, because of lack of definite targets, but are directed instead against the self. The efforts toward discrimination and segregation are (a) an attempt at relieving self-destructive drives by establishing categorical racial differences, thereby making possible hostile drives against external targets, and (b) an attempt toward a rational belief that the self

is wholly and perfectly non-Negro, or perfectly white. Neither of these attempts is successful because both are emotionally and rationally unacceptable to the self.[38]

Kaplow, Stryker, and Wallace made a study of San Juan in which they found discrimination patterns in their data against nonwhite and non-Catholics. They noted: "the arrangement of the new suburban enclave tends to reinforce these latent tendencies to segregation." The newspaper, *Claridad,*[39] reported that a senior citizens' home in Rio Piedras, Morada, Las Teresas, discriminated against black and non-Catholics. The article went on to say that the administrator of the home, Dr. María Teresa Barreras, has gone on record as saying that in the home "no one resides there unless he is 100 percent pro-American." It is ironical that the same newspaper took a picture of an alleged police informant who has very pronounced Negroid features for which the caption under his picture reads (in part), "if this youth only knew how the United States treated those of his race, perhaps he would not work defending Yanqui interest."[40]

Another supports the thesis that racial prejudice is present in Puerto Rico, despite a lack of excessive interracial violence. Juan Rodríguez Cruz reports: "Those who have observed the humble man from the countryside have noticed that many amongst them claim a pure lineage of Spanish descent. These countryside folk express contempt of the black fellow countrymen and they are opposed to the idea that a son or a daughter should contract marriage with one of theirs."[41]

The question of conflict and violence has another important dimension which merits at least brief consideration here. If violence and conflict because of race prejudice is often internalized by Puerto Ricans rather than being externalized, what are the implications of such behavior on the ability of Puerto Ricans to solve the problem of race prejudice in the Island? The fact is that very few Puerto Ricans at all are taking issue with the racial discrimination in Puerto Rico, least of all black and other nonwhites. Is conflict and perhaps violence necessary to solve a problem of race discrimination?

If we agree to look toward Brazil as some kind of reasonable model by which limited comparison can be made with Puerto

Rico, then it would seem that conflict and polarity in the opinion of some observers, might be a better gauge by which to measure the journey toward full integration of individuals suffering the consequences of exclusion because of race prejudice.

Talcott Parsons, while recognizing the dangers of polarity inherent in a policy of polarization, explains:

> Relatively sharp polarization clearly favors conflict and antagonism in the first instance. Providing, however, other conditions are fulfilled, sharp polarization seems on the longer run to be more favorable to effective inclusion than is a complex grading of the differences between components, perhaps particularly where gradations are arranged on a superiority-inferiority hierarchy. To put cases immediately in point, I take the position that the *race relations problem has a better prospect of resolution in the United States than in Brazil,* partly because the line between white and Negro has been so rigidly drawn in the United States because the system has been sharply polarized.[42]

If conflict is a necessary ingredient for a society on the verge of attempting to solve problems of racial discrimination, then Puerto Rican society is in crisis. With few exceptions have members of the scholarly community dared put the issue of race relations before an Islandwide forum. The government, though it commissioned a study in the early 1960s, has not moved toward fulfilling any of the recommendations. Students at the University of Puerto Rico have not made the plight of the poor (white and nonwhite) part of their social concern. The problem of racial discrimination has not been publicly espoused by mulattos, and "the most African-like sectors of the population keep themselves from becoming public activists on guard or against racial discrimination."[43]

If Talcott Parsons is correct about the possibility of the race problem being able to find a solution faster in the U. S. than in Brazil, it becomes apparent to this author that it will probably be solved in the United States and Brazil before it will resolve in Puerto Rico. As one faculty member at the University of Puerto Rico put it, "not only is it impossible to find a black movement in action in Puerto Rico, the fact is that such a possibility has not even been 'contemplated.' "[44]

Black visitors from the mainland have met with indifference and at times with hostility in their visits to the Island. Martin

Luther King complained that Puerto Rican response to his visit was "lukewarm."[45] Stokely Carmichael, invited to Puerto Rico by some "radical intellectuals" to see about the possibilities of a coalition between the Independence Movement in the Island and the aspirations of blacks in the United States, did not meet with success. Leaders of the Independence Movement "threatened to resign" at the possibility of some kind of link between Puerto Rican Independentistas and blacks. "It should be made clear that it was not Carmichael's militant attitude that offended those in the Independence Movement, but his color."[46] A third visitor, a member of the Nation of Islam ("Black Muslim"), visited the Island in 1963 in order to work with black Puerto Ricans. He met with such indifference during his visit that it led him to conclude that Puerto Ricans "are seeking a white identity." The end result, he concluded, was that they have no other choice but to "reject their African roots."[47]

The lack of interest in things "black" and the fact that in Puerto Rico there has never been "any concerted effort or interest" in probing or studying the magnificent African contribution to Puerto Rico has been described by Thomas Mathews as "deplorable."[48]

SOCIAL AND CLASS DISCRIMINATION

Jose Celso Barbosa is an important figure in the history of Puerto Rico.[49] As a black man he became the first of his race to rise to prominence in the affairs of the Island. Celso Barbosa wrote a lot about his beliefs and unlike other prominent black Puerto Ricans, he spoke out on racial issues. One important reason for examining the aspect of "class" and "social" discrimination through the words of Celso Barbosa is that he is often used and quoted as the classic example by Americans and Puerto Ricans who hold the view that there is no prejudice in the Island, simply "social" and "class" discrimination.

As far as Barbosa was concerned, Puerto Rico did not have a problem of color:

> The problem of color does not exist in Puerto Rico. It does not exist in the political life; it does not exist in public life. If a line does exist and it is logical that it should, it is more or less found in the social

life. Not having, then, a problem of color in public life and since the color element has never attempted to cross or to erase the social line, the problem of color does not exist in Puerto Rico.[50]

His formula was simple, "if you stay in your place, you will never have a color problem." His newspaper articles elaborated further his stance. He warned black Puerto Ricans, "never try to confuse social questions with those which are public and political." Again, he wrote that blacks in Puerto Rico must never try "by tolerance or by favor" to break the "social line of division" which existed at that time.[51]

Celso Barbosa was *inconsistent* in his views concerning the problem of race and color in Puerto Rican life. While he said that there was no problem of color, he often wrote about ways of "solving" the problem of color in the Island. He envisioned a solution to the race problem in Puerto Rico through intermarriages between whites and nonwhites. It seemed logical to him that if people who occupied the lowest rung of the social and economic ladder were there because they were black and nonwhite, the solution was simply to make them white, or at least, less black.

The solution was already on the way since, according to him, the "black race had been losing itself with other races." He believed that a man of color in Puerto Rico had three types of blood in his veins: "Each man of color in Puerto Rico is a conglomeration of blue blood (royal lineage), Indian blood and African blood."[52] Evolution was the key to the racial problem of Puerto Rico. The "black" Puerto Rican would become "grifo," the "grifo" would become "mulatto," and the "mulatto" would evolve and become "white," and the "black, black" *(negro, negro)* would disappear. The evolution will continue; and the problem will be resolved."[53]

The belief that there is no race prejudice in Puerto Rico, but simply social or class discrimination has at times weakened scholarly efforts at interpreting the Puerto Rican socio-historical experience. Such is the case with the basic work on the history of slavery in Puerto Rico, by Luis Díaz Soler. The author gathers together in one volume more than enough sources to make a first rate analysis. Somehow convinced that race prejudice is foreign to the Puerto Rican experience, he very selectively chooses a quotation from Celso Barbosa to close a final chapter of his book on slavery.

Although Celso Barbosa's own words indicated a willingness "to accept his place," though he equated "white blood" with "blue blood," Soler gives credence to his assumption by presenting Barbosa as the mouthpiece for blacks in Puerto Rico. Soler writes:

> The certain words of Dr. Barbosa are worthy to close the history of slavery in Puerto Rico. A people which maintained for a period of more than three hundred years an institution of that nature as an integral part of its social and economic structure, nevertheless offered the ex-slave the opportunity to live in equal plane with their fellow citizens enjoying all the rights belonging to free citizens.[54]

Tomás Blanco and Eric Williams are but two more writers who have spread the belief that in Puerto Rico people are discriminated for social and class reasons as opposed to race discrimination. Williams saw the race problem as follows: "legally the Negro is on a footing of equality with the white man. On the social level, however, race prejudice exists today, and is increasing."[55]

Puerto Ricans are insulted if told they are racist. Such an accusation will, if not carefully defined, place them in the same category as the Americans in the mainland. In the United States, laws have been passed to deliberately exclude blacks from full participation in American life after slavery. Such occurrences have not taken place in Puerto Rico. The paradox that exists for the Puerto Rican who is insulted by an accusation which claims he is racist, is that while he denies that he is racist, he is confronted with the social fact of blacks and nonwhites in Puerto Rico occupying inferior positions to whites in Puerto Rico's economic, social and public life.

Explanations for the paradox of a system which favors the white Puerto Rican who pleads innocent to racism cannot be found by linking Puerto Rican social attitudes to those found in the United States. Such a paradox finds a partial explanation in the socio-historical setting which the sociologist Fernandes describes in his adopted Brazil, which in some ways suffers from the same social disease of the "prejudice of having no prejudice."[56]

An explanation will be found by studying carefully the cultural and historical setting of Puerto Rican attitudes towards race and color, where in all fairness one cannot entirely dismiss American influences.

Renzo Sereno's findings in Puerto Rico support Fernandes' thesis while at the same time contrasts the difference in race relations in Puerto Rico when compared to those of the United States.

> Discrimination in Puerto Rico, however, is not the result of deeply inbred prejudice or of a deeply seated conviction of racial inequality. It is a social pattern, automatically followed, which tends to be institutionalized along American lines. But it lacks the personal element of conviction in racial inequality which is part of the American picture.[57]

If there is not a program or plan designed to benefit whites at the expense of nonwhites in Puerto Rico and other Latin American regions, why is it that whites are to be found on top of the social, economic and political pyramid and nonwhites at the bottom?

Because whites in Puerto Rico did not try to compensate the black Puerto Rican after abolition by making him aware of his cultural background which the slavery experience had mutilated and destroyed, the whites unwittingly set up a system which worked against blacks and favored whites. Even though, now, Puerto Ricans speak of "social" and "class" discrimination as opposed to race discrimination, the fact remains that the system set up by whites so much favors them as opposed to the blacks that the term "upper class" in the Island is synonymous with "white,"[58] while the term "lower class" denotes "blackness."[59] In Puerto Rico, "the upper class social strata, or at least its physical ideal, is white, although it continually absorbs a number of coloureds."[60]

In his book, *Los Derechos Civiles En La Cultura Puertorriqueña*, Eduardo Seda studies in depth the problem of race prejudice in the Puerto Rican culture. He focuses on the issue of social and class status as it relates to race:

> If racial discrimination was not a factor in Puerto Rico, we could reason that Puerto Ricans do not recognize or claim for themselves identity or social status that is based on racial factors. Nevertheless, we find in our study that not one single person categorized as "nonwhite"

claimed membership into the upper social stratum, while the proportion of people of color who identify themselves as members of the low social class exceeded our statistical expectations.[61]

It seems reasonable to conclude that since acceptance of new members to the upper class in Puerto Rico is partly determined by a "physical ideal," white skin, apart from educational or economic achievement, and that since this aspect can be labeled as racist, Puerto Ricans find it difficult to claim that what exists in Puerto Rico is simply a process of social and class discrimination.[62]

REFERENCES

1. Flinter, George D.: Examen del Estado Actual de los Esclavos de la Isla de Puerto Rico Bajo el Gobierno Espanol, New York, 1832.
2. Hoetink, H.: *The Two Variants in Caribbean Race Relations*, New York, Oxford University Press, 1967, p. 24.
3. ———: *The Two Variants in Caribbean Race Relations*, New York, Oxford University Press, 1967, p. 24.
4. Tannenbaum, Frank: *Slave and Citizen: The Negro in the Americas*, New York, Knopp Inc., 1946, p. 104.
5. ———: *Slave and Citizen: The Negro in the Americas*, New York, Knopp Inc., 1946, p. 104.
6. Gordon, Maxine: Cultural aspects of Puerto Rico's race problems, *American Sociological Review,* June 1950, p. 383.
7. Hoetink, H.: *The Two Variants in Caribbean Race Relations*, New York, Oxford University Press, 1967, p. 215.
8. Rogler, Charles: The morality of race mixing in Puerto Rico, *Social Forces, 25(1)*:77-81, Oct. 1946.
9. Williams, Eric: Race relations in Puerto Rico, *Foreign Affairs,* p. 308, January, 1945.
10. ———: Race relations in Puerto Rico, *Foreign Affairs,* p. 308, January, 1945.
11. Blanco, Thomas: *El Prejuicio Racial en Puerto Rico,* San Juan, Editorial Biblioteca de Autores, Puertorriquenos, 1942, p. 18.
12. ———: El Prejucio Racial en Puerto Rico, San Juan, Editorial Biblioteca de Autores, Puertorriquenos, 1942, p. 19.
13. Williams, Eric: Race relations in Puerto Rico, *Foreign Affairs,* p. 309, January, 1945.
14. Soler, Luis M. Deaz Para. Una Historia de la Eschavitud en Puerto Rico, *La Torres Revisto General de la Universidad de Puerto Rico, 1(1):* 86, enero-maryo, 1953.
15. Steward, Julian H. (ed.) : *The People of Puerto Rico,* Urbana, University of Illinois Press, 1969, p. 41.

16. Hoetink, H.: *The Two Variants in Caribbean Race Relations,* New York, Oxford University Press, 1967, p. 28.

17. Gordon, Maxine: Cultural aspects of Puerto Rico's race problem, *American Sociological Review,* June 1950, p. 383.

18. Soler, L. Diag: *Historia de la Esclavitud Negra en Puerto Rico,* p. 185.

19. ———: *Historia de la Esclavitud en Puerto Rico,* p. 165.

20. ———: *Historia de la Esclavitud Negra en Puerto Rico,* p. 177.

21. ———: *Historia de la Esclavitud Negra en Puerto Rico,* p. 177.

22. ———: *Historia de la Esclavitud Negra en Puerto Rico,* p. 172.

23. ———: *Historia de la Esclavitud Negra en Puerto Rico,* p. 168.

24. Bryce, Lord: The relation of the races in South America, in *Latin American Panorama,* eds. P. Kramer and R. McNicoll, New York, Capricorn Books, 1969, p. 206.

25. Soler, L. Diaz: *Historia de la Esclavitud Negra en Puerto Rico,* p. 177.

26. Soler, Diaz: *Paua Una Historia de la Esclavitud en Puerto Rico,* La torres Revisto General de la Universidad de Puerto Rico, *1(1)*:83, enero-marzo, 1953.

27. Reuter, Edward B.: *The American Race Problem,* New York, Thomas Y. Crowell, 1966, p. 25.

28. ———:*The American Race Problem,* New York, Thomas Y. Crowell, 1966, p. 25.

29. Memmi, Albert: Are the French Canadians Colonized? *Dominated Man,* Boston, Beacon Press, 1968, p. 188.

30. Wells, Henry: *The Modernization of Puerto Rico,* Cambridge, Harvard University Press, 1969, p. 269.

31. ———: *The Modernization of Puerto Rico,* Cambridge, Harvard University Press, 1969, p. 269.

32. U. S. Bureau of the Census: *National Data Book and Guide to Source* (90th Ed.), Washington, D. C., 1969, pp. 2-3.

33. Rogler, Charles: *Comerio: A Study of a Puerto Rican Town,* Lawrence, University of Kansas publication, 1940, p. 29.

34. Bonilla, Edwardo Seda: *Los Derechos Civiles En La Cultura Puertorriquena,* Rio Piedrias, Editorial Universitaria, 1963, p. 67.

35. ———: *Los Derechos Civiles En La Cultura Puertorriquenas,* Rio Piedros, Editorial Universitaria, 1963, p. 67.

36. Sereno, Renzo: Cryptomelanism: a study of color relations and personal insecurity in Puerto Rico, *Psychiatry, 10*:265, 1947.

37. ———: Cryptomelanism: a study of color relations and personal insecurity in Puerto Rico, *Psychiatry, 10*:265, 1947.

38. Caplow, Theodore; Wallace, Sheldon; and Wallace, Samuel: *The Urban Ambience,* Totowa, Bedmister Press, 1964.

39. *Claridad,* 28 de febrero de 1971.

40. *Claridad,* 28 de febrero de 1971.

41. Cruz, Juan Rodriguez: Las relaciones en Puerto Rico, *Revista de Ciencias Sociales, 9(4)*:385-86, diciembre 1965.

42. Parsons, Talcott: The problem of polarization on the axis of color, in *Color and Race,* John Hope Franklin (ed.) , Boston, Houghton-Mifflin Co., 1968, pp. 351-53.

43. Matthews, Thomas: La cuestion de color en Puerto Rico, mimeograph 1970, p. 23.

44. ———: La cuestion de color en Puerto Rico, mimeograph 1970, p. 23.

45. ———: La cuestion de color en Puerto Rico, mimeograph 1970, pp. 14, 15.

46. ———: La cuestion de color en Puerto Rico, mimeograph 1970, pp. 13, 14.

47. ———: La cuestion de color en Puerto Rico, mimeograph 1970, p. 15.

48. ———: La cuestion de color en Puerto Rico, mimeograph 1970, p. 23.

49. Pedreira, Antonio S.: *Un Hombre del Pueblo: Jose Celso Barbosa,* San Juan, Instituto de Cultura Puertorriquena, 1965.

50. Barbosa, Jose Celso: *Problemas* de Razas, San Juan, Imprenta Venezuela 1937, p. 31, pilan Barbosa de Rosario in series La Obra de Jose Celso Barbosa, *3.*

51. ———: *Problems de Razas,* San Juan, Imprenta Venezuela, 1937, p. 32.

52. ———: *Problems de Razas,* San Juan Imprenta Venezuela, 1937, p. 42.

53. ———: *Problems de Razas,* San Juan Imprenta Venezuela, 1937, p. 42.

54. Soler, Diaz: *Historia De La Esclavitud Negra en Puerto Rico,* p. 380.

55. Williams, Eric: Race relations in Puerto Rico, *Foreign Affairs,* January 1945, p. 308.

56. Fernandes, Florestan: *The Negro in Brazilian Society,* New York, Atheneum, 1971, p. 10.

57. Sereno, Renzo: Cryptomelanism: a study of color relations and personal insecurity in Puerto Rico, *Psychiatry 10:*262-63, 1947.

58. Rogler, Charles: *Comerio: A Study of a Puerto Rican Town,* Lawrence, University of Kansas publications, 1940, pp. 25, 27.

59. ———: *Comerio: A Study of a Puerto Rican Town,* Lawrence, University of Kansas publication, 1940, pp. 25, 27.

60. Hoetink, H.: *The Two Variants in Caribbean Race Relations,* New York, Oxford University Press, 1967, pp. 39, 40.

61. Bonilla, Eduardo Seda: *Los Derechos Civiles En La Cultura Puertorriquena,* Rio Piedras, Editorial Universitaria, 1963, p. 75.

62. Hoetink, H.: *The Two Variants in Caribbean Race Relations,* New York, Oxford University Press, 1967, p. 50.

CHAPTER 4

SOME ASPECTS OF PUERTO RICAN ADAPTATION TO MAINLAND U.S.A.

JUAN CRUZ and GEORGE R. RICKS

Puerto Rico is a Caribbean, West Indies island, 35 miles wide and 100 miles long. It is a Commonwealth,* associated with the United States of America, established in 1954. Its 2,850,000 residents represent a population density of some 714 persons per square mile as compared to a population density of some 57 persons per square mile in the United States.

Culturally, Puerto Rico has been affected greatly by sixty years of contact with the United States. While Iberian (Spanish) cultural heritage has been overshadowed in contemporary times, Puerto Rican national culture is primarily a blend of the culture of Spain and the United States; and is influenced but little by the indigenous Indian culture (Arawak) of the Island. Thus, as compared with some other Latin American countries, Puerto Rico has been considered relatively weak in indigenous folk arts and aboriginal cultural traditions. For example, Indian culture is still meaningful in Mexico and Peru, as is Afro-American culture in Brazil and Haiti. However, in Puerto Rico the Indians were absorbed or were killed off very early and the large population of African slaves (almost half of the population in the early 1860's) retained relatively little of the African cultural survivals that have enriched the cultures of other parts of the West Indies. Examples of the fusion of various cultures in Puerto Rico are quite obvious in aesthetic manifestations of the acculturative

---

* Puerto Rico is a self-governing commonwealth, associated with the United States of America through a voluntary compact. The compact, governing the Federal Government, is founded on Public Law 600. It is the result of a proposal by the people of Puerto Rico that the Congress of the United States provide for the organization of a government by the people of Puerto Rico under a Constitution of their own adoption.

Cruz, Juan, and Rick, George R., "Some Aspects of Pureto Rican Adaptation to Mainland U.S.A.," in *Children Psychology and the Schools* (Eds. Feather and Olson), Evanston, Ill.: Scott, Foresman and Co., 1960.

process. The "plena," for example, represents a fusion of Iberian (Spanish) and African musical elements; while the Puerto Rican "decima" is a Spanish influenced folk-song poetry form.

CULTURAL PATTERNS
Hispanic, African, Indian, American (U. S. A.)

To think of the Puerto Rico culture as an amalgamation of the cultures *per se* would be quite inadequate. Puerto Rico's distinctive colonial position, geographical environment, and location not only caused a selection of features from the Spanish culture; but entailed special adaptation of many of these features. Puerto Rican cultures, especially those of the rural communities, were by no means exact duplicates of those of Spain, and they could not have been duplicate since most forms of population migrated to the island.

Religion

Crown Interest

The power struggle in Puerto Rico's church and state differed from that in Spain in two principal Ecclesiastical patronage. In Puerto Rico the territorial rights belonged exclusively to the crown. Many factors prevented the integration of the bulk of the people into the institutional framework of the church.

During the 18th century and before the opening of the Port of San Juan, traveling over the hazardous route was impossible to accomplish without difficulties. The route conditions in Puerto Rico at this time were pathetic.

Coffee, tobacco, cotton, sugar, minor crops, and livestock, were in the hands of the commercial landowners by the end of the century. The richest men in the island were cattle breeders; owning immense wealth and extensive land.

CREDIT. By 1840 there had not been adequate credit facilities in the island. Agricultural development was by Royal grants or dispensations. The immigration of entrepreneurs with their own capital, or the borrowing of capital from sources outside the island developed the large haciendas. Even the stimulation of the expanding commercial and agricultural activities that would have been provided by a stable currency were absent under Spanish rule.

Labor Forces

Slave labor in Puerto Rico never assumed the great importance which it had in the British and French possessions in the West Indies. Most slave labor concentrated in the coastal region, particularly in the Alluvian Plains. Most of the population was engaged in agriculture of some kind throughout the 19th century.

Government

Government was developed by frameworks dictated by the Spanish Empire. Governors charged to retard or to advance measures which could have important effects on the island's development. Defense and public order also were controlled by the Spanish Parliament.

Deputies and the Provincial Commission

The Deputies elected a small minority that was able to pay the poll tax. Civil Police organized for the purpose of intimidation during the period of unrest.

Sociocultural Groups

By the end of the Spanish regime, Puerto Rico's social status and power were finding a basis of wealth derived from export trade. The trade of coffee and sugar created an aristocracy of wealthy planters who had a considerable investment in land and machinery. Sharp differentiation between large and small farmers was felt on the island.

Puerto Rico became incorporated into the American tariff system in early 1900. As agriculture begins to develop in a commercial basis, the island slowly begins to depend more and more on cash for its agricultural direct competition with other sects, its impact is still deeply felt in the value system and patterns of behavior of the populations. Its stress upon traditional relationships within the social structure gives it strong support from the upper and middle classes in urban areas. The emphasis and sanction on the dominant role of the household (dominant familial role of the father) lends similar support from culturally conservative small-scale farmers in rural areas where the family unit is the most important element in terms of productivity.

Protestant groups affect some 15 percent of the population. Indeed, Protestantism has gained considerable strength since its introduction to the Island in mid-nineteenth century. Its major concentration seems to be in the towns and rural areas and membership chiefly among such faiths as the Evangelical Church, Seventh Day Adventists and the Pentecostal churches which tend to emphasize taboos on smoking, drinking, dancing, sexual promiscuity and an acceptance of strong rhythms and singing to the accompaniment of secular musical instruments (guitar, drum, etc.) as a formidable part of religious services.

Spiritualism, although generally ascribed to lower class and rural people, appears to be quite prevalent among the middle and upper classes on the Island. This belief in the ability of mediums to control cantation by spirits, according to some scholars, occurs primarily among adherents to Catholicism rather than among Protestants. However, it serves mainly as a supplement rather than an alternative to other religious beliefs.

Witchcraft also appears to serve as a supplement to Western religious forms. Although such practices are ascribed to the African derived population in Puerto Rico, research by anthropologists indicate strong influences of witchcraft in culturally conservative areas where the population (Catholic and Protestant) is predominantly non-Negro. Indeed, field research has indicated less influence of spiritualism and black magic in "all-Negro communities" than in other communities.

The Puerto Rican family is in some ways similar to the family-type of peasant Europe. It is patriarchal and authoritarian, with the adult male commanding obedience and respect from all members of the family. However, the Puerto Rican family differs from the European type mainly in the prevalence of consensual or common-law marriage. It is estimated that one quarter of the marriages are of this type, and that as a result, about one third of the births are out-of-wedlock. However, the Puerto Rican's concern for family structure includes legal recognition for children born out-of-wedlock,* and is reflected in the sur-naming custom.

Although the original intent in naming a child was to denote legitimacy and lineage, parents in consensual or common-law marriage also tend to follow this practice. For children born out-of-wedlock, the usual practice was to register the child with the mother's family name only; but in several of the Latin American countries, this practice has been changed by law.

As with all other people, every child has a father and a mother. But among Spanish-speaking people, the child has the father's family name *and* the mother's family name attached to his given or baptismal name or names. Often it is desirable that his lineage be further indicated by adding the family name of an important grandfather or grandmother.

In Puerto Rico, the law requires that the names of both parents, married or not, must be recorded on the birth certificate. Provision is also made permitting the child born out-of-wedlock to use his father's family name. In any case, the continuation of the family name from one generation to the next, is patrilinear.

Both European peasant and the Puerto Rican exhibit concern for the virginity of female children and closely guard their associations with unrelated males. But while the European peasant generally arranged the marriage of his son or daughter to enhance his own condition, Puerto Rican marriages tend to be more a matter of early escape of the young daughter with a man whom her parents had not chosen. There is a pattern of hostility on the part of male members of a family towards would-be suitors. Hence, courtship is most frequently carried on through intermediaries and marriage is made possible by way of elopement of the young lady and her "novio." In spite of obstacles to marriage, the girl (especially among lower classes) of eighteen or nineteen, is expected to have entered wedlock. Indeed, marriage at the age of thirteen and fourteen is not uncommon among peasant and lower

---

* In 1963 the National Association on services to Unmarried Parents reported that 4 percent of the total United States population (about 7 million people) were born out-of-wedlock.

class Puerto Ricans. As a result, many individuals move directly from childhood to adult responsibility; the females have an early experience of child-bearing and males an early responsibility for children.

The family situation in Puerto Rico is perhaps one of the stronger elements in the culture. Men might have children by a number of women, but generally assume responsibility for all of them. Even with relatively high degree of marriage break-ups, there are always places in families for the children. The strong institution of godparents (the "compadre" and "comadre") for each child, provides a second set of parents who are ready to take over if the family of procreation in some way defaults (too many children, death, desertion, etc.). Children are neither resented nor neglected.

WHO ARE THE PUERTO RICAN MIGRANTS? The concept "Puerto Rican" among the majority of mainlanders is that of an "immigrant" or "foreigner.' This point of view is supported by the fact: (1) that Puerto Rico is geographically separated from the mainland, (2) Puerto Rico is not a state, (3) there is a general ignorance of the meaning of the Commonwealth relationship between Puerto Rico and the United States and (4) there is an apparent communication barrier created by the English and Spanish linguistic traditions among Mainlanders and Islanders.

However, Puerto Ricans are American citizens and as such are legally entitled to migrate to the mainland. There are two general types: (1) the Urban Puerto Rican who generally moves from the cities of Puerto Rico to urban centers of the United States and, (2) the rural Puerto Rican who moves from the cane fields of Puerto Rico to perform seasonal labor on the farms of Eastern and Midwestern United States.

Studies of Puerto Rican migration to the United States indicate that in the main, they do not come merely to seek employment. The over-riding factor is desire for a better job. A Columbia University survey has shown that 85 percent of the migrants have quit jobs to come to the mainland, 15 percent had been unemployed at the time of migration, and 71 percent had been fully employed for two years before migration.

Typically, for families with children, the father migrates alone to find a job and living quarters; then brings over the rest of the family, often in stages. This results in a family that is divided between the continent and Puerto Rico and usually creates a situation in which one part of a family is "Americanized" and the other is not. A less typical but not uncommon pattern is the "Fatherless" family in which the mother decides to go to the mainland where jobs are plentiful and a "better life" is offered for women and children. This latter fact partially explains statistics showing that the Puerto Rican mother is more usually employed (though they tend to stay home if possible) here, than in the Commonwealth; the Cook County Department of Public Aid indicates that less than 1 percent of its case load is of Puerto Rican families.

WHAT ARE SOME OF THEIR PROBLEMS OF ADJUSTMENT? The normal Puerto Rican family structure undergoes serious change and stress in the new environment. Even in the case of a complete family (mother-father-siblings), the husband-wife relationship is affected. Where the father is usually the main support of the family, he finds employment difficult or nonexistent while the skills of the wife may bring home as much or more money than her husband's.

In New York and Chicago, for example, it is often easier for women to get jobs in the needlework trades than for their husbands. Or, the women may make $2.50 an hour while her husband can get only $2.00 an hour. This puts his position in jeopardy and many marriage counselors have noted extreme tension in Puerto Rican families resulting from the wife and the depreciated position of the husband. It is harder for him to be the boss when his wife makes more money than he does.

Parent-child relationships also feel the impact of stress and change. A prime factor here is language. Since it is often the case that children have a better command of English than the parents, children may assume a major role in relations between the family and the "outside world," they are no longer "seen but not heard." A by-product of this condition is "second generationitis" where children find themselves torn between two systems of thought and behavior . . . the "old way" of doing things and the new cultural demands of school and society.

Traditionally, male children are given relative freedom in their "growing up" years. Outside of showing respect for the father, the male child is encouraged toward self-discipline. Female children, however, are accorded entirely different treatment. They are carefully guarded with respect to relationships outside the family; a prime consideration being the maintenance of virginity.

The result of conflict between these indigenous culture patterns and new standards of behavior and value has serious consequences. Like other children, Puerto Rican children tend to become about as good or as bad as the children with whom they associate. Left on their own resources in the new environment, boys are frequently exposed to opportunities for falling into "bad company," learning anti-social habits and developing patterns of disrespect and disobedience towards the "illiterate" and "old-time" parent. The girl is frequently seen to rebel against the restrictive patterns of staying at home and dating under the stifling conditions of a chaperon. The desire to emulate the behavior patterns and standards of their classmates and social acquaintances sometimes results in lying to and deception of parents by girls. The settlement house or social center which encourages dancing, for example, may be seen as unwholesome by the parents. Yet, the girls may "steal" time to attend such activities.

Conservative Puerto Rican parents are subject to confusion and shock in the face of such situations. A feeling of inadequacy tends to result in several courses of action. They "give up" their responsibility for the children and often desire that the child be taken over by some institution that will teach it discipline and respect; they exercise even tighter discipline and further alienate or increase the emotional disturbance of the child; or they may send the recalcitrant child back to stay with a relative in Puerto Rico until he is mature and learns to face responsibilities.

An additional difficulty in adjustment lies in the fact that the main task of child-training is traditionally relegated to the mother. Outside of respect and obedience, *the father has little to do with children or management of the home.* Indeed, such a task is considered to be beneath male dignity. Left on her own resources, the Puerto Rican mother is often confused by the variety of patterns of child-rearing she observes in her new cultural setting. Even though she may be amenable to change, she finds herself at a loss to choose a standard of discipline and behavior for her children.

WHAT ROLE DO SOCIAL AGENCIES PLAY? Social agencies often find their programs (and budget) inadequate to deal effectively with newcomers who are plagued with such problems as a divided family (culturally and geographically), a fatherless family, a low social-economic status family, or children in a culture conflict who have little or no command of the English language. Many newcomer families (Puerto Rican and others), embody all of these problems.

With the exception of Protestant sects (mostly store-front churches), social organizations of the grassroots type are of relatively recent origin among Puerto Ricans in mainland United States. In this respect, Puerto Ricans are similiar to other Latin American populations. Such organizations are rapidly increasing. The gap in organizational support and affiliation in the *Puerto Rican community is filled by the Migration Division* of the Department of Labor for the Commonwealth of Puerto Rico. This *agency fills a role for Puerto Ricans similar* to that which the NAACP and the Urban League fills for Negroes in the United States. It does not, however, assume leadership in community organizations, but provides professional services to stimulate and assist the development of "grassroots" leaders. Among other functions this organization serves 1) as an employment agency, 2) as source of orientation, information and education for migrants, 3) as a public relations medium to correct misconceptions about Puerto Ricans, 4) to handle problems of special interest to Puerto Ricans frequently setting policy for the Puerto Rican community, and 5) to develop community resources where they are acutely needed.

There are thirty-eight Puerto Rican civic organizations in Chicago, each of which sends delegates to the advisory committee of the Migration Division. These are primarily "self-help" organizations; some have purchased property for general community and recreational use.

The probability is that language more than any other factor is the greatest handicap to the adjustment of Puerto Ricans in the United States. Even the most unlettered migrant places a high value on education, but school is almost universally a frustrating experience because of the language barrier. Language also presents a problem for the adolescent male of maintaining self-dignity in his attempt to adjust to a new situation. For him it is embarrassing to speak English with an accent. Language too is most frequently a stumbling block to employment and full participation in the daily life of the larger community.

However, the Puerto Rican faces serious problems of adjustment not strictly related to language culture conflict on his arrival in the United States. The Puerto Rican must make adjustments to the weather which is more extreme; very hot in the summer and very cold in winter. The pace of the daily round of life is rapid and no longer leisurely; "time is money." Many a darker-skinned Puerto Rican who does not know discrimination as practiced in the States, suddenly finds that his ability to make a living (or find a home) is frequently related to biology (the color of his skin) and not ability or competence.

Although Puerto Ricans are attempting to adjust to a socio-cultural situation that is somewhat different from the one which earlier immigrant groups adopted, they seem to have chosen the approach of earlier immigrants. This is best seen in the activity of a core of young, educated Puerto Ricans in Chicago and New York. In New York, for example, "ASPIRA" a group of Puerto Rican social workers, professionals, and teachers, have organized to work with students and their parents so that they will make the best possible use of educational opportunities. They run workshops in which they work out plans to get youth through high school or through college, give lectures on professional opportunities, look for money for scholarships, and try to reach parents and community organizations. The young Puerto Rican leaders also run an interesting annual youth conference that gives insight into the concerns of struggles of the young people. They see Puerto Ricans as following in the path of earlier ethnic groups that preceded them and view them as models of imitation, not as targets for attack. In general, the group emphasizes its potential for achievement more than factors of prejudice and discrimination.

THE PUERTO RICAN AND THE SCHOOLS

For Puerto Rican children and youth, school is perhaps the major factor influencing adjustment to the socio-cultural environment of the continental United States. This fact is also true of his experience on the Island. Traditionally, the school in Puerto Rico is considered the second home of the child, and the teacher is considered the second mother of the child. Thus, Puerto Ricans consider school an integral part of the daily round of life, according it great respect and many prerogatives in the handling of children. At the same time, however, they have expectations that the school will assume many responsibilities in the area of child welfare. The school enjoys the rights of corporal punishment, reprimand and influencing family affairs concerning the child. It also is charged with responsibility for identifying and referring children in need of medical aid, clothing, food, and so on. This attitude toward school carries over in the Puerto Rican's experience on the mainland. Puerto Ricans will often send a sick child to school with the expectation that the principal or teacher will care for him. If the child fails to report to school the teacher or principal must show immediate concern for this absence; at least inquire about the progress of his health. In view of his dominant role, all inquiries to the family should be directed to the father. As titular head of the family he may not play the "heavy" role in matters of discipline, but it is he who normally represents the family at PTA meetings and other official matters relating to his family and the "outside world." Even though a child may serve as interpreter, the male adult remains the dominant factor.

It is most desirable that Puerto Rican pupils entering schools feel that the school understands and respects the culture from which he comes. This implies that adjustment is a two-way process and focuses attention on what the school can do to improve and accelerate this two-way process of adjustment.

It is of further importance that differences in cultural and social experience among Puerto Ricans be recognized. Among adults and pupils alike, four general categories may be delineated: 1) island-born, island schooled; 2) island-born, exclusively mainland schooled; 3) mainland-born, Puerto Rican born parents and 4) mainland-born, mainland-born parents.

As with other ethnic groups, one finds multi-problem families that might require the school to learn how to create adult relations; especially while the family is adjusting to the new environment. While in the process, it is particularly noticeable that Puerto Rican parents frequently do not respond to notices from the school or participate in school functions. When they do come, they are apt to huddle shyly in a corner, offering no ideas, and probably will not return. This highlights the fact that such Puerto Rican parents should (as far as possible) be dealt with as individuals.

The Puerto Rican child is generally sensitive in interpersonal and group situations. When faced with criticism or reprimand, a primary grade child may run into a corner to cry rather than have conflict with an authority figure. Older children tend to withdraw into silence. This behavior grows out of a socialization process in which children are taught to respect adults and not talk back; they are also taught not to look at the face of an adult when speaking to him.

However, the Puerto Rican youngster with sophistication in mainland ways may present quite a different attitude. This is especially true of teenagers who have been conditioned to the life-ways of slum areas in large cities. These youngsters are apt to rebel against the authority of parents, teachers and even law-enforcement officers. Their behavior is frequently quite different from the docility exhibited by the youngster who has come directly from Puerto Rico.

When does the Puerto Rican parent come to school? When their children are performing in school assemblies, some parents are eager to help with the activity by sewing of costumes. Others are willing to serve as school escorts, resource persons in the classroom (explaining how sugar is made, etc.), singing Spanish songs accompanied with guitars, or preparing and serving Puerto Rican dishes for classes with children of other backgrounds.

Mothers' clubs conducted in Spanish, for mothers with children in kindergarten-primary grades, are particularly attractive when stress is laid on such practical matters as shopping trips to neighborhood stores (consumer education), knitting lessons, first-aid and instruction in nutrition. Adult evening schools are well attended when the teacher is bilingual. However, English classes for Puerto Rican mothers seem to be more successful when conducted during regular school hours.

The foregoing discussion may be regarded as a brief or rather cursory treatment of some features of Puerto Rican culture that seem to have relevance for the adjustment problems of migrants to the mainland. Nevertheless, it is well to keep in mind the fact that the culture of Puerto Ricans, as the culture of any people, is a dynamic phenomenon subject to rapid and sometimes intense change. The Puerto Rico of today is not the same as the Puerto Rico of ten, fifteen or twenty years ago. The Puerto Rican living in mainland U.S.A., is not quite the same as the Puerto Rican who lives in Puerto Rico. While each may have an essentially similar cultural background, each is reacting to and interacting with a vastly different social and cultural environment. Thus, to understand the Puerto Rican, it is important to view his behavior from the viewpoint of an individual whose background (style of living) is to some degree in conflict with the demands of a new environment.

A major purpose of this article is to highlight certain features of Puerto Rican culture and history; as well as to point up contrasts between Island and mainland culture that affect the process of cultural accommodation by Puerto Ricans in the United States. The adaptation of Puerto Ricans to mainland requirements is indeed not simple nor without stress; it has not been so for any group of people in process of acculturation.

It is incumbent upon those who would (or are so mandated) assist in this process of culture change to develop insights and understandings that will help to meliorate the degree of stress and conflict which is inevitable. Further study through reading, language skill and first-hand knowledge of community life and problems (field trips and interpersonal relations with an open mind) is highly recommended to those who would enjoy an optimum measure of success in this regard.

REFERENCES

Pamphlets

William C. Beggs: *Puerto Rico: Showcase of Development* (reprint), Britanica Book of the Year, Distributed by Migration Division, Puerto Rican Dept. of Labor, 1952.

Juan Cruz: *An Outline History of the Puerto Rican People in America and the United States,* Bureau of Human Relations, Chicago Public Schools, 1967.

————: *The Puerto Rican Newcomer,* Commonwealth of Puerto Rico, Migration Division, Department of Labor, New York, October 1960.

————: *Identifying Names of Spanish Speaking Persons,* City of New York Department of Health, July 1955.

Articles

Joseph Monserrat: Cultural values and the Puerto Ricans, *Selected Papers: Institute on Cultural Patterns of Newcomers,* Welfare Council of Metropolitan Chicago, July 1964.

George Ricks: The Puerto Ricans: Americans in the process of adaptation, *Hexagon* Vol. I, No. 2, The Institute for Educational Theory, 1964.

Clarence Senior: Puerto Rican migrants to the continental United States, in Brown and Roueek, (Ed.), *One America,* Prentice-Hall, 1957.

Books

Clarence Senior: *Strangers then Neighbors,* New York, Freedom Books, 1961.

Julian Steward (Ed.) : *The People of Puerto Rico: A Study in Social Anthropology,* University of Illinois Press, 1956.

CHAPTER 5

CUBAN IMMIGRANTS—THE REFUGEE IMMIGRANTS

PETER BORN

"The Cuba of today is not the Cuba I dream of."
Rodrigo Parajon, Cuban
diplomat explaining his
resignation from Castro's
regime in 1961.

THE CUBAN REFUGEE came to the United States as a different breed of immigrant. Unlike the bulk of those who emigrated from Europe, the Orient, and other parts of Latin America, only a minority of Cubans came here in search of economic opportunity. Some were so well-off in Cuba that they managed to bring their servants with them.

Unlike the Pilgrims and Jews, religious persecution was not the refugees' main motivation, although their Catholicism had become more a handicap than an advantage. And unlike some Canadians, Mexican-Americans, and Puerto Ricans, the Cubans never visit their homeland, even though it is only 90 miles from the continental United States. The 650,000 Cubans who fled their island in the 1960's represent one of the largest groups of political outcasts to ever land in America.

Many of them had considered Fidel Castro a hero in 1959; he had liberated the country from the dictatorial rule of President Fulgencio Batista. But to the horror of the middle and upper classes, the exceedingly popular new government moved rapidly leftward into Communism.

The promised land reform program turned into a Soviet-style land collectivization drive with the small farmer becoming a tenant of the state rather than a man of increased prosperity. Industrial reform became confiscation of private property. Illiter-

Born, Peter, "The Refugee Immigrants," *Tha Latins,* A background report prepared by the Chicago Tribune Educational Services Department, 1972, pp. 17-20.

acy was stamped out, as promised, but only to facilitate the reading of government-sanctioned literature.

Newspapers, television and radio stations were censored at first and then suppressed entirely. Sanitation projects were begun and scenic areas were beautified; but by 1960 food and medicine became scarce and the once-lucrative tourist industry had dried up. In the beginning, "war criminals" were swiftly executed, but the threat of imprisonment for those even slightly suspected of resisting the revolution frightened many Cubans. No parts of the island was too remote to escape government policy.

The Cuban revolution stands alone in the history of the hemisphere as the most fastpaced and thorough period of social, economic, and political change. The Mexicans' revolution was more bloody, but it could not match the swift turnaround of Cuban life. As Castro's personal appeal was dampened by the actions of his government, disillusionment spread through the Cuban establishment. A mere trickle of refugees in 1959 became a flood by 1962. First came the elite-government ministers, judges, professors, plantation owners, and bankers. They were followed by corporate managers, doctors, lawyers, and other professionals.

By 1967 the clerical, skilled, and semiskilled workers were arriving in Miami on the daily freedom flights sponsored by the United States government.

The age and educational level of the refugees continually declined until the self-exiled professor was followed by the grade school teacher and the corporate sales manager by the retail clerk. But the unskilled and rural poor never made up more than 25 percent of the stream.

The majority had been at least comfortable if not rich. In 1958, in pre-Castro Cuba, 60 percent of all employed males made less than $900 a year. A study done among the refugees in 1963 showed that the exiled Cubans had earned between $2,000 and $8,000; and only 23 percent were under the $2,000 mark. Oddly enough only 11 percent of the group said they left because their income was diminished by the Communist regime. Yet two thirds of those interviewed had suffered losses. Economic considerations were apparently seen in context of lost political and social freedoms.

A young man, who had been a bookkeeper in the transport ministry, said he was told to join the militia or face the loss of his job. He was then sent into the fields to cut sugar cane. No one was allowed to be indifferent; people were either participants in the revolution or enemies of the state. "You had to be with them, or they would drive you crazy" another refugee said. And dissent was not tolerated, according to a 35-year-old former sales promotion supervisor. "After I had been taken prisoner twice, demoted in my job from supervisor to peon, and harassed in my house, they (Castro supporters) appeared with a loudspeaker in front of my home to insult us for being against Communism. . . . They informed me that my situation was delicate and that if they took me prisoner again at work, I would never get out of jail."

The government viewed the refugee airlift as a handy escape valve for internal dissent, but it also viewed the exodus as a demoralizing spectacle for those left behind.

Referring to the exiles as "gusanos" (worms), Castro has steadfastly denounced those who abandoned the homeland. "If some more want to go to Miami, let them go to Miami! Each time that a boatload of parasites leaves, the Republic comes out ahead. What do you lose, working men and women who live in the slums, who live in shacks, who live in the poor sections of towns? One less beefsteak eater, one less driver of a fancy car, one drinker less . . . and if he has a good apartment, that apartment will go to a working family that has a lot of children."

If Castro's rhetoric and arbitrary regime gave dissatisfied Cubans a push towards Miami American immigration policies provided the pull. Compared to the restriction placed on the citizens from other Latin American countries, the United States practically enticed the Cubans.

Entry requirements were relaxed to the point of limpness. Once off the freedom flight, the refugees were processed in Miami and, if possible, relocated in other cities and offered retraining or special schooling. Welfare money was funneled into an assistance program designed especially for refugees. This cost the federal government half a billion dollars between 1963 and 1971.

Many exiles who had managed to bring their families were

content to settle down, but others could not escape the ambition of returning to a Communist-free Cuba. Miami with its 350,000 refugees became the nerve center for dozens of secret guerrilla organizations plotting to return home in triumph.

Their desire to return home put the refugees in a quandary. Before Castro turned Marxist, his anti-American stance had been applauded. Suddenly the exiles had to swallow their hatred of past United States intervention in Cuban affairs and go to Washington seeking what they had always claimed to detest.

President John Kennedy sympathized and cooperated to the extent of walking into one of the worst debacles in the history of American foreign policy. In 1961 a small army of 1,400 exiles landed on the southern coast of Cuba, hoping that the population would revolt and come to their aid in overthrowing Castro. Their secret radio transmitted a call to arms: "Alert, Alert. Look well at the rainbow."

But within seventy-two hours the "Bay of Pigs" invasion had collapsed. One hundred invaders were killed outright and the other 1,113 were captured. At first Kennedy took the blame, but the fault was later placed on the Central Intelligence Agency. Acting on misinformation, the CIA had canceled the protective air strikes leaving the exiles nakedly at the mercy of Castro's tiny air force.

The Cuban government finally released the Bay of Pigs prisoners for a ransom price of $49 million worth of medical supplies and other goods.

The dream of driving Castro from power still persisted, however. Various paramilitary groups made scattered raids on the island throughout the 1960s, but direct attempts to topple the regime failed miserably.

A group called Alpha 66 landed troops on the Cuban coast in April and September of 1970 without success. In May of that year the group sank two Cuban fishing boats and took eleven fishermen prisoner. The plan was to wring concessions from Castro, but all the hostages were released two weeks later.

The Miami-based insurgents suffered a setback in the same year when President Nixon "reached an understanding" with the Soviet Union over the building of a Russian submarine base near

Cuba's Cienfuegos Harbor. Bitterly accepting the fact that the United States was not about to invade Cuba, the refugee groups refused to forget their disappointment. Over 500 of them picketed the 1972 Republican convention in Miami with signs reading: "Cuba—Soviet colony under United States protection" and "Mr. Nixon—our demands are not negotiable."

The majority of refugees, though, long ago resigned themselves to rebuilding their lives in America instead of hanging in limbo over politics at home.

The refugees have been called resilient, energetic, and shrewd business people. Spreading their activities outward from Miami, Cubans own one third of the businesses in the 28-community area of Dade County.

Rags to riches stories concerning refugees abound in the area. There are tales of how men begin by washing dishes and driving trucks only to end up owning multi-million dollar construction firms or founding their own banks. Richard Nixon's Key Biscayne neighbor, millionaire, C. G. Rebozo, is an illustration of Cuban refugee success.

Studies show that most Cuban households in Miami have an average monthly income of more than $600. Sixteen percent have earnings of more than $900 a month, and only 18 percent make less than $350. According to a United States census in 1971, they fare better than blacks, Mexican-Americans, and Puerto Ricans.

However, the Cuban experience has not entirely been a sweet song of ringing cash registers. Twelve percent of the refugees in the nation were on welfare in 1971, according to estimates by Paul Lane of the Miami refugee office. And this sad fact has provoked prejudices and rivalries with disgruntled whites and needy blacks.

In practice it is easier for a Cuban refugee to get welfare benefits, partly because the exile aid program is financed completely by the federal government on federal standards, with built-in provisions exclusively for refugees.

Those who are employed are accused of taking jobs away from other minorities. Director Robert Simms of the (Dade) County Community Relations Board has been quoted as saying employers would rather hire white Cubans than black Americans. Despite denials of this from the state employment office, the displacement theory still thrives in the ghettos. The official report on the black riot during the 1968 Republican Convention in Miami tersely cited one cause of the upheaval as "loss of local jobs by blacks over the prior several years to Cuban refugees."

And their Latin cousins in New York City, the Puerto Ricans, have said the Cubans snatched off the opening job opportunities created after years of Puerto Rican political pressure.

The Cubans, however, say they are the ones being discriminated against by being denied their own representatives in local and national government. And evidence exists that they have been exploited by employers.

Harry Tyson, director of the Miami office of the Florida State Employment Service, said "The employers in Dade County have capitalized on these people coming in here and working for less money."

Dr. Reinhold Wolff, an economic research expert, said Dade County, where the bulk of Cubans live, has the lowest industrial wage rate of any metropolitan area in Florida.

CHAPTER 6

AMERICA'S SPANISH-SPEAKING: A PROFILE

HENRY M. RAMIREZ

W HO ARE THE SPANISH-SPEAKING?
Paradoxically, all of them do not speak Spanish. Some speak only Spanish, others only English, and many speak both languages.

Racially, the Spanish-speaking include white people, brown people, and black people. Though they or their ancestors came from Mexico or Puerto Rico for the most part, many originated in Cuba or one of the Central or South American republics.

The main common denominator is a Spanish language heritage. Beyond that they may differ greatly. In microcosm, they are a melting pot—and like the greater United States melting pot, the melting is far from complete.

They are in every state in the Union, and, according to the latest census, 31 states have Spanish-speaking populations of at least 20,000.

They represent roughly 5 percent of the U. S. population, making them our second largest minority group. Physicians, dentists, lawyers, and prosperous businessmen are numbered among the Spanish-speaking, but far too many are poorly paid laborers.

Despite their numbers, the Spanish-speaking have only recently begun to capture the attention of the general public. The national news media during the past decade has become aware of this significant minority, but has continued to reinforce a mixed-to-negative picture of the Spanish-speaking as rural, lazy, sinister, illiterate, and culturally disadvantaged. The Spanish-speaking resent these stereotypes. Though they have dwelled in territory now

Ramirez, Henry M., "America's Spanish-Speaking: A Profile," *Manpower*, September 1972, pp. 311-34.

part of the United States for centuries, they are too often regarded as interlopers and not part of the American mainstream.

In general, Spanish-speaking Americans are severely disadvantaged compared with the dominant Anglo population. In income, occupational status, and unemployment, their status is roughly equivalent to blacks; in education they are far worse off. Discrimination against them remains a major obstacle to their social and economic progress, particularly for poor Chicanos and Puerto Ricans. Lack of English facility and other cultural differences, including a partially self-imposed ethnic isolation common to earlier generations of immigrants, leave a great many Spanish-surnamed people outside the mainstream of economic opportunity.

There is considerable controversy over the actual number of Spanish-speaking people in the United States. Official census figures place the number at more than 10 million in 1970. Nearly three-fifths are of Mexican origin and about one-sixth are Puerto Ricans (not counting the 2.7 million in the Commonwealth of Puerto Rico). But information from local census studies, migrant studies, public school enrollments, the Cuban resettlement program, and other data suggests that the real total may be substantially higher. Informal estimates of some Spanish-speaking spokesmen range up to 16 million.

Numbers Have Increased Substantially

Since World War II, the number of Spanish-speaking have substantially increased, and they have tended to move from the country to the city and to disperse throughout the United States. Although there are still large concentrations in certain areas, 46 United States cities now have Spanish-speaking populations of 10,000 or more.

The areas with the highest concentrations of the Spanish-speaking are:

The southwestern states of Arizona, California, Colorado, New Mexico, and Texas, where the overwhelming majority of Mexican-Americans and 3 out of 5 Spanish-speaking Americans are located.

New York City, where 8 out of 10 of the Puerto Ricans living in the continental United States reside.

Florida, where large numbers of the more than 600,000 persons of Cuban descent have settled along with many immigrants from Central or South America.

This leaves roughly 2 million Spanish-speaking persons who live elsewhere in the nation.

The Spanish-speaking today have a new-found sense of group identity evolving around a common language heritage and similar cultural values. But this should not be permitted to obscure the important differences within this ethnic group.

For the sake of brevity—and at the risk of oversimplifying—let us look at these differences. Mexican-Americans are the largest subgroup. Most of them were born in the United States and large numbers are ill-educated and otherwise disadvantaged. Except for New Mexico and a few locales in California and Texas, they have not reached positions of economic or political power.

The Puerto Ricans, the second largest group, reside primarily in the Northeast, especially New York City. A majority have arrived in recent years. By income, unemployment, education, and similar measures, they are the most severely disadvantaged of the Spanish-speaking. Puerto Ricans have attained little economic or political leverage.

Almost all the Cubans in the United States are foreign born. They entered this country in large numbers in the past 14 years, thanks in part to the excellent Cuban resettlement program, and they are concentrated primarily in the Miami area. Many possess job skills and a profession.

People of Central and South American extraction and other persons of Spanish origin are a large and diverse group, making up about one fifth of the Spanish-speaking population. Most were born in the United States and about half live in the Southwest. They tend to represent a relative economic and social elite, with higher incomes, better jobs, and more education than other Spanish-speaking groups, even Cubans.

Income is the best single determinant of economic and social status. Census figures for 1971 emphasize the difference between the Spanish groups, and their inferior position as a whole to the rest of the United States. Median family income in 1971 was

$7,548 for the Spanish-speaking and $10,285 for all Americans. Puerto Ricans were by far the worst off, with median family income of $6,185, more than $200 less than that for black families.

Most Are in Unskilled, Low-Paid Jobs

Census figures show that some 29 percent of Mexican-Americans and 32 percent of Puerto Ricans are below the poverty level. The comparable figure for all Americans is 13 percent and for blacks 34 percent. Clearly, the Spanish-speaking, and particularly Mexican Americans and Puerto Ricans, are congregated along with blacks at the bottom of the economic ladder in terms of income.

The precarious economic position of the Spanish-speaking is further underscored by the nature of the jobs they hold. About 70 percent of them are in unskilled and low-paid blue-collar, service, and farm jobs. Only 23 percent of Spanish-surnamed men hold white-collar jobs, compared with 42 percent for all American males.

Being relegated to the bottom of the economic heap is a consequence of the educational deprivation suffered by the Spanish-speaking, as well as the discriminatory barriers they face along with other minorities. Persons of Spanish origin have a lower level of educational attainment than any other group in the population. Only about 1 in 5 Puerto Ricans and 1 in 4 Mexican-Americans 25 and older have completed high school. Only 12 percent of all Spanish-speaking Americans 25 and older have attended at least 1 year of college. For Mexican-Americans and Puerto Ricans, the figures are 4 and 6 percent, respectively. The comparable rate for all adults is 21 percent.

Somewhat less measurable but no less real are the cultural differences between the Spanish-speaking and other Americans. The Spanish-speaking have a strong sense of cultural uniqueness, coupled with feelings akin to outrage that the broader society has failed to recognize, accept, or even place a positive value on their contribution to the diverse fabric of American society. To some extent these felt cultural differences result in part from the high proportion of the Spanish-surnamed living in poverty. In this sense, the Spanish-speaking have characteristics in common with blacks, Appalachian whites, or others living in the "poverty subculture."

There are, however, very real differences between disadvantaged Spanish-speaking people and other poor Americans—differences that affect the conduct and success of manpower and other social programs. These differences include language, value orientation, ethnic-isolation, and other social and psychological factors.

Spanish is the most prevalent of all foreign languages in this country and the one with the highest likelihood of surviving here on a permanent basis. Mexican-Americans and Puerto Ricans, unlike earlier waves of immigrants (though strictly speaking the latter arrive as citizens rather than immigrants), persist in using their language over several generations. Access to Spanish language mass media and entertainment permits this pattern to continue. Furthermore, the Spanish-speaking have fewer economic incentives to learn English because their opportunities to advance are limited and the acculturation pressures from children and the rest of society are less severe than in the past.

The result is that roughly 1 Spanish-surnamed adult in 4 is illiterate in English. Many lack a working command of Spanish as well as English. These language barriers and education problems go hand in hand; they feed upon and exacerbate one another. Efforts by manpower and education agencies to cope with language difficulties generally have been inadequate, both in quality and quantity, although in recent months there has been a commendable increase in emphasis on language training in manpower programs.

When it comes to a discussion of value orientations, the danger of stereotyping is always high. Value orientations often differ among the various groups of the Spanish-speaking, as well as between the Spanish-surnamed in general and other Americans. But some cultural attributes that seem to apply to most of the Spanish-speaking can be readily identified:

Relations between individuals are more important than competitive, materialistic, or achievement norms.

Strong family ties.

A sense of solidarity and pride in a unique heritage (a feeling sometimes referred to as La Raza).

Machismo, meaning male dominance, patriarchy, emphasis on man's masculinity.

--Aspirations for professional rather than business or managerial occupations.

To some extent these values reflect an older rural culture. As Spanish-speaking people move to the cities—80 percent now reside in urban areas—they tend to pick up Anglo values. The older values persist, however, and it would be unsafe to assume they will materially change in the present generation. Indeed, there is sharp disagreement within the Spanish-speaking community on the necessity and value of assimilation. Efforts at forcing assimilation, such as the practice of some southwestern schools until recent years of forbidding children to speak Spanish, are generally recognized as unwise.

Ethnic Isolation Linked to Rural Background

The basically rural background of the Spanish-speaking helps explain their ethnic isolation, an isolation more pronounced than that of earlier immigrants. Until World War II, they were congregated in rural areas and held farm jobs, while earlier generations of new Americans generally went to the cities where the pressures of the melting pot were greater. By the time the Spanish-speaking began to urbanize, their numbers were great enough and their subculture strong enough to survive these pressures.

The overwhelming majority of the Spanish-surnamed live in self-contained neighborhoods separated from the rest of the community. Sometimes, this represents a choice of the individual who feels more comfortable in familiar surroundings with people of his own culture and background. All too often, unfortunately, the reason can be found in economic or social discrimination which forces the individual to live in substandard housing in an area having few public services. Such barrios are quite similar to black ghettos. Studies of metropolitan areas such as Los Angeles demonstrate that the chances of a Spanish-speaking person occupying substandard housing are over four times that for an Anglo at a similar income level.

As the Spanish-speaking develop the skills to help themselves, the majority community must make some adjustment in meeting their needs. This is particularly true of institutions providing training and education in an attempt to help the Spanish-surnamed improve their position in the economy.

Manpower policies and programs too often have failed to recognize and deal with the uniqueness of the manpower need of the Spanish-speaking people. The decision makers often do not know enough about the language and cultural characteristics of the people to develop viable and effective programs. The fact that Hispanos speak a foreign language and have different backgrounds is regarded as being their own problem, and the need to establish programs built upon serving people from different cultures is not always recognized.

As a result, while the basic idea of training and education for the disadvantaged may be sound, the policy for implementation has built-in deficiencies which retard success. There must be an urgent, full-scale effort to develop sufficient numbers of skilled Spanish-speaking policymakers and managers and place them at all levels of the delivery system if manpower programs are to serve the Spanish-speaking effectively. Over the last few years substantial increases of funds have been granted to Spanish-speaking manpower delivery organizations such as SER and the Puerto Rican Forum, and this trend must be continued until equity has been achieved.

Giving jobs to the Spanish-speaking on the operational level as interviewers, counselors, trainers, and job developers is not enough. These people would be forced to perform two tasks, delivering services and sensitizing their superiors to the needs of the Spanish-surnamed. They could perform much more effectively if they were relieved of the second task, that is if their superiors as well as their clients were drawn from the Spanish-speaking population.

The Department of Labor, in all fairness, has at least partially responded to this need. Its Manpower Administration has added many Spanish-speaking professionals to its top-level staff. But the number is still relatively slim, equity has by no means been achieved, and we cannot wait for Spanish-speaking counselors and interviewers to work their way up by the usual laborious routes. To overcome the effects of decades of discrimination by the society at large, extraordinary action must be taken now.

The Spanish-speaking want the opportunity to participate in society, to share, learn, and grow—as individuals and as a group. For many centuries, they have been a simple and docile people. This will no longer be true as we move into the 1980's. As Americans they expect to exercise their rights and responsibilities in the context of American society.

PART II

PROBLEMS OF SEGREGATION AND INTEGRATION

CHAPTER 7

RACE AND COLOR IN
MEXICAN-AMERICAN PROBLEMS

JACK D. FORBES

ALL TOO OFTEN SCHOLARS and social workers dealing with Mexican-Americans ignore their Americanoid racial characteristics and regard them as simply another European-type minority
group with certain cultural and linguistic problems; in doing so,
they help Mexican-Americans in *their* tragic escape from the realities of their native American heritage. Thus a recent report for
the U. S. Commission on Civil Rights prepared by Dr. Julian
Samora places considerable emphasis upon the economic, linguistic and educational problems of Mexican-Americans but ignores
completely the question of race and color.[1] Many similar studies
with this failing could also be cited. A "curtain of silence" has
been draped around the questions of the racial characteristics of
Mexican-Americans and how these characteristics might influence
relations with Anglo-Americans. Given the well-known Anglo bias
resulting from the myth of inferiority of all darker-skinned persons, this absence of reference to it is surprising and, indeed, in-
excusable.

The racial character of Mexicans and Mexican-Americans has
long been known. Scholars and laymen south of the border are
cognizant of the scarcity of Spanish-European lineage and of the
predominantly native character of the Mexican population. The
literature and history of the early Anglo-American intrusion into
the Southwest provides many illustrations of this awareness of

Jack D. Forbes is Associate Professor of History at the University of Nevada,
at Reno, after having served as Acting Director of the Center for Western North
American Studies Desert Research Institute, at that institution. His articles on
tribal development and education have been published in various journals. He is
author of "Warriors of the Colorado" and is presently at work on a book about
Mexican-Americans of which this article will eventually be a part.

Forbes, Jack D., "Race and Color in Mexican-American Problems," *Journal of
Human Relations, 16 (1)*:55-68, First Quarter, 1968.

the Mexican's non-European ancestry, and is replete with examples of prejudice against his brown skin color. Paul S. Taylor's studies of Mexican labor,[8-11] (published in the 1920's and 1930's), provide numerous examples of anti-Mexican prejudice based upon color considerations. It is clear that the bulk of Taylor's Anglo informants were quite cognizant of the Mexican's racial differences. Carey McWilliams' *North From Mexico* (1948) also makes frequent reference to the racial heritage of the Mexican and to discrimination based upon the racial considerations which his color involves.

THE WHITE-SPANISH MYTH

In spite of the above, however, many persist in the myth that Mexican-Americans are "Whites with Spanish Surnames" and that their problems are little if any different from those of Polish-Americans or Italian-Americans. Why is this so? There are a number of reasons: (1) the European conquest of Mexico implanted the notion of Caucasian superiority. Natives were treated generally as inferiors and persons of mixed ancestry usually took pride only in their Spanish blood. A cult of "Whiteness" developed in which artificial means (such as the use of powder) were used to lighten the skin, and mestizos sought to be reclassified as "Spanish." This obsession with color eventually led to a neurotic and in some cases near-psychotic concern with "purity of lineage" and racial characteristics. Many Mexican-Americans still participate emotionally in this legacy of the conquest period—they must be referred to as "white" or as "Spanish." (2) Anglo-American color prejudice reinforced the above tendency and caused lighter-skinned Mexicans (in California and New Mexico especially) to deny any non-Caucasian ancestry. (3) Mexican-Americans have generally sought to avoid being associated with Negroes or identified "colored" people in order to keep from having to submit to the discriminatory practices aimed at the latter. Becoming a "white" is, then, a defense mechanism designed to prevent too close a relationship with the Negro. (4) Similarly, being a "white" served to protect Mexicans from being lumped together with the original Americans, the Indians, and thus subject to the discriminatory Anti-Indian feelings and treatment. (5) Finally, many Anglo-Americans, not wishing to "offend" the more sensitive Mexican-Americans, have aided in fostering the "Spanish" and "White" myths.

Regardless of mythology, however, and regardless of the color neuroses of some Mexican-Americans, the fact remains that perhaps 80 percent of the genetic makeup of the average Mexican is Indian or Native American and that only 10 percent is Spanish-European.[2] For practical purposes, then, the average Mexican can be considered as if he were a pure-blood Indian, since his non-native racial heritage is relatively insignificant. In this, he would correspond to a colored person of one-eighth or one-sixteenth white ancestry. The purpose of this article is to examine this myth of White-Spanish origin and the realities of the heritage which account for it, and those of that other heritage which have made the evasion of the true heritage necessary, and to suggest why frank acceptance of these facts instead of continuing this evasion, alone can lead to a satisfactory or human solution of the problems faced by Mexican-Americans or Mexicans within our nation.

THE FLIGHT FROM MEXICAN IDENTITY

There are, of course, individual Mexican-Americans who exhibit nearly-Caucasian, though rarely, wholly Caucasian characteristics. These individuals are exceptions. The problems of the Mexican-Americans remain essentially those of a non-Caucasian population, in terms of realities which have to be faced. Evasion of these realities can only create confusion and tragedy. The lighter-skinned Mexicans often are able to "integrate" themselves into the Anglo community as Spaniards, Californians, or Latins, and they sometimes turn upon their darker-skinned brothers, or at the very least simply leave the latter to flounder by themselves. In addition, the Spanish-Latin myth fostered by the light-skinned group by tending to further disparage the native heritage of the majority of Mexicans isolates them all the more in their in-between, no-culture caste. A study of the San Francisco region notes that

> sub-cultural differences—but much more significantly, panicky status concerns—are focal in the efforts of "Spanish" Mexicans to differen-

tiate themselves from "Indian Mexicans, toward whom only slight objections are felt, and who could scarcely be regarded as partners in a common sense.[3]

Leonard Broom and Eshref Shevky, in a selection in *American Race Relations Today* (1962), recognize the significance of color considerations in this attitude by pointing out that once a Mexican-American has become assimilated into Anglo-American culture and has advanced economically, then "color is the only arbitrary qualification to a ready change in Mexican self-definition." They further state that

> Vertical mobility and loss of identification as Mexicans should theoretically be easier for those who approximate the "Castilian type." It also remains to be discovered to what extent the factor of color is selective in affecting the permanence of settlement in the United States and the secondary movement of Mexicans in this country.[4]

Anglo-Americans have historically favored the "noble Castilian" over the "low greaser" or "half-breed cholo," their contemptious terms for Mexicans in general, because of their dark skin color. It does seem reasonably certain that light-skinned Mexicans are able to relate more easily with the Anglo-American world than their dark-skinned fellow Mexicans, though the subject has not been scientifically explored.

INFLUENCE OF RACIAL HERITAGE: FIXATION WITH LIGHTNESS

There is evidence nonetheless, that Mexican self-esteem has been frequently damaged by anti-Indian prejudice. Some Mexicans appear to be ashamed of their color and wish they were white, a fixation with lightness which is carried to the extreme that even posters depicting the Aztec heritage portray Indians with a near-white skin color. The following selections illustrate this thesis and also provide evidence to support the view that the racial heritage of the Mexican *is* significant and should not be overlooked by the scholar. Needless to state it *cannot* be overlooked by the Mexican-American whose visability brings him into his problem.

During the 1830's Richard Henry Dana visited California and

remarked at some length on the racial character of the Mexican population.

> [The Californians'] complexions are various, depending—as well as their dress and manner—upon their rank; or, in other words, upon the amount of Spanish blood they can lay claim to.
>
> Those who are of pure Spanish blood, having never inter-married with aborigines, have clear brunette complexions, and sometimes, even as fair as those of English-women. There are but few of these families in California; being mostly those in official stations, or who, on the the expiration of their offices have settled here upon property which they have acquired; and others who have been banished for state offenses. These form the aristocracy, inter-marrying, keeping up an exclusive system in every respect. They can be told by their complexions, dress, manner, and also by their speech; for calling themselves Castilians, they are very ambitious of speaking the pure Castilian language, which is spoken in a somewhat corrupted dialect by the lower classes.
>
> From this upper class, they go down by regular shades, growing more and more dark and muddy, until you come to the pure Indian, who runs about with nothing upon him but a small piece of cloth, kept up by a wide leather strap drawn round his waist. Generally speaking, each person's caste is decided by the quality of the blood, which shows itself, too plainly to be concealed, at first sight. Yet the least drop of Spanish blood, if it be only of quadroon or octroroon, is sufficient to raise them from the rank of slaves and entitle them to a suit of clothes—boots, hat, cloak, spurs, long knife, all complete, though coarse and dirty as may be—and to call themselves Espanolos, and to hold property, if they can get any. . . .

The Mexican soldiers in California were, according to Dana, "hungry, drawling, lazy half-breeds."[5]

In the 1840's when the Anglo-Americans were anxious to seize Mexican territory a great many derogatory references to Mexican racial character were made. *The Illinois State Register* (Dec. 27, 1844) asserted that the Mexican population was "but little removed above the Negro." *The Democratic Review* (1847) advocated that the occupation of Mexico was a beneficial development since "the process which has been gone through at the north, of driving back the Indians, or annihilating them as a race, has yet to be gone through at the south." The *Review* was opposed, however, to amalgamation with Mexicans since the latter were a "degraded" race. Later in 1847, as Mexico's land became more attractive to expansionists some Anglo-Americans began to believe that at least a portion of the Mexican population could be "regenerated" and absorbed. As a United States Senator pointed out, however, the three-fourths of the Mexican people who were Indian could never be given full political equality—they were still a "degraded race."[6]

Thus it would appear certain that many Anglo-Americans were influenced in their attitudes towards Mexico during the 1840's by their previous anti-Indian and anti-Negro prejudices. The Mexican people were thought of and dealt with largely as a non-white people.

ANTI-MEXICAN TREATMENT BASED ON COLOR

During the 1850's and thereafter, Mexicans were often the victims of harsh treatment. In 1856 an Anglo-Texan expressed views which help us to understand why the Mexicans were so treated:

> [The Mexicans] are so bigoted and ignorant as the devil's grandchildren. They haven't even the capacities of my black boy [Negro slave]. Why, they're most as black as niggers anyway, and ten times as treacherous. . . .[7]

Anti-Mexican attitudes have endured in spite of continual contact between Anglos and Mexicans. In many areas of the United States, Mexicans came to be recognized as forming a valuable laboring force, as loyal employees, as honest and kind people; at the same time as a biologically inferior, racially different group which should be socially segregated. Paul S. Taylor's studies of Mexican labor (1927-1930) reveal many examples of racial prejudice on the part of Anglos. An Imperial Valley (California) date ranch owner refused to hire Mexican pickers because his customers would not like dates picked by "colored" labor. A restaurant operator would not hire Mexican dishwashers for exactly the same reason. A dark-skinned Mexican chauffeur was refused service at a root-beer stand while his light-skinned passengers were served.

> Even in Calexico, where mingling is general, a cultured man, obviously a mestizo, was refused a rental. . . . The fact that he was not of the

laboring class but a polished gentleman did not alter the fact that he was Mexican, and sufficiently dark-skinned to reveal Indian ancestry, and so was subject to the general prejudice.

At a public auto camp a police officer refused admission to an Anglo man, his Mexican wife, and their children, telling the husband that an Anglo who would "raise a lot of black and tans" was as bad as any Mexican.

Not surprisingly, Taylor refers to the "sensitiveness" of Imperial Valley Mexicans to the "stigma: of being Mexican and non-White."

> Generally the Mexicans of the valley quite unconsciously speak and think of themselves as Mexicans, and as Indian or mestizo. Repeatedly Mexicans have spoken to the writer of the "Mexicans" and the "whites"—in the most casual and matter of fact way. Only twice was objection raised to [these] designations by men who obviously were of part Indian ancestry.

The "sensitiveness" had developed because Anglos used the terms "Mexican" and "Indian" in a derogatory manner.

Finally, Taylor found that the drug stores of the Imperial Valley were handling large amounts of "bleaching cream sold to whiten the complexion—bought, as one druggist reports, furtively, but in large quantities."[8]

Evidences of color prejudice were found also in northeastern Colorado. A light-skinned Mexican girl refused two offers of marriage from Anglo-Americans because "if there should be any dark children, I don't want my husband blaming me and calling them 'my children.' " One Anglo woman stated "We don't believe intermarriage will take place on account of color even if the Mexicans are clean and educated." Another Anglo woman qualified her opposition to Mexicans somewhat:

> The opposition to Mexicans is based on their uncleanliness and their uncivilized way of living. We permit a well-dressed, clean, light complexioned Mexican to eat in our cafe, but not the other Mexicans. I wouldn't go with a Mexican even if he were clean. Negroes, Mexicans, and Japanese are alike but the Negroes are despised the most.

Another Anglo woman opposed intermarriage on the grounds that "—Mexicans are not white. They are the same as the Negroes." An Anglo farmer stated, however, that "I don't believe there will be much mixture with the darker ones but there will be with the lighter ones." An exception to this general trend of thought was that of one Danish-American farmer who thought that intermarriage might take place since the Mexicans "are not black."[9]

Evidence supplied by Taylor also indicated that color prejudice was a factor in discrimination against Mexican-Americans in the Chicago region. As a Mexican states, "The color is the main thing. They don't want to rent to dark Mexicans." A non-Mexican worker justified discrimination by saying, "Some of them are dark, just like the niggers; I wouldn't like to live among them. I want to live among white people." A *Chamber of Commerce* official added, "The Mexicans are lower than the European peasants. They are not white and not Negro; they're Mexicans." Segregation was based upon the idea that

> the Mexicans are not considered white. They are ushered to the first aisle with the colored. White people don't like to sit next to the colored or Mexicans. No, even though they are clean.

Other statements from non-Mexicans of the Chicago region would seem to confirm the above:

> The Italians don't like the Mexicans. One Italian said: "I don't want my kids to associate with the Mexicans. God made people white and black, and he meant there to be a difference . . . there is not much chance of a Mexican mingling with a crowd without recognition because of his color.
>
> [A social worker said:] The Mexicans are mixed with Negro and Indian. When we sent a child for a summer outing to a private home, we tried to bleach the child out. The family expected a Mexican but we didn't want them to think we had sent a Negro. No, [Mexicans] are not regarded as colored; but they are regarded as an inferior class. Are the Mexicans regarded as white? Oh, no! The Mexicans are of a different race; their faces are blacker.
>
> [A social worker reported:] A Mexican at a church supper told me to tell a [somewhat unkempt] Mexican to keep out. He said, "What will the Americans think? He is so dark."
>
> [A Mexican remarked that his wife was "very pretty"] but she is prieta [blackish]; I dark too.

Taylor summarized his findings by noting that

> Recognition of racial difference and the attitudes which so commonly attach to color of skin, hamper free assimilation of the Mexicans, but this barrier . . . is less effective than in the rural West and Southwest. . . . But it is a factor, distinctly additional to those which characteristically have stirred hostility against new groups of European immigrants to the same area.

In response to color prejudice the Mexicans of the Chicago region had to some extent developed a pride in being of "Aztec race." The *Correo Mexicano* (Sept. 6, 1926) noted that "We do not forget that we are descended from a progressive and cultured race, as were our ancestors, the Aztec."[10]

As could perhaps be expected, the Anglo-Americans of south Texas were particularly hostile towards Mexicans on racial grounds. The latter were generally regarded as belonging to a different race, biologically inferior to that of the whites. Various statements should serve to confirm this:

> I feel sorry for these high-class Mexicans who are sometimes refused service at hotels. They are really Spanish and White, but the laborers are Indians. Like the Negroes they were intended to be hewers of wood and drawers of water.
>
> Our people don't recognize [Mexicans] as white people but the law does. There is the same race prejudice here as against the Negro.
>
> The people here regard the Mexicans about the same as they do the Negroes in Louisiana.
>
> [A school official said:] The inferiority of the Mexicans is both biological and class.
>
> The true American even in Mexico holds the best Mexican his inferior. . . . They are a dark race and we don't want to mix.
>
> [The Mexicans] are a mixture, a mule race or cross-breed. The Spaniard is a cross between a Moor and a Castilian, and the Indian is a cross with them. . . . By inter-marriage you can go down to their level but you can't bring them up to yours. . . . When you cross five races you get meanness.
>
> God did not intend [Mexicans] to be [as good as a white man]. He would have made them white if He had.
>
> I went to Eagle Pass to a Rotary meeting to which they invited Mexicans from Piedras Negras. I asked my husband if we were to eat with them; he said they were all right. . . . I told him I did not care

how high-class they were, they looked black to me and I did not want to sit side of them.

They are an inferior race. I would not think of classing Mexicans with whites.

No, I wouldn't object to my children's marrying educated, cultured Mexicans; that is if they weren't too dark in color so there would be any suspicion of negroid ancestry.

The attitude of people here toward the Mexicans is very nearly the same as toward the Negro. Intermarriage is legal but it rarely happens. . . . They wish to maintain purity of the Caucasian race and don't like mixing with dark breeds. . . . I guess they consider that the Mexican has a soul. They have more respect for an American Indian, and the Mexican is a domesticated Indian.

[A tenant farmer opposed to school integration] because a damned greaser is not fit to sit side of a white girl. . . . A man would rather his daughter was dead than that she would marry a Mexican.[11]

A MEXICAN'S REACTION TO COLOR PREJUDICE

The Mexican scholar Manuel Gamio, in his study of Mexican immigration to the United States (1930), devoted considerable attention to the problem of color prejudice. He noted that the Mexicans were familiar with frequent Hispano-Indian and Germanic-Indian intermarriage south of the Rio Grande and, therefore, were "deeply offended" at confronting racial prejudice in the United States. Gamio goes on to state:

If in Texas the pigmentation of the Mexican individuals in a group including idigenes, mestizos, and whites were arranged in a series according to the Broca tables, the result would be a theoretical scale of prejudices which would conform fairly to the actual situation. The darkest-skinned Mexican experiences almost the same restrictions as the Negro, while a person of medium-dark skin can enter a second-class lunchroom frequented also by Americans of the poorer class, but will not be admitted to a high-class restaurant. A Mexican of light-brown skin as a rule will not be admitted to a high-class hotel, while a white cultured Mexican will be freely admitted to the same hotel, especially if he speaks English fluently. . . .

Gamio asserts that this color prejudice arose quite early, when Anglo-Americans first came into contact with Indians, Spaniards, and "Indo-Spaniards" in the Southwest. He also contends that the fact of color difference has served to render the assimilation of

Mexican-Americans more difficult than that of other immigrant groups, such as German and Italians.

As an extension or reflection of this racial prejudice, individuals of Mexican origin but of white skin are also socially discriminated against. The stigma of indigenous blood is so deep that the word "Mexican," which implies a little or a great deal of Indian blood and the corresponding pigmentation, has acquired in the South a derogatory character. In general, to distinguish between white and brown Mexicans, the whites are euphemistically called "Spanish," and they themselves adhere to this distinction. The head of one large family, established in the United States for more than two hundred years, but whose color and features showed marked indigenous blood, answered to discreet questioning about his family antecedents: "I am Spanish; my ancestors were Spaniards who were in Mexico and later came to New Mexico. They were relatives of Cabeza de Vaca."

Gamio also comments upon the then lack of intermarriage between Mexican and Anglos and remarks that

the only enduring conquest is racial conquest, since any other after a time is not conquest but exclusion. If racial prejudice had not existed in the United States, there would be at present no citizens nominally American but really Mexican, for they would long ago have become part of the nation racially. Moreover, the Mexican border states would have at present a population predominately American, whereas, as a matter of fact, not only is this population Mexican but within the United States there exists a vast zone parallel to the boundary line, inhabited by nominally American but really Indo-Spanish or Mexican, who although they have adopted American customs and American material civilization, remain racially, sentimentally, and traditionally one with Mexicans on the other side of the Rio Grande and a part of the whole body of the Indo-Spanish people.[12]

THE FUTURE OF THE MEXICAN-AMERICAN

Carey McWilliams summed up the situation rather well in 1948:

Three cultures, not two, have fought for supremacy in the Southwest: Anglo, Hispano, *and* Indian. . . . Indians were a conquered race despised by Anglo-Americans. Mexicans are related to Indians by race and culture with the Indian part of their cultural and racial inheritance being more important than the Spanish. Mexicans are consistently equated with Indians by the race-conscious Anglo-Americans. Quite apart from the question of how much Indian blood flows in the veins of the Mexican minority, Mexicans are regarded as a racial minority in the Southwest.[13]

The future of the Mexican in the United States, in brief, can never be satisfactory until the problem of race is solved, for feelings of color prejudice and color inferiority are still very much alive. The words of the Santa Barbara, California, Mexican woman who in 1853 apologetically asserted in court that "I am ugly; I am black; I am poor . . ." are echoed silently today.[14] Her style of self-denigration is also occasionally vocalized, as in the case of a Mexican-American girl who recently asserted that she would marry only an Anglo-American because she did not want her children to be as dark as she was.[15]

The eradication of the sense of color inferiority found among Mexican-Americans is a pressing necessity, not only because it poisons the lives of large numbers of denigrated dark-skinned persons, but also because it impedes the political and organizational collaboration of Mexican-Americans with Tribal Americans and Negroes. The process of giving a positive value to the brown-skinned native heritage of Mexico has already commenced south of the border, but Mexican-Americans are still only partially affected by that trend. In this connection, a young leader in southern California, E. Cardoza Orozco, is currently spearheading the "Mexica Movement" (pronounced "Meschica" in the Aztec fashion) to provide a nonambiguous identity for persons of Mexican background who are United States citizens. The latter are to be referred to as "Mexicas" even as Japanese-Americans of United States birth are called "Nisei." Mr. Orozco lays great stress upon the native Mexican heritage and its worth in his articles, and the Mexica concept itself is Indianist in inspiration.[16] This removal of feelings of color inferiority and color prejudice cannot, of course, be accomplished without changing attitudes on the part of the non-Mexican community. Fortunately, the process of giving greater status to the native heritages of both the United States and Mexico has begun. What remains is to translate the romantic and artistic fascination with the Aztec-Sioux heritage into a meaningful connection with the living descendants thereof. This process can be greatly facilitated if the Mexican-American community stops its futile evasion of its true origin and places great emphasis upon the quality of its largely indigenous origin; however, this process will also demand that the Anglo-dominated public schools devote more attention to the important non-European aspects of contributions to the American heritage.

Finally, color prejudice against brown-skinned Mexican-Americans and Indian Americans will not completely disappear, in the writer's opinion, until the brown-skinned Negro is also made a social equal of the white. In short, the problem of racial prejudice is a single problem and all groups must share in a common assault upon the color barrier. Those scholars and leaders, on whatever side who ignore the racial aspect of the "Mexica's" struggle for equality, or of any other colored group, are not helping to solve the problem; they are merely giving tacit approval to an escapist avoidance of all the issues, and thereby contributing to the postponement of any final or human solution.

REFERENCES

1. Staff paper-Spanish speaking people, United States Commission on Civil Rights, February 5, 1964 (draft).
2. Drwer, Harold: *Indians of North America*. Chicago, University of Chicago Press, 1961, p. 602.
3. Record, C. Williams: Intergroup conflict in the Bay area. Public Affairs Report Bulletin of the Institute of Government Studies, *4(4):5*, Berkeley, University of California, August 1963.
4. Raab, Earl Ed.: *American Race Relations Today*. New York, Doubleday, 1962, p. 167.
5. Dana, R. H. Jr.: *Two Years Before the Mast*. New York, Burt (no date), pp. 72-73, 160.
6. Weinberg, Albert K.: *Manifest Destiny*. Chicago, Quadrangle Books, 1963, pp. 165-77.
7. Olmsted, Frederick Law: *A Journey Through Texas*. Dix, Edwards, 1857, p. 126.
8. Taylor, Paul S.: Mexican labor in the United States: Imperial Valley. *University of California Publications in Economics, 6(1):89-93*.
9. ———: Mexican labor in the United States: valley of the South Platte, Colorado. *University of California Publications in Economics, b(2): 230-32*.
10. ———: Mexican labor in the United States: Chicago and Calumet region. *University of California Publications in Economics, 1(2):227-28, 232, 234-37, 280*.

11. ———: Mexican labor in the United States. Dimmit County, Winter Garden district, South Texas. *University of California Publications in Economics.*

12. Gamio, Manuel: *Mexican Immigration to the United States.* Chicago, University of Chicago Press, 1930, p. 52-56.

13. McWilliams, Carey: *North from Mexico: The Spanish Speaking People of the United States.* New York, Lippincott, 1940, pp. 208-209.

14. Huse, Charles E.: In Ellison, W. H. (ed.) : Diary trans. by Frances Price. Typewritten manuscript. Santa Barbara, University of California, 1953, p. 54.

15. Personal Communication, 1963.

16. Orozco, Cardoza: Mexica: An identity for Mexican Americans, mimeographed article, no date.

CHAPTER 8

MEXICAN-AMERICANS AS A LEGAL MINORITY

U. S. COURT OF APPEALS

On August 2, 1972, the U. S. Court of Appeals for the Fifth Circuit ruled in Cisneros v. Corpus Christi, a school segregation case involving, among other things, the question whether Mexican-Americans constitute an identifiable ethnic group in desegregation proceedings. The affirmative answer is embodied in the following extracts from the decision. For ease of reading, footnotes and most legal citations have been omitted. The opinion was written by Judge David W. Dyer.

IN THIS DESEGREGATION class action brought against the Corpus Christi Independent School District and its Board of Trustees, the district court held that the city's Mexican-American and black children were segregated from Anglo children in the public school system as a result of official action of the Board in violation of the mandate of *Brown v. Board of Education*, 1954, 347 U.S. 483. *Cisneros v. Corpus Christi Independent School District*, S.D. Texas 1970, 324 F.Supp. 599 *(Cisneros I)*. The court ordered an immediate reassignment of the District's teaching staff, consideration of the achievement or preservation of a "reasonable mixture" of Mexican-American and black students with other students in construction of new schools, the filing of a revised student assignment plan for the purpose of creating "a unitary school system," and the creation of a Human Relations Advisory committee. Subsequently, after extended hearings, the court formulated and ordered into effect a student assignment plan to achieve integration of the school system in accordance with contemporary constitutional guidelines. This order was stayed by Mr. Justice Black, sitting as Circuit Justice, pending consideration of the merits of the Board's appeal by this Court.

This is a novel school desegregation case. A large number of

"Mexican Americans as a Legal Minority," *Integrated-Education*, March-April 1973, pp. 68-74.

Mexican-American children attend the public schools of Corpus Christi. Although they are now and have been historically separated in fact from Anglos in the schools of the city, this separation has never had a statutory origin. Therefore, unlike cases involving the traditional black-white dual systems, the question is whether the segregation of Mexican-American children who are not the victims of statutorily mandated segregation is constitutionally impermissible. We hold that it is, and affirm the district court's finding that the Mexican-American children of Corpus Christi are segregated in violation of the Constitution. For reasons hereinafter explicated, however, we disagree with the remedy prescribed by the district court and require it to be modified.

Although we are faced with a tri-ethnic school population, the determination below that the relatively few black students in the school system were segregated contrary to law is basically uncontested in this appeal. The district court must, however, also reconsider the remedy with regard to black students in accordance with this opinion.

The Corpus Christi Independent School District encompasses the metropolitan area of Corpus Christi, Texas. The district is crescent-shaped extending approximately 11 miles in length from its southeast to its northwest corner, and varies in width from three to four miles. Following the curvatures of Corpus Christi and Nueces Bays, it is bounded by water on its north, east, and south sides.

SCHOOL NUMBERS

In the school year 1969 to 1970, upon which the statistics in this case are based, there were 46,023 scholastics in the public school system. In terms of total ethnic distribution, 47.4 percent of the school children were Anglo, 47.2 percent Mexican-American, and 5.4 percent black. There are 61 public schools in the school system, 45 elementary schools, 12 junior highs, and 5 senior highs. In terms of ethnic distribution by grade level, of the 24,389 elementary students, 43.4 percent were Anglo, 50.8 percent Mexican-American, and 5.7 percent black. Of the 11,793 junior high students, 48 percent were Anglo, 46.7 percent Mexican-American, and 5.25 percent black. Of the 9,841 senior high school students, 56.4 percent were Anglo, 38.9 percent were Mexican-American, and 4.6 percent were black.

The ethnic distribution figures further show that in 1969 to 1970, one third of the district's Mexican-American high school students attended Moody High School, the enrollment of which was 97 percent Mexican-American and black (11% black). Another one third of the Mexican-American high school students attend Miller High, which is 80 percent Mexican-American and black (14% black). One third of the district's Anglo high school students attend King High, the enrollment of which is over 90 percent Anglo. Another 57 percent of the Anglo high school students attend either Carroll or Ray high schools, each of which is over 75 percent Anglo.

In the junior high schools, approximately 61 percent of the Mexican-American students attend three junior highs which are over 90 percent Mexican-American in enrollment. Over 50 percent of the Anglo junior high students attend junior highs that are over 90 percent Anglo in enrollment. Of the 24,389 elementary level students, approximately 10,178 Mexican-Americans and blacks (1,250 blacks) attend elementary schools in which over 90 percent of the enrollment is non-Anglo-American. Approximately 6,561 Anglo elementary students attend schools in which the non-Anglo-American enrollment is less than 20 percent. The enrollment in eleven of the 45 elementary schools in the school system is over 90 percent Mexican-American, over 75 percent Mexican-American in three others, over 90 percent Mexican-American and black in four other schools, over 90 percent Anglo in six schools, and over 80 percent Anglo in nine other schools.

At the elementary level alone, twenty-nine of the forty-five schools, or almost a full two-thirds, are clearly identifiable as consisting of one ethnic derivation. The same total figure comparisons can roughly be made with regard to the junior and senior high schools of the school system.

Highly relevant to these enrollment statistics are the historic and established residential patterns of the city. There is today and has traditionally been substantial residential concentration by ethnic groups in Corpus Christi. The Mexican-American and black population of the district is concentrated in a narrow area that comprises the middle part of the district, running roughly southwest to northeast, bordered on the south side by a major city artery, Ayres Street. This residential concentration is referred to throughout the litigation as the Mexican "corridor." To the south of Ayres Street, as the corridor boundary, the relative number of Mexican-Americans and blacks as opposed to Anglos, drops sharply. The southern part of the district exists almost exclusively as an Anglo residential area.

DEZONING

Since before 1938, the district has assigned Anglo children to schools according to a neighborhood school plan composed of geographic attendance zones. Students of Mexican-American descent have always been classified as Anglo by the school board. Generally, students attend school at all levels at the school nearest their home. Thus, the imposition of neighborhood school zones over the pattern of marked residential segregation in Corpus Christi has, inevitably, resulted in Mexican-American and Anglo children being substantially separated in the public schools.

The city's high schools provide a striking example. The first public high school built in the district still in existence is Miller High, built in 1928, and rebuilt in 1966. It is located at the north end of the Mexican "corridor," although not in the area of highest Mexican-American concentration. Its attendance zone until 1968 comprised all the northern part of the school district. In 1949, its enrollment was 78 percent Anglo, 22 percent Mexican-American. In 1950, Ray High School was built approximately in the center of the school district, to the southeast of the Ayres Street artery which has served as the "corridor" boundary. It opened with an enrollment that was 87 percent Anglo. A significant number of Anglo students was then withdrawn from Miller into Ray High School. In 1958, Carroll was opened in the south central part of the district, again south of Ayres Street, and served an attendance zone that extended beyond Ayres north into the heart of the Mexican-American corridor. It opened, however, as a 78 percent Anglo school. While Ray remained fairly constant at its 87 percent Anglo enrollment figure, Miller now had a majority of Mexican-American students. In 1965, King High School was opened in the southernmost corner of the district, with an enrollment that was 95 percent Anglo (90% in 1969-70). By this time Miller High had become 71 percent Mexican-American, and 8 percent black.

In 1968, Moody High School was opened in the heart of the Mexican-American corridor as a 96 percent Mexican-American-black school (11% black). Its southernmost boundary was Ayres Street. Its attendance zone encompassed the great majority of the Mexican-American concentration of the corridor, sequestering all of that area north of Ayres that once was included in the Carroll, Miller and Ray schools, their inclusion in the Moody zone now locked over two thirds of the city's Mexican-American high school students into two high schools located in the non-Anglo residential area of the city each of which was clearly identifiable as a minority group high school. Importantly, the drawing of the new boundary lines after the building of Moody, in furtherance of the neighborhood school concept, with its withdrawal of significant numbers of Mexican-American and black students from Carroll, Ray, and Miller into Moody, decreased the degree of integration in those schools, increased their reflected ethnic identity, and further locked the residents of the corridor into their racially and ethnically homogeneous high schools.

ALLEGED DISCRIMINATION

With this background we briefly trace the protracted litigation in this case. The suit was filed on July 22, 1968, by the parents of black and Mexican-American children alleging that the local school authorities had operated the schools of the district in a discriminatory manner which resulted in the unlawful segregation of black and Mexican-American students from whites. In *Cisneros I, supra,* June 4, 1970, the court found that *de jure* segregation existed in Corpus Christi. The court held that Mexican-Americans constituted an identifiable, ethnic-minority group entitled to the Fourteenth Amendment guarantee of equality in public education, and that both Mexican-Americans and blacks were unconstitutionally segregated in the public schools of Corpus Christi, as a result of official action by the defendant Board.

In *Cisneros II,* July 2, 1971, a court-designed student assignment plan was promulgated, based upon various parts of plans submitted by the District and the Department of Health, Education and Welfare. The court directed that the plan be implemented by the commencement of the fall, 1972 school term. The plan, in essence, required the pairing of elementary schools in two levels, a complete revision of high school attendance zones, and further reassignment of specific groups of school children throughout the system to aid in the dismantling of identifiable ethnic group schools. The district court found that extensive busing would be required to implement the new plan, as it contemplated the transportation of approximately 15,000 school children at an initial estimated cost ranging from $1,400,000 to $1,700,000. The school district then had a total of only nine buses transporting 400 students. On July 13, 1971, the Board moved for a stay of the July 2 order insofar as it concerned Mexican-American desegregation. On July 16, 1971, a different district judge granted the partial stay. That stay was vacated by an order of this Court on August 5, 1971, but was reinstated by Mr. Justice Black on August 19, 1971. This appeal followed.

The district court's finding that the black students were segregated as a result of constitutionally impermissible state action was not contested at argument. It is clearly supported by the record. The stay order of the district court, entered August 23, 1971 against that portion of the district court plan requiring the immediate integration of the black plaintiffs in this case must be vacated.

Main Appeal Thrust

We now turn to the main thrust of this appeal. Although Brown arose in the context of segregation by state law, often termed "classical or historical *de jure* segregation," we think it clear today beyond preadventure that the contour of unlawful segregation extends beyond statutorily mandated segregation to include the actions and policies of school authorities which deny to students equal protection of the laws by separating them ethnically and racially in public schools. Such actions are "state action" for the purposes of the Fourteenth Amendment, and result in dual school systems that cannot be somehow less odious because they do not flow from a statutory source. The imprimatur of the state is no less visible. The continuing attempt to cast segregation that results from such action as *de facto* and beyond the power of the court to rectify is no longer entitled to serious consideration.

Thus, we discard the anodyne dichotomy of classical *de facto* and *de jure* segregation. We can find no support for the view that the Constitution should be applied antithetically to children in the north and south, or to Mexican-Americans *vis-à-vis* Anglos simply because of the adventitious circumstance of their origin or the happenstance of locality. Time has proven the soundness of the view expressed in dissent in *Jefferson II*, which, in focusing upon *de facto* dicta in *Jefferson I,* said:

> The Negro children in Cleveland, Chicago, Los Angeles, Boston, New York, or any other area of the nation which the opinion classifies under *de facto* segregation, would receive little comfort from the assertion that the racial make-up of their school system does not violate their constitutional rights because they were born into a *de facto* society, while the exact same racial make-up of the school system in the 17 Southern and border states violates the constitutional rights of their counterparts, or even their blood brothers, because they were born in a *de jure* society. All children everywhere in the nation are protected by the Constitution, and treatment which violates their constitutional rights in one area, also violates such constitutional rights in another area.

The Board, however, conceding the existence of severe racial and ethnic separation in the Corpus Christi public schools, nevertheless maintains that another type of *de facto* segregation exists here, arguing that this separation is not a result of school board actions and policies but rather of housing patterns, geographic fluctuations, and other social and economic factors prevalent in the city. Moreover, it urges, even if the imbalance could be traced to Board action, it does not fall within constitutional proscription because it has not acted with a discriminatory motive or purpose.

We must also reject this type of continued meaningless use of *de facto* and *de jure* nomenclature to attempt to establish a kind of ethnic and racial separation of students in public schools that federal courts are powerless to remedy. Such attempts are confusing and unnecessary. The decision in *Brown* is the clear embodiment of the legal framework for the resolution of these important issues.

Brown prohibits segregation in public schools that is a result of state action. It requires simply the making of two distinct factual determinations to support a finding of unlawful segregation. First, a denial of equal educational opportunity must be found to exist, defined as racial or ethnic segregation. Secondly, this segregation must be the result of state action.

We need not define the quantity of state action or the severity of the segregation necessary to sustain a constitutional violation. These factual determinations are better dealt with on a case by case basis. We need only find a real and significant relationship, in terms of cause and effect, between state action and the denial of educational opportunity occasioned by the racial and ethnic separation of public school students.

Real Segregation

We affirm the finding of the district court that action by the school district here has, in terms of cause and effect, resulted in a severely segregated school system in Corpus Christi. We need find nothing more. Discriminatory motive and purpose, while they may reinforce a finding of effective segregation, are not necessary ingredients of constitutional violations in the field of public education. We therefore hold that the racial and ethnic segregation that exists in the Corpus Christi school system is unconstitutional—not *de facto,* not *de jure,* but unconstitutional.

In limine, we note that there is no serious challenge to the district court's finding that Mexican-Americans in the Corpus Christi school system are an identifiable, ethnic-minority class entitled to the equal protection guarantee of the Fourteenth Amendment. The Board does contend, however, that segregation of Mexican-American children in Corpus Christi is not a result of Board action.

The explicit holding of *Cisneros I,* which we now affirm, was that actions and policies of the Board, had, in terms of their actual effect, either created or maintained racial and ethnic segregation in the public schools of Corpus Christi. The district court found that

... [A]dministrative decision by the school board in drawing boundaries, locating new schools, building new schools and renovating old
schools in the predominantly Negro and Mexican parts of town, in
providing an elastic and flexible subjective, transfer system that resulted in some Anglo children being allowed to avoid the ghetto, or "corridor" schools, by bussing some students, by providing one or more
optional transfer zones which resulted in Anglos being able to avoid
Negro and Mexican-American schools, not allowing Mexican-Ameri-
rans or Negroes the option of going to Anglo schools, by spending
extraordinarily large sums of money which resulted in intensifying
and perpetuating a segregated, dual school system, by assigning Negro
and Mexican-American teachers in disparate ratios to these segregated
schools and further failing to employ a sufficient number of Negro
and Mexican-American school teachers, and failing to provide a ma-
jority-to-minority transfer rule, were, regardless of all explanations
and regardless of all expressions of good intentions, calculated to, and
did, maintain and promote a dual school system.

Each of these findings is clearly supported by the record. But
in our view the use of the neighborhood school plan is the direct
and effective cause of segregation in schools of the city.

Here, the Board, by a rigid superimposition of a neighborhood
school plan upon the historic pattern of marked residential segregation that existed in Corpus Christi equated the residential
homogeny to ethnic and racial homogeny in the public school system, producing inevitable segregation. That there was an absence
of state action involved in creating the city's residential patterns
is of no significance. The Board imposed a neighborhood school
plan, *ab initio,* upon a clear and established pattern of residential segregation in the face of an obvious and inevitable result.

Neighborhood School

We have considered the Board's claim that its neighborhood
school plan was established on racially or ethnically neutral criteria and impartially administered, and is therefore not beyond
the pale. This contention, that treatment of Mexican-Americans
the same as Anglos lends a patina of nonsegregated respectability
to the system is, when analyzed, not as pristine as it appears. The
Supreme Court made it plain in *Swann* that

As assignment plan is not acceptable simply because it appears to be
neutral; such a plan may fail to counteract the continuing effects of

past school segregation resulting from discriminatory location of school sites or distortion of school size in order to achieve or maintain an artificial racial separation. When school authorities present a district court with a "loaded game board," affirmative action in the form of remedial altering of attendance zones is proper to achieve truly nondiscriminatory assignments. 402 U.S. at 28.

The Board nevertheless argues that unlawful segregation in the constitutional sense cannot exist in the absence of actions by the Board that are intentionally designed to achieve segregation, and that such a discriminatory purpose is absent here. It iterates that in the absence of a malevolent motive, *de facto* and not *de jure* segregation exists.

While there is admittedly no catholicity of viewpoint in the Circuits on the question of intentional state action, this Court has never tempered its prohibition of school board actions that create, maintain, or foster segregation by the requirement that a discriminatory intent be shown. The underpinning of our decisions is a determination of the unlawful effect of state action upon the existence of unitary school systems.

This principle has now become the law of the land. In *Wright v. Council of the City of Emporia*, 1972, —— U.S. —— [40 U.S.L.W. 4806, June 20, 1972], the Supreme Court held that the city could not create a new school district separate from that of the surrounding county where "its effect would be to impede the process" of court-ordered dismantling of a dual school system, id. at 4812, finding that under its previous decisions in *Green v. County School Board*, 1968, 391 U.S. 430, and *Monroe v. Board of Commissioners*, 1968, 391 U.S. 450, school board action must be judged "according to whether it hinders or furthers the process of school desegregation." Id. at 4809. Citing with approval our decisions in *Lee* and *Stout, supra,* the Court rejected the "dominant purpose" test adopted by the Fourth Circuit decision in the case, focusing rather "upon the effect—not the purpose or motivation—of a school board's action in determining whether it is a permissable method of dismantling a dual system. . . . [T]his 'dominant purpose' test," said the Court, "finds no precedent in our decisions." Id. at 4810.

Importantly, the dissent voiced no opposition to the discarding of purpose and motivation, but objected only to the majority's factual determination that the action of the city in creating its own school district would impede the progress of desegregation.

School cases serve to emphasize the correctness of this principle, for regardless of motive, the children that suffer from segregation suffer the same deprivation of educational opportunity that *Brown* condemns. No one would suggest that the validity of a segregation law depends upon the legislators' motives in enacting it, or that such a law is unconstitutional only when it can be ascribed to racial animus. Why then the distinction between types of school board action that produce segregation? "[T]he factor of malevolent motivation is farther from the core of invidiousness that condemns explicit racial discrimination than are the odious effects produced."

Next we direct our attention to the hiring and reassignment of Mexican-American teachers. The district court held that the faculty and administrative staff of the system were more segregated than the schools, and used this finding as further evidence of an unlawfully segregated school system. The Board was directed to assign black and Mexican-American teachers throughout the system on the same ratio of percentages they comprise of the total teacher and staff population. This finding is clearly supported by the record and the court's order is necessary to bring the Board into compliance with *Singleton v. Jackson Municipal Separate School District,* 5 Cir. 1970, 419 F.2d 1211, 1218 (en banc), *Ellis v. Bd. of Public Instruction of Orange County,* 5 Cir. 1970, 423 F.2d 203. The requirement of percentage assignments of faculty was presaged by the decision of the Supreme Court in *United States v. Montgomery County Board of Education,* 1969, 395 U.S. 225, in which the Court held that as a goal, the ratio of white to black teachers be substantially the same in each school as the ratio of white to black teachers throughout the system. This method of faculty desegregation has been endorsed by the Court in *Swann, supra* at 19-20.

The trial judge further found, and we agree, that the Board had discriminated against Mexican-Americans by failing to employ Mexican-American teachers in the system, and ordered that it move immediately to employ more. In order for the dual nature of the system to be realistically dismantled, faculty composition must more truly reflect the ratio of Mexican-American students to the total scholastic population of the school district. The Board therefore must continue its efforts, which we acknowledge as substantial, toward the achievement, as a goal, of a ratio of Mexican-American teachers to total faculty that approaches the ratio of Mexican-American students to the total student population. In *United States v. Texas Education Agency*, 5 Cir. 1972, F.2d (en banc) [No. 71-2508, July 31, 1972], today decided, we pointed out, however, that "[t]he school board need not, of course, lower its employment standards. A showing of a good faith effort to find sufficient qualified Mexican-American teachers to achieve an equitable ratio, will rebut any inference of discrimination." Id. at ——.

CONCLUSIONS

We turn now briefly to the position of the United States, the invited intervenor in this case. Essentially, it argues that we are confronted with *de facto* segregation with "maybe something more than isolated discrimination." The intervenor contrasts this with traditional dualism where the segregation is systemwide because that is what the law required, and thus the remedy had to be systemwide. But here, it is suggested, the remedy should be applied only to the areas which have become segregated by Board action.

Such an approach is untenable here in view of our holding that over two-thirds of the public school students in Corpus Christi are the victims of unconstitutional ethnic and racial segregation. There is established here an overwhelming pattern of unlawful segregation that has infested the entire school system. To select other than a system-wide remedy would be to ignore system-wide discrimination and make conversion to a unitary system impossible.

CHAPTER 9

LA RAZA EN NUEVA YORK:
SOCIAL PLURALISM AND SCHOOLS

GLENN HENDRICKS

As a major and visible social institution, schools cannot help but reflect, in their operation, organization, and structure, the stresses of the society of which they are a part. At present, a significant shift in ethnic relationships is occurring in New York City, indicative of a larger national shift: a tripartite social pluralism based upon categories that are both physical (racial) and cultural is emerging. As a result, institutions are changing to reflect a pluralism not heretofore characteristic of the modern urban American experience.

The intention of this paper is to describe the development of an Hispano-American culture in New York,* and to indicate how the politicization of ethnicity which results is affecting the New York City schools.

---

* The term Hispano is used here to mean all persons originating from countries which are the bearers of a culture complex that originated in Spain and who make use of the Spanish language. This includes Puerto Ricans, Cubans, South Americans, as well as persons from Spain. There is no term in Spanish or English to cover just those persons who originate in Hispanic countries other than Puerto Rico. Therefore, it is necessary to use the awkward phrase beginning with the descriptor "other." Official records usually now break the categories down into "Puerto Ricans" and "other Spanish surnames." Until a few years ago this latter group was lumped into the "other" category meaning all persons who were not Negro, Oriental, or Puerto Rican, thus further concealing this growing non-Puerto Rican Hispano segment. Still, Hispanos living in the United States lack a generally agreed upon generic term. Mexican-Americans use the term Chicano to distinguish a particular subset of this group. What is needed is a term covering the entire set of Hispanos. Although used in a derogatory sense, the Mexican term *pocho* (literally faded out or bleached) to denote Americanized approaches the term that will undoubtedly some day be coined.

Glenn Hendricks is assistant professor of anthropology at the University of Minnesota. The research project from which this article was drawn was supported by a grant from the Horace Mann-Lincoln Institute, Teachers College, Columbia University.

Hendricks, Glenn, "La Raza en Neuva York: Social Pluralism and the Schools," *Teachers College Record*, 74(3):379-93, February 1973.

A great deal has been written about cultural and social pluralism. It is beyond the scope of this paper to reconstruct its theoretical basis. In brief, however, the proponents of the plural society model argue that institutional differences serve to distinguish differing cultures and social units. One of the difficulties inherent in this viewpoint is its inability to specify the operational level at which institutional differences become such markers. Despres distinguishes between minimal (e.g. kinship) and maximal (e.g. market structures) institutions as ideal types and argues that to the degree maximal structures serve specific culture groups the society may be labeled pluralistic.

> It is suggested the definition of the plural society must take into account two related sets of facts: (1) the extent to which the specific groups are culturally differentiated in terms of specific institutional activities, and (2) the level at which institutional activities serve to maintain cultural differentiation as the basis for sociocultural integration.[1]

Pluralism has been examined most often within multi-ethnic colonial or postcolonial situations. Implicit in these discussions has been the political dimension and consequent emergence of social pluralism as ethnic groups vie for access to sources of power. Vincent rightfully points out that "cultural pluralism then becomes politically relevant when differential access to positions of differing advantage is institutionalized in ethnic terms."[2] One area in which this ethnic competition is visibly expressed is within the public school system of New York City. The black-white-brown lines become ever more rigidly drawn as each group cajoles, pleads, and threatens for programs developed specifically to meet its particular social and cultural circumstances.

New York City, as the primary port of entry for millions of immigrants into the United States, historically has been a polyglot of diverse ethnic groups exhibiting various stages of assimilation into that culture complex labeled "American." In the past several decades, we have come to recognize, however, that the popularized conception of the dominant pattern of American assimilation, the so-called melting pot theory, has proved to be an inadequate framework in which to describe what has actually taken place. Persistence of ethnic identity for large segments of almost every immigrant section for generations after it was assumed to have been lost[3] indicates the inadequacy of the melting pot formulation. Political activities based upon "ethnic arithmetic" continue to exist and reward the patient political practitioner. Nevertheless, however persistent this ethnic consciousness may be, it would be both unfair and inaccurate not to recognize the American experience as having woven the fabric of a viable society from very diverse ethnic strands.

Immigrant populations of the nineteenth century, who are usually included among those having successfully integrated, shared two important attributes: (1) they were phenotypically white-skinned, and (2) they came to the United States as citizens of another sociopolitical unit to assume residence in the United States. Upon arrival, citizenship rights were not necessarily automatically conferred, and until they were given, these immigrants were seldom in a position to make overt political demands. They could only indirectly affect public policy.

THE HISPANOS. The passage of the first immigration laws in 1924, restricting numbers and national origins of potential immigrants, was of tremendous importance in changing the nature of the incoming stream of immigrants. The elimination of the national quotas in 1968 and the placement of a ceiling for the first time on immigrants from other countries of North and South America will also dramatically change the immigrant stream. The impact of this change is just beginning to emerge and is not yet adequately documented. However, during the last half century a new pattern of internal migration developed as the agrarian economy of the United States changed and large numbers of persons were forced to leave the land and seek urban employment. The shifting economy of the South had special implications for New York as the city became one of the target areas for millions of blacks who migrated northward. A later but parallel internal migration was that of the Spanish-speaking Puerto Rican. As his island home began to feel the effect of burgeoning population growth, he found economic relief by seeking employment in New York. Not unlike some previous immigrants, both the blacks and Puerto Ricans arrived as members of socially subordinate groups, subject to the vicissitudes of American racism, unskilled and often functionally illiterate, speaking a completely foreign language or nonstandard form of English, and bearers of a cultural pattern that was to varying degrees contrastive to the mainstream dominant culture. But (and an important but) they shared two latent powers: American citizenship and significantly large numbers.

In the last decade a third large immigrant group has arrived on the New York scene. But because the wider society misidentifies them as Puerto Rican, the magnitude of this immigration has been almost unnoticed. This is the mix of nearly a million Spanish-speakers from the Caribbean Islands of Cuba and the Dominican Republic and a variety of South American countries. The size of this group is difficult to ascertain because it has arrived since the 1960 decennial census.† The growth of this "other than Puerto Rican Hispanos" segment is the result of both internal events in the countries of origin as well as United States relationships to those events. Since the takeover of Cuba by the Castro government, daily flights from Havana to Miami have been airlifting three to four thousand Cubans monthly to mainland United States. Large numbers have settled in New York and continue to do so in spite of massive government attempts to settle them out of the New York and Miami areas. The Dominican diaspora began shortly before the death of Trujillo in 1961 and was reinforced by the political instability that has occurred in the decade since, including the intervention and landing of United States forces in the Dominican Republic for the third time in the twentieth century. Estimates of the total Hispano population in New York generally place it at slightly under two million, only half of whom are of Puerto Rican origin.[4] This is in contrast to a 1970 preliminary census estimate of 1.7 million blacks living in the city.[5] At minimum it can be said that black and Hispano populations are of approximately the same size. Togeth-

---

† At the time of this writing, even preliminary reports of New York's 1970 count of the Spanish speaking population have not been released. The fact that the count of blacks was released less than three months after the count was made is perhaps indicative of the relative political clout carried by blacks vis-à-vis the Hispano population.

er they represent 3.5 million persons or 40 to 45 percent of the city's population.

A necessary legal distinction must be made between the Puerto Rican and the "other Hispano" in that Puerto Ricans are legal citizens of the United States and have the same legal right to enter and exit New York as a New York resident has to move to Miami. The others have passed through the screen of United States immigration law (or illegally by-passed it) and by and large still retain citizenship in their native countries. This fact not only disenfranchises most of them from participation in United States political events, but also results in a population of large but unknown numbers who are in a precarious illegal situation similar to the large number of "wetbacks" in the Southwest. Their presence has important consequences not only for them but also for the nature of the interaction between the entire non-Puerto Rican Hispano segment and the wider American society. While Cubans as political emigres are not in quite the same position, they have as yet failed to obtain United States citizenship in large numbers. The result of this disenfranchisement is that even when political units acknowledge that Puerto Ricans are but one segment of the total Hispano group, they are of necessity forced to recognize the Puerto Ricans as the spokesmen for the larger Hispano segment.

Not unlike the members of most immigrant groups, the Hispano immigrant most often considers his new residence to be only temporary and assumes he will one day return to his native country. However, this assumption is a far more realistic one for the Hispano than for previous immigrants who arrived earlier and from more distant countries. Modern forms of transportation plus the proximity of San Juan, Santo Domingo, or even Caracas to New York make ingress and egress relatively simple. Ties to kinsmen and friends in the countries of origin need not be severed or even attenuated. (Here we must except the Cuban who at this time cannot return. However, very often his kinsmen have also arrived in the United States.) For many Dominicans migration to New York is but one segment of the individual's life, and a portion of their active social field remains geographically located in the Dominican Republic. This failure to make a permanent commitment to immigrate to the United States has significant consequences to the patterns of assimilation and acculturation that take place. I use the word commitment purposefully to imply intention rather than actual behavior patterns.

Most of the Hispano settlers in New York come from areas of Latin America where there has been a massive infusion of Negro phenotypic characteristics into the population's genetic pool. A smaller segment is generated out of areas where the mixture includes Indian characteristics, both physical and cultural. The majority of the native population pools of the three most significant segments of Hispanos (Puerto Rican, Cuban, and Dominican) in New York are consequently classified as mullato. While racial consciousness and discrimination is indigenous in these societies, it is of a far different order than that practiced in the United States, where little distinction is made between brown and black. One of the first problems the immigrant faces upon arrival is the encounter with his new social classification as a person of "color." The unsolicited inclusion in a common category of black and Puerto Rican is acceptable to neither blacks nor Hispanos.‡ The Hispanos have reacted defensively, not only retaining Hispanic characteristics, especially the language, but accentuating them in order to avoid classification as Negroes. Since both groups are often competing with each other for available economic and political resources (e.g. poverty program grants, positions as minority representatives on committees and commissions, and special school programs), the cleavage and the tensions between these two groups are great.§ By the same token, to be a Puerto Rican is said to carry with it a more socially subordinate stigma that to be "South American," and therefore "other Hispanos" are often careful to point out that they are not Puerto Rican but Cuban or Dominican or whatever.

‡ So frequent is the term "black and Puerto Rican" (actually meaning Hispano) used together as another synonym for "the poor" that it is often pronounced as a single unbroken morphemic unit, "Blackandpuertorican."

§ I have been witness to public arguments between black and Puerto Rican representatives who base the argumentation for acceptance of their particular point of view on the fact that they as a group are more discriminated against than is the other.

LA RAZA. A further factor which must be considered is the ethnocentrism that is a prominent part of the Hispanic culture. The Hispano is quite conscious of the concept *la raza,* literally meaning the race, but actually connoting a complex of ethnocentric values which imply the inherent superiority of Hispano lifeways. Superimposed is a nationalistic attachment that is expressed in far more emotional terms than is found in American culture. Therefore, despite acculturation into United States society, strong ties are still retained to the country of origin. Thus a politicized Puerto Rican is often more concerned about statehood for Puerto Rico than about his position in New York. This is even more true of political emigrés from Cuba and the Dominican Republic. Almost all political activity found among Dominicans in New York is bound up with events in Santo Domingo and not New York. During the Dominican elections of 1970 the key political speeches of President Balaguer were broadcast in New York simultaneously with their transmission in the Republic. Colombians formed long lines before their Consulate in order to vote in their presidential elections in 1970.‖ In the case of Puerto Ricans, this pattern is slowly changing as second and third generations are born on the mainland and there is an emergence of an identification with Puerto Rican problems here. Attempts to coalesce as a national group are often negated by charges and countercharges of individuals gaining political advantage in the home country. A recent election of a New York Puerto Rican Day Parade President, a prestigious position among Puertoriqueños, was punctuated by charges that the election was being used to promote the individual's political position in the San Juan government.[6]

In spite of the divisive social and political factors operating to prevent its coalescence as a formal corporate group, the sheer number of Spanish speakers, sharing a largely similar cultural complex, has led to the development of a very visible if not vi-

---

‖ According to a *New York Times* account of the affair the more than 5,000 persons who voted in New York "turned the area on 57th Street in front of the Colombian Center into a fiesta." One participant is quoted, "For us, Colombia is all that is important in our hearts. America can give us jobs, but it cannot give us a heart. *New York Times,* April 20, 1970, p. 3.

able Hispanic subculture in New York City. Two daily newspapers in the Spanish language are published in New York. Two television stations and at least a half dozen radio stations broadcast primarily to a Spanish speaking audience. Dozens of Spanish language movie theaters are to be found in the areas of Hispano settlement. Innumerable stores, especially those selling food, either cater exclusively to this population or have whole sections devoted to footstuffs preferred by Caribbean- and Latin-Americans: plantains, yucca, rice, beans, and condiments. (A slang term for Puerto Ricans among this population is that of *Goya,* actually a trade name for a popular brand of processed foodstuffs originally aimed at the Puerto Rican market.) At least three banking institutions identified as Puerto Rican have opened numerous branches in New York and aggressively pursue business of the Spanish speaking population. A credit card system catering to the Hispano customer has been launched by one of them.

ETHNIC IDENTITY. Cohen's analysis of the Hausa living in Yoruba towns of Nigeria provides one theoretical framework in which to consider the growing Hispano segment in New York. He notes that the Hausa adjusted to the new social situation not by rapidly losing their cultural distinctiveness, but by:

... adjust[ing] to the new realities by reorganizing its own traditional customs, or by developing new customs under traditional symbols, often using traditional norms and ideologies to enhance its distinctiveness within the contemporary situation.[12]

This process he labels retribalization, as opposed to detribalization.

Obviously, value systems do undergo significant changes upon arrival in New York. Life in the major metropolitan area of the United States is not that of San Juan, a rural Dominican village, not an Ecuadorian provincial town. But the process of the cultural shift is often, to use Spicer's definition, more integrative than assimilative;[8] that is, new culture traits are taken on and integrated in such a way to conform to the meaningful and functional relations within the individual's ongoing culture system, rather than his accepting the totality of a new system. The new life in New York makes certain functional demands upon the individual. He obviously must learn to use the subways and conform to the rigidity of time requirements of factory employment. Again using Spicer's typology, these elements are more likely to be isolative or compartmentalized than assimilative. *El Boss* is part of the American's way of life and at the end of the day one retreats to family and friends where *compañerismo* is the basis of social relationships.

The newly arrived Hispano immigrant at this point in time enters an ongoing social system that is significantly different from that of the dominant culture but is so encompassing that the pressures to assimilate to the dominant culture have been effectively mitigated. A virtually complete subsociety of a New York variant of Hispano culture has been erected. The immigrant does change, but this change is most often best characterized as retribalization. Presently this process is most apparent in subsets of the total segment (e.g. Puerto Ricans or Dominicans), but it still can be documented for the total Hispano group.

Among the group I am most familiar with, Dominicans, movement to New York carries with it possibilities for great upward economic and social mobility. This is especially so for the *campesino* who in his own country has little opportunity to gain employment even by moving to urban areas of the Republic. Settlement in New York provides opportunities not only for a job but the ability to acquire quantities of capital most middle-class Dominicans are hard pressed to accumulate. However, his economic success in North American terms is relatively unimpressive. In New York he is usually classified as poverty stricken and is often a slum dweller. But if he views himself in terms of his former position in his native society, he has indeed achieved much. Thus the frame of reference by which to measure his success must come in relationship to other Dominicans either in the Republic or among his fellow countrymen in New York. Hence the New York dweller finds sources for reinforcement of his retention of Hispanic cultural attributes by the very nature of the rewards system. Attendance at an English language public school represents higher social status in Dominican terms for at least two reasons. First, mere attendance of school, especially at the secondary level, is a privilege for a relative few in his own country. Secondly, large numbers of the social and economic leading classes have for generations sent their children to schools in the United States. Bilingualism is not seen as an opportunity to become an American, but rather a functional skill which allows greater economic and social maneuverability as either a Dominican or a Hispano. However, attendance at a typical New York public school is not accepted without some reservations. For many parents and even children the school is seen as an instrument of "Yankee imperalism," robbing the Hispano child of some of the basic values of his own culture.

A genuinely successful product of the New York experience is seen as the individual who gains the economic, social, and political power to return to the island home with enhanced status. Among the politically oriented Dominicans in New York a significant lesson is to be found in the experience of the current President of the Republic, Joachim Balaguer, who is alleged to have rebuilt his political power base on 57th Street in a Horn and Hardart cafeteria while in political exile following the assassination of Trujillo. Among the Dominican *campesinos* with whom I worked in New York, the true success story was the individual who returned home after a purgatorial sojourn to New York with sufficient capital accumulation to live a comfortable existence. This New York experience allows him to gain access to many material items: automobiles, refrigerators, television sets, and medical care, items that are not unknown in his own culture; but which because of his socioeconomic status, were seldom available to him. Traditional values in marriage patterns, kin relationships, and religious beliefs undergo only slight transition in the Dominican move to New York. Marriages are contracted exclusively with other Hispanos, usually their own countrymen and often among persons from their own village. This is true even for young persons who have been reared primarily in New York.

While the majority of the total immigrant population of Hispanos is recruited from either the urban lower class or from the rural peasantry, significant numbers are drawn from the middle and even the upper class of some countries. Upon arrival in New York few, if only because of the language barriers, possess employable skills and thus all tend to be thrown into the same labor pool, working, for example, as factory operators (machine operators in the garment industry) or in service occupations (restaurant workers, especially dishwashers). The mastery of English, and hence occupational mobility, is usually a function of previous education, which in turn reflects to some degree the socioeconomic segment of the society from which the Hispano has come. Within a short period of time the social stratification system of the home country begins to re-emerge. By the same token there is a stratification system emerging between national groupings. Cuban immigrants, large portions of whom were drawn from the enterpreneurial class of their home society, seem to have re-emerged as the most successful economically. An often quoted joke among Hispanos is that a Cuban arrives in a Spanish speaking establishment to begin work as the floor sweeper and by the end of the year he has become the manager. The relative obscurity of Cubans in visible positions of leadership among the Hispano segment is a function of both their recent arrival and their lack of citizenship and hence political enfranchisement. However, there is every reason to believe that future leadership will emerge from among Cuban-Americans. Cross cutting relationships within the Hispano population have developed as marital unions are formed between members of these national groupings. Based upon my observations of Dominicans as well as a survey of marriage announcements made in the Spanish press, the tendency is for these unions to be formed along class lines even when national lines are crossed for mate selection. It is possible that a lower class Dominican may find a marital partner from among a higher placed Honduran, but seldom would the mobility take place through mate selection from members of his own nationality. Far most common is the linking of middle-class individuals from different countries through marital unions.

ETHNIC TENSIONS. Tensions do exist between the national segments which must be recognized in any description of the Hispanos of New York. Even though Spanish is the common language, each national grouping has variants of it, if only in pronunciation or in specific vocabulary terms. These variations are most pronounced in the spoken rather than in the written language. Radio and television stations face the difficulty of carefully balancing the nationalities of their announcers due to criticism over what is "correct" Spanish. The organizers of a block association party in a Hispano neighborhood with which I was familiar had to carefully balance the choice of musical groups in order to avoid offending either the Puerto Rican or Dominican participants. In a similar fashion, several years ago the Hispano banking institutions in New York were accused in the Spanish press of undergoing a process of "Cubanization." This intragroup competition is a significant factor in the schools. As more Spanish speaking individuals are recruited to teaching positions within the school systems (both public and private), the middle-class, educated Cuban, often a former teacher in Cuba, most often fulfills the requisite educational requirements. This has led to resentments among Puerto Ricans who claim their children are not being taught "their own" Spanish.

Previous periods of large scale single ethnic group immigration by the Germans, Italians, and East European Jews have led to attempts by sensitive socially conscious individuals and groups, both public and private, to alleviate their problems and accommodate to their needs. But underlying these activities was the assumption that the newcomers would eventually assimilate to the language and values of the dominant American society. What is unique about the current Hispano experience is that portions of the social and legal systems which heretofore operated to impose the dominant culture's norms are now utilized to reinforce and retain the Hispano's separate cultural identity. Judicial decisions at all levels plus administrative policy (which is both a result of and independent of judicial decree), bolstered by a value system that pays at least lip service to the "right of individuals to maintain their own culture," have led to the emergence of an intrastructural pattern which not only permits but encourages the development of cultural and social pluralism. Literacy in English is no longer a requirement for voting. Driver's license examinations are now administered in Spanish—a social reality that intimately touches thousands of Hispanos. In New York State, consumer credit contracts must be written in Spanish as well as in English, and courts are required to furnish bilingual interpreters in Spanish and English for those cases requiring it. Most widely used municipal forms, such as those applicable to rent control, are written bilingually. When feasible, and of necessity, governmental offices which serve the general public are staffed by bilingual individuals. Subway warning signs are now routinely posted in both Spanish and English. Recognition of both the political power as well as the legal and moral right for representation is demonstrated by the now almost standard practice of seeking out black and Hispano representatives on any commission, delegation, or committee that seeks an image of widespread representation. The first United States Congressman identified with the Puerto Rican segment of New York City's population has been re-elected, and undoubtedly there will be more following. This recognition has not evolved without some degree of militancy on the part of the Hispanos themselves as they first sought recognition and then equality. The activities of the Young Lords, an ethnically oriented separatist movement of mainland born and reared Puerto Ricans, represent at least one direction that this new Hispano self-consciousness might take.

The degree to which the Hispano now constitutes a recognized segment is seen in the growing practice of bilingual advertising. Thus in a great many places in New York Coca Cola's "Es la cosa real" is seen as frequently as "It's the real thing." A growing advertising and public relations industry caters exclusively to Hispanos. The newly created New York City Betting Commission aimed a specific advertising program at the Spanish speakers (another separate program was aimed at the black).

Settlement patterns of the Hispano group are dominated by the shortage of all types of housing in New York, which is especially severe among low priced rental units. However the propensity of Hispanos to live in concentrated groups is as much a result of their desire to live near familiar persons as it is a result of the competition to secure any kind of housing at prices they can afford. The concentration of many individuals in a single living unit is an outgrowth of their own behavioral patterns of living in relatively limited space, as well as an efficient way of mobilizing sufficient resources to pay the relatively high rents demanded for even minimal accommodations.

The most widely known residential area for the Hispano population is *el Barrio,* the eastern part of Harlem located on the Up-per East Side of Manhattan. However, this area is almost exclu-sively Puerto Rican and contains only a small segment of the to-tal population. Hispanos can be found throughout the city, with the heaviest concentration in Manhattan and the Bronx, but in-creasingly in Brooklyn. Table 9-I indicates school population characteristics and provides as reliable an index to relative settle-ment patterns as any currently available.# In addition to the 68,-500 Hispano children in the Borough of Manhattan public schools, almost fourteen thousand more attend Catholic parochi-al schools in the Manhattan diocese. This writer, however, would argue that use of school statistics for total population projec-tions is still erroneous since the "other Hispanos" have just start-ed to establish households and marital unions in New York. Be-cause of their recent arrival, their children have yet to reach the schools in large numbers. In addition, many do not enter the im-migrant stream until after they are past school age. A further caveat is that the large number of illegal residents seldom are ac-companied by school age children. However, what the table does indicate is that, with the exception of Staten Island, significant numbers of Hispanos reside in all boroughs of the city.

PLURALISTIC SCHOOLS. I should like to turn now to a brief dis-cussion of the impact all of this has had upon the schools of New York City. As Table 9-I indicates, at least 25 percent of the public school population of the city is of Hispano origin, com-ing from family units that retain varying degrees of that unique cultural identity. Were these 25 percent distributed throughout

---

Board of Education of the City of New York. *Annual Census of School Popu-lation,* October 31, 1969. The problems inherent in making such a census leave the reliability of these figures open to question. Teachers were left to make these determinations without asking the pupils. The Central Office of Educational Pro-gram Research and Statistics specifically instructed that each school was to make its own interpretation of these categories without consulting their office. A number of Dominicans, for example, do not carry Spanish sounding surnames. Lack of information makes it difficult for a non-Spanish speaking teacher to determine the place of origin of a child and thus everyone who speaks Spanish is Puerto Rican. This is not a problem unique to New York City. In Minneapolis the ethnic census is referred to as the "sight count" and is literally based upon the observa-tory powers of the teacher.

TABLE 9-I

ETHNIC ENROLLMENT IN ALL NEW YORK CITY SCHOOLS, 1969-70

Borough and Level	Number of Pupils							Per Cent of Total Register					
	Puerto Rican	Other Sp. Amer.	Negro	Amer. Indian	Oriental	Others	Total	Puerto Rican	Other Sp. Amer.	Negro	Amer. Indian	Oriental	Others
Manhattan	57,974	10,675	67,934	50	7,592	28,798	173,023	33.5	6.2	39.3	0.0	4.4	16.6
Brooklyn	89,813	6,467	156,741	148	3,089	157,242	413,500	21.7	1.6	37.9	0.0	0.8	38.0
Bronx	89,706	5,265	78,073	36	1,483	56,897	231,460	38.8	2.3	33.7	0.0	0.6	24.6
Queens	8,304	10,679	66,459	53	3,707	160,390	249,592	3.3	4.3	26.6	0.0	1.5	64.3
Richmond	1,110	392	4,221	2	204	41,862	47,862	2.3	0.8	8.8	0.0	0.5	87.6
Special schools	2,148	96	3,520	—	19	1,945	7,728	27.8	1.3	45.5	—	0.2	25.2
City-wide	249,055	33,574	376,948	289	16,094	447,205	1,123,165	22.2	3.0	33.6	0.0	1.4	39.8

TABLE 9-II

ELEMENTARY PUPILS WITH LANGUAGE DIFFICULTIES

Borough	*Total Puerto Ricans Registered*	*With Language Difficulties*	*% of Puerto Ricans Registered*	*Total Other Spanish Surnames*	*With Language Difficulties*	*% of Other Spanish Surnames Registered*
Manhattan	32,233	15,168	47.0	6,799	4,504	62.2
Bronx	57,304	24,573	42.9	3,391	1,780	52.5
Brooklyn	55,914	23,648	42.3	3,872	1,987	51.3
Queens	3,945	1,103	28.0	6,494	3,476	53.5
Richmond	662	113	17.0	250	40	16.0
Total	152,181	64,605	42.9	20,898	11,787	56.4

the system their impact would undoubtedly be of a different order. In both Manhattan and the Bronx, however, they constitute 40 percent of the population, and were these figures broken down by district and school, one would find individual schools with 80 to 90 percent Hispano registrants.

Among the catalogue of problems this large population brings to the schools is the obvious one of language. A special language census in 1969 revealed that 95,482 Hispano children attending New York public schools faced language difficulties ranging from moderate (i.e. they speak English hesitantly) to severe (they speak little or none) (see Table 9-II).[9]

A wide variety of experimental programs has been proposed and in some cases implemented in attempts to cope with this very real language problem. In the past few years there have developed a number of pilot experimental programs due to the infusion of federal aid funds under the Bilingual Education Act of 1968.** The most radical of these are at least two schools in the

** It might be noted here that the Bilingual Aid Act grew out of problems existing in the Southwest among Mexican-Americans and was eventually funded only because President Johnson made special efforts to see that it was pushed through Congress. Implicit in the discussion of this paper is the significance of recent decisions on the national level to further aid the Spanish speaking portion of the American population as well as court rulings requiring equality of treatment for Spanish speaking citizens.

Bronx in which Spanish is the language in which all major subject matters are taught and English is introduced as a foreign language. Variations on this concept exist in many schools depending upon the number and kind of Spanish speaking teachers who can be recruited. Besides deliberate proposals for separate secondary schools catering to the Spanish speaker, de facto segregation in certain areas is also leading to high schools which are largely Hispano. George Washington and Benjamin Franklin High Schools in upper Manhattan have increasingly large numbers of Spanish speaking students. The opening of Maria Hostos Community College, as part of the city's two year college program, is an overt attempt to create an institution of higher education specifically aimed at this population.

A discussion of the merits of such programs is not my purpose here; rather it is to note the consequences such programs, if fully implemented, might have. Burnett raises the issue of the significance of schools as instruments of developing pluralism.

> I question whether the objects of cultural pluralism can be pursued in the presence of highly centralized political and economic control of schools. The recent posture of teachers' unions has added to my doubts.[10]

In New York City, part of the current battle over decentralization is over just such issues. The degree that each district achieves autonomy, especially in the recruitment of its teachers, will affect the implementation of Spanish language programs. If our definition of ethnic pluralism, especially in a sociological sense, includes the construction of "maximal" institutions that serve to socialize individuals into separate language (hence ethnic) segments, it would seem obvious such Spanish language schools are inherently part of this social movement towards pluralism. The selection of the first Puerto Rican District Superintendent, by a knowledgeable and militant board, who is dedicated to the development of these truly bilingual schools is evidence of how far this movement has progressed. One can only speculate how far such a development might proceed before the intercession of other countervaling forces. However, both the possibility and the direction already taken is clearly demonstrable.

Vincent's argument that ethnicity becomes politically salient when it involves a competition for access to available strategic resources is pertinent here. If separate schooling facilities for the Hispano population indeed become an alternative to which a significant number have access, it is possible to foresee further coalescence of this ethnic segment and the accentuation of ethnic divisions. This is particularly true in the division between blacks and Hispanos as they press for schools emphasizing their particular cultural points of view.

A usual rebuttal to the kind of argument presented in this paper is that other ethnic sections in New York, notably the Jews, have passed through the school system and used it as a route toward acculturation. Greer, in a recent historical examination of the role of the schools in New York in the processes of assimilation, raises the serious question that this centrality ever existed. Rather he posits that:

> Public education was the rubber stamp of economic improvement; rarely has it been the bootstrap . . . the key factor is more probably the indigenous grounding of the unit within the ethnic boundary— the establishment of an ethnic middle class before scaling the walls of the dominant society.[11]

As I have said, it can be further argued that historical analogy cannot be used in the Hispano case because neither their position vis-à-vis the political structure nor the dominant society's at least token acceptance of cultural pluralism was previously present.

The legal position of the majority of Hispanos, their great numbers, American racial attitudes, and the Hispanos' historically demonstrated penchant for retaining major cultural traits in spite of pressures toward acculturation are all salient conditions which combine to aid the emergence of new forms of social organization and structures in New York City. Certainly, the direction of this pluralistic development is not irreversible, and even at present a considerable number of persons of Hispano heritage choose to assimilate into the dominant society. Others may situationally select when to be American and when to be Hispano. And further, policy decisions made by political and educational leaders concerning the school's response to societal change will obviously affect the future course of events. What is clear, however, and what I have attempted to demonstrate, is that the situation is a dynamic one in which dynamic processes of culture and social change are in full operation.

REFERENCES

1. Despres, Leo A.: *Cultural Pluralism and Nationalist Politics in British Guiana,* Chicago, Rand McNally, 1967, pp. 21-22.
2. Vincent, Joan: The politics of ethnicity, paper delivered at the 29th annual meeting of the Society for Applied Anthropology, Boulder, Colorado, April, 1970, p. 2.
3. Glazer, Nathan, and Moynehan, Daniel Patrick: *Beyond the Melting Pot,* Cambridge, the MIT Press, 1963.
4. New York State Division of Human Rights: Puerto Ricans in New York State, 1969, mimeo.
5. Carmody, Deirdre: True black count urged in census, *New York Times,* February 11, 1970, p. 35.
6. Navarey, Alfonso A.: Aide to be named by Puerto Ricans, *New York Times,* November 29, 1970, p. 57.
7. Cohen, Abner: *Custom and Politics in Urban Africa,* Berkeley, University of California Press, 1969.
8. Specer, Edward H.: Types of contact and processes, in Specer (ed.), *Perspectives in American Indians Cultural Change,* Chicago, University of Chicago Press, 1961, pp. 517-544.
9. Board of Education of the City of New York: Survey of pupils who have difficulties with the English Language, Publications 334, September 1970.
10. Burnett, Jaquetta H.: Culture of the school: a construct for research and explanation in education, *Counsel on Anthropology and Education Newsletter, 1(1):*11, 1970.
11. Greer, Colin: Immigrants, Negroes and the public schools, *Urban Review,* January 1969.

CHAPTER 10

ETHNIC STUDIES OF THE MELTING POT

FRANCES CASTAN

W ITH THE EXCEPTION of the blacks, who were brought here against their will, and the American Indians, whose reasons for coming predate recorded history, everyone has come to this land seeking something better. And that *something better* is economic well-being. Of course, politics, religious discomforts, impending conscription, and lack of educational opportunities also play a role, but the prime mover of people to North America has been economics.

Do the immigrants find their dream? Do they succeed? The answer, for many, is yes. Others raise their children to succeed where they failed.

Always, the first task is learning the new language. Next comes adopting local manners and shedding evidence of foreignness as quickly as possible. Those whites willing to rend and wrench themselves from their roots in this way find it possible to gain acceptance, to assimilate in accordance with the melting pot theory. Whites can *pass*, become invisible. But the blacks, American Indians, Orientals, Chicanos and brown-skinned peoples find that it is impossible to become invisible. No matter how they speak, dress, or behave, their skin color shows through and identifies them as different.

Yes despite this truth, the melting pot myth continued. "Melting" was everyone's goal. Step right up; jump right in; swim around a little and you'll come out right—spelled *white*.

However, people aren't metals in a crucible or vegetables in a stew pot—and besides, they're incapable of being uniform. Today in the United States we have (according to the 1970 census) 177,748,975 whites; 22,580,289 Negroes (the census still uses the

---

Frances Castan, a former teacher of English, is an assistant editor of *ST*.

Castan, Frances, "Ethnic Studies Out of the Melting Pot," *Scholastic Teacher,* April 1972, pp. 8-11.

word Negro); 792,730 American Indians; 591,290 Japanese; 435,-062 Chinese; 343,060 Filipinos, and All Others (Koreans, Hawaiians, Aleuts, Eskimos, Malayans, Polynesians, etc.) number 720,520. Some stew!

Though each ethnic group has a readily identifiable set of values and customs, some of them shared by other groups, the original melting pot idea implicitly called for a *preferred* set of values—those of the white Anglo-Saxon Protestant. And the closer a person comes to matching this ideal, the better his chances for success here.

America's schools helped to bring about the acculturation of immigrants. By 1911, in the public schools alone, over 57 percent of the students in 37 of the largest cities were children of immigrants. By 1918, all states had attendance laws making it compulsory to remain in school until age 14. The audience was captive and the task was clear—teach them English and Anglo customs.

For Indians on nontaxable lands (which don't contribute to the support of public schools) the solution was federally operated (Bureau of Indian Affairs) schools. Most of these were boarding schools. Today, although the majority of Indian children attend public schools, 25 percent are still in BIA schools.

The trauma of change, particularly for a person from a racial group long isolated from the mainstream, is reconstructed by an Indian woman born on a reservation of about 300 people.

As a preschooler she'd play with her friends and spend hours listening to the legends told by the elders as they smoked their pipes. Then:

> This rather casual and cozy existence came to an end when I was six and was sent to a boarding school in a small town 70 miles from the reserve. At the time we had no school on the reserve. There was a school in the village some three miles away, but there was no school bus, and the roads were in a pretty bad condition. . . . Living on the reserve I had naturally thought that all people were the same and spoke the same language. I did not know that I was an "Indian" and that there were a lot of important people in the world that were "white." . . . I remember huddling together with a lot of frightened little girls of my own age. Many of us came from different reserves and did not even speak the same Indian language. Besides we were forbidden to speak our own languages and were punished for doing so, if we were caught. . . . I stayed for four years, and I don't think I ever stopped

being scared and lonely. I was scared of being caught speaking Indian, scared because I didn't understand the English of the teachers and could not follow the lessons, scared that I would get punished for wetting my bed, scared that I would not wake up in time for the six o'clock mass. I also remember being beaten up for many of these things.[1]

A variation of this theme also obtains for the blacks, Chicanos, and Puerto Ricans of today's ghettos. They, too, are enticed or coerced into changing their ways and latching onto the preferred set of values, but somehow, like the Indians, they don't quite gain acceptance. They receive a double message: This is a land of freedom and opportunity for everyone (everyone but *you*).

This dream of acceptance, dangling just out of reach, is expressed by Jack Agueros, 38-year-old son of Puerto Rican immigrants to New York's Harlem:

The neighborhood had its boundaries. Third Avenue and east, Italian. Fifth Avenue and west, black. South, there was still a hill on 103rd Street known locally as Cooney's Hill. When you got to the top of the hill, something strange happened: America began, because from the hill south was where the "Americans" lived. Dick and Jane were not dead; they were alive and well in a better neighborhood.

When, as a group of Puerto Rican kids, we decided to go swimming to Jefferson Park Pool, we knew we risked a fight and a beating from the Italians. And when we went to La Milagrosa Church in Harlem, we knew we risked a fight and a beating from the blacks. But when we went over Cooney's Hill, we risked dirty looks, disapproving looks, and questions from the police like, "What are you doing in this neighborhood?" and "Why don't you kids go back where you belong?"

Where we belonged! Man, I had written compositions about America. Didn't I belong on the Central Park tennis courts, even if I didn't know how to play? Couldn't I watch Dick play? Weren't these policemen working for me too?[2]

Orientals—primarily the Chinese and Japanese—experienced a special brand of discrimination. The Chinese were the scapegoat's scapegoat. After rushing the West Coast in great numbers, responding to exaggerated claims of gold, they needed alternate means of economic survival. They worked on the railroad, washed laundry, made clothing—in short, competed against all the other immigrants who had come West. The competition was keen. Though many of the white immigrants may not have had all the preferred traits of the Anglos, they were certainly closer to that ideal than these yellow-skinned non-Christians. What followed, in addition to individual persecutions, was the Chinese Exclusion Act (1882), which denied immigration for 10 years to Chinese laborers. It was renewed in 1892, and in 1902 immigration was suspended indefinitely for these people. The exclusion act also served to deny citizenship to those Chinese not born on United States soil.

During World War II, people of Japanese extraction in the states of California, Washington, and Oregon were moved to ten internment centers in the U. S. interior. The remaining thinly scattered Japanese-American population was subject to search, questioning, and harassment. Prior to the war, they didn't get the best treatment either. In the early 1900's, the San Francisco Board of Education had ordered all Japanese, native- or foreign-born, to attend the segregated Oriental school in Chinatown on the premise that all Orientals are the same. After this, in 1908, a "Gentlemen's Agreement" was arrived at between the United States and Japan. It called for a ban on Japanese laborers and farmers immigrating to the United States.

Jade Snow Wong, the fifth daughter of Chinese immigrants to San Francisco, who managed to keep her family traditions and language as well as join the mainstream of American life as a ceramist and author, compares her experiences of discrimination with those of her children:

> The difference of being Chinese was not always lovely. One day after junior high school classes (I was one of only two Chinese faces there), a tormentor chased me, taunting me with "Chinky, chinky, Chinaman . . ." and tacked on some insults. Suddenly, I wondered if by my difference, I was inferior. This question had to be resolved again and again later: when I looked for my first job, when I looked for an apartment, when I met with unexplained rejection. It was a problem I felt I could not discuss with my parents.
>
> It is a problem which has not diminished with the years. Only a few years ago, my two youngest children came home from their walk to the neighborhood library with the story that some boys had physically attacked them as they passed the schoolyard, insulting them because they were Chinese. Immediately, I took them with me and looked for

the schoolyard's director, who called the culprits. There were defensive denials and looks of surprised guilt. But our children will not be wondering for years if being Chinese means being inferior.[3]

Like Jade Snow Wong, members of visible ethnic minority groups are speaking out, demanding an equal place in society. Blacks, Chicanos, American Indians, and Puerto Ricans are notable examples. They want "in" on the *single* message—that this is a land of freedom and opportunity for everyone *including* them.

By speaking up for their rights—and getting results—these groups have elevated their self-esteem all the way to "Black is beautiful!" "Viva La Raza!" and "Indian Power!" As they reexamine their histories, and check their data against widely used texts, these least-preferred groups are finding discrepancies. Textbooks sometimes gloss over difficulties and atrocities as they patriotically unfold the story of America from the preferred point of view.

These discoveries lead to the call for ethnic studies—black studies, American Indian studies, Chicano studies—to provide ego repair to maligned and mistreated groups. It's a call "to tell it like it is" from the other side. To have their own people tell it and to correct the Anglo history books. There is also a call for local control of schools and, sometimes, separatism. This turn is particularly ironic in the case of blacks who lived so long in seggregated schools and fought a hard-won battle for integration. A battle that they won on the grounds that separate is *not* equal.

In typically human "me-too" fashion, some white members of ethnic minority groups are requesting ethnic studies. "If the publicly supported schools are teaching black studies to the black kids, they better teach [Polish, Jewish, Italian, Irish] studies to my [Polish, Jewish, Italian, Irish] kid."

Multi-ethnic studies, covering a range of cultures, seem to be less in evidence at present than ethnic studies relating to a particular group. Like courses in social studies, they attempt to expand students' understandings of minority groups and their contributions to the United States. Multi-ethnic studies are offered in schools with homogeneous majority populations as well as in schools populated by diverse minority groups.

Today the schools have come full-circle in their role of educating immigrants. First called upon to teach for similarity and uniformity—to reinforce the use of the English language and American ways—schools today are also called upon to teach about our differences, our unique values and contributions. To instill in us a sense of pride in our ancestral culture, rather than in a "melted" mass culture. Instead of *melting pot,* today's phrase, in school and out, is *cultural pluralism*—or *cultural mosaic.* The image evoked is that of distinct individuals making a cohesive whole as opposed to the indistinct, uniform melting pot people.

Isn't this going to make matters worse? Like jumping from the melting pot into the fire. Won't the emphasis in our differences tend to separate us more as a nation? What was wrong with the idea of all of us being one?

"There is nothing wrong with this eventual goal of one nation and one people," says Antonio Gabaldon, principal, Charles W. Sechrist Elementary School, Flagstaff, Arizona. "However, to force people to lose their identity by giving up their cultures and especially their pride, even before it has been established, is despicable. Once a person has gained this pride in his group culture and his group identity, let it become an individual matter as to how he or she will navigate within the mainstream of the large current."[4]

If it isn't dangerously destructive to our nation to go back to our beginnings and find our roots again, is it the job of the schools to take us there? Some people think it's up to the parents and the community to provide ethnic background and pride. They make an analogy between teaching ethnicity and teaching religion. They feel neither is the job of the schools, that the schools should stay out of such family matters.

James A. Banks, associate professor of education at the University of Washington, Seattle, disagrees: "Ethnic studies are needed by *all* students to help them to understand themselves and the social world in which they live. The minority experience is part of the human experience, and education should deal with the *total* experience of man."[5]

Despite disagreements and doubts, several kinds of programs are going on under the heading *Ethnic Studies.* Bilingual programs attempt to help Indians and recent immigrants—often Puerto Ricans, Cubans, Chicanos—learn English and United States culture while they learn subject matter in their native language. These programs usually result from community demands. (Parents feel it is unfair for their children to lose time in school, sometimes several years, as they try to master English.) Massachusetts recently became the first state to make bilingual education mandatory. Next September every Massachusetts school district with 20 or more children of limited English-speaking ability must provide native-language instruction.

Another type of program has evolved for ethnic minority groups who may know English and be able to function here, but need the sort of ego repair which can be gained through a positive cultural identity. A number of these programs exist for Chinese, blacks, Indians, and Jews. Often the ancestral language is taught as much for a feeling of cultural heritage as for communication with elders. Native music, literature, food, and art forms are explored. History and tradition are also reviewed.

A third type of program comes under the category of multi-ethnic or polyethnic studies. In this program one can find members of less populous or more obscure minority groups who don't quite have the numbers to warrant a class of their own (Koreans, Welsh, French). Also enrolled in multi-ethnic studies are members of the majority (white Anglo-Saxon Protestants) who want to gain understanding of the spectrum of cultures making up the United States. Multi-ethnic studies superficially acquaint students with aspects of diverse cultures, and attempt to right some of the misconceptions or omissions of which old history texts are guilty.

A number of leaders in the field of education agree with Professor Banks' and Principal Gabaldon's views that ethnic studies are important and that the schools should help provide them, but fear that the whole thing may go bad if it's jumped on like a bandwagon or followed slavishly like a fad, without any forethought. These critics of some current practices, but not of the theory behind them, feel that much of today's ethnic studies courses concentrate on minority leaders and their contributions. Though they agree that this is important, and certainly better than nothing at all, they'd like to see inquiry into the subtleties of why members of certain ethnic groups behave, think, and feel the way they do.

In the meantime, ready or not, programs are underway. One very interesting experiment was going on until recently on the grounds of an abandoned orphanage in the outskirts of San Francisco. There, at the Multi-Culture Institute, Frances Sussna directed a radical foundation-supported program until the orphanage buildings were scheduled for demolition. The Institute's program goes like this: During each morning the students (3 to 12 years old) attend integrated classes for math, reading, and other major academic subjects. After lunch, they divide into ethnic groups. At last count, there were six: Jewish, Irish, black, Chinese, Spanish, and polyethnic. In these groups they learn an appropriate language (Hebrew, Cantonese, Swahili), cook ethnic foods, explore cultural history, and fill their music and art requirements by studying the music and art of their ancestors. The purpose of the separate afternoon groups is to generate an understanding of, and pride in, the individual student's cultural background. An understanding he can then share with others. When a group celebrates a holiday, performs some program, or prepares food, another group is invited in to share the experience.

The purpose of all this is not to create an angry superiority, but a healthy pride. It is an attempt to face differences squarely, not deny their existence. It is also an attempt to show the common threads running through all human cultures—pride, dignity, love, loyalty, family structure, the need for faith and for self-expression through work and art.

When asked how the children group themselves during free time, Miss Sussna's assistant, Judy Mings, said that the younger children, or those who have spent less time at the institute, seem to gather in ethnic groups more than the older, more experienced kids who seem to select friends on more objective grounds—common interests, skills, and talents.

There is a strong indication that a number of schools around the country will soon duplicate aspects of Miss Sussna's pilot project. Of course, there is no guarantee that this experiment, or others like it, will ultimately take us out of the seething melting pot we created. At the very least, the pursuit of ethnic studies is a sign of recognition, rather than denial, of our problems. At best, it is an *attempt* to solve them.

REFERENCES

1. Manitouwabi, Edna: Ojibwa girl in the city. *This Magazine Is About Schools, 4(4)*.
2. Agueros, Jack: Halfway to Dick and Jane. In Wheeler, Thomas (ed.): *The Immigrant Experience*. Dial Press, 1971.
3. Wong, Jade Snow: Puritan from the Orient. In Wheeler, Thomas C. (ed.): *The Immigrant Experience,* Dial Press, 1971.
4. *Educational Leadership, 29(2):123*, November 1971.
5. *Educational Leadership, 29(2):113*, November 1971.

PART III

EXPECTATIONS AND SELF-CONCEPT: A PROFILE

CHAPTER 11

THE NEGATIVE SELF-CONCEPT OF MEXICAN-AMERICAN STUDENTS

THOMAS P. CARTER

MOST EDUCATORS WHO DEAL with Mexican-American children are convinced that the group contains a larger than normal percentage of individuals who view themselves negatively. This negative self-image is seen as being a principal reason for the group's lack of school success. Contacts with Mexican-American youth in one area of California, however, do not support the notion that they perceive themselves more negatively than do their "Anglo" peers.

What causes the individual Mexican-American's self-image to be negative? The usual answer stresses that such a child is marginal, caught between two ways of life—the Mexican and the American. This marginality presents the individual with more than normal difficulty in establishing his self-identity, leading the child to assume he is inferior. Often not accepted by the "Anglo" group, he concludes that he is as that group views him— lazy, unambitious, not very intelligent, etc. It is assumed that the child internalizes the "Anglo" stereotype of the "Mexican." Other causes are seen as contributing. Constant frustration and disappointment in school are regarded by Prof. Manuel as promoting feelings of inferiority. He contends that the child caught in such a syndrome of failure withdraws from the battle and assumes the inferior feelings ascribed to him by the school.[1] The child is perceived as judging himself against the "Anglo" school's norms of success.

The search for identity is real and traumatic for most youth in our kinetic world. The search for self for the marginal youth is, without doubt, more real and more traumatic. The Mexican-

---

Reprinted from *School & Society*, March 30, 1968, by permission of the author and publisher.

American suffers many frustrations and problems. Yet, experience indicates that such youth are quite resilient as a group, and seem fairly successful in withstanding the temptation to think of themselves negatively. Rather than judge themselves solely by "Anglo" standards, they appear to judge by norms established by their own peer society or by the Mexican-American society of which they are part. They seem to reject "Anglo" society's and the school's opinion of them, and maintain individual integrity at least as well as their "Anglo" peers. A strong suggestion must be made that the supposed negative self-image of the Mexican-American is, in reality, our own stereotype projected onto him. "Anglos" tend to think of Mexican-Americans in negative ways, and conclude they see themselves in the same light.

From September, 1964, to June, 1966, the author conducted research in the secondary schools of one of California's rich agricultural valleys. The study involved the feeder seventh- and eighth-grade schools and the one union high school. School population in the area is approximately 65 percent Mexican-American, the vast majority are children of low-paid agricultural workers. The "Anglo" school population's parents follow a much more normal distribution of occupations and income. During the study, parents, students, teachers, and administrators were interviewed, some a number of times. Classes were observed repeatedly. Three sets of socio-psychological instruments were administered. Nothing supported the belief that the Mexican-American students saw themselves more negatively than "Anglo" students. However, it was very obvious that teachers and administrators believed them to be inferior and to conclude they saw themselves that way.

A demonstration of self-concept parity between the two ethnic groups was the analysis of data collected from a questionnaire administered to 190 Mexican-American and 98 "Anglo" high school ninth graders. It was hypothesized that important components of self-image involved the elements of personal intelligence, goodness, happiness, and power. The individual student rated himself on a five-point semantic differential. The adjectives used were: good-bad, wise-foolish, happy-sad, and strong-weak. Students told how they felt about themselves by indicating where they fell on the five-point continuum between the two adjectives. Little or no difference, in self-view as assumed to be measured by the instrument, was found to exist between the two groups.

Percentages of the two groups rating themselves on each of the five points between the four sets of differentials were calculated. In some cases, the Mexican-Americans had a slightly larger percentage rating themselves on the positive extreme. For example, 21 percent of the Mexican-Americans, contrasted to 13 percent of the "Anglos," rated themselves on the extreme good side of the good-bad differential. Even on the wise-foolish continuum, a slightly larger percentage of the Mexican-Americans than of "Anglos" saw themselves as extremely wise. On the other dimensions, both groups had similar percentages. Median scores for the two groups were very close. On the good-bad scale, both groups had a median score of 3.1. On the wise-foolish and strong-weak scales, the differences were practically nil. Mexican-American median on the intelligence item was 2.9, as contrasted to 2.8. The power item reflected the same magnitude of difference—the Mexican-American median being 2.2, the "Anglo" 2.1. Only on the happy-sad scale did a larger difference exist, the Mexican-American median being 3.6, a little less happy than the "Anglo" 3.3.

The students interviewed supported the notion that as a group they did not suffer from a negative view of themselves. Admittedly, individuals did. Yet, the Mexican-American students were well aware of the way teachers and others viewed their group. They knew the stereotype. Numerous students reported examples of derogatory statements about "Mexicans" made by teachers and fellow students. Many were school failures—having long histories of low achievement, poor grades, and repeated years. Yet, the majority of these children appeared to be doing a magnificent job of maintaining a positive view of themselves against the onslaught of the beliefs of the "Anglo" and the judgments of the school.

Two societies, the Mexican-American and the "Anglo," exist in the area served by the schools studied. The school, its teachers, content, and methods, represent the middle-class "Anglo" culture. The Mexican-American child often sees much of what is taught as irrelevant or in conflict with what he learns at home. The child caught between the home and school culture readily learns his reference group's methods of coping with the conflict situation. The reference group of most Mexican-Americans is their own sub-society. Such actions as a boy hanging his head and playing dumb often are interpreted by teachers as manifesting a negative self-view, yet well may be "tricks" developed by the subordinate group in order to coexist with the "Anglo." From the boy's point of view, the action may insulate and protect the boy's feelings. The apparent submissiveness of some Mexican-American girls often is judged as reflecting the girl's negative view of herself. However, this behavior may be well established in the girl's home culture as normal and desirable. Educators tend to interpret a minority's behavior from the "Anglo" frame of reference. Actions which may manifest negative self-view in one society are interpreted equally in children from another ethnic group.

The Mexican-American child may remove himself subjectively from the environment that depreciates him, and place himself in the valid community that supports and maintains the individual. What becomes relevant to him is either his ethnic peer group, the adult Mexican-American community, or both. This point was well taken by José Villarreal when he stated, ". . . discrimination, prejudice and poverty have not made him [Mexican-American youth] feel inferior. He can be traumatized by these things, but he is not broken by them. The Anglo may lull himself into believing the opposite, but the boy who is forced to drop out of the eighth grade because he was ignored, discouraged, or misdirected does not feel inferior."[2] Such a youth is lucky, as he has a sanctuary in a society existing adjacent to the "Anglo" world. The child's home and peer society teaches him who he is and what is expected of him. The Mexican-Americans studied seem to follow a rather normal distribution in regards to how well they perceive of themselves as meeting these standards.

The limitations of this research must be recognized. The area studied is rural and agricultural, with a numerical majority of Mexican-Americans. Other situations, where percentages are different, where there is a less close-knit Mexican-American community, or where the setting is urban and industrial, may present other findings as to how the Mexican-Americans view themselves. While no definite conclusions can be reached, a few assumptions are suggested. Every school and community is distinct; each must be examined carefully. Generalizations concerning Mexican-American students are misleading at their best. Mexican-Americans are a very heterogeneous group of people. Mexican-American youth does not necessarily internalize the "Anglo's" image of him, nor does he necessarily judge himself against school norms of success and failure. Educators must re-examine the school and the students they serve to test such currently held beliefs as the group negative self-image concept. Too ready acceptance of such notions serves to protect educators from the in-depth examination of other problems relative to the success and failure of Mexican-American students in the "Anglo" School.

REFERENCES

1. Manuel, Herschel, T.: *Spanish Speaking Children of the Southwest.* Austin, University of Texas Press, 1965, p. 189.
2. Villarreal, Jose: Mexican-Americans and the leadership crisis. *Los Angeles Times West Magazine*, September 25, 1966, p. 45.

CHAPTER 12

THE MUTUAL IMAGES AND EXPECTATIONS OF ANGLO-AMERICANS AND MEXICAN-AMERICANS

A NUMBER OF PSYCHOLOGICAL and sociological studies have treated ethnic and racial stereotypes as they appear publicly in the mass media and also as held privately by individuals.[1] The present paper is based on data collected for a study of a number of aspects of the relations between Anglo-Americans and Mexican-Americans in a South Texas community, and is concerned with the principal assumptions and expectations that Anglo- and Mexican-Americans hold of one another; how they see each other; the extent to which these pictures are realistic; and the implications of their intergroup relations and cultural differences for the fulfillment of their mutual expectations.*

The Community

The community studied (here called "Border City") is in South Texas, about 250 miles south of San Antonio. Driving south from San Antonio, one passes over vast expanses of brushland and grazing country, then suddenly comes upon acres of

Based on an address at the annual meeting of the Mexican Christian Institute at San Antonio in 1958.

* The term "Anglo-American," as is common in the Southwest, refers to all residents of Border City who do not identify themselves as Spanish-speaking and of Mexican descent. The Anglo-Americans of Border City have emigrated there from all parts of the United States and represent a wide variety of regional and ethnic backgrounds. The terms "Mexican-American" and "Mexican," as used here, refer to all residents of Border City who are Spanish-speaking and of Mexican descent. The term "Spanish-speaking" is perhaps less objectionable to many people, but for present purposes is even less specific than Mexican or Mexican-American, since it also refers to ethnic groups that would have no sense of identification with the group under consideration here.

Simmons, Ozzie G., "The Mutual Images and Expectations of Anglo-Americans and Mexican-Americans," *Deadalus*, 90(2):286-300, The American Academy of Arts and Sciences, Spring, 1961.

138

citrus groves, farmlands rich with vegetables and cotton, and long rows of palm trees. This is the "Magic Valley," an oasis in the semidesert region of South Texas. The Missouri Pacific Railroad (paralleled by Highway 83, locally called "The longest street in the world") bisects twelve major towns and cities of the Lower Rio Grande Valley between Brownsville, near the Gulf of Mexico, and Rio Grande City, 103 miles to the west.

Border City is neither the largest nor the smallest of these cities, and is physically and culturally much like the rest. Its first building was constructed in 1905. By 1920 it had 5,331 inhabitants, and at the time of our study these had increased to an estimated 17,500. The completion of the St. Louis, Brownsville, and Mexico Railroad in 1904 considerably facilitated Anglo-American immigration to the Valley. Before this the Valley had been inhabited largely by Mexican ranchers, who maintained large haciendas in the traditional Mexican style based on peonage. Most of these haciendas are now divided into large or small tracts that are owned by Anglo-Americans, who obtained them through purchase or less legitimate means. The position of the old Mexican-American landowning families has steadily deteriorated, and today these families, with a few exceptions, are completely overshadowed by the Anglo-Americans, who have taken over their social and economic position in the community.

The Anglo-American immigration into the Valley was paralleled by that of the Mexicans from across the border, who were attracted by the seemingly greater opportunities for farm labor created by the introduction of irrigation and the subsequent agricultural expansion. Actually, there had been a small but steady flow of Mexican immigration into South Texas that long antedated the Anglo-American immigration.[§] At present, Mexican-Americans probably constitute about two-fifths of the total population of the Valley.

In Border City, Mexican-Americans comprise about 56 percent of the population. The southwestern part of the city, adjoining

§ For the historical background of the Valley, see Frank C. Pierce, *A Brief History of the Lower Rio Grande Valley,* Menasha, George Banta Publishing Company, 1917; Paul S. Taylor, *An American-Mexican Frontier,* Chapel Hill, University of North Carolina Press, 1934; and Florence J. Scott, *Historical Heritage of the Lower Rio Grande,* San Antonio, The Naylor Company, 1937.

and sometimes infiltrating the business and industrial areas, is variously referred to as "Mexiquita," "Mexican-town," and "Little Mexico" by the city's Anglo-Americans, and as the *colonia* by the Mexican-Americans. With few exceptions, the *colonia* is inhabited only by Mexican-Americans, most of whom live in close proximity to one another in indifferently constructed houses on tiny lots. The north side of the city, which lies across the railroad tracks, is inhabited almost completely by Anglo-Americans. Its appearance is in sharp contrast to that of the *colonia* in that it is stictly residential and displays much better housing.

In the occupational hierarchy of Border City, the top level (the growers, packers, canners, businessmen, and professionals) is overwhelmingly Anglo-American. In the middle group (the white-collar occupations) Mexicans are prominent only where their bilingualism makes them useful, for example, as clerks and salesmen. The bottom level (farm laborers, shed and cannery workers, and domestic servants) is overwhelmingly Mexican-American.

These conditions result from a number of factors, some quite distinct from the reception accorded Mexican-Americans by Anglo-Americans. Many Mexican-Americans are still recent immigrants and are thus relatively unfamiliar with Anglo-American culture and urban living, or else persist in their tendency to live apart and maintain their own institutions whenever possible. Among their disadvantages, however, the negative attitudes and discriminatory practices of the Anglo-American group must be counted. It is only fair to say, with the late Ruth Tuck, that much of what Mexican-Americans have suffered at Anglo-American hands has not been perpetrated deliberately but through indifference, that it has been done not with the fist but with the elbow.[2] The average social and economic status of the Mexican-American group has been improving, and many are moving upward. This is partly owing to increasing acceptance by the Anglo-American group, but chiefly to the efforts of the Mexican-Americans themselves.

Anglo-American Assumptions and Expectations

Robert Lynd writes of the dualism in the principal assumptions that guide Americans in conducting their everyday life and identifies the attempt to "live by contrasting rules of the game" as a characteristic aspect of our culture.[3] This pattern of moral compromise, symptomatic of what is likely to be only vaguely a conscious moral conflict, is evident in Anglo-American assumptions and expectations with regard to Mexican-Americans, which appear both in the moral principles that define what intergroup relations ought to be, and in the popular notions held by Anglo-Americans as to what Mexican-Americans are "really" like. In the first case there is a response to the "American creed," which embodies ideals of the essential dignity of the individual and of certain inalienable rights to freedom, justice, and equal opportunity. Accordingly, Anglo-Americans believe that Mexican-Americans must be accorded full acceptance and equal status in the larger society. When their orientation to these ideals is uppermost, Anglo-Americans believe that the assimilation of Mexican-Americans is only a matter of time, contingent solely on the full incorporation of Anglo-American values and ways of life.

These expectations regarding the assimilation of the Mexican are most clearly expressed in the notion of the "high type" of Mexican. It is based on three criteria: occupational achievement and wealth (the Anglo-American's own principal criteria of status) and command of Anglo-American ways. Mexican-Americans who can so qualify are acceptable for membership in the service clubs and a few other Anglo-American organizations and for limited social intercourse. They may even intermarry without being penalized or ostracized. Both in their achievements in business and agriculture and in wealth, they compare favorably with middle-class Anglo-Americans, and they manifest a high command of the latter's ways. This view of the "high type" of Mexican reflects the Anglo-American assumption that Mexicans are assimilable; it does not necessarily insure a full acceptance of even the "high type" of Mexican or that his acceptance will be consistent.

The assumption that Mexican-Americans will be ultimately assimilated was not uniformly shared by all the Anglo-Americans who were our informants in Border City. Regardless of whether they expressed adherence to this ideal, however, most Anglo-Americans expressed the contrasting assumption that Mexican-

Americans are essentially inferior. Thus the same people may hold assumptions and expectations that are contradictory, although expressed at different times and in different situations. As in the case of their adherence to the ideal of assimilability, not all Anglo-Americans hold the same assumptions and expectations with respect to the inferiority of Mexican-Americans; and even those who agree vary in the intensity of their beliefs. Some do not believe in the Mexican's inferiority at all; some are relatively moderate or skeptical, while others express extreme views with considerable emotional intensity.

Despite this variation, the Anglo-Americans' principal assumptions and expectations emphasize the Mexicans' presumed inferiority. In its most characteristic pattern, such inferiority is held to be self-evident. As one Anglo-American woman put it, "Mexicans are inferior because they are so typically and naturally Mexican." Since they are so obviously inferior, their present subordinate status is appropriate and is really their own fault. There is a ready identification between Mexicans and menial labor, buttressed by an image of the Mexican worker as improvident, undependable, irresponsible, childlike, and indolent. If Mexicans are fit for only the humblest labor, there is nothing abnormal about the fact that most Mexican workers are at the bottom of the occupational pyramid, and the fact that most Mexicans are unskilled workers is sufficient proof that they belong in that category.

Associated with the assumption of Mexican inferiority is that of the homogeneity of this group—that is, all Mexicans are alike. Anglo-Americans may classify Mexicans as being of "high type" and "low type" and at the same time maintain that "a Mexican is a Mexican." Both notions serve a purpose, depending on the situation. The assumption that all Mexicans are alike buttresses the assumption of inferiority by making it convenient to ignore the fact of the existence of a substantial number of Mexican-Americans who represent all levels of business and professional achievement. Such people are considered exceptions to the rule.

Anglo-American Images of Mexican-Americans

To employ Gordon Allport's definition, a stereotype is an exaggerated belief associated with a category, and its function is to justify conduct in relation to that category.[4] Some of the Anglo-American images of the Mexican have no ascertainable basis in fact, while others have at least a kernel of truth. Although some components of these images derive from behavior patterns that are characteristic of some Mexican-Americans in some situations, few if any of the popular generalizations about them are valid as stated, and none is demonstrably true of all. Some of the images of Mexican-Americans are specific to a particular area of intergroup relations, such as the image of the Mexican-American's attributes as a worker. Another is specific to politics and describes Mexicans as ready to give their votes to whoever will pay for them or provide free barbecues and beer.† Let us consider a few of the stereotypical beliefs that are widely used on general principles to justify Anglo-American practices of exclusion and subordination.

One such general belief accuses Mexican-Americans of being unclean. The examples given of this supposed characteristic most frequently refer to a lack of personal cleanliness and environmental hygiene and a high incidence of skin ailments ascribed to a lack of hygienic practices. Indeed, there are few immigrant groups, regardless of their ethnic background, to whom this defect has not been attributed by the host society, as well as others prominent in stereotypes of the Mexican. It has often been observed that for middle-class Americans cleanliness is not simply a matter of keeping clean but is also an index to the morals and virtues of the individual. It is largely true that Mexicans tend to be much more casual in hygienic practices than Anglo-Americans. Moreover, their labor in the field, the packing sheds, and the towns is rarely clean work, and it is possible that many Anglo-

---

† For an analysis of Mexican-American value orientations and behavior in the occupational and political spheres, see Ozzie G. Simmons, Anglo-Americans and Mexican-Americans in South Texas: A Study in Dominant-Subordinate Group Relations (unpublished doctoral dissertation, Harvard University, 1952).

Americans base their conclusions on what they observe in such situations. There is no evidence of a higher incidence of skin ailments among Mexicans than among Anglo-Americans. The belief that Mexicans are unclean is useful for rationalizing the Anglo-American practice of excluding Mexicans from any situation that involves close or allegedly close contact with Anglo-Americans, as in residence, and the common use of swimming pools and other recreational facilities.

Drunkenness and criminality are a pair of traits that have appeared regularly in the stereotypes applied to immigrant groups. They have a prominent place in Anglo-American images of Mexicans. If Mexicans are inveterate drunkards and have criminal tendencies, a justification is provided for excluding them from full participation in the life of the community. It is true that drinking is a popular activity among Mexican-Americans and that total abstinence is rare, except among some Protestant Mexican-Americans. Drinking varies, however, from the occasional consumption of a bottle of beer to the heavy drinking of more potent beverages, so that the frequency of drinking and drunkenness is far from being evenly distributed among Mexican-Americans. Actually, this pattern is equally applicable to the Anglo-American group. The ample patronage of bars in the Anglo-American part of Border City, and the drinking behavior exhibited by Anglo-Americans when they cross the river to Mexico indicate that Mexicans have no monopoly on drinking or drunkenness. It is true that the number of arrests for drunkenness in Border City is greater among Mexicans, but this is probably because Mexicans are more vulnerable to arrest. The court records in Border City show little difference in the contributions made to delinquency and crime by Anglo- and Mexican-Americans.

Another cluster of images in the Anglo-American stereotype portrays Mexican-Americans as deceitful and of a "low" morality, as mysterious, unpredictable, and hostile to Anglo-Americans. It is quite possible that Mexicans resort to a number of devices in their relations with Anglo-Americans particularly in relations with employers, to compensate for their disadvantages, which may be construed by Anglo-Americans as evidence of deceitfulness. The whole nature of the dominant-subordinate relationship does not make for frankness on the part of Mexicans or encourage them to face up directly to Anglo-Americans in most intergroup contacts. As to the charge of immorality, one need only recognize the strong sense of loyalty and obligation that Mexicans feel in their familial and interpersonal relations to know that the charge is baseless. The claim that Mexicans are mysterious and deceitful may in part reflect Anglo-American reactions to actual differences in culture and personality, but like the other beliefs considered here, is highly exaggerated. The imputation of hostility to Mexicans, which is manifested in a reluctance to enter the *colonia,* particularly at night, may have its kernel of truth, but appears to be largely a projection of the Anglo-American's own feelings.

All three of these images can serve to justify exclusion and discrimination: if Mexicans are deceitful and immoral, they do not have to be accorded equal status and justice; if they are mysterious and unpredictable, there is no point in treating them as one would a fellow Anglo-American; and if they are hostile and dangerous, it is best that they live apart in colonies of their own.

Not all Anglo-American images of the Mexican are unfavorable. Among those usually meant to be complimentary are the beliefs that all Mexicans are musical and always ready for a fiesta, that they are very "romantic" rather than "realistic" (which may have unfavorable overtones as well), and that they love flowers and can grow them under the most adverse conditions. Although each of these beliefs may have a modicum of truth, it may be noted that they tend to reinforce Anglo-American images of Mexicans as childlike and irresponsible, and thus they support the notion that Mexicans are capable only of subordinate status.

Mexican-American Assumptions, Expectations, and Images

Mexican-Americans are as likely to hold contradictory assumptions and distorted images as are Anglo-Americans. Their principal assumptions, however, must reflect those of Anglo-Americans —that is, Mexicans must take into account the Anglo-Americans' conflict as to their potential equality and present inferiority, since they are the object of such imputations. Similarly, their images of Anglo-Americans are not derived wholly independently, but to some extent must reflect their own subordinate status. Consequently, their stereotypes of Anglo-Americans are much less elaborate, in part because Mexicans feel no need of justifying the present intergroup relation, in part because the very nature of their dependent position forces them to view the relation more realistically than Anglo-Americans do. For the same reasons, they need not hold to their beliefs about Anglo-Americans with the rigidity and intensity so often characteristic of the latter.

Any discussion of these assumptions and expectations requires some mention of the class distinctions within the Mexican-American group.‡ Its middle class, though small as compared with the lower class, is powerful within the group and performs the critical role of intermediary in negotiations with the Anglo-American group. Middle-class status is based on education and occupation, family background, readiness to serve the interests of the group, on wealth, and the degree of acculturation, or command of Anglo-American ways. Anglo-Americans recognize Mexican class distinctions (although not very accurately) in their notions of the "high type" and "low type" of Mexicans.

In general, lower-class Mexicans do not regard the disabilities of their status as being nearly as severe as do middle-class Mexican-Americans. This is primarily a reflection of the insulation between the Anglo-American world and that of the Mexican lower class. Most Mexicans, regardless of class, are keenly aware of Anglo-American attitudes and practices with regard to their group, but lower-class Mexicans do not conceive of participation in the larger society as necessary nor do they regard Anglo-American practices of exclusion as affecting them directly. Their principal reaction has been to maintain their isolation, and thus they have not been particularly concerned with improving their status by acquiring Anglo-American ways, a course more characteristic of the middle-class Mexican.

Mexican-American assumptions and expectations regarding Anglo-Americans must be qualified, then, as being more characteristic of middle- than of lower-class Mexican-Americans. Mexi-

---

‡ See *ibid.,* for a discussion of the Anglo-American and Mexican class structures.

cans, like Anglo-Americans, are subject to conflicts in their ideals, not only because of irrational thinking on their part but also because of Anglo-American inconsistencies between ideal and practice. As for ideals expressing democratic values, Mexican expectations are for obvious reasons the counterpart of the Anglo-Americans'—that Mexican-Americans should be accorded full acceptance and equal opportunity. They feel a considerable ambivalence, however, as to the Anglo-American expectation that the only way to achieve this goal is by a full incorporation of Anglo-American values and ways of life, for this implies the ultimate loss of their cultural identity as Mexicans. On the one hand, they favor the acquisition of Anglo-American culture and the eventual remaking of the Mexican in the Anglo-American image; but on the other hand, they are not so sure that Anglo-American acceptance is worth such a price. When they are concerned with this dilemma, Mexicans advocate a fusion with Anglo-American culture in which the "best" of the Mexican ways, as they view it, would be retained along with the incorporation of the "best" of the Anglo-American ways, rather than a one-sided exchange in which all that is distinctively Mexican would be lost.

A few examples will illustrate the point of view expressed in the phrase, "the best of both ways." A premium is placed on speaking good, unaccented English, but the retention of good Spanish is valued just as highly as "a mark of culture that should not be abandoned." Similarly, there is an emphasis on the incorporation of behavior patterns that are considered characteristically Anglo-American and that will promote "getting ahead," but not to the point at which the drive for power and wealth would become completely dominant, as is believed to be the case with Anglo-Americans.

Mexican ambivalence about becoming Anglo-American or achieving a fusion of the "best" of both cultures is compounded by their ambivalence about another issue, that of equality versus inferiority. That Anglo-Americans are dominant in the society and seem to monopolize its accomplishments and rewards leads Mexicans at times to draw the same conclusion that Anglo-Americans do, namely, that Mexicans are inferior. This questioning of their own sense of worth exists in all classes of the Mexican-American group, although with varying intensity, and plays a substantial part in every adjustment to intergroup relations. There is a pronounced tendency to concede the superiority of Anglo-American ways and consequently to define Mexican ways as undesirable, inferior, and disreputable. The tendency to believe in his own inferiority is counterbalanced, however, by the Mexican's fierce racial pride, which sets the tone of Mexican demands and strivings for equal status, even though these may slip into feelings of inferiority.

The images Mexicans have of Anglo-Americans may not be so elaborate or so emotionally charged as the images that Anglo-Americans have of Mexicans, but they are nevertheless stereotypes, overgeneralized, and exaggerated, although used primarily for defensive rather than justificatory purposes. Mexican images of Anglo-Americans are sometimes favorable, particularly when they identify such traits as initiative, ambition, and industriousness as being peculiarly Anglo-American. Unfavorable images are prominent, however, and, although they may be hostile, they never impute inferiority to Anglo-Americans. Most of the Mexican stereotypes evaluate Anglo-Americans on the basis of their attitudes toward Mexican-Americans. For example, one such classification provides a two-fold typology. The first type, the "majority," includes those who are cold, unkind, mercenary, and exploitative. The second type, the "minority," consists of those who are friendly, warm, just, and unprejudiced. For the most part, Mexican images of Anglo-Americans reflect the latter's patterns of exclusion and assumptions of superiority, as experienced by Mexican-Americans. Thus Anglo-Americans are pictured as stolid, phlegmatic, cold-hearted, and distant. They are also said to be braggarts, conceited, inconstant, and insincere.

Intergroup Relations, Mutual Expectations, and Cultural Differences

A number of students of intergroup relations assert that research in this area has yet to demonstrate any relation between stereotypical beliefs and intergroup behavior; indeed, some insist that under certain conditions ethnic attitudes and discrimination can vary independently.[5] Arnold M. Rose, for example, concludes that "from a heuristic standpoint it may be desirable to assume that patterns of intergroup relations, on the one hand, and attitudes of prejudice and stereotyping, on the other hand, are fairly unrelated phenomena although they have reciprocal influences on each other. . . ."[6] In the present study, no systematic attempt was made to investigate the relation between the stereotypical beliefs of particular individuals and their actual intergroup behavior; but the study did yield much evidence that both images which justify group separatism and separateness itself are characteristic aspects of intergroup relations in Border City. One of the principal findings is that in those situations in which contact between Anglo-Americans and Mexicans is voluntary (such as residence, education, recreation, religious worship, and social intercourse) the characteristic pattern is separateness rather than common participation. Wherever intergroup contact is necessary, as in occupational activities and the performance of commercial and professional services, it is held to the minimum sufficient to accomplish the purpose of the contact.[7] The extent of this separateness is not constant for all members of the two groups, since it tends to be less severe between Anglo-Americans and those Mexicans they define as a "high type." Nevertheless, the evidence reveals a high degree of compatibility between beliefs and practices in Border City's intergroup relations, although the data have nothing to offer for the identification of direct relationships.

In any case, the separateness that characterizes intergroup relations cannot be attributed solely to the exclusion practices of the Anglo-American group. Mexicans have tended to remain separate by choice as well as by necessity. Like many other ethnic groups, they have often found this the easier course, since they need not strain to learn another language or to change their ways and manners. The isolation practices of the Mexican group are as relevant to an understanding of intergroup relations as are the exclusion practices of the Anglo-Americans.

This should not, however, obscure the fact that to a wide extent the majority of Mexican-Americans share the patterns of living of Anglo-American society; many of their ways are already identical. Regardless of the degree of their insulation from the larger society, the demands of life in the United States have required basic modifications of the Mexicans' cultural tradition. In material cultural, Mexicans are hardly to be distinguished from Anglo-Americans, and there have been basic changes in medical beliefs and practices and in the customs regarding godparenthood. Mexicans have acquired English in varying degrees, and their Spanish has become noticeably Anglicized. Although the original organization of the family has persisted, major changes have occurred in patterns of traditional authority, as well as in child training and courtship practices. Still, it is the exceedingly rare Mexican-American, no matter how acculturated he may be to the dominant society, who does not in some degree retain the more subtle characteristics of his Mexican heritage, particularly in his conception of time and in other fundamental value orientations as well as in his modes of participation in interpersonal relations.[8] Many of the most acculturated Mexican-Americans have attempted to exemplify what they regard as "the best of both ways." They have become largely Anglo-American in their way of living, but they still retain fluent Spanish and a knowledge of their traditional culture, and they maintain an identification with their own heritage while participating in Anglo-American culture. Nevertheless, this sort of achievement still seems a long way off for many Mexican-Americans who regard it as desirable.

A predominant Anglo-American expectation is that the Mexicans will be eventually assimilated into the larger society; but this is contingent upon Mexicans becoming just like Anglo-Americans. The Mexican counterpart to this expectation is only partially complementary. Mexicans want to be full members of the larger society, but they do not want to give up their cultural heritage. There is even less complementarity of expectation with regard to the present conduct of intergroup relations. Anglo-Americans believe they are justified in withholding equal access to the rewards of full acceptance as long as Mexicans remain "different," particularly since they interpret the differences (both those which have some basis in reality and those which have none) as evidence of inferiority. Mexicans, on the other hand, while not always certain that they are not inferior, clearly want equal opportunity and full acceptance now, not in some dim future, and they do not believe that their differences (either presumed or real) from Anglo-Americans offer any justification for the denial of opportunity and acceptance. Moreover, they do not find that acculturation is rewarded in any clear and regular way by progressive acceptance.

It is probable that both Anglo-Americans and Mexicans will have to modify their beliefs and practices if they are to realize more nearly their expectations of each other. Mutual stereotyping, as well as the exclusion practices of Anglo-Americans and the isolation practices of Mexicans, maintains the separateness of the two groups, and separateness is a massive barrier to the realization of their expectations. The process of acculturation is presently going on among Mexican-Americans and will continue, regardless of whether changes in Anglo-Mexican relations occur. Unless Mexican-Americans can validate their increasing command of Anglo-American ways by a free participation in the larger society, however, such acculturation is not likely to accelerate its present leisurely pace, nor will it lead to eventual assimilation. The *colonia* is a relatively safe place in which new cultural acquisitions may be tried out, and thus it has its positive functions; but by the same token it is only in intergroup contacts with Anglo-Americans that acculturation is validated, that the Mexican's level of acculturation is tested, and that the distance he must yet travel to assimilation is measured.[9]

Conclusions

There are major inconsistencies in the assumptions that Anglo-Americans and Mexican-Americans hold about one another. Anglo-Americans assume that Mexican-Americans are their potential, if not actual, peers, but at the same time assume they are their inferiors. The beliefs that presumably demonstrate the Mexican-Americans' inferiority tend to place them outside the accepted moral order and framework of Anglo-American society by attributing to them undesirable characteristics that make it "reasonable" to treat them differently from their fellow Anglo-

Americans. Thus the negative images provide not only a rationalized definition of the intergroup relation that makes it palatable for Anglo-Americans, but also a substantial support for maintaining the relation as it is. The assumptions of Mexican-Americans about Anglo-Americans are similarly inconsistent, and their images of Anglo-Americans are predominantly negative, although these are primarily defensive rather than justificatory. The mutual expectations of the two groups contrast sharply with the ideal of a complementarity of expectations, in that Anglo-Americans expect Mexicans to become just like themselves, if they are to be accorded equal status in the larger society, whereas Mexican-Americans want full acceptance, regardless of the extent to which they give up their own ways and acquire those of the dominant group.

Anglo-Americans and Mexicans may decide to stay apart because they are different, but cultural differences provide no moral justification for one group to deny to the other equal opportunity and the rewards of the larger society. If the full acceptance of Mexicans by Anglo-Americans is contingent upon the disappearance of cultural differences, it will not be accorded in the foreseeable future. In our American society, we have often seriously underestimated the strength of tenacity of early cultural conditioning. We have expected newcomers to change their customs and values to conform to American ways as quickly as possible, without an adequate appreciation of the strains imposed by this process. An understanding of the nature of culture and of its interrelations with personality can make us more realistic about the rate at which cultural change can proceed and about the gains and costs for the individual who is subject to the experiences of acculturation. In viewing cultural differences primarily as disabilities, we neglect their positive aspects. Mexican-American culture represents the most constructive and effective means Mexican-Americans have yet been able to develop for coping with their changed natural and social environment. They will further exchange old ways for new only if these appear to be more meaningful and rewarding than the old, and then only if they are given full opportunity to acquire the new ways and to use them.

REFERENCES

1. Harding, John, Kutner, Bernard, Proshansky, Harold, and Chein, Isidor: Prejudice and ethnic relations, in Lindzey, Gardner (ed.), *Handbook of Social Psychology*, Cambridge, Addison-Wesley, 1954, Vol. 2, pp. 1021-1061; and Kleinberg, Otto, *Tension Affecting International Understanding*, New York, Social Science Research Council, 1950, Bul. 2.
2. Tuck, Ruth D.: *Not with the Fist,* New York, Harcourt Brace, 1946.
3. Lynd, Robert S.: *Knowledge for What?* Princeton, Princeton University Press, 1948.
4. Allport, Gordon W.: *The Nature of Prejudice,* Cambridge, Addison-Wesley, 1954.
5. Merton, Robert K.: Discrimination and the American creed, in Maclver, R. M. (ed.), *Discrimination and National Welfare,* New York, Harper, 1949, pp. 99-128; Harding, John, Kutner, Bernard, Proshansky, Harold, and Chein, Isidor, op cit.; Rose, Arnold M.: Intergroup relations vs. prejudice: pertinent theory for the study of social change, *Social Problems,* 4:173-176, 1956; Williams, Robin M. Jr.: Racial and cultural relations, in Gittler, Joseph B. (ed.), *Review of Sociology: Analysis of a Decade,* New York, John Wiley, pp. 423-464.
6. Rose, *op cit.*
7. Simmons, *op cit.*
8. For cultural differences and similarities between Anglo-Americans and Mexicans, see Simmons, op cit.; Tuck, op cit.; Saunders, Lyle, *Cultural Difference and Medical Care,* New York, Russell Sage Foundation, 1954; Edmonson, Munro S., *Los Manitos; A Study of Institutional Values,* New Orleans, Middle American Research Institute, Tulane University, 1957, Publication 25, pp. 1-72; and Clark, Margaret, *Health in the Mexican American Culture,* Berkeley, University of California Press, 1959.
9. Broom, Leonard, and Kitsuse, John I.: The validation of acculturation: a condition to ethnic assimilation, *American Anthropologist,* 57:44-48, 1955.

CHAPTER 13

PRIDE AND PREJUDICE: A MEXICAN-AMERICAN DILEMMA

EDWARD CASAVANTES

Lately, there has been increasing discussion about the "ethnic pride" of minority groups, including the Mexican-American. Such discussions, however, are sometimes handicapped because of confusion about what it is that makes a person a member of an ethnic group—whether it is his culture, his national origin, his language, his skin coloration, or some combination of these factors.

THE CONFUSION IS PARTICULARLY pronounced in discussions about the Mexican-American. For example, can one be middle class and still be called a Mexican-American? Or can one be an intellectual and still be a Mexican-American? The answer to both these questions is, of course, yes but an accurate ethnic definition of a Mexican-American has been clouded because of the wide acceptance of a wide range of stereotypes that project a false image of what it is that constitutes being Mexican-American.

Basically, there are three sets of qualities, or attributes—often hard to define—associated with being a Mexican-American. The first set is not true at all; the second is true, in that it does describe the essence of the Mexican-American; and the third is true in a limited sense, insofar as it does describe many Mexican-Americans, but has really nothing to do with their being Mexican-American.

With rare exception, every time social scientists have studied "Mexican-Americans," they have ended up describing *poor* Mexican-Americans, not Mexican-Americans as they exist *in toto*. These social scientists have chosen to study that segment of the Chicano (an expression probably derived from "Mexicano," cur-

Mr. Casavantes, a psychologist, is Deputy Chief of the Mexican-American Studies Division of the U. S. Commission on Civil Rights.

Casavantes, Edward, "Pride and Prejudice: A Mexican American Dilemma," *Civil Rights Digest,* Winter 1970, pp. 22-27.

rently being used to designate the Mexican-American) population that Ralph Guzman refers to as "the quaint," ignoring Mexican-Americans who are middle class. The net result of this extraordinary scientific oversight is the perpetuation of very damaging stereotypes of the Mexican-American.

Table 13-I shows those qualities which have been invalidly attributed to Mexican-Americans as part of their ethnicity.

In reality, as the title of the chart indicates, the attributes are actually those of people in poverty but these regularly cut across ethnic lines.

The first item says that, in general, Mexican-Americans spend a larger proportion of their socialization time with relatives and with other people living nearby than do individuals from the middle class. And, indeed, a certain proportion of Mexican-Americans do possess this attribute. Two, Mexican-Americans are

TABLE 13-I

CHARACTEROLOGIC OR INTERPERSONAL STYLES: ATTRIBUTES OF
MOST PEOPLE LIVING IN THE CULTURE OF POVERTY

1. Their life within the context of an extended family incorporates a *larger proportion* of available time (than is true of middle and upper class individuals) in interaction with relatives and with other people living nearby.

2. They are nonjoiners of voluntary associations, including fraternal, church-related, and political associations.

3. They have a preference for the old and the familiar, demonstrated by a reluctance to engage in new situations, or to form new social relationships, especially to initiate interactions with strangers.

4. They demonstrate a marked anti-intellectualism, which expresses itself in little admiration for intellectuals, professors, writers, artists, the ballet, symphonies, etc., as well as in lack of support for schools or for the school activities of their children.

5. Males demonstrate "machismo." This is seen as opposite behavior to being intellectual or engaging in such activities as the ballet. Males who demonstrate "machismo" brag a great deal about their male conquests, and refuse to engage in any behavior which is associated with femininity, such as diaper-changing dishwashing, cooking, etc.

6. There is a great deal of use of physical force, for example, to settle arguments or in the use of physical punishment with disobedient children.

7. They appear unable to postpone gratification. The tendency to live on a day-to-day basis looms extremely prevalent, and few provisions are made for long-range activities.

8. They are extremely fatalistic in their view of the world, feeling that they have very little control over nature, over institutions, or over events.

Adapted from: Albert K. Cohen, and Harold M. Hodges, *Characteristics of the Lower-Blue-Collar Class.*

said not to generally join voluntary associations, which include educational, fraternal, church, and political associations. (Fortunately, though, the Mexican-American is increasingly learning to join political organizations.)

Three, Mexican-Americans are said to prefer the old and the familiar. They are reluctant to engage in new situations or to form new social relationships. They appear to be especially hesitant to initiate social interactions with strangers. Four suggests that they generally demonstrate an anti-intellectual attitude and have little admiration for writers, intellectuals, artists, college professors, and the like. Thus, Mexican-Americans are seen as demonstrating a lack of behavioral support for the school activities of their children.

Five, the male of the species is said to demonstrate manliness, "machismo." "Machismo" comes from the word "macho," which simply means "male." The average Mexican-American male is supposed to demonstrate a great deal of "machismo" instead of, for instance, intellectualism or interest in the arts. Men who show "machismo" are alleged to brag a great deal about their male conquests, and to regularly refuse to do womanly things such as dishwashing, cooking, diaper-changing, or minding the children.

Six, Mexican-Americans are often said to use physical force to settle arguments or to punish disobedient children.

Seven, Mexican-Americans have been described as being unable to postpone gratification. Most are said to live on a day-to-day basis and few make plans or provisions for long-range activities.

Lastly, the Mexican-American is said to be very fatalistic in his view of the world, feeling that he has very little control over nature, over institutions, over people, or over events.

As I stated earlier, *while these eight attributes have been used to characterize Mexican-Americans, they are really characteristic of people living in poverty, in the lowest socioeconomic level.* In this context they do have validity. The danger lies in assigning these attributes as the unique possession of one ethnic group— as has been done with the Mexican-American—instead of viewing them in their proper light, as the products of the "Culture of Poverty," a phrase borrowed from Oscar Lewis.

By "Culture" in the phrase "Culture of Poverty," Lewis means, in part, the ready-made set of behavioral solutions for everyday problems that continually emerge: a style of life, a way of thinking, a series of attitudes and beliefs which emerge when an individual is forced to get along in his everyday activities without money. He does this by a unique and different way of using people. "Using" is not meant in a derogatory negative sense, but rather utilizing them. The reason is simple: *If you don't have money, you have to have people.* They simply do what they can to help each other. To give of themselves to each other, to lend emotional support, to help physically, this is the poor person's "money." Consequently, when poor Mexican-Americans, or for that matter poor blacks or poor Puerto Ricans, don't have money, generally they must spend a larger portion of their time with relatives and other people living nearby than do middle-class people.

Similarly, the poor generally don't join voluntary associations. The reason for this is probably wrapped up with the whole business of hopelessness which will be discussed in detail later. Thus poor Mexican-Americans feel that joining an association will not do any good, because they have learned to live with hopelessness. In the past few years, however, Mexican-Americans, as well as other ethnic groups, have increasingly been joining action groups when they have found that at times it does pay off.

Because they have had a poor education—thus a narrow and limited exposure to the world and its experiences—many seem to prefer the old and the familiar, rather than striking off in new directions, with new dimensions and new ideas. And, they don't like to form new social relationships, probably for the identical reasons that the more educated person sometimes feels awkward when walking into a completely new situation. Only the poor have many more such instances.

Poor people evidence anti-intellectualism in part because they haven't been well educated. People in poverty settings typically have no more than an eighth grade education, and quite often even less. It would be unusual for a man to be an intellectual without having had a relatively good exposure to "book learning." True, many poor have read a great number of books. But, in the main, the large portion are nonintellectual or antiintellectual. Consequently, they don't have the feeling that school is really that necessary for success in life. Certainly, a high proportion will not see a college degree as necessary for success.

The males demonstrate manliness, "machismo," perhaps as an overcompensation. *A man is his work.* But what kind of work does a man who lives in poverty have? Poor work, if any. He does not often have a job that he can be genuinely proud of; he does not have a vocation. Thus, he does not have a full identity. A man is supposed to be a working man, one who provides for his family, a protector, a giver of care and sustenance. Instead, the poor man has a low-paying job, or a half-time job, or maybe no job at all. Few men can live comfortably with the feeling of not being a good provider, and consequently, they often overcompensate and by this demonstrate that they nevertheless are strong and powerful. Therefore, they show excessive "machismo." This is probably what leads to the refusal to have anything to do with things that are "womanly."

What's wrong with "machismo," with being "macho"? There's nothing terribly wrong with it. It's only in the exaggeration, in the male demonstrating too much of a good thing, in the excess, that this becomes a dysfunctional thing. Perhaps dysfunctional "machismo" is best defined in terms of the motivation. If it is a greatly exaggerated overcompensation for feeling inadequate, and the overcompensation takes the form of excessive fighting, drinking, or bragging about conquests, then it is a dysfunctional "machismo."

Inability to delay gratification is due, at least in part, to realizing the fact that if you don't have money, it is very difficult to adequately plan for the future. How can you plan for the future when you don't know what's going to happen tomorrow? When you don't even know if you will have a job? Even if a poor man wanted to plan for the future, and he had a relatively steady job, it is usually not a well-paying one. Thus, he would have few provisions—that is, tangible financial provisions—for long-range planning of activities. So then, it becomes a day-to-day existence, but not necessarily because of some perverse quality in poor people, but because, in the past, planning and its attendant postponement of immediate gratification of needs has been experienced as futile.

Fighting in order to settle arguments, or to punish disobedient children, probably comes about partly as a function of the same business associated with being "muy macho," which in turn stems, at least in large measure, from the many frustrations associated with a man's lack of ability to hold a job.

Fatalism is a basic feeling, attitude, or belief that does affect—and may be very damaging to—people living in the culture of poverty. If you had lost the game many times, if you had never been able to make headway, if you had never been able to get a good job and hold it, if you had planned for a lot of things that never came true, I suspect you would lose hope too. This is regularly what happens to a man who comes from a poverty home. He simply has stopped trying because it has not done him—and others he has seen—a great deal of good to have tried.

The eight qualities just outlined are then basically the qualities or attributes of people from the culture of poverty, not the culture of Mexico. These same qualities have been used to describe blacks, American Indians, and Puerto Ricans.

From a combination of these stereotypes have arisen some totally false attributes of the Mexican-American. And these stereotypes do not escape even the Mexican-American himself. The following is a statement made by a Mexican-American writer:

> The Mexicano, or mestizo, a racial amalgamation of resigned stolid Indians and lighthearted Spaniards, has based his romanticism on the reality of the present and its relation to the past. The future is attacked with a fatalism, an indefinite term, mañana, which expresses a remoteness missing from "tomorrow." He lives an improvised, spontaneous existence. He never puts off for tomorrow what can be enjoyed only today. He is not lazy, but he works only enough to support his meager needs.

What then are the *real* qualities of being a Mexican-American? Or, to put it another way, what constitutes the second set of attributes noted at the beginning of this article, those that accurately describe the essence of being Mexican-American?

One, they have come or their parents or grandparents have

come from Mexico (or from Spain in the case of the Hispano of northern New Mexico and southern Colorado) and brought with them many customs and many traditions. Secondly, they speak Spanish and many have a noticeable accent. These two qualities alone, I feel, comprise the major portion of the essence of being Chicano or Mexican-American.

On another level, but also within the valid set of attributes, we know that the vast majority of Mexican-Americans is Catholic. Of course, as is true of any group, insofar as it practices a given religion, much of its behavior is influenced by that religion. So, much of the behavior of the Mexican-American is allied with his Catholicism. A simple example of this might be the "Dia de Santo," the Saint's Day, where a small feast is planned to honor the Saint on whose day the youngster was born. It is very much like a birthday feast.

Lastly, in the group of five attributes, many Mexican-Americans have darker skin and hair, and thus they are easily distinguishable. Many have what sociologists call "high visibility."

Here are in review—in my mind anyway—the true qualities or attributes of most Americans: They have come from Mexico, or perhaps from Spain via Mexico; they speak Spanish, many with an accent; they are Catholic; and, many have dark skin and hair. These are the things that a "true Chicano," a "real Mexican" must possess. These attributes are the things that make him Mexican.

Viewing three of these from a different perspective, however, we can see that you don't have to be a Catholic to be a Chicano; even less so, have darker skin, because dark skin is not a criterion for being Mexican, although many Mexicans have it. More essence comes from the first two characteristics: that their ancestors came—with their many customs and traditions—from Mexico and Spain and that they spoke Spanish.

Is it not the custom and language that make most people a particular people? If you are of Greek descent and you share Greek customs and speak Greek, then you can be said to be a Greek-American. If you are Chinese, and you share Chinese customs and speak Chinese, then you are a Chinese-American. Likewise, should a Mexican-American identify himself as being Mexican-American, the essential qualities that he must have are the language and customs that he has brought, or his forefathers have brought, from Mexico: *that is his heritage.* Some of the more *tangible* items from this heritage are reflected in such things as the Mexican music that Mexican-Americans love so dearly, and obviously, Mexican food.

The third and final set of attributes are those that are true for the majority of Mexican-Americans, but only in a limited sense. The first of these is that perhaps 80 percent of their five to six million live in the five Southwestern States of Texas, New Mexico, Colorado, Arizona, and California. The second is that the average Mexican-American (over age 25) can be described as having an educational level of less than 8 years. Now mind you, that says *average,* which really means that roughly 50 percent have even less than an eighth grade education, an appalling situation. The third is that between 30 and 40 percent of the families earn less than about $3,500 per year and thus are seen to be living in the culture of poverty.

With that I conclude the third of three different types of attributes of the Mexican-American. The first was a set of false attributes usually ascribed to him because he is poor and or because he is perhaps from a rural locale. The second group has to do with his national origin, and this is the set of true attributes: that his parents—with their culture and customs—come from Mexico, that he speaks Spanish, that he is Catholic, and that he is dark. This set usually does define Mexican. The third set of attributes is potentially irrelevant. It describes many Mexican-Americans, that's true. However, a black man could live in one of the five Southwestern States and be poorly educated and be living in the culture of poverty. These characteristics have little to do with ethnicity or national origin.

Perhaps we can now come to some important conclusions. One of them is that it is poverty, much more than ethnicity, that seems to account for so many of the "failures" of Mexican-American children in the classrooms; and of their fathers' "failure" in vocational endeavors. "Failures," not because they are black or brown, but because they are so badly educated and so poor.

While the Mexican-American cannot erase prejudice overnight, a great deal can be done to diminish the effect and impact of prejudice by helping the Mexican-Americans become well educated and achieve adequate employment.

For it is lack of education with its attendant poverty that helps keep Mexican-Americans (and other ethnic groups) in the possible situation we see today.

It is clear that the main element which acts as a barrier to the full development of the Mexican-American is prejudice. Countless instances of both gross and subtle discrimination have been documented. See, for example, "The Mexican-American," U. S. Commission on Civil Rights, 1968; "Civil Rights in Texas," U. S. Commission on Civil Rights, Feb. 1970; "Hearing Before the U. S. Commission on Civil Rights: San Antonio, Texas, Dec. 9-14, 1968."

Some of this prejudice arises directly out of the acting-out of felt stereotypes such as those we have been trying to help destroy in his discussion. Other discriminatory practices are simply the result of obvious racist attitudes. When some or both of these are found in our schools, and deter or impede the adequate education of Mexican-American children, forceful and decisive steps *must* be taken to eliminate them. For it is the school that offers the single best path out of poverty for the vast majority of Mexican-Americans.

While racism and prejudice have no place in any part of our country, the practice is especially contemptible in American schools, for it is these very institutions that, with "forked tongue," *teach* the story of democracy and equal opportunity and then *act out* patterns of individual and wholesale discrimination.

Secondly, prejudice and discrimination in the schools are especially contemptible because they communicate to a child—that is, to an as yet not fully developed organism—feelings that suggest to him he is inferior, a notion that is false. Both common sense and some very recent highly sophisticated social science investigations thoroughly document the fact that the *native* capacity of the Mexican-American child is fully equal to that of anyone else.

We also need to constantly stress to the individual Mexican-

American that he can make it; that many competent Chicanos have come from the ghettos, have come from small farms, from migrant camps; that he, too, has a good chance. Further, he needs to know that chances for success in life are becoming increasingly more open to him.

We must work to improve the self-image of the Mexican-American so that neither he nor those he encounters act out a negative self-fulfilling prophecy.

It is clear, then, that there is literally nothing wrong with the Mexican-American, except that he is economically poor and poorly educated.

Thus, it is also totally clear that, if the Mexican-American is to develop his true potentialities, all barriers to his development must be erased.

The Mexican-Americans' Ethnic Pride, of which we spoke at the very beginning, is totally and completely legitimate, for we are confident that being Mexican-American is something of which we can be proud. We need only to banish our poverty and our ignorance.

If prejudice and discrimination stand in our forward thrust toward those ends, then we will need to take action against that prejudice and discrimination.

CHAPTER 14

PUERTO RICAN YOUTH

SAMUEL BETANCES

Puerto Rican young people in the United States feel very confused about their identity as it relates to the issue of race and color. The confusion and psychological trauma experienced by second generation Ricans is partly caused by conflicting social definitions that place Puerto Ricans in a "no man's land," neither black nor white. This crisis, while sometimes masked, causes ambivalence, anxiety, and bitterness which often turns against the self.

The following article by Samuel Betances is but a beginning effort to place in a larger forum a very important issue confronting young Ricans in the States.

RACE AND THE SEARCH FOR IDENTITY

P UERTO RICANS are sometimes white, they are sometimes black, and they are sometimes Puerto Ricans—and so they are quite often confused. This holds particularly true for the second generation Puerto Ricans in the U.S. mainland. The single most crucial issue burning deep in the souls of many young, second generation Puerto Ricans in the United States is that of the wider identity— the search for ethnicity.

Puerto Rican youth in America in search of their ethnic identity have often faced the stark reality of having to relate to critical issues solely on the basis of black and white. In other words, it becomes impossible simply to be "Puerto Rican" or "Latin" or a "Third World Type" or "Spanish" in a society that demands categories based on black and white.

To a large degree, Puerto Rican youth who come from a racially mixed background believe that in America they can choose whether they want to be black or white. Some have decided not to suffer the plight of becoming black. It is hard for them to be a Puerto Rican without becoming black as well, the assumption being that one can choose with which group to relate.

Betances, Samuel, "Puerto Rican Youth: Race and Search for Identity," *Rican*, Fall 1971, No. 1, pp. 4-13.

Erik Erikson suggests that Negro creative writers are in a battle to reconquer for their people a "surrendered identity." He states:

> I like this term because it does not assume total absence, as many contemporary writers do—something to be searched for and found, to be granted or given, to be created or fabricated—but something to be recovered. This must be emphasized because what is latent can become a living actuality, and thus a bridge from past to future.[1]

If what Erikson says is true, then the Puerto Rican adolescent's search for a wider identity becomes even more complicated in the light of some historical facts that are uniquely Puerto Rican.

Puerto Rico at present has no definite political status. The island is neither a state of the union, nor is it an independent nation. It is no more than a "perfume colony," as a critic of the present system has described it. Puerto Ricans are considered "Americans" by their Latin American cousins and "Latins" by the Americans. They have never been in control of their island and during a period of nineteen years, between 1898 and 1917, were citizens of no country.[2]

Dr. Roman Lopez Tames, a careful student of the Puerto Rican experience, has noted that there is insecurity in the island. Puerto Ricans are forever asking themselves, "What am I?" ("que soy?"), and "What are we?" (que somos?"). He notes that "for the North Americans the island is hispanic, this is to say, strange sister to what they call Latin American." But on the other hand, "Latin American countries without having a very concrete notion about the island, quite frequently reject her considering her North Americanized, lost to the great family."[3] Puerto Rico has been likened by Dr. Lopez Tames to the plight of the bat who is rejected by birds and by rodents, belonging to neither family in any concrete way, who is condemned to live a solitary life between two worlds, misunderstood by both.

To some degree, the seeds of insecurity toward ethnicity are already planted in the minds of first generation Puerto Ricans. Thus, a youngster who has parents who have some doubt as to their own identity has to face new problems which indicate further that he is neither black nor white. He is neither American nor Latin American. He comes from an island which is neither a state nor a nation. Is it possible for Puerto Ricans to find their "surrendered identity"? Or is it not a fact that to some degree the historical experience indicates that there is nothing there which is latent, nothing that can come alive, nothing that can serve as a bridge from the past to the future, since Puerto Rico, as a geographical entity, has been molded in an experience of dependency, first to Spain and then to the United States?

Confusion, ambivalency, and contradictions are present in the lives of Puerto Rican adolescents as they relate to the issue of race and color. Some Puerto Ricans learn English very quickly and refuse to speak Spanish in hopes of finding acceptance in the larger society. Others who are dark-skinned deliberately keep their Spanish, lest they be mistaken for American Negroes. Still others will hide their dark-skinned grandmother in the kitchen while introducing their potential spouses to their lighter-skinned parents.[4] The more successful the Puerto Rican, the more "European-looking" his wife tends to be. It's an interesting commentary that the first book[5] out of East Harlem, *Down These Mean Streets*, based on the second generation experience, was written by Piri Thomas, a Puerto Rican who is very concerned with the crucial issue of identity. One chapter in his book is entitled, "How to Be a Negro Without Really Trying." Others are, "Hung Up Between Two Sticks" and "Brothers Under the Skin."

The migrant Puerto Rican, whose children are the focus of this paper, have brought with them certain experiences and outlooks on the issue of race and color that have influenced to some degree the lives of their children. The first generation grew up in an island which historically has experienced "whiteness" as a positive value and "blackness" as a negative one. "White is right," in Puerto Rico, too. While blackness may not be as negative as in America, it is still negative enough to be a source of embarassment in many instances of Puerto Rican life.

Puerto Rico has a problem of color; America has a problem of race.[6] That is the critical difference between discrimination in Puerto Rico and in the U.S. mainland.

Discrimination in Puerto Rico is based on color. As such, color is a physical characteristic which can be altered and/or changed in several generations. Marrying someone lighter-skinned than one-self immediately alters the way in which the offspring of such a union would be described. A Negro-Puerto Rican who marries a non-Negro Puerto Rican will have children which will be described as non-Negro.

If the pattern is continued through several generations, a Negro Puerto Rican can live to see his "white" great-grandchildren. The negative physical element, color, can be eliminated or be made to play a less embarrassing role in the lives of those who seek to make things "better for their children."[7]

Not so in America where discrimination is based on the concept of race. It has to do with a deep-seated conviction about one group being superior to another. In the United States, the element of racial inequality is prevalent. Racism has to do with the issue of the "purity of the blood," a kind of changeless, hereditary disease or blessing which is transmitted from parent to offspring. In America many gain their sense of being and power from their membership in the "superior" white race. The most deprived white man can think of himself as "better than any Nigger." It doesn't really matter what his position or educational background may be: "No matter how you dress him up, a Nigger is a Nigger," a racist will tell you.

To be black in America is such a serious handicap that a person with "one drop" of Negro blood is considered Negro. Negro blood is a kind of reverse and negative "black power," which haunts a person reminding him that he is inferior—at best, a mere shadow of white figure. Such are the "deep-seated, anxiety-rooted, sadomasochistic drives"[8] which account for much of the racial problems in America. Is it any wonder that in the United States inter-marriage is considered the unpardonable social sin?

Puerto Rican discrimination based on color as opposed to race can be labeled as a "milder" type of discrimination. It has, nevertheless, influenced the outlook of the people, including those who journeyed to the mainland with notions that blackness is a negative aspect in a person's life and whiteness is a positive value.

So that the non-Negroid Puerto Rican may look upon his darker skinned counterpart as a person with certain drawbacks, a descendant of slaves whose physical features, texture of hair and/or color of the skin may leave something to be desired. He is not necessarily someone to hate, to control, or to fear, but perhaps to avoid in certain social contexts.

And it is not always a matter of color that determines desirability in certain social contexts. Negroid features: full lips, kinky hair ("pelo malo") may play a much more crucial role in terms of "good" hair, but dark skin ("un trigueño de pelo bueno") may be more desirable than a light-skinned but kinky-haired individual. Color gives way to other physical characteristics at times. Distinction, however, may not be made verbally, so that when individuals refer to a person of "color," they may be really referring to "Negroid" features as opposed to complexion—although they may still relate to the question as one of "color."

Puerto Ricans believe that "trigueñas" or "morenas" (women of dark complexion) make better lovers than those who are non-dark. The belief that color plays a positive role in sex is somewhat different than the racist connotations found in such belief in America. One observer has noted, "this is not the expression of a neurotic fear of sexual insufficiency but an accepted and openly stated commonplace."[9]

Alex Rodríguez, a Puerto Rican spokesman in the city of Boston and past director of the Cooper Community Center in Lower Roxbury, was recently interviewed in the *Boston Globe* on the role of color and race in Puerto Rican life. Rodríguez noted that most Puerto Ricans, while identifying themselves as non-white, quickly learned the advantages of being "white" in a racist society. He suggests that in Puerto Rico, blackness is thought of as a beautiful trait. He used the following examples: "One of the most affectionate terms in Spanish is 'negra,' which means Dear or Darling, but literally translated means 'black one.' "

Rodríguez's example is used quite frequently by people of Latin America who would imply racial equality by citing it. The term "negrita" *does* imply intimacy and affection in the usage that Rodríguez gave it. But there is some difference between "intimacy" and "affection" with "equality" which should be considered. A Peruvian newspaper quoted Velarde who held to the same interpretation on this matter as Alex Rodríguez. Pitt-Rivers brings focus to that difference:

> The implication of racial equality that he drew from his examples invites precision. Such terms do not find way into such context because they are flattering in formal usage, but because they are not. Intimacy is opposed to respect; because these terms are disrespectful, they are used to establish or stress a relationship where no respect is due. The word "Nigger" is used in this way among Negroes in the United States, but only among Negroes. Color has, in fact, the same kind of class connotation in the Negro community as in Latin America: pale-skinned means upper class. Hence, Nigger, in this context dark-skinned or lower class, implies a relationship that is free of obligation of mutual respect.[10]

It is true that Puerto Rico has never had a race riot. But the assertion made by Puerto Rican spokesmen[11] that all is well in this matter of race and color in the island, or that Puerto Rico is one thousand years ahead of America on this issue is misleading. The fact that there is discrimination against those who would embrace the "Afro-Antillean cultured tradition"[12] or those who are dark-skinned, certainly enough discrimination to make those who are black wish that they were not, indicates all is not well in Puerto Rico.

Those who damned the United States race riots and point to the superior culture which does not have race riots in Puerto Rico, have not been as zealous in explaining the problem of color that does exist in the island. As a result many citizens on the mainland, including such noted sociologists as Nathan Glazer,[13] believe the problem to be less serious than in reality.

The point being suggested here is that the problem of color is serious enough in Puerto Rican life to complicate further the second generation's search for ethnicity in the mainland. As the second generation looks toward the island and toward their homes, they don't find a people who have solved the problem of black and white. Instead they find further reasons for added anxiety, confusion, and feelings of uncertainty. Pointing out that Puerto Rico does not have race riots does not solve the problem of a youngster who must not only deal with a world outside of his home which is unsympathetic and at times cruel, but he also must confront his family and Puerto Rican neighbors who for reasons all their own seem to be making efforts toward concealment of color.

In the early part of 1970, sixty young second generation Puerto Ricans were interviewed concerning this issue of race and color as it affected their search for ethnicity in the U.S. mainland. Thirty of the youth resided in the South Bronx in New York City; fifteen of them resided in the Division Street area of Chicago's Northwest Side; and fifteen live in the South End of Boston. Their response to the questionnaire and their willingness to have their answers taped when requested, provided perspective in attempting to understand this very crucial issue. A close look at their responses indicates the problem to be much more complicated than previously imagined.

One young Puerto Rican in Boston, when asked how she was perceived by other people in a downtown store or in a crowded bus or walking through the busy streets of Boston, answered that most people would consider her "white." She quickly added, "an Eastern European type or Italian."

When asked how she described herself—"say that you were applying for a job and you had to fill out a blank which demanded some definition on your part"—she said, "Negro." Why? She explained that people on the streets tend to look at her very superficially. Since she has a light complexion and long, black hair, she could "pass" in that kind of situation. However, when applying for a job, she explained, employers tend to take a second look, even a third look, especially if the job requires one to be visible, like office work. By filling the blank "Negro," she felt the employer would probably say to himself that she was not really black. If he detected an accent, he would be sure that she was not really black. But he would probably be happy to hire such a nice, light-skinned, safe Negro.

On the other hand, if she filled in the blank "white," the employer would probably think her dishonest since she was not really white. He probably would not forgive her for trying to "pass." The chances of his objecting to one's describing oneself "Negro" are less than the other way around.

Here is a case of a nineteen-year-old Puerto Rican youth trying desperately to psyche out the society in which she lives, anticipating the moods of people she somehow must not offend if she is to make it in racially tense America in the 1970's. It is difficult to ascertain just what psychological price she and many like her are paying in their attempt to survive without arousing people's prejudices.

Several youths, when asked whether they thought people in America were prejudiced towards them because they were Puerto Ricans, answered, "no." They explained that prejudice stemmed from the fact of their dark skin color. Somehow in their minds they had carefully separated their skin color from their Puerto Ricanness.

Answering another question, this time on the issue of intermarriage between American Negroes and Puerto Ricans, one of the interviewees from New York answered:

> Puerto Ricans are on the bottom of the social ladder in this country; blacks are even worse off. Blacks should not marry Puerto Ricans since two wrongs don't make a right!

While most of those interviewed said that when it comes to marriage it should really be up to the people involved, it would appear that the "two wrongs don't make a right" answer is closer to the feeling of those questioned. Deeper probing indicated that while most of them "prefer" not to marry American Negroes, they would not voice "opposition" to such marriages.

The question of intermarriage is a very difficult one for Puerto Rican youth to answer. Admitting that one has reservations, or voicing opposition to marriage with American Negroes, is in effect, admission of prejudice based on cultural and color differences. To agree even in principle with a stance against Negroes having a choice on who should be their potential spouses is to undermine the Puerto Rican position. If it is possible for a Puerto Rican to be prejudiced against Negroes in America, then it is possible for American-Anglos to be prejudiced towards Puerto Ricans, for similar reasons. This the second generation does not want.

What makes it difficult, then, is the fact that Puerto Ricans *do* express preference in regard to skin color. Deep inside they know that Americans have "legitimate" reasons for prejudice toward Puerto Ricans since they have, perhaps themselves, reasons why they discriminate against blacks. The feelings of insecurity are there.

Interestingly enough, second generation Ruerto Ricans believe that even marrying a darker Puerto Rican than oneself is not desirable. Most of the youth simply stated that they expected to marry someone lighter-skinned, but not darker than themselves. Most of them knew of Puerto Rican neighbors or had parents or relatives who would oppose their children marrying anyone, whether American Negro or Puerto Rican, who happened to be darker than they were, who could be described as "real black."

In the area of mutual cooperation with American Negroes in pursuit of better wages and against social discrimination, most Puerto Rican youth answered affirmatively. One youth in the Bronx voiced the opinion by stating that while Negroes experienced 100 percent prejudice, Puerto Ricans experienced about 99 percent prejudice; so they should work together. Five young Puerto Ricans in Chicago who had actually worked together in an organization with blacks were a little more cautious on the matter. They wanted to know what "together" meant. One young man in Chicago simply said that as long as there is a "fifty-fifty" cooperation at the top of such an organization that is all right, but not otherwise.

One response was somewhat bitter; a young man who obviously had some experience in black endeavors snapped at the question by saying:

> When blacks need an extra pair of feet to march, they welcome the Puerto Rican cooperation. When they need an extra voice to shout against injustice, they welcome Puerto Rican cooperation. When they need another head to bleed in the struggle, cooperation is welcomed from their "Latin brothers." But when, as a result of the shouting, the marching, and the bloody head, there is an extra pocket to fill, the Puerto Ricans are suddenly not black enough.

When asked if Puerto Ricans should work with white Anglos in the same way that they would work with Negroes, most of them said, "yes." As one Puerto Rican put it, "Puerto Ricans should work with blacks and whites. The blacks have the power (aggressiveness) and the whites have the money; by working with both groups we can come out on top.'

Another dimension in the trials of young Puerto Ricans' search for identity and ethnicity is the issue of just how black can a Puerto Rican become? Afro-American youth see their ultimate unity revolving around the issue of "blackness." The cry is "I am black and beautiful." Puerto Ricans who participate in all black meetings find themselves apprehensive when the anti-white rhetoric reminds them that the "white devil" is just as much a part of his experience as the heritage and concern which make it possible for him to be allowed into such organizations. As Piri Thomas puts it, "It wasn't right to be ashamed of what one was. It was like hating Momma for the color she was and Poppa for the color he wasn't."[14]

If one can be a "Negro" without really trying as Thomas would suggest,[15] then it is quite another matter to be "black." The politics of race in the black movement at times make a distinction between those who are described as "colored," those who are described as "Negroes," and those who are "black." If the society at large determines that racially mixed Puerto Ricans are Negro (using the "one drop" formula), where will the black movement place them? Can Puerto Ricans ever be "black" enough for such groups and still be Puerto Rican?

Puerto Ricans in Chicago, those who had some experience in black organizations, complained that the "black power" movement is too obsessed with "blackness" and not enough with "power," thereby writing off some potential energy from Puerto Ricans who up to that time wanted to embrace their African heritage.

Most Puerto Rican youth interviewed expressed pessimism about their ability to resolve the issue of race and color and identity in their own lives. They have felt that for too long they have been in the middle of blacks and whites receiving the worst from both sides. They were relieved to learn that other Puerto Rican youth were having similar problems over the issue of identity. Some were also glad to hear that an adult, the interviewer, was having a difficult time as well; that while the problem has not been resolved, one can still function and have self-respect. Perhaps that in itself is a very important beginning at resolving the destructive trauma which creates so much confusion in the lives of second generation Puerto Rican adolescents.

It's a good feeling to know that one is not alone when facing critical problems. If more Puerto Rican adults would but share some of their ambivalency and their confusion and end "the conspiracy of silence," it could lead to more second generation Puerto Ricans to the conclusion that given the historical experience of Puerto Ricans in the island and in the "barrios" in the mainland, confusion and ambivalency may not be as abnormal as all that.

At a time when the governor of Puerto Rico is desperately trying to coin the phrase, "Puerto Rico is our fatherland, but the United States is our nation," confusion and ambivalency may indeed not be as abnormal as all that!

REFERENCES

1. Erikson, Erik H.: *Identity, Youth and Crisis.* New York, W. W. Horton and Company, Inc., 1968, p. 297 (emphasis added). The phrase "surrendered identity" was borrowed by Erikson from Van Woodward.

2. The U. S. Government declared the residents of Puerto Rico citizens on the eve of the First World War, in 1917.

3. López Tames, Román: *El Estado Libre Asociado de Puerto Rico.* Oviedo, Publicaciones del Instituto Jurídico, 1965, pp. 14, 15.

4. Fortunato Vizcarrondo popularized the problem in his famous poem "Y tu agüela onde ejta?" Literally translated, it means, "And your grandmother, where is she?"

5. While Jesús Colón's book, *A Puerto Rican in New York: And Other Sketches,* was published in 1961, several years before *Down These Mean Streets,* the treatment he gives his sketches suggests more of a first generation view of New York rather than a second generation approach. Colón's formative years were spent in Puerto Rico; see pages 11 to 15 of his book.

6. Williams, Eric: Race Relations in Puerto Rico and the Virgin Islands. *Foreign Affairs,* 23:308, 1945. As quoted in Sereno, Renzo: Cryptomelanism: A Study of Color Relations and Personal Insecurity in Puerto Rico. *Psychiatry,* X:264, 1947.

7. Pitt-Rivers, Julian: Race, Color and Class in Central America and the Andes. *Daedalus: Journal of the American Academy of Arts and*

Sciences (Cambridge, Mass. *96:556,* Spring, 1967), "Color is an ingredient, not a determinant of class. It can, therefore, be traded for other ingredients. It is something that can be altered in the individual life, but it is something that can be put right in the next generation."

8. Pitt-Rivers: op. cit., p. 547.

9. *Ibid.,* p. 550.

10. Joseph Monserrat is guilty of this one-sided type of analysis. See his report, *School Integration: A Puerto Rican View.* New York, the Commonwealth of Puerto Rico, 1966, p. 5.

11. Lewis, Gordon K.: *Puerto Rico: Freedom and Power in the Caribbean.* New York, Harper & Row, 1963, p. 286.

12. Glazer, Nathan: *Beyond the Melting Pot.* Cambridge, Mass., M.I.T. Press, 1963, p. 132. "The Puerto Rican introduced into the city a group that is intermediate in color, neither all white nor all dark, but having some of each, and a large number that show the physical characteristics of both groups. (They) carry new attitudes toward colors—and attitudes that may be corrupted by continental color prejudice but it is more likely, since this is in harmony with terms that are making all nations of a single world community, that the Puerto Rican attitude to color, or something like it, will become the New York attitude."

13. Thomas, Piri: *Down These Mean Streets.* New York, Signet Book, The New American Library, Inc., 1967, p. 122.

14. *Ibid.,* pp. 124-126.

PART IV

THE SCHOOLS
AND THE
SPANISH-SPEAKING

CHAPTER 15

THE CHALLENGE OF THE NON-ENGLISH-SPEAKING CHILD IN AMERICAN SCHOOLS

FRANCESCO CORDASCO

IN AN OPEN-ENDED American society, education has afforded the essential entry point into the mainstream of American identity. Education has provided social mobility, and it has extended opportunity. In the peopling of the American continent and the creation of a democratic society, the schools have served as a basic vehicle of cohesion; in the transmission of a society's values, the American schools have ministered to children who brought with them myriad cultures and a multiplicity of tongues. More often than not (almost always in the urban immigrant citadels), the American school found its children in poverty and neglect; increasingly, the schools recognized that their success in the absorption of the child lay not only in meeting his cognitive needs, but equally in confronting the reality of the social context in which the child was found. A definite correlation existed between the cognitive achievement of the child *vis-à-vis* the socioeconomic disadvantagement which he suffered.

The cornucopia of Federal legislation of the last few years did not discover poverty as a new or rare phenomenon in American society. What the Congress perceptively recognized was that many of our social institutions (particularly, our schools) only partially were successful, and that many of our democratic ideals were mauled severely in the grim pathology of social disaffection, cultural assault, and enforced assimilation. It was not that our schools failed, but rather that their recorded failures were to be measured in the inadequacy of their response to the child who

---

Reprinted from *School & Society*, March 30, 1968, by permission of the author and publisher. Based on testimony before the Committee on Education and Labor, U. S. House of Representatives, Washington, D. C., June 29, 1967.

came to them formed in the context of another heritage, or in the articulation of a strange tongue. If there is a common denominator which must be sought in the millions of American children who presented themselves to a society's schools, it is poverty. And its ingredients (within the parameters of this poverty) were cultural differences, language handicaps, social alienation, and disaffection. In this sense, the Negro in-migrant rural poor huddled in the urban ghettoes of the 1960's, the Puerto Rican migrant poor who seek economic opportunity on the mainland, and the Mexican-American poor, largely an urban minority, are not newcomers to the American schools, nor do they present American educators with new problems. The American poor, traditionally, are the ingredients out of which our social institutions have fashioned the sinews of greatness.

A vast literature on the schools and poor children is being assembled.* The children of poverty have been described euphemistically as "culturally deprived," "disadvantaged," "disaffected," "alienated," "socially unready"; yet, what most educational historians have not seen and have not recorded is the continuing historical confrontation of American social institutions and the poor. The American "common" school evolved in a free society to train citizens "to live adequately in a republican society and to exercise effectively the prerogatives of citizenship . . . ,"[1] and in the process it encountered many difficulties. The greatest of these difficulties lay in its treatment of the "minority child" whose minority status was affirmed by his cultural, ethnic, religious, and linguistic differences, and all related to his presence in a social sector of severe socioeconomic disadvantagement.

In its efforts to assimilate all of its charges, the American school assaulted (and, in consequence, very often destroyed) the

---

* See Yeshiva University, Informational Retrieval Center on the Disadvantaged, *Bulletins;* also, *The Education of Disadvantaged Children: A Bibliography . . .* (Washington: Office of Education, U. S. Dept. of Health, Education, and Welfare, Aug. 15, 1966) ; and Helen Randolph, *Urban Education Bibliography* (New York: Center For Urban Education, 1967). We are witnessing a proliferation of books (mostly collections of articles) on the schools and the children of the poor, the best of which is the review of current issues and research edited by Harry L. Miller, *Education for the Disadvantaged* (New York: Free Press, 1967) .

cultural identity of the child; it forced him to leave his ancestral language at the schoolhouse door; it developed in the child a haunting ambivalence of language, of culture, of ethnicity, and of personal self-affirmation. It held up to its children mirrors in which they saw not themselves, but the stereotype middle-class, white, English-speaking child, who embodied the essences of what the American child was (or ought) to be. For the minority child, the images which the school fashioned were cruel deceptions. In the enforced acculturation, there was bitterness and confusion, but tragically, too, there was the rejection of the wellsprings of identity and more often than not, the failure of achievement. The ghettoization of the European immigrant, in substance, is exactly analogous to the ghettoization of the Negro, Puerto Rican, and Mexican-American poor. A long time ago, Louis Wirth called attention to the vitality of the ghetto in its maintenance of the life-styles, languages, and cultures of a minority people assaulted by the main institutions of a dominant society.

The schools, if only because of the sensitivity of their role, measured their successes sparingly; for it increasingly became apparent that, if the schools truly were to be successful, they would have to build on the strengths which the children brought with them—on ancestral pride, on native language, and on the multiplicity of needs and identities which the community of the children afforded.[†]

The imposition of immigration quotas from 1920 to 1924

---

† It is instructive to note that the immigrant Catholic minority of the 19th century created its own schools as a direct response to the social disenfranchisement of its children by the dominant society. See J. A. Burns and Bernard Kohlbrenner, *A History of Catholic Education in the United States* (New York: Bennziger, 1937). For an in-depth study of the acculturation of a minority's children, ethnicity and the American school, and the context of poverty and its challenge to the schools, see Leonard Covello, *The Social Background of the Italo-American School Child: A Study of the Southern Italian Mores and Their Effect on the School Situation in Italy and America*, edited and with an introduction by F. Cordasco (Leiden [The Netherlands]: E. J. Brill, 1967). A graphic picture of the failings of the school in meeting the needs of children of the immigrant poor is in the address of Jane Addams before the National Education Association in 1897 (*Proceedings*, 1897, pp. 104-112).

largely ended the confrontation of the American school and the European immigrant bilingual child. In the course of the past quarter-century, the bilingual child in America, in the main, has been Spanish-speaking, encountered in growing numbers in the classrooms of American schools. In the major cities of the U. S. at the present time, it is the Spanish-speaking child (Mexican-American or Puerto Rican) who is the bilingual child, almost inevitably found in a context of poverty and reflecting a constellation of unmet myriad needs.

Faye L. Bumpass, Texas Technological University, recently testified before a Senate subcommittee on bilingual education. She observed: "In the five state area [Texas, New Mexico, Colorado, Arizona, and California], there exist today at least 1.75 million school children with Spanish surnames, whose linguistic, cultural and psychological handicaps cause them to experience, in general, academic failure in our schools or at best limit them to only mediocre success."[2] The average number of school years completed by the Anglo child in the Southwest is 12.1 years, for the Negro it is nine years, and for the Mexican-American it is 7.1 years. "The problems of the group [Mexican-Americans] include all of the interrelated complexities of low income, unemployment, migration, school retardation, low occupational aspirations, delinquency, discrimination and all of the problems that attend the intrusion of one culture upon another."[‡] The Mexican-American child classically demonstrates that an almost inevitable concomitant of poverty is low educational achievement.[§]

The Commonwealth of Puerto Rico neither encourages nor discourages migration. As an American citizen, the Puerto Rican moves between the island and the mainland with complete freedom. If his movement is vulnerable to anything, it fluctuates only with reference to the economy on the mainland. Any eco-

---

‡ From a development proposal submitted to the U. S. Commissioner of Education by the Department of Rural Education, National Education Association. Reported in *Congressional Record*, Jan. 17, 1967, p. S 357. See generally, Sen. Ralph Yarborough, "Two Proposals for a Better Way of Life for Mexican-Americans of the Southwest," *Congressional Record*, Jan. 17, 1967, pp. S 352-S 361.

§ The best source on the educational problems of Mexican-American children is Herschel T. Manuel, *Spanish Speaking Children of the Southwest: Their Education and the Public Welfare* (Austin: University of Texas Press, 1958).

nomic recession or contraction graphically shows in the migration statistics.‖ How the Puerto Rican child has fared in the mainland schools is best illustrated in the experience in New York City, where Puerto Ricans have the lowest level of formal education of any identifiable ethnic or color group. Only 13 percent of Puerto Rican men and women 25 years of age and older in 1960 had completed either high school or more advanced study. Among New York's nonwhite (predominantly Negro) population, 31.2 percent had completed high school; and the other white population (excluding Puerto Ricans) did even better. Over 40 percent at least had completed high school.# In 1960, more than half (52.9%) of Puerto Ricans in New York City 25 years of age and older had less than an eighth grade education. In contrast, 29.5 percent of the nonwhite population had not finished the eighth grade, and only 19.3 percent of the other whites had so little academic preparation.** Clearly, the critical issue for the Puerto Rican community is the education of its children, for the experience in New York City is a macrocosm which illustrates all the facets of the mainland experience.

‖ The best source on Puerto Rican migration is the Migration Division of the Department of Labor, Commonwealth of Puerto Rico, which maintains a central mainland office in New York City and offices in other U. S. cities. It also maintains an office in Puerto Rico to carry out a program of orientation for persons who intend to migrate to the mainland. See Joseph Monserrat, *Puerto Ricans in New York City* (New York: Department of Labor, Migration Division, Commonwealth of Puerto Rico, 1967) . See also *Bibliography on Puerto Ricans in the United States* (New York: Department of Labor, Migration Division, Commonwealth of Puerto Rico, April, 1959) . In 1964, the New York City Department of Health placed the Puerto Rican population in New York City at 701,500, representing 9.3% of the city's population. A projection of this study by the Migration Division of the Puerto Rico Department of Labor estimated the 1966 Puerto Rican population at 762,000.

\# The statistical indices of Puerto Rican poverty (and the related needs) are assembled best in *The Puerto Rican Community Development Project* (New York: Puerto Rican Forum, 1964) , pp. 26-75. See also Monserat, op. cit.

** *The Puerto Rican Community Development Project*, pp. 34-35, 39-41, and tables, pp. 43-44; see also F. Cordasco, "Puerto Rican Pupils and American Educations," *School & Society*, Feb. 18, 1967, pp. 116-119; and F. Cordasco, "The Puerto Rican Child in the American School," *Journal of Negro Education*, 36:181-186, Spring, 1967.

In the confrontation of the problems faced by Mexican-American and by Puerto Rican children, educators have not been without specific proposals. If one allows for these essential differences which relate to the history of both groups and their relationships *vis-à-vis* the dominant American society, the major problem presented to the American schools has been the legacy of poverty and the context of debilitating deprivation in which the children are found. In this sense, it cannot be reiterated too strongly that the Spanish-speaking child is not unlike the child of poverty who presented himself to the American school in other eras. It is not that the school is inadequate to the needs of these children; the tragedy lies in the failure to use the experience gained by the schools, and the lessons learned, in the many decades past.

A persistent theme in all of the literature which deals with the minority child is the *absolute necessity* for the school to build on the cultural strengths which the child brings to the classroom: to cultivate in him ancestral pride; to reinforce (not destroy) the language he natively speaks; to capitalize on the bicultural situation; to plan bilingual instruction in Spanish and English for the Spanish-speaking child in the cultivation of his inherent strengths; to make use of a curriculum to reflect Spanish (and Puerto Rican) as well as American traditions; and to retain as teachers those trained and identified with both cultures. Only through such education can the Spanish-speaking child be given the sense of personal identification so essential to his educational maturation.†† We only can lament the lost opportunities of other

---

†† See Herschel T. Manuel, op. cit.; also, "Bilingualism and the Bilingual Child: A Symposium," *Modern Language Journal, 49:*143-239, March-April, 1965; Yarborough, op. cit., particularly, pp. S 358-S 361. Eight colleges and universities in Texas are cooperating to develop a model for teaching Mexican-American children. Teachers from selected Texas public school systems attended a 1967 summer institute (NDEA, Title XI) at St. Mary's University, San Antonio, followed by inservice training during the school year, in the use of Spanish and English in first-grade teaching of children of Mexican ancestry. The institute is the first step toward the establishment of a number of demonstration centers featuring bilingual schooling. A New York City-sponsored Puerto Rican conference (April 15-16, 1967) called for bilingual education programs for Puerto Rican children, and the inclusion of Puerto Rican history and culture in the curriculum of the schools (*The New York Times,* April 17, 1967) .

eras;‡‡ there is no excuse for failure at this historical and critical juncture in our society.

Congress has put forward a number of proposed bills to deal with the critical problem of the non-English-speaking child. In addition to H.R. 9840, introduced by Rep. James H. Scheuer (D.-N.Y.), bills have been introduced by Rep. Edward R. Roybal (D.-Calif.), Rep. Henry B. Gonzalez (D.-Tex.), and by others in the House, and by Sen. Ralph Yarborough (D.-Tex.). These bills seek to amend the Elementary and Secondary Education Act of 1965 to provide assistance to local educational agencies in establishing bilingual education programs.

In essence, the bills confront the basic problems of the non-English-speaking child in our schools. The bills seem to agree in the critical needs, not only in the categoric allocation of funds, but in the provision of programs which would promote closer home-school cooperation and provide high quality educational opportunities for children from non-English-speaking homes. If any basic difference exists in the bills, it remains primarily in the proposed Yarborough bill's limitation of its provisions to Spanish-speaking students, and its recommendation that Spanish be taught as the native language and English as a second language.

Neither of these differences is irresolvable. The limitation of the Yarborough bill to Spanish-speaking children quite obviously is a recognition that it is the Spanish-speaking child in our schools who, in the main, is non-English-speaking; and this is true not only in the Southwest, but in the major cities and many of the rural areas of America. However, nothing is lost by extending our definition to ". . . children from non-English-speaking, low income families" (H.R. 9840). On the matter of which

---

‡‡ See Covello, *The Social Background of the Italo-American School Child.* Look ing back over a near half-century of service in the New York City public schools, Dr. Covello recently observed: "The Italian Department at the DeWitt Clinton High School began with one class in 1920 and by 1928 had a register of 1,000 students with a full four year course, and two 4th year classes. Cooperating with the Italian Teachers Association, parity for the Italian language was established in 1922 after a ten year campaign. *For during that period school authorities felt that having Italian students study the Italian language would segregate them from other students and retard their 'Americanization'—an old and often repeated story—an idea with which we very definitely took issue.*" (*Congressional Record*, May 16, 1967 [italics added]) .

primacy of language for instruction (Spanish or English?), attention must be paid to the needs of the children involved. It really is not a problem of which language is to be used, but rather of which language is most effective use to be made. It long has been an "ethnocentric illusion" in the U. S. that for a child born in this country English is not a foreign language, and virtually all instruction in schools must be through the medium of English.[§§] All of the bills provide for planning and development of programs, including pilot projects to test the effectiveness of plans. Against this provision, the provisions of a final bill should allow for that flexibility out of which sound and effective programs will evolve. It really is not the primacy of language in the instructional process, but rather how a child is to be moved into an area of effective educational growth which will dictate practice.

The Scheuer Bill (H.R. 9840) provides a practicable vehicle to confront the critical needs of the non-English-speaking child. It provides for planning and development of programs, including pilot projects to test the effectiveness of plans, and the development and dissemination of special instructional materials; preservice and in-service training programs for teachers and teacher aides involved in bilingual education programs; programs to upgrade the quality of the entire program of schools where large proportions of the children come from non-English-speaking, low-income families, including construction, remodelling, or renovation of facilities; intensive early childhood programs; and bilingual and bicultural education programs for elementary and secondary school children to acquaint students from both English-speaking and non-English-speaking homes with the history and culture associated with each language. It also provides a whole range of supportive service for students, with participation by full-time nonpublic school students assured.

For millions of disadvantaged children, a Bilingual Educational Act promises fuller participation in a free society.

[§§] See A. Bruce Gaarder, "Teaching the Bilingual Child: Research, Development, and Policy," in "Bilingualism and the Bilingual Child: A Symposium," loc. cit., pp. 165-175.

REFERENCES

1. Cremin, Lawrence A.: *The American Common School: An Historic Conception.* New York, Bureau of Publications, Teachers College, Columbia University, 1951, pp. 213-214.
2. *The New York Times.* June 18, 1967.

CHAPTER 16

PUERTO RICAN PUPILS AND AMERICAN EDUCATION

FRANCESCO CORDASCO

IN 1960, SOME 900,000 Puerto Ricans lived in the United States, including not only those born on the island, but also those born to Puerto Rican parents in the states. Until 1940, the Puerto Rican community numbered only 70,000, but, by 1950, this had risen to 226,000, and over the decade of 1960, the net gain due to migration from the island amounted to nearly 390,000. The census of 1950 began the recording of second-generation Puerto Ricans (those born on the continent to island-born parents) and counted 75,000; in 1960, the figure stood at 272,000, so that, by 1960, three out of every 10 Puerto Rican residents in the U. S. were born in the states.

Although there has been a dispersal of the migration outside greater New York City, the overwhelming number of Puerto Ricans are New Yorkers; the 1960 census showed 612,574 living in New York City (68.6% of the U. S. total). New York City's proportion had dropped from 88 percent in 1940, to 83 percent in 1950, and to 69 percent in 1960. If there is no serious setback in the American economy, the dispersion undoubtedly will continue.*

The Commonwealth of Puerto Rico neither encourages nor discourages migration. As an American citizen, the Puerto Rican moves between the island and the mainland with complete freedom. If his movement is vulnerable to anything, it fluctuates

Reprinted from *School & Society*, February 18, 1967, by permission of the author and publisher. Based on a paper presented at 61st annual convention, American Sociological Association, Miami, Fla., August 30, 1966.

* U. S. Bureau of the Census, *U. S. Census of Population: 1960 Subject Reports. Puerto Ricans in the United States.* Final Report, PC (2) -1 D. (Washington, D. C.: U. S. Government Printing Office, 1963.) The 1960 census reported Puerto Rican born persons living in all but one (Duluth-Superior) of the 101 Standard Metropolitan Statistical Areas of over 250,000 population.

only with reference to the economy on the mainland. Any economic recession or contraction graphically shows in the migration statistics.[†] It is invidious at best to suggest that "The Puerto Rican migration to *Nueva York*, unchecked by immigrant quotas, is a major source of the island's prosperity," but there is truth in the appended observation that the migration ". . . upgraded the migrants, converted them from rural to urban people, relieved the island of some of its labor surplus, and sent lots of cash back home."[1]

For the mainland schools, the Puerto Rican migration presented a distinct and yet, in many ways, a recurrent phenomenon. With the imposition of immigration quotas in the early 1920's, the non-English speaking student gradually had disappeared. The great European migration and the manifold educational problems to which the American schools had addressed themselves had been resolved in a manner; with the increasing Puerto Rican migration and the recurrent pattern of the ghettoization of the new arrivals, the migrant child, non-English speaking and nurtured by a different culture, presented the schools with a new, yet very old, challenge.[‡]

The Puerto Rican "journey" to the mainland has been (and continues to be) the subject of vast literature.[§] For the most part, the Puerto Rican child reflects a context of bitter depriva-

---

[†] See, in this connection, migration figures for 1953-54. The best source on Puerto Rican migration is the Migration Division of the Department of Labor, Commonwealth of Puerto Rico, which maintains a central mainland office in New York City and offices in other U. S. cities. It also maintains an office in Puerto Rico to carry out a program of orientation for persons who intend to migrate to the states.

[‡] Although one of the greatest achievements of the American common school has been the acculturation and assimilation of the children of non-English speaking immigrants (largely European), it has received little study. See F. Cordasco and L. Covello, *Educational Sociology: A Subject Index of Doctoral Dissertations Completed at American Universities, 1941-1963* (New York: Scarecrow Press, 1965). Of over 2,000 dissertations listed, only a few clearly concern themselves with the non-English immigrant child, or generally with the educational problems of the children of immigrants.

[§] One of the best accounts is Clarence Senior, *The Puerto Ricans* (Chicago: Quadrangle Books, 1965), which includes an extensive bibliography. See also Christopher Rand, *The Puerto Ricans* (New York: Oxford, 1958); Don Wakefield, *Island in the City* (Boston: Houghton Mifflin, 1959); Elena Padilla, *Up From*

(Continued on page 190)

tion, poor housing, high unemployment, and a record of disappointing educational achievement. It is the poverty context, to which the Puerto Rican community has been relegated, that explains its problems and graphically underscores its poor achievement in the schools. Not only is the Puerto Rican child asked to adapt to a "cultural ambience" which is strange and new, but he remains further burdened by all the negative pressures of a ghetto milieu which educators have discerned as inimical to even the most rudimentary educational accomplishment.‖

How the Puerto Rican child has fared in the mainland schools is illustrated best in the experience in New York City, where Puerto Ricans have the lowest level of formal education of any identifiable ethnic or color group. Only 13 percent of Puerto Rican men and women 25 years of age and older in 1960 had completed either high school or more advanced education. Among New York's non-white (predominantly Negro) population, 31.2 percent had completed high school; and the other white population (excluding Puerto Ricans) did even better. Over 40 percent at least had completed high school.[2]

In 1960 more than half—52.9 percent—of Puerto Ricans in New York City 25 years of age and older had less than an eighth-grade education. In contrast, 29.5 percent of the nonwhite population had not finished the eighth grade, and only 19.3 percent of the other whites had so low an academic preparation.

If the schools in New York City were to correct all of this (the numbers in the second generation who have reached adult years is still small, only 6.4% of persons 20 years of age and older in 1960), there is still evidence that Puerto Rican youth, more than any other group, is handicapped severely in achieving an educa-

Puerto Rico (New York: Columbia University Press, 1958); Jesus Colon, *A Puerto Rican in New York and Other Sketches* (New York: Mainstream Publications, 1964); an older, but invaluable documented study of Puerto Ricans in New York City is that of C. Wright Mills, Clarence Senior, and Rose Kohn Goldsen, *The Puerto Rican Journey* (New York: Harper, 1950).

‖ For a graphic commentary on the debilitating environmental pressures and the "ghetto milieu" see David Barry, *Our Christian Mission Among Spanish Americans,* mimeo., Princeton University Consultation, Feb. 21-23, 1965. The statistical indices of Puerto Rican poverty (and the related needs) are assembled best in *The Puerto Rican Community Development Project* (New York: Puerto Rican Forum, 1964), pp. 26-75.

tion in the New York City public schools. A 1961 study of a Manhattan neighborhood showed that fewer than 10 percent of Puerto Ricans in the third grade were reading at their grade level or above. The degree of retardation was extreme. Three in 10 were retarded one and one-half years or more and were, in the middle of their third school year, therefore, reading at a level only appropriate for entry into the second grade. By the eighth grade the degree of retardation was even more severe, with almost two-thirds of the Puerto Rican youngsters retarded more than three years.

Of the nearly 21,000 academic diplomas granted in 1963, only 331 went to Puerto Ricans and 762 to Negroes, representing only 1.6 percent and 3.7 percent respectively, of the total academic diplomas. In contrast, Puerto Ricans received 7.4 percent of the vocational school diplomas, and Negroes, 15.2 percent. For the Puerto Rican community, these figures have critical significance, since Puerto Rican children constituted, in 1963, about 20 percent of the public elementary school register; 18 percent of the junior high school register; and, in keeping with long-discerned trends, Puerto Rican youngsters made up 23 percent of the student body in vocational schools and 29 percent of that in special (difficult) schools.

Clearly, the critical issue for the Puerto Rican community is the education of its children, for the experience in New York City is a macrocosm which illustrates all the facets of the mainland experience.

In the last decade, a wide range of articles have reported special educational programs to meet the needs of Puerto Rican children. Although many of these have been of value, the more ambitious theoretic constructs have come largely from the school boards and staffs which have had to deal with the basic problem of communication in classes where a growing (and at times preponderant) number of Spanish-speaking children were found. As early as 1951 in New York City, a "Mayor's Advisory Committee on Puerto Rican Affairs" turned its attention to this major problem of communication; and this problem was periodically re-examined during the years which followed.

In New York City, as in other cities, the Board of Education turned its attention to the Puerto Rican child because communications *had* to be established, and, in this context, the most ambitious study of the educational problems presented by the Puerto Rican migration became (for New York City) ". . . a four-year inquiry into the education and adjustment of Puerto Rican pupils in the public schools of New York City . . . a major effort . . . to establish on a sound basis a city-wide program for the continuing improvement of the educational opportunities of all non-English speaking pupils in the public schools."[3]

If the major emphasis of *The Puerto Rican Study* was to have been the basic problem of language (English), its objectives soon were extended to include the equally important areas of community orientation and acculturation. The *Study*'s objectives were summed up in three main problems: What are the more effective ways (methods) and materials for teaching English as a second language to newly arrived Puerto Rican pupils? What are the most effective techniques with which the schools can promote a more rapid and more effective adjustment of Puerto Rican parents and children to the community and the community to them? Who are the Puerto Rican pupils in the New York City public schools? For each of these problems, *The Puerto Rican Study* made detailed recommendations. The third problem, above, largely an ethnic survey, resulted in a profile of characteristics of pupils of Puerto Rican background and fused into Problems I and II.

Problem I: How Effectively to Teach English as a Second Language?

The Puerto Rican Study concluded that an integrated method (vocabulary method; structured or language patterns method; and the functional situations or experiential method) was to be employed, and it developed two series of related curriculum bulletins, keyed to the prescribed New York City course of study. But, in the course of its considerations, it dealt with the ancillary and vital need ". . . to formulate a uniform policy for the reception, screening, placement and periodic assessment of non-English speaking pupils." It recommended, until such time as the

Bureau of Educational Research may find or develop better tests or tests of equal value, the use of the USE Test—Ability to Understand Spoken English; the Gates Reading Test—Primary and Advanced; and the Lorge-Thorndike Non-Verbal Test. It proposed, also, three broad categories of class organization; considered the need of adequate staffing (Substitute Auxiliary Teachers [SAT]; Puerto Rican Coordinators; School-Community Coordinators and Other Teaching Positions [OTP]; and guidance counselors, particularly in the senior high schools), and found essential the ". . . coordinating [of] efforts of colleges and universities . . . to achieve greater unity of purpose and effort in developing both undergraduate and graduate programs for teachers who will work with non-English speaking pupils. . . ."

Problem II: How to Promote a More Rapid and More Effective Adjustment of Puerto Rican Parents and Children to the Community and the Community to Them?

In this recognition of this problem, *The Puerto Rican Study* struggled with providing answers to the basic anxieties and preoccupations of a group of people beset with problems of housing, adequate employment, health, and "assimilation." That the study found difficulty in providing answers is perhaps explained in its inability to relate the answers it found most effective to the mandate of the school. If it were possible to revise curricula and discern the problems implicit in the learning experience of the Puerto Rican child, it remained an altogether different matter to attempt the solution of broad socio-economic problems, or to attend the amelioration of community ills. In essence, the following statement suggests how far the schools have retreated from the community: "On the relation of Puerto Rican parents to schools, *The Puerto Rican Study* holds that because Puerto Rican parents are preoccupied with problems of learning English, finding apartments, finding employment, and with problems of providing their families with food, clothing, and proper health protection, they are not ready to set a high priority on their children's school problems. The schools can't wait until they are ready."

If *The Puerto Rican Study* is not thought of as a finished guide to the solution of the problems it investigates, but rather as a beginning, it must be characterized as the best assessment of the educational challenges which the Spanish-speaking child poses to the mainland school. In this sense, it is both a guide and a blueprint for effective reform.

Basically, the Puerto Rican child is not a newcomer to the continental school. In many ways, he presents himself to a school and a society whose very nature is heterogeneous and variegated, and to which the non-English speaking child is no stranger. In this sense, the acquisition of English for the Puerto Rican child (if necessary and inevitable) is not a great problem; certainly, it is a soluble problem to which the American school brings a rich and successful experience, the *The Puerto Rican Study* affirms how successful and resourceful American schools can and have been. What is more important to the Puerto Rican child and to American society is the process of acculturation. How does the Puerto Rican child retain his identity, his language, and his culture? In substance, this remains the *crucial* problem, and, in this crucial context, the role of the school in American society needs to be assessed carefully. If the Puerto Rican child is sinned against today, the tragedy lies in the continued assault against his identity, his language, and his cultural wellsprings. In this sense, his experience is not different fundamentally from that of millions of other children to whom the American school was a mixed blessing. This is in no way a deprecation of the egalitarianism of the American common school, but, rather, a reaffirmation of the loss of the great opportunity that a free society afforded its schools to nurture and treasure the rich and varied traditions of its charges. The melting pot theory is, at best, an illusion measured against the realities of American society and a true discernment of its strengths.

In another light, the Puerto Rican child is the creature of his social context—its opportunities or lack of opportunities. If his needs are to be met, they only can be met effectively insofar as the needs of this context are met. A school which is not community-oriented is a poor school. If this is so for the middle-class suburban school, it is even more so for the urban school, which is the heir of the myriad complexities of a rapidly deteriorating central city. More important than the Puerto Rican child's lack of English is the lack of that economic security and well-being that relates him to a viable family structure. If the Puerto Rican child's major disenchantment does not result from segregated schools into which his poverty has placed him, still one would have to deplore the school's inability to cope with the alienation that segregation spawns and the bitter destitution that poverty brings to its children. Perhaps, the "great society" really emerges from a strengthening of the school by its joining hands with all the creative agencies of the community.

REFERENCES

1. Sexton, Patricia: *Spanish Harlem: Anatomy of Poverty,* New York, Harper & Row, 1965, p. 15.
2. *The Puerto Rican Community Development Project.* New York, Puerto Rican Forum, 1964, pp. 26-75.
3. Morrison, J. Cayce: *The Puerto Rican Study (1953-1957): A Report on the Education and Adjustment of Puerto Rican Pupils of the City of New York.* New York, Board of Education, 1958, p. 1.

CHAPTER 17

EDUCATION FOR THE NEEDS OF CUBAN REFUGEES

J. MICHAEL DAVIS

THOUSANDS OF CUBANS have been forced to flee their homeland because of political upheaval in recent years. Over 320,000 immigrants from Cuba have officially registered at the Cuban Refugee Emergency Center in Miami, Florida, during the past decade.[1] Many have been resettled throughout the United States with friends and relatives, with nearly half the Cuban refugee population in this country residing in the greater Miami area.[2] A recent survey noted that the current population of Cuban exiles represents 26 percent of the residents of the city of Miami.[3] This number represents a dramatic contrast to the 20,000 population figure of Cubans in the Miami area before 1960.[4] Their arrival has changed the complexion of all facets of life in the South Florida area.

The first stage of the Cuban refugee movement began shortly after Fidel Castro's accession to power in 1959 and continued until commercial flights were suspended in 1962. The second stage of the exodus was the period between the Cuban missile crisis in 1962 and the beginning of the authorized flights in 1965. During this time, refugees arrived in the United States only by third countries or clandestinely in small boats.[5] The third stage was represented by the recent air flights from Cuba. Ten flights a week brought 4,000 Cuban refugees from Cuba each month in search of freedom to the United States,[6] until the flights were suspended late in 1971.

Cubans who had specialized training in education, English, law, accounting, science, engineering, pharmacy, and philosophy and literature came on these flights, but were unable to resume

Davis, Michael J., "Education for the Needs of Cuban Refugees," in *Education and the Many Faces of the Disadvantaged* (Eds. W. W. Brickman and Stanley Lehrer), New York: John Wiley & Sons, Inc., pp. 205-208.

their careers upon entry into the United States. Many found employment in the United States as private school teachers, tutors, teachers aides, factory workers, garment makers, hairdressers, taxi drivers, sales clerks, secretaries, translators, and waitresses.

The influx of Cuban refugees in such large numbers was not expected, and most of the children and the adults spoke little or no English. They created special problems for the community and the school system. Miami community leaders were sympathetic towards these homeless persons and were determined to demonstrate to them in a practical way how a democratic society could adjust to meet their needs.

American and Cuban cultures made up of numerous subgroups with different backgrounds, interests, and customs came together. During the first years, the local residents and newly arrived exiles went through an unique orientation period. Schools, churches, agencies, and the total community felt the influence of the migration and resettlement of Cuban refugees. Neighborhood compositions changed, as well as church congregations and school memberships. The local labor market experienced profound changes as an ever-increasing number of employable people entered the labor force at different levels.

A good example of this change can be illustrated by the growth in school enrollment of Cuban children. At the conclusion of the 1967-1968 school year, there were 24,360 Cuban refugee pupils enrolled in the Dade County public schools.[7] This represented 11.27 percent of the total pupil membership in the Dade County schools. It has been estimated that between 30,000 and 35,000 Cuban children are currently attending schools in the South Florida area. Dade County school officials contend that the number of Cuban refugee pupils almost certainly will continue to increase.

Programs were implemented to begin meeting the unique educational needs that became evident throughout the area. A brief review of a few programs indicate how the community and its educational systems began to meet this challenge of resolving present and potential difficulties.

During the early 1960s, an agreement was concluded between

the Dade County School Board and the United States Department of Health, Education, and Welfare. This subsequent "agreement" served to supplement previous federal assistance to the school system in order to provide for the educational needs of the ever-increasing number of Cuban students (children and adults).

Arrangements were completed so that free public education was furnished to the Cubans to the same extent and manner as it was to the children who were permanent residents of the country.[8] The government underwrote public education costs which included facilities, equipment, materials, supplies, transportation, and other related services for Cuban refugees in the Dade County area.

Non-English-speaking students were scheduled into special courses of study depending on their ability to speak and understand English, not on intelligence or academic achievement. Pupils concentrated on English instruction and then began taking additional subjects in the curriculum in which achievement was measured in terms of performance rather than verbal ability. As language proficiency was acquired, more of the regular program was included in their daily schedule.[9]

Another program developed exclusively for the refugee children was a tuition-free summer school. The summer program made it possible for newly arrived refugees to participate in an English program before school commenced in September.[10]

With the assistance of foundation money, a unique bilingual education program was implemented and has since been expanded. English was the medium of instruction for all pupils for half a day and Spanish during the other half in a select number of elementary and junior high schools. The staffs were composed of native Spanish-speaking teachers and native English-speaking teachers.

Extensive adult vocational training and educational programs were started to provide for the needs of refugees who wished to improve themselves. English instruction on different levels of competency was provided to adults in evening and day school centers throughout the county. Specific training in marketable skills was provided at special adult training centers (e.g., secretarial, upholstery, child care, welding, commercial sewing, and clerical).

In addition to providing instruction to the pupils, in-service training programs were offered in order to certify teachers and assist Cuban teacher aides. Workshops were designed to improve instruction in teaching Spanish as a vernacular language.

Bilingual Cuban teacher aides were recruited from among the refugee teachers living in Dade County. The aides assisted American teachers and administrators by performing vital services in the school offices and participating in the execution of the instructional program in the classrooms. Their performance has proven to be exceptional and their contributions to the educational process have been extremely helpful.

During the early 1960s, the demand for bilingual teachers who could communicate effectively with the large number of Spanish-speaking children became acute. A large number of teachers had to be employed to teach these pupils.[11] To help meet this need, the University of Miami initiated the Cuban Teacher Retraining Program in 1963 with a grant from the U. S. Office of Education utilizing funds allocated from the Cuban Refugee Program appropriations.[12] The purposes of the program were to help meet the demands for bilingual teachers in the Dade County School System and to assist displaced Cuban refugee professionals in the resumption of their teaching careers. During the past seven years the Cuban Teacher Program has served to place over 300 Cuban refugees in useful and responsible positions in approximately 90 schools.

Exiles interested in becoming full-time students for undergraduate or graduate degrees could participate in the college student loan program for Cubans. Allocations were made to institutions of higher education under the National Defense Education Loan Program. Funds were distributed by colleges and universities in South Florida to those Cuban students who were eligible.

Numerous programs could have been mentioned, but this brief review of a few education programs illustrates how a community has begun to meet particular problems resulting from the Cuban exodus. All educational needs have not been resolved, but an excellent start has been made by public and private education. Important lessons have been learned by educators, residents, and refugees.

Surveys, observations, and program evaluations continue to highlight the fact that the influx of Cubans to South Florida has provided the area with an invaluable asset. This community asset is due in large measure to the high motivation and exemplary performance of the exiles. Another instrumental factor was the cooperative efforts of the Cuban Refugee Program, the U. S. Department of Health, Education, and Welfare, the Dade County School Board, and the University of Miami.

REFERENCES

1. U. S. Cuban Refugee Program: *Resettlement Recap,* Miami, Cuban Refugee Emergency Center, 1969.
2. Wooten, Clyde C., and Sofen, Edward: *Psycho-Social Dynamics in Miami,* Coral Gables, University of Miami, 1969.
3. *Psycho-Social Dynamics in Miami,* Coral Gables, University of Miami, 1969.
4. U. S. Dept. of Health, Education and Welfare: The Cuban Immigration 1959-1966 and Its Impact on Miami—Dade County, Florida, prepared by the Research Institute for Cuba and the Caribbean Center for Advanced International Studies, Coral Gables, University of Miami, 1967.
5. Stoutamire, Barney W., and Wey, Herbert W.: Cuban teachers train for service, *Florida Education, 46:*20-23, November 1968.
6. Davis, Michael J.: The relationship of selection factors in the Cuban teacher retraining program to the effective classroom performance of Cuban teachers, unpublished Ed.D. dissertation, University of Miami, 1969.
7. Dade County Public Schools: Cuban refugee report—number seven, Miami, Florida, Dade County Administrative Research, 1969, p. 3.
8. Dade County Public Schools: Cuban refugee report—number seven, Miami, Florida, Dade County Administrative Research, 1969, p. 3.
9. Wooten, Clyde C., and Sofen, Edward: *Psycho-Social Dynamics in Miami,* Coral Gables, University of Miami, 1969, pp. 314-323.
10. Dade County Public Schools: Cuban refugee report—number seven, Miami, Florida, Dade County Administrative Research, 1969, p. 3.
11. Richardson, Mabel W.: An evaluation of certain aspects of the academic achievement of elementary pupils in a bilingual program, unpublished Ed.D. dissertation, University of Miami, 1968.
12. Wey, Herbert W.: The professional preparation and placement of Cuban refugee teachers, annual report, Coral Gables, University of Miami, 1968, pp. 6-19.

CHAPTER 18

AS I SEE SPANISH-SPEAKING STUDENTS

RUTH H. MATTILA

Drawing upon twenty-six years' experience in teacher education, and her work with Spanish-speaking students in the Southwest, Ruth Mattila compares Spanish-speaking children with Anglos of similar background, age and intelligence. Her description here is based solely on personal observation. The author is professor of education at New Mexico Highlands University.

THE TENDENCY TOWARD uncritical acceptance of expert opinion frequently lulls teachers into operating in an atmosphere of pedagogical stereotypes. Teacher insight then gives way to guided observation—a concentrated effort to see what the experts say should be there—and, accordingly, contrary evidence is discounted. The case of the disabled reader provides excellent examples. Three widely accepted generalizations responsible for much formula teaching will serve to illustrate the point. These are:

Nearly all children come to school wanting to learn to read.

Children who fail to learn to read soon develop emotional reactions which then become barriers that further complicate and impede the learning process.

Children who fail at reading develop numerous symptoms which reflect their difficulty and enable teachers, specialists and counselors to identify them quickly and provide the help they need.

Perhaps these generalizations once held true for large groups of middle-class children but in may be argued that there are today many middle-class children to whom the generalizations do not apply and certainly there are many others to whom the generalizations never applied.

Middle Class Bias

An examination of the three assumptions reveals their obvious

Mattila, Ruth, "As I See Spanish-Speaking Children," *The Reading Teacher,* *26(6)*:605-09, March 1973.

middle class bias. Education has long been revered by the middle class as the road to upward mobility and no group in our society has been more strongly set on the path of upward mobility than the solid middle class. Furthermore, the ability to read—literacy —is recognized by all members of this group as the first giant step on the educational ladder.

However, it may be contended that this pattern is now being broken for many reasons. First, the middle class value system is seriously threatened, as the strong middle class following in drug culture, commune living and draft evasion quite dramatically attest. Second, today's society is increasingly mobile. This mobility is reflected in changing goals—goals which are set in terms of peer group orientation. Thus, today's youth tends to be much less single-minded with regard to school achievement and much less willing to accept adult evaluations of achievements, whether it be from teachers or other adults.

Third, independent thinking among even the very young is today a reality. Children are much less docile about accepting the way to do anything, in school or out of school. Fourth, television and other mass media have increased the expectation for being entertained and for enjoying any pursuit in which one chooses to engage. Fifth, civil rights measures have changed the complexion of the schools, loosening community pressures and controls over students, clouding issues of accountability for both faculty and students, and for the time being at least, confusing all as to goals and sense of direction.

Sixth, complexities of today's problems, at home and abroad, have eroded confidence levels and have frequently paralyzed constructive action in schools and in school communities. Consequently, teachers and administrators are no longer sure where they are or should be going and children, sensing the faltering leadership drop out.

Reexamination Required

In this milieu, then, it seems reasonable to assume that student needs and the reading programs designed to serve them require reexamination. To date at least, the writer's experience with Spanish-speaking students in northern New Mexico has served to reinforce this conclusion. It should be emphasized that the conclusions drawn here apply to children of middle class background who are of normal intelligence, are from fifth to eighth grade level in school and have reading disabilities.

In comparing Spanish-speaking children who fit this description with English-speaking children of similar socioeconomic background the writer has noted some interesting contrasts and comparisons:

The Spanish-speaking children are not disturbed in their social adjustment. Not being able to read is accepted as normal. Many of their friends, as well as many adults whom they respect and admire, either cannot or do not read. Therefore, Spanish-speaking retarded readers have friends at school and relate well to their peers. Lack of reading ability, at least well into the junior high school levels, does not cut them off from normal social participation. (At the senior high school levels the picture tends to change but that, of course, depends on the high school attended.)

There is a notable absence of nervous symptoms—bitten fingernails, nervous ticks—commonly noted among so-called Anglo children who are retarded readers. However, clowning and distractive techniques designed to pull attention away from reading and toward other activities are tactics common to both groups.

Spanish-speaking children are more social in their relationships to adults than are children of the Anglo middle class. Apparently, the extended family relationships which most Spanish-speaking children enjoy have made them more accepting of adults and given them a better base for establishing friendships with adults.

Spanish-speaking students are strongly aware of themselves as Spanish-speaking citizens and on the alert for any reaction, particularly any note of disapproval or reservation in accepting them or their culture. They reject any teacher who does not like them, whether or not that teacher speaks Spanish. They work well with teachers who like them and not at all with teachers who do not, but they seem to have a special hostility for the Spanish-speaking teachers who do not like them.

They are less verbal than their Anglo counterparts—less fluent in all areas of language, less aware of what reading is all about and, consequently, much less strongly motivated toward improvement in reading.

They work well together and poorly alone. The immediate social application of learning is seemingly much more important to them than to their Anglo middle class peers.

They are supersensitive to changes in social climate. A new member of a group must be assimilated before work can move forward. A new teacher must be assessed as a person before his suggestions can be fully accepted.

Spanish-speaking students are politically more astute, showing much stronger interest in government at all levels—local, state, national—than their Anglo counterparts.

Though reading may seem relatively unimportant to them, speech does not. The Spanish-speaking person who can speak out in public, make himself heard and show himself to be forceful and fluent in public meetings is much admired. The substance of his speech is often less important than the fact of his speaking and his persuasiveness is gauged by his ability to hold his own against English speakers in English-speaking groups.

Spanish-speaking students are authoritarian and male-oriented in their leadership expectation. Consequently, permissiveness tends to be interpreted as weakness and the verbal, positive leader who knows what *he* wants is easily accepted. Women teachers are all right; women principals are suspect.

Spanish-speaking students are more strongly tied to ritual and protocol than their Anglo counterparts. Form is important. Knowing the right thing to say and the right thing to do counts for much. Forms are also useful to hide behind. Sometimes they are useful for delaying unwanted action.

Once they have assessed the reading task and set goals for themselves Spanish-speaking students show patterns of ups and downs in motivation and attitude that are indistinguishable from patterns shown by Anglo children. There is the early cockiness with initial progress, the slump when the realization of how far behind they really are strikes them, the leveling off and digging in when they decide that the job can be done after all and the growing self-assurance as they hit their stride and begin to make steady progress.

Once they are on the road to success, Spanish-speaking students are just as competitive as their Anglo counterparts but probably more responsive to praise and more sensitive to criticism. Their sensitivity to loss of face in front of a group is far greater than that of the typical Anglo student and they are less likely to have a ready defense against sarcasm or unfair criticisms.

It should be reemphasized that the above generalizations are meant to apply only to those children who have developed a middle class orientation. However, with this particular group there are strong teaching-learning assets available to the teacher. Perhaps the greatest of these assets is a refreshing absence of generation gap. Seemingly these students have not yet been turned off by adults and they offer both a challenge and friendship to teachers who sincerely want to help them.

PART V

PROBLEMS OF
LANGUAGE AND LEARNING:
A CHALLENGE

CHAPTER 19

SOCIO-CULTURAL FACTORS IN EDUCATING DISADVANTAGED CHILDREN

PATRICIA G. ADKINS

THERE IS AN INCREASING amount of educational concern for the students who do not fall within the criterion of the middle-of-the-road curriculum designed for monolingual standard-English-speaking middle-class pupils.

We may use the terms "bilingual," "bidialectal," or "impoverished" to describe these students, but the semantics of the terms fail to encompass the situation.

"Bilingual" may not carry the linguistic connotation of equal proficiency in two languages, as linguists and teachers of English as a Second Language define it. It may describe the student who comes from a Spanish-speaking home, has a Mexican surname, and is culturally and experientially divergent. "Bidialectal" may often mean a single dialect outlawed and rejected by the school environment. "Impoverished" may be applied to black, brown, red and white alike. It is not solely an economic factor but is inextricably woven into the pattern of environment and opportunity. Regardless of label, it is futile to attempt to educate these children in the same manner as their more advantaged counterparts.

Editorials take educators to task for failing to understand the problems of slums, crowded conditions, lack of privacy, insufficient diet, lack of help and interest on the part of the parents, and lack of understanding of the English language on the part of both the parents and the pupils. "The odds are that such youngsters will drop out of school eight or ten years later with little to show for it but the experience of failure."[1]

Responsible educators are awakening to the fact that the na-

Patricia G. Adkins (Ph.D., University of Colorado, 1966) is Director, Education Professions Development, Region XIX Education Service Center, El Paso, Texas.

Adkins, Patricia G., "Socio-Cultural Factors in Educating Disadvantaged Children," *Education, 93(1)*:32-35, Sept./Oct. 1972.

tion cannot afford to waste the potential productivity of thousands of citizens nor cope with the complex problems that uneducated majorities create.

One of the largest geographic areas of educational concern lies along the border of United States and Mexico. The problematic situation of the student revolves around the socio-cultural milieu affecting his learning.

Perhaps the most obvious result of an educational handicap is the economic problem which results. Henry Munoz, an official of the Political Association of Spanish-speaking Organizations, studied the economic conditions of thousands of persons of Mexican descent, concluding in his findings that "illiteracy in English" was causative of the lack of job opportunities.[2]

When Mexican-Americans or other ethnic groups seek employment which demands communication in English beyond a minimum, they find themselves vocationally handicapped. They are restricted to such jobs as cooking, cleaning, gardening, or painting because they do not "qualify" for "white collar" employment. Regardless of native intelligence or assets of personality, they cannot apply for position as clerks, office workers, or foremen if they cannot speak the language of the country in which they live.

The University of Texas at Austin, concerned with educational conditions and related income, conducted a study of the economic conditions of "Anglo" families and those with Spanish surnames in Texas. The per capita median annual income of "Anglos" in Texas in 1959 was $4,137, that of Spanish-surname Texans, $2,029. It did not increase appreciably in the intervening ten years to 1969. The figure falls far below the poverty index of $3,000 determined in the federal surveys of low-income disadvantaged.

The economic plight of the parents has a direct influence upon the education of the children in these homes. Welfare workers in the border states frequently report the disappearance of the husband and father when he cannot support his family on his meager wage. This often results in the children dropping out of school and taking odd jobs to contribute to the support of the mother and the younger members.[3] Loyalty is strong among Spanish-speaking people; a boy whose mother is working to support the family wants to assist her as soon as he can be dropping out of school and finding a job.

His lack of education leads directly to his continuing poverty, with which the United States government is concerned today. He is likely to be a welfare case, a burden to his community, and a failure in his own estimation and in that of his peers. If he feels inferior and outside the world of the monolingual English-speaking American, then contempt, hate, and unrest are likely to breed. A segregated society is a restless society.

The educational goal of this country must be to fully include all students. This is not always through acculturation and assimilation.

There is a mutual benefit to be gained when cultural exchange is effected. The rich heritage of Mexico is infused in the Mexican-American of the border in the form of art, music, and language. A sense of pride in a Mexican background is not to detract from a good American citizen. Rather, it brings to the United States a warmth of friendship and understanding from Mexico which is highly desirable. If we fail to educate the Mexican-American student to the fullest of his capabilities, we lose the cultural exchange as well as the potential of his thinking and leadership. One of the basic goals of education is to produce an enlightened electorate, able to provide the leaders in a democratic society. One responsibility to the Mexican-American must be that he succeed in this area, for he is often a member of a majority group rather than a minority group and should take his rightful place in the politics of his community.

It seems logical to assume that students with divergent backgrounds have the problem of trying to decide who they are, what they are, and where they actually fit into the scheme in the United States. If they belong to the country, but are still attached to another language, one of the greatest difficulties is the attitude toward the problem. If English is spoken in the home where it is likely to be ridiculed, if peers tease about attempts to be Americanized, if resentment of the American culture is deeply ingrained, resistance may create a psychological barrier which will be a strong deterrent to learning English as a Second Language. A sense of loyalty to culture, family, friends, and first language may be tantamount. This is an American, but he is segregated outside of the realm of the monolingual English-speaking American. His deficiency in the English language may cause him to feel insecure, uneasy, and inferior. He may have misgivings about his own ability. He alienates himself from his family and his friends by speaking a tongue whose native speakers may or may not accept him. He may naturally be confused and filled with doubts concerning the advantage of his new language. Such psychological handicaps unquestionably help to complicate his difficulties. Dr. Horacio Ulibarri, Southern Methodist University, describes the bilingual in the Southwest as a *marginal man*. Dr. Ulibarri explains his term in this manner: "He is marginal because he is neither here nor there, but in between."

The burden rests squarely upon the schools and the teachers to demonstrate to the Mexican-American student that he is not only present, but that he actually belongs. He must be made to feel that his native culture is important; he must recognize the qualities of both Spanish and English, while also recognizing that English is essential for success in the United States.

Dr. Bruce Gaarder, speaking in his private capacity and without official support of the United States Office of Education inferred, states that linguistic, pedagogical, psychological, and social barriers all combine and function in complicated interrelationships to slow and lessen the scholastic achievement of the Spanish-speaking child. He adds that while the linguistic component can be isolated in print and talk, in reality it is inseparable from the others.[4]

This viewpoint is substantiated by Robert Lado, Dean of Linguistics, Georgetown University, who states that when the bilingual child goes to an English-speaking school, he faces a different set of social and cultural patterns as well as a different language.[5]

These factors tend to put the child at a disadvantage with his monolingual English-speaking peers. Few schools have found means to compensate for the social disadvantages of their students and this ever-widening gap becomes more obvious as the child progresses in the school.

The cultural differences in the backgrounds of the Mexican- and Spanish-American and that of the native-born English-speaking American are distinct and varied. Often there is little understanding between the two. Lado stresses the importance of the recognition of cultural differences in bilingual persons. "Because human personality has evolved a variety of ways of life, ways which we call cultures, we are constantly misinterpreting each other across cultures."[6]

Language is one key to the solution of the problem. However, if the student accepts the English language as an answer to his immediate and long-range needs, there must come the understanding on the part of teachers and administrators that his social, economic, psychological, and pedagogical problems are all inextricably interwoven. Hunt observes that children of poverty lack many opportunities to develop cognitive skills, they lack especially the circumstances which foster linguistic skills, and the syntax of standard language in which the abstractions of cognitive content are couched.[7]

Teaching must be approached in a different manner. Additional lecture-type instruction is not the key; a change in curriculum may be the remedy. Teachers must be trained to handle the education of the individual. Changes must be effected whereby bilingual pupils may be taught with materials designed for their special needs rather than approaches primarily selected for teaching native English-speaking children. These reflect a middle-class environment and contain little with which the Spanish-speaking pupil can identify. If there is a lack of relevancy in his curriculum, he is not being furnished an equal educational opportunity.

The internalization that exists in the mind of the Spanish-speaking student as to his language, his family, his social position, and his ultimate economic realization provides the incentive that he has to continue his education. Understanding and empathy on the part of his teachers and administrators is a tremendous factor. The teacher is not in the business of failing students. If the educator is successful, the student is successful.

There must be continual free-flowing communication between the student and the teacher. There must be continuous program evaluation and elimination of inadequate program content.

The educational problems of the "culturally divergent" student can be solved by teachers, principals, supervisors, and administrators working together as a team. Such differentiated staffing will produce an awareness of needs and a curriculum designed to insure a successful educational experience for all pupils.

REFERENCES

1. Editorial, El Paso *Times.* December 11, 1964.
2. McGown, Tom: San Antonio *Light.* Sunday, November 24, 1963, p. 10-A.
3. Cline, Marion Jr.: Realistic education needed in slum barrios. *Rocky Mountain Social Science Journal,* II, No. 2, 1964, p. 222.
4. Gaarder, Bruce: Address to Southwest Council of Foreign Language Teachers, El Paso, Texas, 1965.
5. Lado, Robert: Linguistic and pedagogical barriers. In *Our Bilinguals.* El Paso, Texas, Second Annual Conference of Foreign Language Teachers, November, 1965, p. 14.
6. Lado, Robert: *Linguistics Across Cultures.* Ann Arbor, University of Michigan Press, 1957, p. 6.
7. Hunt, J. McVicker: *The Challenge of Incompetence and Poverty.* Urbana, University of Chicago Press, 1969, p. 204.

CHAPTER 20

INTERFERENCE PHENOMENA IN LANGUAGE TEACHING: THEIR NATURE, EXTENT, AND SIGNIFICANCE IN THE ACQUISITION OF STANDARD ENGLISH

MURIEL R. SAVILLE

Fewer than half of the English speakers in the world learned English as a native language. Those who did somehow internalized its sound system and most of its grammatical structures before they came to school—without any help from specialized English teachers. Each year, however, thousands of students first encounter English as a foreign language when they enroll in school, even within the United States. Thousands more learn English as a native language in their preschool years but find it is a variety which is unacceptable to their teachers from the first grade on.

These are our linguistically different learners, often our disadvantaged. Because of an apparently high correlation between linguistic divergence from standard English and low achievement in our schools, considerable research on this population has been conducted by educators and linguists. The increasing implementation of bilingual programs has interested psychologists, anthropologists, and sociologists as well, with some resultant gains in our understanding of first- and second-language acquisition, cultural differences in styles of learning and motivation, and additional speculation about the relationship of thought and language.

It is time for those of us in education to carefully assess the questions and answers which the social sciences have directed to the problems of teaching English. This report will focus on the

This is a preprint from a forthcoming NCRE pamphlet.

Saville, Muriel R., "Interference Phenomena in Language Teaching: Their Nature, Extent, and Significance in the Acquisition of Standard English," *Journal of Elementary English*, XLVIII(3):396-405, March 1971.

identification of interference phenomena: the factors in a student's personality or culture which may get in the way of his acquisition of standard English.

LINGUISTIC INTERFERENCE

A common manifestation of interference is the switching of linguistic codes. These codes have usually been thought of as distinct languages, but they may be variants of a single language, or dialects. Hymes[24] maintains that no speaker is limited to a single linguistic code, and that all switch to a code appropriate for signaling social intimacy or distance. If such switching is to be understood, emphasis must be placed on the interaction of language and its social contexts. Gaarder comments on the significance of intralingual interference:

> The interference between two closely related dialects—such as a nonstandard dialect and standard English—is far greater than between two completely different languages, and the socially significant differences between the standard and nonstandard forms may be overshadowed by the similarities and fail to present a real challenge to the students.[19]

The nature of the linguistic interference phenomena is provided by structural analyses of nonstandard Negro speech and standard English. These contrastive studies provide the same predictive and explanatory functions for areas of interference in monolingual English speakers as contrastive studies of two languages do for bilinguals.

Probably the most valuable resource for educational use is Labov's *The Study of Non-Standard English*.[28] He discusses the nature of the language and makes direct application of the description to the classroom teacher. His emphasis is on preparing teachers to recognize points of linguistic interference and to adapt methods and materials to the actual problems of students.

Labov and others[30] produced a more technical study of the structural differences between the nonstandard Negro English of the northern ghetto areas and standard English. They explain such interference phenomena as the following as differences in low-level rules which affect surface structure.

1. Simplification of consonant clusters, sometimes causing the deletion of past -ed suffix (e.g. *walk* for *walked*).

2. The negative concord rule, distributing the underlying negative particles to a wide range of environments (e.g. *Don't say nothing*, for *Don't say anything*).
3. The absence of third person singular *-s* and the possessive suffix (e.g. *He go*, for *He goes*).

Many of the speakers they tested could understand both nonstandard and standard forms but produced only the nonstandard. For these native English speakers, interference between linguistic codes is occurring for the most part only at the productive level. While English-as-a-second-language techniques may be applicable to teaching standard English as a second dialect, this study shows us that the nature and scope of the students' interference is probably different enough to make standard ESL material inappropriate.

Labov and Cohen[29] prepared still another contrastive analysis of phonology and grammar including verb tenses, noun forms, negatives, pronouns, embedded questions, and count and mass nouns. They describe important interference areas in terms of general rules which differentiate nonstandard and standard forms.

The only extensive analysis of southern Negro speech surveyed is Williamson's[64] study of high school students in Memphis, Tennessee. She provides no suggestions for language teachers, but her listing of structures would be helpful in preparing instructional materials for students in the southeast. Southern Negro speech is also the primary source of data for Smith[56] in his discussion of cross-code ambiguity as a form of grammatical interference. This is a plausible reason for the persistence of some nonstandard forms, and one which emphasizes the importance of teacher understanding of students' language.

Smith and Truby[55] treat the interference of nonstandard English with the acquisition of reading skills, specifically the sound-symbol correspondence. They conclude that this interference can be minimized if the teacher either teaches his correspondence in terms of the students' dialect or teaches the standard dialect prior to reading.

Rystrom[50] also explores the idea of the nonstandard Negro dialect as a source of interference in acquiring reading skills. He hypothesizes that Negro children could be taught to use specified elements of standard English in eight weeks, and that this would have a significant positive influence on their word reading score when the relationship between letters and sounds was controlled. Pre- and post-testing in two first grade classrooms cause these hypotheses to be rejected. The experiment is potentially interesting but needs to be replicated with a larger sample and with more attention given to teaching methods used. Since the first hypothesis is rejected (the children did not learn to use the elements of standard English), the rejection or affirmation of the influence of these elements on reading seems meaningless.

We can clearly see that contrastive analysis is still considered a useful tool in identifying and explaining points of linguistic interference. It is quite obviously not sufficient, however, to explain all of the performance errors made by speakers learning English as a second language or standard English as a second dialect. While the contrastive linguistic model may be improved by the application of current theoretical principles and techniques, there will be a continuing demand for sensitive teachers in each classroom. And valuable as it may be, the contrastive approach has seldom been applied to the construction of instructional material, nor would it be sufficient in determining content. As Rivers[48] reminds us, areas of contrast are points where we must combat native language interference, but the contrasting element should be taught as it functions in the language system—not just at the point of contrast.

PSYCHOLOGICAL INTERFERENCE

The psychologist's specialized definition of *interference* does not coincide exactly with the linguist's but is limited to phenomena in forgetting and inhibition when first-language habits modify the learning of a second.

Carroll[6] reviews theories of psychological interference and reports many psychological factors which may get in the way of second-language acquisition and are, therefore, of central interest to the language teacher. Interference can occur at the cognitive level (in selection among possible responses), or at the psychomotor level (resulting in a "foreign accent"), or it may result from "unguided imitative behavior." Factors affecting degree of interference include aptitude and intelligence, motivation, age (young children are less subject to interference than older learners), and teaching methods and materials.

Ervin-Tripp[14] provides another general discussion of the psychological factors in bilingualism. She discusses probable differences in language learning due to the age of the student and suggests looking at performance errors as a distinct type of interference which requires analysis of the learner's linguistic system as well as a contrastive analysis of the languages involved. Many of the factors which interfere with the linguistic performance of a speaker learning English as a second language are the same as those affecting a monolingual speaker of English (for example, fatigue, stress, sentence length, and grammatical complexity), but some are due to the more complex linguistic and sociolinguistic rules which the bilingual must learn to control. This suggestion is reinforced by Nemser.[40]

Diebold[12] makes the distinction between "coordinate" and "compound" bilinguals and describes relevant research by Lambert and others. He uses this distinction in describing different types of relationships between word-pairs in the speaker's language systems and their referents. This model should show areas and degrees of semantic interference beyond those available through contrastive linguistic techniques.

Diebold also discusses the possibility that cognitive conflict may accompany semantic interference in bilinguals. This follows from the hypothesis that languages differ from each other in their selection of critical semantic features and in their lexical groupings, or categorization. The nature of this conflict has been explored in discussions of the "Whorfian hypothesis" but its extent and significance to language teaching have received little objective attention. One controlled study is Sisson's[54] use of the Stroop Word Test in a bilingual context to measure degrees of interference.

Niyekawa[42] applies more extensive tests to the influence which the first language has on perception, thinking, and second language learning. Interference phenomena in translation to the second language are partially accountable in terms of the cognitive framework related to the first language. The cognitive framework associated with a particular language and culture

> . . . has adjustment and survival value in that it enables us to econo-mize our effort in perceiving only relevant material and organizing this material in a culturally meaningful way.[42]

This also suggests an interference factor for students learning a second language which may be impervious to any of our teaching techniques.

Cognitive factors are also explored by Spolsky[59] who restates some questions regarding the possible differences in conceptualization in speakers of different languages and the possible effects of bilingualism on language development. While tentative in his conclusions, he suggests a possible loss in linguistic ability when two languages are learned. One type of interference which may operate in second language learning (according to the "balance theory") is that only a certain amount of language learning ability may be available to any one individual. If this is divided between two languages, then each will be weaker.

The discussion of the "coordinate-compound" distinction is renewed by Macnamara[36] as it relates to the language learning contexts. Interference may be taught to students by parents or teachers, although effective teaching eliminates as much of it as possible. One way interference can be minimized is to keep the language of instruction predictable—once started in a language, continue to follow the rules of that language.

The interference potential from negative attitudes and motivation has been widely recognized. Cowan[11] reports that Japanese students who have high integrative motivation (who tend to be somewhat "Americanized") learn English better. Low integrative motivation interferes with language learning. Taylor and others[62] support the hypothesis that the ability to pronounce a second language is related to "empathetic capacity" or sensitivity to interpersonal cues. Others to stress the importance of attitude and motivation include Gardner[19] and Zintz.[66]

Dugas[13] reviews some of the findings reported above and states the implications these have for language teaching. Because integrative motivation lessens interference, for instance, the teacher should look for elements in the English-speaking community with which the students might want to relate and make positive references to bilingual speakers.

Interference phenomena in language learning have been of considerable interest to psychologists in recent years, and reports of their findings are available in such sources as the *Journal of Verbal Learning and Verbal Behavior*. Considering its relevance to instructional materials and methodology, it seems unfortunate that so little in this area is readily available to educators in a less technical form.

CULTURAL INTERFERENCE

Language is essentially a social phenomenon, learned in a social context, and used to communicate with others in a society. Some social factors also interfere with language learning or, at least, inhibit the use of standard English. Labov and Cohen[29] define the conflict between dialects of English as

> . . . the problems that follow from the different uses of language and attitudes toward language that are characteristic of these two forms of English.

They may prove to be even more important to the acquisition of standard English in some contexts than linguistic interference factors discussed above.

Diebold[12] lists as potential interference phenomena the language loyalty sentiments of the speaker, the acculturation pressures being applied, the dominant or more prestigious status of English, socioeconomic conditions, and the ambivalent sentiment in the United States toward bilingualism. Christian[10] accuses the Anglos of a lack of respect for human values and lists this and their impatience with different cultures as causes of interference and Anglo unpopularity. Zintz[66] stresses the importance of teachers perceiving differences in values and custom as well as in the languages of their students. He includes examples from Mexican American, Navajo, Alaskan Indian, and Zuni cultures and a useful bibliography of minority group studies.

Ervin-Tripp[14] lists possible areas of interference as beliefs about the appropriateness or ease of becoming bilingual and feelings of social identity. She reports Labov's observation that working class boys in New York may have trouble learning the speech features of their women teachers because of this last factor.

Bilingual students may not speak English acceptable for classroom use because they contact only the bilingual community and have no model or social support for standard English. The type of linguistic interference manifested in switching between linguistic codes may be normal language usage in the community, with the switching itself carrying social meaning. This phenomenon is convincingly documented by Lance.[34]

If a speaker has mastered the appropriate code-switching rules, the interference phenomena deterring the use of standard English are not so much linguistic (the use of native-language forms in place of English) as social (identity with the bilingual rather than monolingual community). If the choice of codes includes standard English for use when that is appropriate (as in school), the term *interference* may no longer accurately describe code-switching.

Labov and others[31] deal with the functional differences of nonstandard Negro English and standard forms. They describe the relationship of school performance and reading to the vernacular culture, overt attitudes toward language, and other social factors. They find the cultural conflict between the value systems of the two groups a greater contributor to reading failure than the structural conflict between the linguistic systems. It is also noteworthy that Labov finds much greater verbal capacities in ghetto children than do other studies.

Dugas[13] argues that language functions need to be taken into account in preparing teaching material, but his suggestions may be called into question using the same criteria. Dugas claims language material should be on a more informal level to permit social mobility. This will be true if the purpose of language instruction is complete acculturation to a monolingual society, but, if the student lives in a bilingual community, he needs the more formal English of teachers and books. He may not need or want to use the style of English appropriate only with family or friends.[63]

Many have recognized the importance of collecting and disseminating more information about social factors affecting language learning, and some specific procedures have been suggested. Rudnyckyj[49] suggests a model for comparing "cultures in contact" similar to a linguistic model for contrastive analysis. He identifies the interference from conflicting cultural patterns as "cultural accents."

The conference report on *Styles of Learning Among American Indians* (1969) provides a basic resource for teachers of culturally diverse students, although presenting many more questions than answers. It points out how little we know about different learning styles and conflicting value systems and social structures. The primary value of this document to educators may be in pointing out that there *are* such basic differences which are potential points of interference in learning. The recommendations for background studies, related research projects, direct studies and research, and pilot projects should also provide an outline for research with other ethnic minorities.

Unfortunately, reports of research following these guidelines are either past due or not yet readily accessible through such channels as ERIC.

EDUCATIONAL INTERFERENCE

There are several factors in schools themselves which get in the way of students learning English. Where these exist, they include unsuitable instructional material, bad teaching methods, educational segregation of minority groups, and negative attitudes on the part of school personnel.

Some of these negative attitudes toward linguistically and culturally diverse students are also recorded in ERIC documents:

> ... that sardonic chicano sense of humor ...
> ... the touchy pride of the chicano ...
> ... the chicano herd instinct ...

We find an educator rejecting the students' native language:

> If (the student) elects to speak English in a school where the majority use Spanish, it takes a strength of will few possess.
> Under normal circumstances the bilingual teacher or coach who speaks Spanish to the student and encourages the student to speak Spanish in return is likely doing the student a disfavor since it does

nothing to promote his linguistic ability and can easily confuse him in his attitudes.

Professors, too, sometimes make value judgments on students' language:

> He speaks Spanish with his playmates. But it is an impoverished Spanish, a language which has been culturally "beheaded" by its forced separation from its own literary heritage.
> The fact that the pupil's home language is a colloquial Spanish may be only one additional handicap, no more important than other cultural handicaps.

Gaarder[19] states that the greatest barrier to the Mexican-American child's success in school is that those schools want him to grow up as another Anglo.

> This he cannot do except by denying himself and his family and his forbears, a form of masochism which no society should demand of its children.[19]

The extent of such interference phenomena cannot be determined by a survey of the literature, but partial remedies are available. In a collection of reports, Gaarder[19] and Lado[32] make concrete suggestions about how such educational interference may be overcome.

1. Do not legislate against using the native language; this builds hostility toward English.
2. Establish bilingual programs, in which English is taught as a second language.
3. Understand dialect variations in English and the students' language, including their functions in society.
4. Teach dialect switching, not replacement of "incorrect" with "correct."

The understanding of dialects is also important in the development of instructional material. Gumperz[22] points out the hazards of relying solely on contrastive analyses of standard languages spoken by "ideal speakers living in a homogeneous community."[8] Material prepared in English or the first language of the student needs to take into account the regional and social dialect which he speaks—or still another "foreign language" is added to his linguistic milieu, often without being recognized as such by educators.

Heffernan-Cabrera[23] provides an easy to understand review of traditional ESL methodology, suggests scope and sequence for content at varied levels of instruction, and includes a checklist for the evaluation of texts.

Reading methodology and materials for speakers of nonstandard English are presented by Baratz and Shuy.[2] Materials are prepared so that sounds and words associated with written symbols will correspond with sounds and words in the students' speech. They recommend using only forms the students use and hear.

Labov and Cohen[29] also provide teaching suggestions for speakers of nonstandard Negro English. They stress keeping in mind the systematic distinction made in each dialect, rather than the actual sounds themselves. Trying to correct each "mistake" rather than deal with systematic differences is ineffective and will frustrate students. It should be remembered that this analysis and the teaching suggestions are directed to the urban northeast. The reported merger of *pin* and *pen*, for instance, cannot be treated as a nonstandard feature in parts of Texas, where the vowels are not distinguished in standard speech.

Of all areas of possible interference surveyed, ERIC is most helpful in providing extensive bibliographies of instructional material for teaching English as a second language at every age level. More information is needed on teaching standard English as a second dialect, but this need has obviously been recognized and is being met through these channels by Labov, Shuy, and other highly competent sociolinguists.

No static body of information on interference phenomena would suffice in this time of rapid change in linguistic theory, new emphasis on cultural factors in education, experimental teaching models, and ambivalent feelings toward diversity in classrooms. The ERIC document reproduction service now offers the fastest and most complete single resource on these varied factors. The very bulk of currently available material, however, makes the idea of more preselection and evaluation of documents by experts in the fields attractive to busy educators. It may soon be essential if efficiency and effectiveness are to be maintained.

REFERENCES

1. Baehr, Timothy J.: Toward the Quantitative Analysis of Deviant Articulation, in *Development of Language Functions, A Research Program.* Ann Arbor: University of Michigan Department of Psychology, 1967. ED 022 173.

2. Baratz, Joan C. and Shuy, Roger W., eds.: *Teaching Black Children to Read.* Urban Language Series No. 4. Washington, D. C., Center for Applied Linguistics, 1969. ED 025 761.

3. Bilingual Education in Three Cultures. *Annual Conference of the Southwest Council for Bilingual Education.* Las Cruces, N. M., 1968. ED 027 515.

4. Briere, Eugene J. et al.: *A Behavioral Study of the Syllable.* Los Angeles, University of California, 1967. ED 012 442.

5. Burton, James: Our Bilinguals: Social and Psychological Barriers, in *Our Bilinguals—Social and Psychological Barriers, Linguistic and Psychological Barriers.* El Paso, Southwest Council of Foreign Language Teachers, 1965, pp. 31-36. ED 019 899.

6. Carroll, John B.: Contrastive Linguistics and Interference Theory, in *Report of the Nineteenth Meeting on Linguistics and Language Studies.* Washington, D. C., Georgetown University Press, 1968, pp. 113-22. ED 022 159.

7. Catford, J. C.: Contrastive Analysis and Language Teaching, in Report of the *Nineteenth Meeting on Linguistics and Language Studies.* Washington, D. C., Georgetown University Press, 1968, pp. 159-74. ED 022 160.

8. Chomsky, Noam: Current Issues in Linguistic Theory, in *Readings in the Philosophy of Language,* edited by J. A. Fodor and J. J. Katz. Englewood Cliffs, N. J., Prentice-Hall, Inc., 1964, pp. 50-118.

9. ———: *Aspects of the Theory of Syntax.* Cambridge, Mass., M.I.T. Press, 1965.

10. Christian, Chester C., Jr., et al.: Our Bilinguals: Social and Psychological Barriers, in *Our Bilinguals—Social and Psychological Barriers, Linguistic and Pedagogical Barriers.* El Paso, Southwest Council of Foreign Language Teachers, 1965, pp. 7-11. ED 019 899.

11. Cowan, Susie: English Proficiency and Bicultural Attitudes of Japanese Students, *The English Teachers' Magazine, 17:*9, 1968. ED 027 529.

12. Diebold, Richard A., Jr.: The Consequences of Early Bilingualism in Cognitive Development and Personality Formation. Paper prepared for symposium on The Study of Personality. Houston, Rice University, 1966. ED 020 491.

13. Dugas, Don: Research Relevant to the Development of Bilingual Curricula. Report presented at Conference of Foreign Language Teachers. El Paso, Tex., November, 1967. ED 018 298.

14. Ervin-Tripp, Susan: An Issei Learns English, *The Journal of Social Issues, 23*:78-90, April 1967. ED 024 034.

15. ———: Becoming a Bilingual. Paper read at National Conference on Linguistics. New York, 1968. ED 018 786.

16. Ferguson, Charles A.: Contrastive Analysis and Interference Theory, in *Report of the Nineteenth Meeting on Linguistics and Language Studies*. Washington, D. C., Georgetown University Press, 1968, pp. 101-12. ED 022 158.

17. Fillmore, Charles J.: *On the Notion of Equivalent Sentence Structure*. Columbus, The Ohio State University, Research Foundation, 1965. ED 012 009.

18. Fishman, Joshua A.: Bilingualism With and Without Diglossia; Diglossia With and Without Bilingualism, *The Journal of Social Issues, 23*:29-38, April 1967. ED 024 034.

19. Gaarder, A. Bruce: Our Bilinguals: Linguistic and Pedagogical Barriers, in *Our Bilinguals—Social and Psychological Barriers, Linguistic and Pedagogical Barriers*. El Paso, Southwest Council of Foreign Language Teachers, 1965, pp. 17-25. ED 019 899.

20. ———: Organization of the Bilingual School, *The Journal of Social Issues, 23*:110-20, April 1967. ED 024 034.

21. Gardner, R. C.: Attitudes and Motivation: Their Role in Second-Language Acquisition, *TESOL Quarterly, 2*:141-50, September 1968. ED 024 035.

22. Gumperz, John J.: On the Linguistic Markers of Bilingual Communication, *The Journal of Social Issues, 23*:48-57, April 1967. ED 024 034.

23. Heffernan-Cabrera, Patricia: *A Handbook for Teachers of English to Non-English Speaking Adults*. Washington, D. C., Center for Applied Linguistics, ERIC Clearinghouse for Linguistics, 1969. ED 033 335.

24. Hymes, Dell: Models of the Interaction of Language and Social Setting, *The Journal of Social Issues, 23*:8-28, April 1967. ED 024 034.

25. *Journal of Verbal Learning and Verbal Behavior*. New York, Academic Press.

26. Kinzel, Paul F.: Lexical and Grammatical Interference in the Speech of a Bilingual Child, in *Studies in Linguistics and Language Learning, I*, 1964. ED 029 273.

27. Kloss, Heinz: Bilingualism and Nationalism, *The Journal of Social Issues, 23*:39-47, April 1967. ED 024 034.

28. Labov, William: *The Study of Non-Standard English*. Center for Applied Linguistics, 1969. Champaign, Ill., National Council of Teachers of English, 1970. ED 024 053.

29. ——— and Cohen, Paul: *Some Suggestions for Teaching Standard En-*

glish to Speakers of Non-Standard Dialects. New York, Columbia University, 1967. ED 016 948.

30. ———, et al.: *A Study of the Non-Standard English of Negro and Puerto Rican Speakers in New York City, Volume I: Phonological and Grammatical Analysis.* New York, Columbia University, 1968a. ED 028 423.

31. ———, et al.: *A Study of the Non-Standard English of Negro and Puerto Rican Speakers in New York City. Volume II: The Use of Language in the Speech Community.* New York, Columbia University, 1968b. ED 028 424.

32. Lado, Robert: Our Bilinguals: Linguistic and Pedagogical Barriers, in *Our Bilinguals—Social and Psychological Barriers, Linguistic and Pedagogical Barriers.* El Paso, Southwest Council of Foreign Language Teachers, 1965, pp. 14-16. ED 019 899.

33. Lambert, Wallace E.: A Social Psychology of Bilingualism, *The Journal of Social Issues, 23:*91-109, April 1967. ED 024 034.

34. Lance, Donald M.: *A Brief Study of Spanish-English Bilingualism: Final Report,* Research Project ORR-Liberal Arts 15504. College Station, Tex., Texas A&M University, College of Liberal Arts, 1969. ED 032 529.

35. Lee, W. R.: Thoughts on Contrastive Linguistics in the Context of Language Teaching, in *Report of the Nineteenth Meeting on Linguistics and Language Studies.* Washington, D. C., Georgetown University Press, 1968, pp. 185-94. ED 022 161.

36. Macnamara, John (ed.): *The Journal of Social Issues, 23:* April 1967. ED 024 034.

37. ———: The Bilingual's Linguistic Performance—A Psychological Overview, *The Journal of Social Issues, 23:*58-77, April 1967a. ED 024 034.

38. ———: The Effects of Instruction in a Weaker Language, *The Journal of Social Issues, 23:*121-35, April 1967b. ED 024 034.

39. Nash, Rose: *Intonational Interference in the Speech of Puerto Rican Bilinguals, An Instrumental Study Based on Oral Readings of a Juan Bobo Study.* San Juan, Puerto Rico, Inter-American University, 1968. ED 024 939.

40. Nemser, William: *Approximate Systems of Foreign Language Learners.* Washington, D. C., Center for Applied Linguistics, 1969. ED 026 639.

41. Nicklas, Thurston Dale: English for Speakers of Choctaw, in *Teaching English to Speakers of Choctaw, Navajo and Papago,* edited by Sirarpi Ohannessian and William W. Gage. Washington, D. C., Center for Applied Linguistics, 1969.

42. Niyekawa, Agnes M.: *A Study of Second Language Learning: The Influence of First Language on Perception, Cognition and Second Language Learning—A Test of the Whorfian Hypothesis. Final Report.*

Honolulu, University of Hawaii, Educational Research and Development Center, 1968. ED 024 026.

43. Ohannessian, Sirarpi: English for Speakers of Papago, in *Teaching English to Speakers of Choctaw, Navajo and Papago*, edited by Sirarpi Ohannessian and William W. Gage. Washington, D. C., Center for Applied Linguistics, 1969.

44. Olstad, Charles: Our Bilinguals: Linguistic and Pedagogical Barriers, in *Our Bilinguals—Social and Psychological Barriers, Linguistic and Psychological Barriers*. El Paso, Southwest Council of Foreign Language Teachers, 1965, pp. 37-38. ED 019 899.

45. *Our Bilinguals—Social and Psychological Barriers, Linguistic and Pedagogical Barriers*. El Paso, Southwest Council of Foreign Language Teachers, 1965. ED 019 899.

46. Pedtke, Dorothy A. and Oswald, Werner: English for Speakers of Navajo, in *Teaching English to Speakers of Choctaw, Navajo and Papago*, edited by Sirarpi Ohannessian and William W. Gage. Washington, D. C., Center for Applied Linguistics, 1969.

47. Ritchie, William C.: *On the Explanation of Phonic Interference*. Ann Arbor: University of Michigan, Center for Research on Language and Language Behavior, 1968. ED 021 234.

48. Rivers, Wilga M.: Contrastive Linguistics in Textbook and Classroom, in *Report of the Nineteenth Meeting on Linguistics and Language Studies*. Washington, D. C., Georgetown University Press, 1968, pp. 151-58. ED 023 074.

49. Rudnyckyj, J. B.: Formulas in Bilingualism and Biculturalism. Paper read at conference of Linguistic Circle of Manitoba and North Dakota. Grand Forks, N. D., 1967. ED 026 623.

50. Rystrom, Richard: *The Effects of Standard Dialect Training on Negro First-Graders Learning to Read*, Final Report. Concord, Calif., Diablo Valley College, 1968. ED 029 717.

51. Saville, Muriel R.: *Curriculum Guide for Teachers of English in Kindergartens for Navajo Children*. Washington, D. C., CAL, English Speakers of other Languages Program, 1969. ED 030 122.

52. ―――― and Troike, Rudolph C.: *A Handbook of Bilingual Education*. Washington, D. C., Center for Applied Linguistics, 1970. ED 035 877.

53. Sharp, John M.: Our Bilinguals: Linguistic and Pedagogical Barriers, in *Our Bilinguals—Social and Psychological Barriers, Linguistic and Pedagogical Barriers*. El Paso, Southwest Council of Foreign Language Teachers, 1965, pp. 27-30. ED 019 899.

54. Sisson, Cyrus R.: *Foreign Language Experience and Color Word Interference*. Ann Arbor, University of Michigan, Center for Research on Language and Language Behavior, 1968. ED 021 235.

55. Smith, Kenneth J. and Truby, Henry M.: *Dialectal Variance Interferes*

with Reading Instruction. Miami, Fla., Communication Research Institute, 1968. ED 026 199.

56. Smith, Riley B.: Interrelatedness of Certain Deviant Grammatical Structures in Negro Nonstandard Dialects. From paper read at meeting of American Dialect Society. New York, December 1968. 1969. ED 030 877

57. Soveran, Marilylle: *From Cree to English. Part One: The Sound System.* Saskatoon, Saskatchewan, University of Saskatchewan, Indian and Northern Curriculum Resources Centre, 1968. ED 025 755.

58. Spalatin, Leonardo: *Formal Correspondence and Translation Equivalence in Contrastive Analysis.* Washington, D. C., Zagreb University, 1969. ED 025 766.

59. Spolsky, Bernard: Some Psycholinguistic and Sociolinguistic Aspects of Bilingual Education. From a paper read at the Conference on Teaching the Bilingual Child, University of New Mexico, November 1968. ED 028 412.

60. Sturm, Virginia J.: Applied French Linguistics. Paper read at Conference on Language for the Teachers of Falls Church, Virginia Public Schools. Falls Church, Spring 1965. ED 029 526.

61. *Styles of Learning Among American Indians: An Outline for Research.* Washington, D. C., Center for Applied Linguistics, 1969.

62. Taylor, Linda L., et al.: *Psychological Variables and Ability to Pronounce a Second Language.* Ann Arbor, University of Michigan Center for Research on Language and Language Behavior, 1969. ED 028 439.

63. Troike, Rudolph C.: TESOL and Joos' Five Clocks, *TESOL Quarterly,* 5 March 1971, to appear.

64. Williamson, Juanita V.: *The Speech of Negro High School Students in Memphis, Tennessee. Final Report,* 1968. ED 021 210.

65. Young, Robert W.: *English as a Second Language for Navajos, An Overview of Certain Cultural and Linguistic Factors.* Window Rock, Ariz., U. S. Bureau of Indian Affairs, 1968. ED 021 655.

66. Zintz, Miles V.: *What Classroom Teachers Should Know About Bilingual Education.* Albuquerque, University of New Mexico College of Education, 1969. ED 028 427.

CHAPTER 21

THE REGULATORY FUNCTION OF LANGUAGE IN BILINGUAL CHILDREN

H. JOHN VAN DUYNE and GEORGE GUTIERREZ

ABSTRACT

The authors investigated the development of the ability of 4-, 5-, 6-, and 7-year-old bilingual children to perform a complex perceptual-motor task when they were given only Spanish or English verbal instructions. Results indicated that children perform better when given Spanish instruction. This was especially true of the 5-year-olds. Results also indicated that performance under both languages increased with age, and that a stable system of perceptual-motor connections was established by verbal instruction under the Spanish treatment at age 6 and under the English treatment at age 7.

THE ABILITY TO DECODE verbal instructions and encode them in other forms of behavior, such as perceptual-motor, may be basic to other forms of language behaviors. The purpose of this study was to examine the development of the above mentioned ability in bilingual children.

Luria[3, 4] demonstrated that children from 3½ to 4½ years old regulate their perceptual-motor behavior by means of the non-specific impulse aspect of language. From the ages of 4½ to 5½ years, the regulatory function of language is transferred from the nonspecific impulse aspect to the analytic system of specific elective significative connections which are produced by verbal rules. Language begins to play an important role in the establishment of new connections which enable the child to control his behavior within new situations. Under verbal instructions, 4-year-olds could press a balloon to a red light and not to a green one. More difficult tasks such as pressing a balloon twice to a red light and not to a green light could only be performed by 5-year-olds.

Duyne, H. John Van, and Gutierrez, George, "The Regulatory Function of Language in Bilingual Children," *The Journal of Educational Research, 66(3)*:122-124, November 1972.

Luria's findings have been essentially replicated by Birch,[1] Joynt and Cambourne,[2] and Van Duyne.[5]

Van Duyne[5] found a significant difference in performance between 3-, 4-, and 5-year-olds when they were given verbal instructions as their only training in performing a complicated two-association perceptual-motor task (pressing a square block to a blue light and a round block to a yellow light). The performance of the children was consistent with Luria's findings concerning the development of the specific elective significative aspects of language. The purpose of the present study was to examine the development of the specific elective significative aspects of language in Spanish and English in 4-, 5-, 6-, and 7-year-old bilingual children in terms of their performance on a two-association perceptual-motor task when the only training was verbal instructions given in either Spanish or English.

METHOD

The S's were twenty-four Mexican-American migrant workers' children who are now residents of DeKalb County, Illinois. Their parents had been permanent residents of the area for the past nine months. The children of school age are enrolled in the DeKalb school system, they have been attending school for four months prior to the experiences. The parents speak Spanish and some English.

Six children were randomly selected from each of four age groups. Mean ages for each group were 53 months (three males and three females), 64 months (three males and three females), 76 months (four males and two females), and 91 months (four males and two females).

The equipment was a gray vertical panel with an aperture through which a yellow and blue light were shown in random sequence. In front of the vertical panel was a gray horizontal panel with two lever-press mechanisms. Mounted on one of the levers was a square block 1 inch on a side and $\frac{1}{2}$ inch thick, and on the other a round block 1 inch in diameter and $\frac{1}{2}$ inch thick. The stimulus interval was 1.96 seconds, the interstimulus interval 2.04 seconds. Stimuli and responses were recorded on a digital recorder.

PROCEDURE

This study was a repeated measure, within subject comparison design. The children were randomly assigned to receive either the English or Spanish treatment on the initial task and the other language treatment on the second task. All children were given operant conditioning of color and form discrimination and labeling in both languages to a criterion of four consecutive correct responses for square, round, yellow, and blue. The reinforcement used was candy and balloons. All children performed to criterion.

The experimenter was a bilingual Spanish-American of Peruvian descent who had worked with the children and their families for the past six to nine months. He is employed by state and federal authorities to work with migrant workers in DeKalb County.

The initial task was to press the square to a blue (or yellow) light and the circle to a yellow (or blue) light. The task consisted of thirty-eight stimulus events: nineteen blue and nineteen yellow lights in random sequence. Within the treatment cells the color-form associations were randomized to control for preferential associations.

The verbal instructions for the English treatment on the initial task were as follows:

> We are going to play a game twice and you may win some candy and balloons if you do well. I will tell you how to play the game. When the blue (yellow) light comes on, press the square (circle). What do you do when the blue (yellow) light comes on?

The instructions and questions were repeated until the child made four consecutive correct verbal responses for each stimulus. Once the child had reached criterion, he was asked to play the game. The verbal instructions for the Spanish treatment were the same as those for the English treatment except in Spanish. Children responded to the experimenter in Spanish.

On the second task, the children received whichever language treatment they had not previously had. The color-form associations of the initial task were reversed for the second task. The verbal instructions for the English treatment were as follows:

This time we are going to change the game. When the yellow (blue) light comes on, press the square (circle). What do you do when the yellow (blue) light comes on?

The instructions and questions were repeated until the child could give four consecutive correct responses for each stimulus. The verbal instructions and questions for the Spanish treatment followed the same format. When the child reached criteria, he was asked to play the game.

After both the initial and second task, the children were given some candy and balloons. They were also told that they did a very good job.

RESULTS

The scoring for both treatments of the task was the number of correct responses out of thirty-eight stimulus events. A correct response was a single appropriate response for the particular stimulus. The mean correct scores for the treatments are given in Table 20-I.

A two-way analysis of variance for repeated measures was performed. A significant difference was found between language treatments, $F = 4.298$ (1,40); $p < .05$. The children performed better under the Spanish than under the English treatment. A significant difference was observed between age levels, $F = 22.13$ (3,40); $p < .01$, their performance increased with age. No significant interaction was found.

A subanalysis was performed using the Scheffe test following a significant F-ratio. It was determined that 5-year-olds scored significantly higher under the Spanish treatment than the English treatment at the .05 level of confidence. Other differences be-

TABLE 20-I

MEAN SCORES

Age Groups	Treatments	
	English	Spanish
4-years-old	1.6	.4
5-years-old	13.00	24.6
6-years-old	25.8	33.8
7-years-old	33.8	35.8

tween treatments were not significant, although all age groups scored higher under the Spanish treatment.

Collapsing across language treatments, the Scheffe test revealed a significant difference at the .01 level between 4- and 5-year-olds, 4- and 6-year-olds, 4- and 7-year-olds, and 5- and 7-year-olds, and a significant difference at the .05 level between 5- and 6-year-olds. No significant difference was found between 6- and 7-year-olds.

Using the Scheffe test applied to the English treatment scores, significant differences at the .01 level were found between 4- and 6-year-olds, 4- and 7-year-olds, and 5- and 7-year-olds, and a significant difference at the .05 level between 5- and 6-year-olds. No significant differences were found between 4- and 5-year-olds and 6- and 7-year-olds.

Performing a Scheffe test on the Spanish treatment scores, significant differences at the .01 level were found between 4- and 5-year-olds, 4- and 6-year-olds, and 4- and 7-year-olds, and a significant difference at the .05 level between 5- and 7-year-olds. No significant differences were found between 5- and 6-year-olds and 6- and 7-year-olds.

DISCUSSION

According to Luria,[3] it is not until a child has developed the specific elective significative function of language that one may elaborate a stable system of perceptual-motor reactions by means of verbal instructions alone in children. When the specific functions of language are developed, the child regulates his behavior by means of the internalized verbal rule which is recoded into complicated excitatory and inhibitory connections within the perceptual-motor system.

The present task required a stable system of complex perceptual-motor reactions. The S had to respond to the blue light pressing the square block and simultaneously inhibit pressing the round block; and when the yellow light appeared he had to reverse pressing the round block and simultaneously inhibit pressing the square. Since the children all learned to discriminate and label the shapes and colors, and could verbalize the rules, it is assumed that the development of or the lack of development of performance was due to the elective significative aspects of speech.

The results indicated that the children of the sample performed better when given Spanish treatment than when they received English treatment. The difference in performance of the two total language groups was due mainly to the 5-year-olds who scored significantly higher under the Spanish treatment. This suggests that within the 5-year-olds of this sample the ability to decode verbal instructions and encode them into specific perceptual-motor connections is more fully developed in Spanish than English.

When the scores for both languages are collapsed, the results suggest that the period from 5 to 6 years may be the transitional stage when the regulatory function is transferred from the non-specific impulsive aspects to the specific elective significative aspects of language. Luria and others[1, 3-5] found this transitional period in monolingual children occurred between 4 and 5 years old. These results indicate that the children of this sample are approximately one year retarded in this language development.

When the results were analyzed for the treatments separately, two different developmental sequences were observed. The results of the English treatment indicate that 5- and 4-year-olds are essentially functioning by means of the nonspecific aspects of language. Six-year-olds appear to be at a transitional stage in which the specific aspects of language are being developed. Seven-year-olds exhibit a stable system of perceptual-motor connections under verbal English instructions. The results of the Spanish treatment indicate that 4-year-olds are functioning at a level of the nonspecific aspects of language while 5-year-olds are at a transition stage in their development from nonspecific to the specific aspects of language. Six- and 7-year-olds appear to be controlling their behavior by a stable system of perceptual-motor connections established by verbal Spanish instructions.

Results indicate that the Mexican-American children in this study were approximately one year delayed in Spanish and two years delayed in English in their development of the specific elective significative aspects of language. This conclusion appears to be substantiated when the results of the present study are compared with the findings of Van Duyne[5] using the same task with monolingual suburban children. In that study, 5-year-olds (mean score 33.6) were controlling their perceptual-motor behavior by means of a stable system of connections produced by verbal instructions. The Luria[3] and Birch[1] findings also indicate that 5-year-olds have developed the specific aspects of speech while 4- to 5-year-old children are at a transitional stage between the nonspecific and specific aspects of language.

REFERENCES

1. Birch, D.: Verbal control of nonverbal behavior, *Journal of Experimental Child Psychology, 4*:266-275, 1966.
2. Joynt, D., and Cambourne, B.: Psycholinguistic development and control of behavior, *British Journal of Educational Psychology, 38*:249-260, 1968.
3. Luria, A. R.: *The Role of Speech in the Regulation of Normal and Abnormal Behavior,* New York, Liveright Publishing Corporation, 1961.
4. Luria, A. R.: The genesis of voluntary movements, in O'Connor, N. (ed.): *Recent Soviet Psychology,* New York, Liveright, 1961, pp. 165-185.
5. Van Duyne, H. J.: The development of the control of adult instructions over nonverbal behavior, *Journal of Genetic Psychology,* in press.

CHAPTER 22

THE EDUCATIONAL PROBLEMS OF ATYPICAL STUDENT GROUPS: THE NATIVE SPEAKER OF SPANISH

LUIZ F. S. NATALICIO and DIANA S. NATALICIO

A GOOD DEAL OF ATTENTION has been given in the past few years to the problems of the "culturally disadvantaged" student populations *vis-à-vis* their educational encounters in the school systems of many of our large urban centers. In broad terms, the issue in question relates to the education of those pupils who differ, along one or more significant dimensions (e.g. language of the home, sociocultural background), from the modal student for whom the curriculum is designed and who is responsive, in general terms, to the pedagogy underlying curriculum implementation. In this particular instance, the problems being addressed are those associated with the education of the native speaker of Spanish.

The general character of this discussion is the product of an analysis of the possible etiology of the problem and is directed at such causative factors, e.g. linguistic and social handicaps in relation to the dominant culture. To better substantiate the arguments that follow, the inclusion of relevant data for a sample of the population in question was deemed appropriate.

An Example

The relative distribution of the total population in Bexar County, Texas (which includes San Antonio as the only major metropolitan area) and in the state of Texas according to the ethnic group categories (1) Anglo, (2) Spanish Surname, and (3) Nonwhite is described by the 1960 census thus:

Natalicio, Luiz F. S., and Natalicio, Diana S., "The Educational Problems of Atypical Student Groups: The Native Speaker of Spanish," *Urban Education*, 4:262-72, October 1969.

POPULATION DISTRIBUTION BY ETHNIC GROUPS

	Anglo	*Spanish Surname*	*Nonwhite*
Bexar County	57.8	37.4	4.8
Texas	72.6	14.8	12.6

Such figures reveal the high percentage of Spanish-surnamed population located in this region. When coupled with data on his educational attainment (median school years completed, dropout rate, etc.) and his economic status (average family income, unemployment rate, etc.), the position of the Mexican-American citizen in Texas must be recognized as a severely disadvantaged one compared to that of the Anglo.

A recent household survey conducted by the Department of Labor in cooperation with the Texas Employment Commission indicates that for the San Antonio Metropolitan Area the unemployment rate is 4.2 percent—as compared with 3.7 percent for the United States as a whole. More serious than this, however, was the discovery that one of the major slum areas on the "West Side" of San Antonio had an unemployment rate of 8 percent and a subemployment rate of 47.4 percent. The survey showed that several general characteristics of the population group examined were directly relevant to the situation:

—70 percent of the unemployed did not graduate from high school
—48 percent of the unemployed did not go beyond the eighth grade
—6.5 percent had not gone to school at all.

It seems important to note that 84 percent of the people in this neighborhood were Mexican-Americans, or Spanish-surnamed. In conclusion, the study stressed several basic facts, among them:

. . . unemployment and subemployment in these slums are— much more than in other areas a matter of *personal* rather than *economic* condition. No conceivable increase in the gross national product would stir these backwaters. The problem is less one of inadequate opportunity than of inability, under existing conditions, to use opportunity. Unemployment in these areas is primarily a story of inferior education, no skills, discrimination, fatherless children, unnecessarily rigid hiring practices and hopelessness.[14]

Fundamental to the problem seem to be the linguistic barriers Mexican-Americans must face when confronting the educational system, the labor market, and society in general. The Spanish-speaking child in the Southwest has traditionally been "taught" with almost complete disregard for the fact that his native language is not English. Census data for 1960 graphically illustrate the extremely low educational attainment of the Spanish-surnamed population in Texas. (Table 21-I presents information relative to ten sample counties.) Although a more realistic and enlightened attitude toward the problem of this ethnic group has begun to develop, the fact remains that the majority of Mexican-American children in Texas repeat the first grade at least once and drop out of school by the fourth grade.

TABLE 21-I

CHARACTERISTICS OF THE SPANISH-SURNAMED POPULATION OF
TEN SAMPLE COUNTIES IN TEXAS (1960)

County	Total Population 1960	Spanish Surnamed Population 1960	Percent Spanish Surname of Total Population 1960	Median School Years Completed Persons (25+)[a] 1960	Median Family Income (Dollars)[a] 1960
Atascosa	18,828	8,545	45.4	2.5	2,809
Bexar	687,475	257,090	37.4	5.7	3,446
Dimmit	10,095	6,760	67.0	2.3	1,721
Frio	10,112	6,250	61.8	2.3	1,666
LaSalle	5,972	3,832	64.2	1.4	1,585
Maverick	14,508	11,253	77.6	3.9	2,047
Medina	18,904	6,998	37.0	3.0	2,185
Uvalde	16,814	8,002	47.6	3.7	2,478
Wilson	13,267	4,911	37.0	3.1	2,277
Zavala	12,696	9,440	74.4	2.3	1,732

SOURCE: (1) *Persons of Spanish Surname,* 1960, Tables 14 and 15. (2) *Number of Inhabitants, Texas, 1960,* Table 7.

Above table extracted from *A Statistical Profile of the Spanish-Surname Population of Texas,* Harley L. Browning and S. Dale McLemore (Austin: Bureau of Business Research, The University of Texas) , 1964, pp. 69-79.

[a] Spanish surnamed.

The Teacher's Role

Many have attributed this pattern to the teacher's lack of understanding of the child's culture and his or her inadequate training in an appropriate pedagogy for teaching these students to understand, speak, read and write the language of the dominant culture. Apparently, it has been suggested, the roots of the problem lie at the level of teacher training.[4] Howsam[7] has pointed out that such programs as Operation Head Start have demonstrated what can be accomplished with very young children; the difficulty, he claims, lies in the fact that teachers in the regular school system are not adequately trained to capitalize on this preschool progress.

Although not explicit, the fallacious assumption inherent to most teacher training programs is that the training provided makes possible satisfactory teacher performance regardless of learner characteristics. However, in order to ensure effective performance on the part of the teacher and, thus, adequate achievement on the part of the learner, the particular characteristics of the student must be accounted for at some point in the training or retraining of his instructors.

The teaching of reading and writing in any language, for example, presupposes an oral foundation in the target language on the part of the learner. Child development studies indicate that the average child has met the oral foundation requirement in his native language by approximately four years of age.[9] Here lies the tragedy in the educational experience of the Spanish-speaking child who, upon entering school at the age of six, has considerably less verbal competence in English than his English-speaking counterpart. In addition, it should be noted that this child has not had the advantage of the dominant culture's socialization practices to which the curriculum and all other activities that take place in the school are geared. The environment of the poor, Bangs[2] has indicated, produces pupils whose language and behavior mark them as subnormal in comparison with their middle-class schoolmates. The result is that their teachers treat them as "slow" children, rather than as culturally different children.

Teacher Training and Retraining

There is an urgent demand to provide already experienced teachers, as well as new teachers with training in linguistics, for the teaching of English as a second language (TESL). That materials are not lacking in this field is evidenced by its vast bibliography.* However, a point too often disregarded is that the linguistic principles upon which such materials are based are generally unfamiliar to the teacher for whose use they were intended. The great majority of elementary school teachers attended college and became certified long before courses in contrastive and applied linguistics were considered an essential part of the preparation of persons teaching minority groups whose native language is other than English, e.g. the Mexican-Americans of the Southwest. Even today, course requirements of teacher-training programs fail to reflect this need.[1] The average teacher has little or no understanding of the principles underlying the development or the sequence of the materials available for teaching English as a second language. Furthermore, the appropriate use of such materials presupposes a knowledge of the methodology applicable to them.

Teachers are, on the whole, being held responsible for the educational plight of the Spanish-speaking child. This is, perhaps, unfair since they are not always equipped with the necessary tools to cope with the problems with which they are faced. A survey carried out by TENES (the association of Teachers of English to Non-English Speakers) revealed gross inadequacies in the preparation of the majority of teachers engaged in teaching English to speakers of other languages as evidenced by their performance, especially in the critical primary grades.[1] The average teacher working with the Spanish-speaking child is neither prepared nor is she actively endeavoring to teach the student oral English (understanding and speaking) systematically.

Mention has been made of the need of training teachers in TESL methodology. A word of clarification seems appropriate. TESL is a broad designation for a set of procedures and does not represent, by any means, a panacea designed for universal

---

* See, for example, TESOL Newsletter, vol. 1, no. 1, 1967, pp. 10 ff.

application. Each instance of utilization calls for adaptations that must reflect the unique characteristics of the particular sociolinguistic situation. As has been pointed out:

> . . . one perceives the sounds of another language in terms of the structure of sounds of one's own. This phenomenon—perception of another system in terms of one's own—has been studied by linguists as interference between two systems, most notably by Weinreich of Columbia University in his book *Languages in Contact*. When both systems in question are known, it is possible to predict quite accurately where and what kind of interference will occur and what kinds of substitutions and interpretations will be made, as speakers of one language learn the other. In consequence, it is possible to design materials for the teaching of one language specifically for speakers of another, and to anticipate the particular advantages and disadvantages their own system will confer in the task.[8]

The teacher's clear understanding, for example, of the phonology (sound system) of both the learner's native tongue and the target language is required, not only to train verbal proficiency in the latter (English), but also to preclude the conditioning of failure on the part of the student. The learner effectively *does not hear* the sound differences between what he is verbalizing and the model provided him by the teacher. Needless to say, the problem is not physiological (e.g. auditory) but cultural in nature, yet as McDavid pointed out: ". . . too often in the schools it is not recognized that the child whose parental language lacks the phonemic contrasts between /s/ and /z/ constitutes a different kind of problem from one with a cleft palate."[12]

If the teacher does not recognize the cause of the child's inability to imitate the model correctly, her efforts to endow him with verbal mastery of the sound in question will be random, and she will be unable to create the conditions required to increase the probability of the child's achieving success and, thus, his learning which aspects of his behavior are likely to meet teacher expectations. If, on the other hand, she is aware of the linguistic interference underlying the child's inability to produce a given sound in the target language, she can use appropriate techniques to bring about learner success. For example, if the child fails to produce the English /th/ as in *this,* the teacher, rather than accepting the native Spanish-speaker's problems with the so-called th sound in English as insurmountable, might draw on her knowledge of Spanish phonology where the sound /th/ often occurs in words such as "padre," "verdad," "sábado," and the like.† In this case, the teacher who uses applicable contrastive techniques makes it possible for the child to succeed and, hence, conditions success rather than failure. Of great importance is the fact that the child is at the beginning of his educational experience; the ratio of his successes and failures will be reflected in his future academic achievement and his attitude toward education in general. Educational research has shown that the greater the number of successes the child experiences, the higher his level of aspiration and his academic motivation; repeated failure tends to produce pessimism, resignation, and reduction of effort.[11]

The recognition of this need to analyze the phonology of two given languages (e.g. Spanish and English) in order to insure effective learning of the second language is now new: ". . . a given language cannot be successfully taught in an identical way to pupils of different language backgrounds . . . every different native language causes a different combination of problems in learning a given secondary language."[13] However, the implications of this observation relative to insuring the academic success of linguistic minority groups whose native language is not the official language of the school has not been fully realized.‡ The problem is not solely one of unfamiliarity with the language of the dominant culture, but also the fact that this lack predisposes and often

---

† In any example such as this, dialectical variations must, of course, be taken into consideration.

‡ The importance of phonology in this discussion cannot be overemphasized, for in the words of H. A. Gleason (1961: 343) : Incorrect pronunciation of even a very rare phoneme or cluster can render speech conspicuously strange or even objectionable. It can interpose a serious social barrier between the speaker and the members of the speech community. Of course, some deviations from the general usage are tolerated much more readily than others. While it is often possible to avoid the use of troublesome words or constructions, there is seldom any possibility of manipulating the conversation so as to avoid certain phonemes or phonemic combinations. A speaking knowledge of a language therefore, requires very close to *one hundred percent control of the phonology* and control of from fifty to ninety percent of the grammar, while one can frequently do a great deal with one percent or even less of the vocabulary [emphasis ours].

leads to educational failure, limited occupational opportunities and their logical consequences. Whereas it is important that special programs be provided for the dropouts, the unemployed, the underemployed, and other borderline members of society to make them productive members thereof, it must be recognized that such programs are no more than belated efforts to remedy failures of the past. This vicious circle can be broken only if effective action is directed at the root of such social problems, i.e., education.

It seems obvious that the Spanish-speaking child must first be provided the prerequisite oral foundation in the English language (i.e., understanding and speaking) before any attempts are made to teach him reading and writing skills. He must be verbally competent in English before he is required to cope with even the most elemental aspects of the school curriculum, which presuppose native competence in that language.[§] In order for him to acquire such prerequisite skills the school must have within its ranks adequately trained personnel to carry out this task. The need for teachers qualified in TESL was recognized by the U. S. Office of Education with the inclusion of this area of study in the provisions of the National Defense Education Act Title XI Institutes for Advanced Study.[‖]

The School as an Institution

The problems associated with teaching a child who is a native speaker of Spanish, however, are but one aspect of the larger educational question of how to instruct children who differ cul-

---

[§] See Bell (1965: 101): Until materials are available for beginning reading instruction, the teacher should use the methods and the materials, with some basic modifications, with which he is most familiar. Basically, these modifications must enable a pupil, through the oral practice session, to learn how to say what he is expected to read. If the child must read, "Spot can run," he should be able to say, "Spot can run," before he tackles the problem of reading it. Furthermore, the teacher should not expect the child to be able to talk about what he has read unless he has been taught the language necessary to express these ideas.

[‖] While the focus of this discussion has been on linguistic factors, it is worth noting that most NDEA Institutes for Advanced Study give appropriate recognition to sociocultural variables—e.g., values and attitudes—in the education of the atypical student, by including in their programs lecture series or actual courses in such areas as cultural anthropology, sociology and/or history.

turally or linguistically from the "average English-speaking child," for whom the practices of the educational system are designed. While many have blamed the teacher, citing her inadequate preparation, poor attitude, etc., for the failure of children who are, in one respect or another, different from the "average child," it should be remembered that ". . . a teacher is both a person and an office, both a human being and an element within a vast educational system."[5] However, since the *institutional role* of teachers is always the most evident in their contacts with non-academic personnel, the latter are tempted to conclude that the limiting factor upon teachers' effectiveness is inherent to the educational system. The responsibility in this case is placed with the administrators. Clearly, there is room for improvement at both administrative and teaching levels, and it seems unwise to assign causative responsibility for the failure of atypical student groups to either level; it would be of no consequence in terms of coping with the educational problem in question.

Accepting the above as a given, to provide teachers with special training and guidance aimed at enabling them to be effective in their teaching of atypical student groups, without due consideration being given to the administrative aspects of special programs that the teachers might want to introduce, would greatly diminish the potential effect of the training provided them. By the same token, administrative adaptation, as an attempt to cope with the problems inherent in the education of such atypical groups, without providing the teachers with the special training required, would also prove to be an effort of limited success. Administrative reassessment, as well as teacher training, must be a part of any program proposed to examine a solution for the educational problems unique to groups differing in one or more characteristics from those which the school is normally equipped to handle. This approach should result in a concentrated effort on the part of *both* administrative and teaching personnel toward the solution of the problem, the nature of which would then be, hopefully, clearly understood by all concerned, thus increasing the probability of the attainment of their common goal. Furthermore, such a total school effort would permit a more objective evaluation of the instructional program itself, by precluding the assignment of the responsibility for its success or failure to either teachers or administrators.

Regarding the specific problem of the Spanish-speaking child, the introduction of special programs should be considered. It is a matter of established policy in the schools today to provide programs for children with various handicaps such as blindness, deafness, etc. The child who enters school in the first grade unable to function in English suffers from a cultural handicap relative to the language of the dominant culture. Nonstandard speech patterns are as much a handicap, socially speaking, as a cleft palate, deafness, etc. are in organic or physical terms. This type of handicap can be effectively overcome by intelligent diagnosis and special instruction directed at the correction of the problem facing the child, that is, not understanding or speaking English. As McDavid[12] has stated: "The earlier in the school career a positive language program is introduced, the sooner students will be able to perform as equals regardless of race or ethnic background. . . ." One important result of such a special program would be to diminish greatly the performance differentials evident in the classrooms—due to the inability of some students to function in the language in which instruction is offered —thus, facilitating the task of the teacher and raising the achievement level of the class as a whole.

The sole emphasis here has been to make explicit those aspects that must be considered in any attempt to cope with educational problems of the magnitude and scope of the one discussed. It should be stressed, in conclusion, that past experience strongly suggests that one-shot, two or three month training or retraining programs of teachers who work with atypical students provide an inadequate solution to this multifaceted problem. It would appear that a more realistic strategy should involve both the instructional and administrative staff of the school and evolve from their joint analysis and planning, implementation being, thus, the realization of their integrated efforts.

REFERENCES

1. Allen, H. B.: Challenge to the profession. *TESOL Q. 1*:2, 1967.
2. Bangs, T. and Howsam, R.: Testimony to Texas Senate Interim Poverty Study Committee. San Antonio Express, December 3, 1967.

3. Bell, P. W.: An instructional program for Spanish-speaking elementary school pupils. In V. F. Allen (ed.) On Teaching English to Speakers of Other Languages, Series 1. (Papers presented at the TESOL Conference, May 8-9, Tucson, Arizona), 1965.

4. Bowen, J. D.: Teacher training for TESOL in degree and certificate programs. In C. J. Kreidler (ed.) On Teaching English to Speakers of Other Languages, Series 2. (Papers presented at the TESOL Conference, March 12-13, 1965, San Diego, California), 1966.

5. Gleason, H. A.: Language in the institutes. Address delivered to the NDEA Special Institute, February 9, Minneapolis, Minnesota, 1967.

6. ———: *An Introduction to Descriptive Linguistics.* New York, Holt, Rinehart & Winston, 1961.

7. Howsam, R.: Testimony to Texas Senate Interim Poverty Study Committee. *San Antonio Express,* December 3, 1967.

8. Hymes, D. H.: Functions of speech: an evolutionary approach. In F. O. Gruber (ed.) *Anthropology and Education.* Philadelphia, Univ. of Pennsylvania Press, 1961.

9. Lenneberg, E. H.: *Biological Foundations of Language.* New York, John Wiley, 1967.

10. ———: Understanding language without ability to speak: a case report. *Journal of Abnormal Social Psychology 65,* 1962.

11. McCandless, B. R.: *Children: Behavior and Development.* New York, Holt, Rinehart & Winston, 1967.

12. McDavid, R. I., Jr.: Differences in an urban society. In W. Bright (ed.) *Sociolinguistics.* The Hague, Mouton, 1966.

13. Reed, D. W., Lado, R., and Shen, Y.: The importance of the native language in foreign language learning. *Language Learning 1:*1, 1948.

14. U. S. Department of Labor: Sub-employment in the Slums of San Antonio. Washington, D. C., Government Printing Office, 1965.

CHAPTER 23

LEARNING FOR TWO WORLDS

RON RODGERS with DIEGO RANGEL

Y OU ARE 11 YEARS OLD and enrolled in an elementary school far from your former home in Puerto Rico, and you are confronted by a teacher who speaks a language you do not understand. You feel intimidated and lonely, and the situation appears so impossible that you are already considering the attractions of dropping out.

Three years later your parents receive an invitation to your graduation from the eighth grade of a most unusual public school: Chicago's Juan Morel Campos Bilingual Center. As with the classes you have been attending and the material you have been studying, the invitation is presented in both Spanish and English. Learning does not seem such a formidable proposition now, and, as a high school freshman, you have decided that a diploma may not be beyond your grasp after all.

The Juan Morel Campos Bilingual Center had its modest beginnings in 1968 on the third floor of Lafayette public elementary school on Chicago's near Northwest Side. Opening as a "school within a school," it had four teachers paid with funds provided under Title I of the Elementary and Secondary Education Act and 45 students selected from grades six, seven, and eight in schools in District Six. The following year the Lafayette Bilingual Center (as it was then known) expanded to 80 students when ESEA Title VII money was added and the teaching staff reinforced. Then in the fall of 1971 the center acquired its own building by leasing a former Catholic school, and its present name—honoring the 19th century Puerto Rican composer whose *danzas* and songs are still highly popular "back home" and with the children at the center. Two thirds of these youngsters were

Ron Rodgers with Diego Rangel, American Education, U. S. Dept. of Health & Welfare, Office of Education, November 1972, pp. 28-32.

Rodgers, Ron, and Rangel, Diego, "Learning for Two Worlds," *American Education,* 8:28-32, November 1972.

born in Puerto Rico, and 90 percent had been in the country less than two years when they enrolled in the bilingual program.

One of ten national models selected for the Right to Read "Target for the 70's" project, Juan Morel Campos today has 90 students and a full-time teaching and administrative staff of nine, a clerk, a school-community representative, and two teacher aides. Two teachers are paid with funds from Title VII of the Elementary and Secondary Education Act, and seven by the Chicago Board of Education.

While the center has had its limitations as well as its successes, checkups show that none of its graduates in the past two years has disappeared into the street corner society of high school dropouts, and many of its students are at or near grade level achievement by the time they leave the center. Juan Morel Campos Bilingual Center is in short a model of progress rather than perfection. And its director, Natalie Picchiotti, emphasizes that no matter what language may be involved, good teaching is still the heart of good education.

"If you follow good teaching procedure, you'll succeed," she says, "and in doing so you will make bilingual education good for *all* children. What we have here is standard education in a bilingual format."

That format does not simply mean the translation of compensatory education into Spanish. As viewed by at least some educators during the 1960's, compensatory education seemed bent on trying to adjust children to the demands of the school. At the Juan Morel Campos center the focus is on the child, and on his particular needs. Thus the first step in establishing the center was a reassessment of the ability of District Six schools to meet the needs of children in a rapidly changing neighborhood where Italian and Polish families were being replaced by immigrants from rural Puerto Rico, Mexico, and several South and Central American countries.

More than 75 percent of the children now in District Six schools speak Spanish at home. As a principal of one of the district's schools, Miss Picchiotti (who speaks fluent Spanish and Italian herself) argued that these children were being shortchanged and that there should be a center where they would be taught in Spanish while they learned English. Gradually, she said, these children could become citizens of two worlds—the one into which they were born and the one in which they now live. She won the immediate support of her district superintendent, Edmund Daly, and now, in addition to her duties as principal, Miss Picchiotti directs the Juan Morel Campos Bilingual Center.

As visitors to the center are usually quick to note, the classes are small and the students spend much of their time talking rather than "studying" in the conventional sense. Classes are kept at from 10 to 12 students, grouped according to their ability to learn in English, the idea being to encourage active and spontaneous participation by putting the students on an equal linguistic footing. Oral communication is the first step toward full citizenship in those two linguistic worlds they inhabit, Miss Picchiotti says.

"I believe children must learn to speak a language—any language—idiomatically before they can learn to read and write it. Most of these children have learned to speak Spanish idiomatically at home, but until they can also speak English conversationally, it will always be a second language to them. That means teachers must be trained and conditioned to encourage the students to talk while they themselves listen."

Toward that end the teachers at Juan Morel Campos center have originated a variety of drills, dialogs, materials, and approaches designed to use speaking as a foundation for reading. Catherine Sullivan, the head teacher at the center and a former exchange teacher in Puerto Rico, says students may spend their first few months in English-as-a-second-language (ESL) classes talking, reciting, recording, and listening before they are asked to read. Meanwhile, they study arithmetic, science, social studies, and culture in Spanish with teachers qualified to teach at the elementary school level in both Spanish and English.

When the student arrives at the center, he goes through a series of pretests—oral, for the most part, and chiefly in Spanish—to identify his abilities in each subject in both languages. Most of the students speak almost no English when they arrive, and many show very skimpy skills in Spanish. They often are, in short, illiterate in two languages. Moreover, along with their educational handicaps, there are economic and social handicaps to be considered. Two thirds of the students are from families on welfare, and parents who do manage to find work usually hold marginal, low-paying jobs in nearby factories. Most of the youngsters are thus confronted not only by the assortment of disadvantages that hamper other urban children from low-income homes but by the complicating disadvantage of a language barrier.

This emphasis on student skills is reflected in the evaluation program developed under the guidance of District Superintendent Daly. This program falls into three main parts: self-evaluation and pretesting of each student when he arrives at the center, post-testing to determine how far he has come each year, and followup visits to high schools to measure and observe progress once he has left the center.

Making this system work, Miss Picchiotti says, meant "setting up our objectives first and concentrating on how to achieve them. Our original idea was to recruit students and keep them until they were completely functional in English, but we later dropped that. We still want children to be completely bilingual and bicultural, but we also are dealing with the social pressures teenagers apply to one another. Being out of one's age group can be embarrassing. So if a child is 14 years old and can become functional in English during high school, we won't keep him another year. Now we work toward getting the youngsters into high school at a reasonable age with enough preparation to give them a solid chance for success there."

Cultural diversity among students and staff is another important objective at the center. District Six principals nominate Spanish-speaking students for the bilingual program on the basis of teacher recommendations, but the center also recruits about ten "anglo" youngsters who are at or above grade level in their home schools and want to learn in a bilingual setting. These students study Spanish while their friends are in ESL classes, and gradually the two groups join in genuinely bilingual classes.

Likewise, four of the nine teachers at the center are anglo. "All our teachers are bilingual, but they don't all need to be bicultural," Miss Picchiotti says. "I prefer that our teachers reflect the community in which the children will live. I want the children to have an absolutely anglo accent when they speak English just as I want them to have a perfectly Spanish accent when they are speaking Spanish. They have to become acquainted with the culture of other than Spanish-speaking people. They must learn the point of view of the anglos in the community in which they live, and they can hardly get it unless they are with teachers and classmates truly representative of that point of view."

The emphasis is on what Miss Picchiotti refers to as "orchestration rather than assimilation or integration." The idea, she says, is that "children need to know about and understand their own customs and heritage as well as those of their adopted country, and how the two cultures harmonize." Classes in the history, geography, and culture of Puerto Rico, Mexico, the South and Central American countries, and the United States encourage children from these varied backgrounds to share their talents and experiences with their center classmates. Thus a recent birthday celebration for Juan Morel Campos featured a program of skits, songs, *danzas,* original poems, and recitations representing a blend of American and Spanish folkways.

Three other federally assisted programs reinforce this cultural exchange. An orientation and language development center (located in two classrooms in the school) helps children still newer to the city than those in the Juan Morel Campos program. It functions as a "port of entry" into the school system for children who speak absolutely no English when they arrive in Chicago, and is one of five such centers funded under ESEA Title I as part of the Chicago Board of Education's ESL program. A second program uses ESEA Title III funds for a bilingual-bicultural center that operates from 3 p.m. to 9 p.m. daily in the school and in four mobile classrooms parked next door. Children and adults in the community come to this center for tutoring, guidance and recreation programs directed by a Puerto Rican head teacher recommended by the community and appointed and paid by the Board of Education.

The third source of cultural exchange is an arrangement that provides Juan Morel Campos with teaching interns from the Bilingual Education Program at the Chicago Circle Campus of the University of Illinois. That program is for natives of Puerto

Rico who had entered teaching on the island after two years of college but need another two years of training in order to qualify to teach in mainland schools. Three or four interns usually are assigned to the center each semester, and by their backgrounds and experience they bring special perceptions to the students and a pragmatic view of the center's operation. One of their strongest opinions is that familiarity with Spanish and English is not of itself sufficient qualification for an effective bilingual teacher, a point also consistently advanced by Miss Picchiotti.

"Some people think anyone who can teach high school Spanish would obviously make a good bilingual teacher at the elementary school level," she says, "but that's far from the truth. Bilingual teachers must be qualified to teach not only reading but math and science or social studies and to do so at the elementary school level, where teaching techniques vary greatly from those used in high school. The fact is that courses don't exist in how to teach elementary school subjects in a bilingual setting so we do a lot of inservice work to help our teachers improve their skills. In any case, the point is that it takes special, specific training to produce an effective bilingual teacher." And it takes a special kind of attitude, she adds, for "we become almost an extension of the family. Teachers and parents become partners for the child."

The interns unanimously endorse these principles but have reservations about allowing students to graduate when they are not at grade level in every subject in both English and Spanish.

It would be easy if all our students were good students in Spanish before they arrived here, Mrs. Sullivan says, but we cannot assume that at all. You have to determine each child's achievement level in his own language in every subject and build your program from there. Content subjects—science, history, and the like—must be taught in the language and at the level suitable for the individual children in each class. If a lesson can be explained and understood in English, then that day's lesson will be taught in English. But if the children aren't ready for concepts or materials in English, they may spend all or part of that day's lesson learning in Spanish.

"Children in Puerto Rico must know their lessons before they go on to the next grade," one intern says. "Some of the students here do not know how to add and subtract and read and write at grade level when they graduate. The main problem is language, and for many students that problem remains unsolved when they leave. I know that the bilingual approach is better than putting them in classes where everyone speaks only English, but I think these children need to be taught in the full sense of the word 'teach.' I don't think they should leave here until they are at grade level."

Mrs. Sullivan and Robert Alexander, science teacher and the center's family liaison coordinator, do not dismiss that line of reasoning, but they point out that the situation is not as unequivocal as the criticism seems to suggest. For one thing, the teen-age pressure of keeping abreast of one's peers cannot be ignored without inviting some severe psychological scars. Equally important, the students leave the center only when they display a reasonably good chance of making it through high school academically and socially. Moreover, the teacher-parent-student partnership continues, and the staff seeks to place graduates in high school programs that let them continue, if necessary, one or two additional years of bilingual classes, tutoring, ESL, and other special help. In practice the majority of Juan Morel Campos center graduates attend Tuley High School in District Six, where ESL programs and Spanish-speaking teachers are available to continue "orchestrating" the students' further learning in both English and Spanish.

Meanwhile the center's program is constantly being refined on the basis of information gathered through followup contacts and other checkups. Posting scores for the 22 students in a recent graduating class, for example, shows some serious deficiencies in vocabulary and reading skills but somewhat greater progress in computation and problem-solving skills, a clear indication of the problem that language continues to present. The result has been greater emphasis on the use of English in all subjects.

On the other side of the coin, Alexander was especially pleased during his followup visits by the attitudes he found toward school in general and completion of high school in particular. All but two or three were demonstrably interested in their studies, doing well enough to keep their heads above water academically and looking forward to getting their high school diplomas. Most important they *were* in school, and they *were* learning.

"Perhaps their achievement wasn't sparkling," Alexander says, "but they had average to near-average grades, *and* they were moving ahead. The center doesn't put them at the top of their class in high school, but our graduating class enters high school with considerably more facility with English than when they first arrived here."

Still, Miss Picchiotti and members of the staff see the bilingual education concept as being only one part of the lasting complicated, and baffling puzzle of how to make education succeed in the innercity. Thus, they say, the importance of ventures such as Juan Morel Campos must be viewed not just in terms of immediate results but in terms also of the hints they provide as to how that puzzle may one day be put together. The center would seem to demonstrate, Miss Picchiotti, says, that a child's native language, culture, and customs can serve as invaluable reference points for his adaptation to a new language and a new culture. In short, "Harmony and orchestration may be far more rewarding than assimilation and integration have been."

Nevertheless, she adds, the fact is that American educators have not yet discovered ways to teach the children of poverty how to succeed in middle-class affluent society, even when those children speak English exclusively. "When that riddle is successfully dealt with, bilingual education will consist essentially of enabling children of Spanish-speaking backgrounds to struggle with the disadvantages of poverty in two languages rather than one. That is an important and useful advance, but it surely should not be mistaken for the solution to the larger puzzle."

Readers with questions about this model program may write to Miss Natalie Picchiotti, Juan Morel Campos Bilingual Center, 1520 North Claremont Ave., Chicago, IL. 60622.

Readers may also write directly to the Office of Education. For general information about reading programs, address Right to Read, U. S. Office of Education, 400 Maryland Avenue, S.W., Washington, D. C. 20202. With specific inquiries about bilingual education, please write to Dr. Albar Pena, Director, Bilingual Education, U. S. Office of Education, 400 Maryland Avenue S.W., Washington, D. C. 20202.

PART VI

ACHIEVEMENT AND
INTELLIGENCE:
CULTURAL INFLUENCES

CHAPTER 24

EDUCATION FOR THE SPANISH-SPEAKING: MAÑANA IN MOTION

ARMANDO RODRIGUEZ

YA BASTA, ES EL GRITO del pueblo Chicano. Ya basta, es el grito de todos los de hoy y los de ayer! Ya basta, de no tener los mismos privilegios que goza la mayoría de los cuidadanos en los Estados Unidos! Ya basta, de no tener la educación que queremos! Ya basta, de no tener el trabajo que necisitamos! Ya basta, de no tener la libertad que merecemos! Ya basta, de no tener los derechos civiles que debemos tener! YA BASTA!

If you did not understand the preceding paragraph, you experienced some of the same frustration and bewilderment that Spanish-speaking (and indeed all non-English-speaking) children undergo each day of their lives in the classrooms of this nation —classrooms where children are permitted to hear and speak only English and are forbidden the use of their native language.

The 1970 Federal Government Census will identify more than 10 million Spanish-speaking persons in the United States. The census process is designed to break down this ethnic count into Mexican-Americans, Puerto Ricans, Cubans, and other Latinos. The Mexican-American grouping will include Spanish-Americans, Latin-Americans, and a more recent and fast growing term, *Chicano*. The term *La Raza* also has been increasingly used in recent years to refer to the people and the cultural spirit of the Spanish-speaking.

Each of these terms denotes a particular philosophy regarding self-identification. To consider the Spanish-speaking a homogeneous group with a given set of characteristics and qualities is to

Education for the Spanish-speaking: mañana in motion. A. Rodriquez, National Elementary Principal *49*:52-6, Feb. '70.

Armando Rodriguez is Chief, Office for the Spanish-Speaking, U. S. Office of Education, Washington, D. C.

259

stereotype. In focusing on education in the United States, the term Spanish-speaking is more accurate than any other, including Spanish-surname, for the basic elements of educational difficulties are language and culture.

Of the 10 million Spanish-speaking population in the United States in 1970, the census will show that more than 6 million are Mexican-Americans, more than 2 million are Puerto Ricans, more than 1 million are Cubans, and the remaining 1 million Latinos are from other Spanish-speaking countries. Until 1965, the geographical placement found most Mexican-Americans in the five Southwestern states of Arizona, California, Colorado, New Mexico, and Texas; the Puerto Ricans in the New England and Middle Atlantic States; and the Cubans in Florida and the New York metropolitan area. During the period from 1965 to 1970, however, massive migrations of Mexican-Americans and Puerto Ricans, and to a lesser extent Cubans, took place into the Midwest states of Illinois, Michigan, Indiana, Ohio, and Wisconsin. Recent estimates indicate more than 400,000 Spanish-speaking people in the Chicago area alone. In addition thousands of Mexican-Americans dropped out of the migrant stream of the Southwest during this same five-year period, resulting in substantial Mexican-American population concentrations in Utah (50,000 in one valley near Salt Lake City), Missouri, Iowa, Kansas, and other states. In many cases, the newly arrived Chicanos joined second and third generation families in these areas.

Today more than 80 percent of the Spanish-speaking population live in urban environments. More than a million Puerto Ricans live in the New York metropolitan area. And more than 700,000 Mexican-Americans are living in Los Angeles, which ranks only behind Mexico City and Guadalajara in concentration of population. These concentrations find the Spanish-speaking population leading all groups in percentage of population under 20 years of age—more than 60 percent. These movements into our urban areas have raised an even heavier challenge to the inner-city school's responsibility for equal educational opportunity for all students.

The history of the education of the Spanish-speaking in the United States is filled with tragedy. With the treaty of Guadalupe Hidalgo, concluding the Mexican-American War of 1846 to 1848, automatic American citizenship was given to all those living in the territory included in the treaty for the most part, portions of the five Southwest states of Arizona, California, Colorado, New Mexico, and Texas.

Unfortunately, full-fledged citizenship did not give them a right to be educated. The diversity among the Anglos, Mexicans, and Indians in customs, traditions, aspirations, and attitudes was tremendous. With the absence of any program of acculturation by the United States government, even though the majority were Spanish-speaking and Indian, this population remained linguistically and culturally isolated and rejected. They were unassimilated citizens, subject to the political dominance of a foreign culture—the Anglo-American culture.

By 1870, with the coming of the railroads, the West had become a prime target for economic exploitation. The need for labor was great, and the nation turned to Mexico and the Far East for manpower. The increased population which came about as a result gave little help to a growing country whose eyes were not on creating institutions to meet rising problems. George Sanchez, in his paper, "Spanish in the Southwest," says, "Virtually no thought was given to the educational, economic, or political rehabilitation of these Spanish-speaking peoples. After 1910, the opportunity passed."

It was not until during the decade of the 1950's that the critical educational needs of the Spanish-speaking surfaced prominently and then the primary impetus came from two sources. For the Mexican-Americans, it was the entrance of a large number of Mexican-American male teachers into education. The G.I. Bill of Rights gave college opportunity to thousands of Mexican-American veterans, many of whom entered the field of education. They quickly realized—having been both student and teacher—that the public educational process was not designed to provide equal educational opportunity for success to bilingual-bicultural children. As these Mexican-American educators moved into positions of experience and administration, they began to raise the question of the failure of the schools.

The other source of stimulation came from the impact of

thousands of Puerto Rican youngsters descending upon the schools of New York City and other Eastern cities. Here American citizens sought equal educational opportunity on the mainland from a school system whose previous response to non-English-speaking students was limited, for the most part, to a few language classes for the foreign born. Coinciding with this movement was the influx of Cubans into Florida and later to other parts of the East Coast.

As a result, the public school system from coast to coast was faced with an additional educational challenge never before faced with such force. The three-pronged attack by the Mexican-Americans in the Southwest (still living to a great extent in the status of the conquered, both educationally and economically), the Puerto Ricans (newly discovered American citizens demanding full rights of citizenship in the mainland schools), and the political refugees from Cuba (seeking educational opportunities needed for a new life in the United States) severely shook the traditional school approach designed to deal with the monolingual, monocultural client.

By 1963, following the release of the educational information from the 1960 census, it was clear that the schools were failing the bilingual-bicultural child. The median level of education among Mexican-Americans was 8.6 years of school as compared with 10.5 for the Negro and 12.1 for the Anglo and "others." As late as 1964, 18 percent of the Mexican-American men and 22 percent of the Mexican-American women were classified as "functionally illiterate." This compared with 9 percent for Negro men and 4 percent for Negro women. The real tragedy in the education of the Spanish-speaking was revealed, however, in the dropout rate. As late as 1969, more than 50 percent of the Mexican-American students in two predominantly Mexican-American high schools in Los Angeles left school before graduation. Approximately the same situation was true in predominantly Mexican-American high schools, in San Antonio and El Paso. In many cases, the reason the students gave for dropping out was simply, "The quality of education I received, even if I had a high school diploma, prepared me for little real economic opportunity."

Texas found that along the Mexican border more than 90 percent of the Mexican-American students dropped two grades behind by the fourth grade. Tom Carter of the University of Texas at El Paso estimates that, until recently, more than 80 percent of Mexican-American youngsters starting school in Texas did not finish. By 1965, more than 80 percent of all Mexican-Americans were living in Texas and California, placing heavy educational responsibility for change upon those state departments of education and the local school districts they serve.

Spurred by the dismal picture of educational attainment of the Spanish-speaking revealed by the 1960 census, a number of studies focusing on this problem were started during the 1960's. The most notable early study was *The Mexican-American Study Project* developed by the Graduate School of Administration, Division of Research, University of California at Los Angeles, through a Ford Foundation grant. The study dealt with the educational, economic, housing, employment, and allied areas of life of the Mexican-American. While not proposing any solutions, it effectively identified the major areas of human distress for the bilingual-bicultural person. In 1966, a survey by the California State Department of Education, through its Bureau of Intergroup Relations, disclosed that more than 14 percent of the public school enrollment was Spanish-surname; yet less than 1 percent of the student enrollment at the seven university campuses was Spanish-speaking.

A recurring portrait of the educational difficulties of the Spanish-speaking began emerging by 1965. The basic problem was the inability of the school to cope with the language and cultural assets of the Spanish-speaking youngster. Many Spanish-speaking children came to school speaking Spanish with a limited or nonexistent communication skill in English. Frequently the youngster was functionally noncommunicative in both languages. Yet here was a client with a high potential to become a bilingual member of society. The general approach of the school was to place the youngster in an English as a Second Language class. The purpose, obviously, was to teach the child sufficient English to enable him to learn in the English-dominated classroom environment. The Spanish-speaking child might spend more than two years learning English, isolated from the rest of his class-mates and any subject matter learning for a large part of the school day. As a means of hastening the acquisition of English, the speaking of Spanish was forbidden at school.

The result was inevitable. The child was caught in a language and culture conflict between his home and the school. He began to doubt his identity as a member of a family with a treasured language and culture and suspect the motives of the school in in-sisting that he reject his linguistic and cultural diversity in order to meet the standards of the system. He dropped behind his classmates because he was taught little subject matter—only En-glish. He found little or nothing in the school curriculum and materials—especially in the books—that he could identify with his role in this country. Even more frustrating for him was the fact that far too often the teacher of English as a Second Lan-guage did not speak Spanish. Probably one of the most destruc-tive aspects of his educational experience was the general atti-tude of the school toward its responsibility for developing an educational program to meet the needs of the bilingual-bicultur-al child. Certainly few, if any, schools until recently considered it one of their responsibilities to prepare their constituents to live in a pluralistic linguistic and cultural society. An immediate outgrowth of this attitude has been the massive movement in both colleges and high schools for ethnic and racial studies pro-grams during the past three years.

Where are we today and where must we go? Education for the Spanish-speaking today—and this is really mañana in motion—is moving forcefully in several promising directions. The Chicano Youth Movement which has raised so eloquently the cry, "Ya Basta," has focused its efforts on destroying the belief that the bilingual-bicultural person is "disadvantaged." The participants are striking at the long-held debilitating syndrome that the school can educate only those whose mold fits the curriculum. They are saying that if that is the extent of the school's capacity then truly the school is a "disadvantaged" institution. They are main-taining that if the school, which really means society, talks about "disadvantaged children," this is in essence saying they are in-

ferior and not a great deal can be expected of them. This leads
to a self-fulfilling prophecy where children are put into "disadvantaged," that is, "inferior" programs.

If, on the other hand, we focus on "disadvantaged institutions," this implies accepting the responsibility for inadequate
institutions or "institutional deprivation." A child who doesn't
learn to read by the age of 5 or 6 may later learn to read. However, if he is taught that he is "disadvantaged," that is, "inferior"
at 5 or 6, he may never overcome it.

I am constantly shocked when I hear about the thousands of
Spanish-speaking youngsters who have been tabbed as "disadvantaged" merely because they did not come to school speaking
English. What we fail to realize is that they came to school with
a rich potential to be a bilingual-bicultural person—a highly desired personal and national value in almost every country in the
world except ours. The school must predicate this whole picture
of attitude change by recognizing that high morale, which is one
of the characteristics of any effective institution, is related to
"value infusion" and "pride." *Few effective institutions consider
their participants "disadvantaged."* This means that the school
must accept the Spanish-speaking youngster based on these principles:

1. The Spanish-speaking child can learn. The language barrier
   or the cultural conflict is a false apology for the failures of
   the school.
2. The Spanish-speaking child and his parents have the same
   high aspirations and expectations as the Anglo and the
   black.
3. Language—Spanish in the case of the Spanish-speaking
   youngster—is an effective tool for learning. To destroy a
   child's language is to destroy him as a person with identity
   and self-esteem.
4. Cultural heritage—a rich resource in the Spanish-speaking
   child—must be a visible, viable part of his school experience. Cultural cognizancy must be a continual curriculum
   entity.
5. Training programs should be established which will enable

the teacher and administrator to have confidence that they can be successful with the bilingual-bicultural child.

6. The parents and the community must be involved in the decisions that direct the education of their child. Spanish-speaking parents do want to be a part of this process.

The direction in the education of the Spanish-speaking is tied completely to the acceptance of diversity in our society. The National Advisory Committee on Mexican-American Education, a committee created by the U. S. Office of Education, in its first report to the Secretary of Health, Education, and Welfare, *The Mexican-American: Quest for Equality,* documents the disaster of education for the Spanish-speaking and makes these observations and recommendations:

> The melting pot ideology that we speak of so proudly has not produced a moral climate in which all citizens are accepted on the basis of individual worth. . . . Educators, especially, must search their consciences for an answer to the question: Is only a monolingual, monocultural society acceptable in America?
>
> We must immediately train at least 100,000 bilingual-bicultural teachers and administrators.
>
> We must agitate for priority funding by the U. S. Office of Education to develop educational programs immediately.
>
> We must see that testing instruments are developed that will accurately measure the intelligence and achievement potential of the bilingual-bicultural child.
>
> We must provide assistance, through federal funds, to Spanish-speaking students in the pursuit of a college education.
>
> We must help the various states to recognize the need for statewide programs in bilingual-bicultural education.

For the bilingual-bicultural child, his experiences in the first few years in school are far more important in determining his future educational success than they are with the Anglo or the black. He must bridge that linguistic and cultural chasm. Bilingual education programs are a must. Bilingual education, in which the child is taught in his native language—Spanish—until he is able to communicate in English—and then using both languages for learning, is the path that will lead him to acquire the tools for educational success. For most schools, the use of Title I, ESEA funds will provide the financial resources necessary to develop a program. And the use of these funds in a positive program to achieve learning capability at the beginning is a far wiser and more profitable investment than the remedial programs later on. If there must be one priority for early childhood education for the Spanish-speaking, it is bilingual education on the very first day of school.

The second area of need for the Spanish-speaking involves the relationship of the elementary school to the community. For many years to come, there will be a shortage of bilingual-bicultural teachers. As a result, the Anglo teacher and the black teacher and administrator will be faced with a real challenge in understanding the feelings of their Spanish-speaking constituents. Simply put, do not try to mold the Spanish-speaking child into your cultural values. Preservation of the cultural values, attitudes, customs, and traditions of the Spanish-speaking is imperative in developing a successful teaching-learning environment. By promoting diverse cultural and linguistic values we will strengthen, not weaken, a school's educational programs.

I have not made an effort in this article to delve in depth into the education of the Spanish-speaking. Instead, I hope that future issues of this journal will contain observations by experts on many of the educational challenges and ways of meeting them. In the meantime, I would recommend that any reader dealing with the education of Spanish-speaking youngsters in early childhood education programs obtain a copy of *Disadvantaged Mexican-American Children and Early Educational Experiences,* published by the Southwest Educational Development Corporation, Austin, Texas. This booklet provides some provocative observations on teaching the bilingual-bicultural child and has an excellent bibliography.

The poet, Alberto Alurista, portrays the spirit of the movement for education for the Spanish-speaking today:

> *Mis ojos hinchados*
> *flooded with lágrimas*
> *de bronce*
> *melting on the cheek bones*
> *of my concern*
> *razgos indigenos*

the scars of history on my face
and the veins of my body
that aches
vomito sangre
y lloro libertad
I do not ask for freedom
I am freedom

Spanish-speaking peoples repudiate the idea of rehabilitation as a condition for their share in the American Dream. Education has the highest responsibility to strike a blow at that idea by using all its resources to instill in all people, but particularly those going through the schools and those employed in the schools, the vital fact that the United States is a country united. The bonds of unity are strengthened by the richness of differences—the linguistic and cultural diversity—that make each individual a sacred entity whose destiny is bound to every other person by our American belief that the worth of the individual is paramount.

CHAPTER 25

CULTURE CONFLICT AND MEXICAN-AMERICAN ACHIEVEMENT

NEAL JUSTIN

IT APPEARS THAT THE least-educated citizens in the U. S. are the Mexican-Americans. Nearly 1,000,000 Spanish-speaking children in the Southwest never will go beyond the eighth grade.[1] In some areas, up to 90 percent of the Mexican-Americans fail to complete high school.[2]

What are some of the causes of deprivation and failure among the Mexican-Americans? Four closely related areas are of concern: language, discrimination, lower socioeconomic status, and culture.

The most obvious identifying characteristic of the Mexican-Americans is their language. The Tucson Survey of the Teaching of Spanish to the Spanish-Speaking by the National Education Association placed great emphasis on the influence of the Spanish language and its use as related to academic achievement.[3] In fact, the language barrier currently is given more attention than any other factor affecting Mexican-American achievement.

The use of the Spanish language by the Mexican-Americans has played a definite role in the isolation and discrimination of these people by the Anglos. The preservation of the Spanish language has been interpreted by the dominant group as "a persistent symbol and instrument of isolation."[4] While the Anglo tends to consider the use of Spanish as an indication of foreignness, the Mexican-Americans consider it a symbol of their unity and loyalty to *La Raza.*[5]

In his discussion on barriers to Mexican integration, Officer stated that "the greatest hindrance to complete cultural assimilation of Tucson's Mexicans is the language problem."[6] Apparent-

Reprinted from *School & Society,* January 1970, by permission of the author and publisher.

ly, this opinion has been shared widely by educators, if we can judge from the adjustments made for Mexican-Americans in curricula.

There is evidence that the language barrier, although important, may be overrated. Available research shows that language need not be an insurmountable barrier to the academic and intellectual achievement of youngsters who come from foreign language-speaking homes.[7] Henderson points out that "the current mania for structural linguistics as a panacea for educational problems of Mexican-American children is another example of a language centered curriculum emphasis."[8] Moreover, he shows that the Mexican-American pupils who spoke the most Spanish also could speak the most English.[9] Nevertheless, most educators consider the language barrier as the major obstacle to the Mexican-American's success and achievement in school.

There is substantial evidence, however, that the greater emphasis should be placed on the socio-cultural problems of the Mexican-American. The ugly factors of discrimination and prejudice have played and continue to play an important role in keeping the Mexican-Americans in a subservient position. The Mexican coming to the U. S. is confronted with a double problem of prejudice. In Mexico, class discrimination is commonplace, but discrimination against color is unusual. Here, unfortunately, discrimination and prejudice commonly are based on both class and color.

Prejudice against the Mexicans and Mexican-Americans in the Southwest generally follows this pattern: lack of job opportunities, lack of educational opportunities, segregation in housing, lack of equality before the law, and various kinds of social discrimination.[10] Among the major reasons for this situation are a strong history of lower socioeconomic status, darker skin color, language, conflicting cultural traits and customs, and religion.

For the most part, discrimination against the Mexican-Americans is subtle in nature. While the Mexican-American enjoys all the legal rights of citizenship, he is the victim of extralegal discrimination. It is this special type of discrimination which led Tuck to call her book *Not with the Fist*. In it, she comments: "Rather than having the job of battering down a wall, the Mexican-American finds himself entangled in a spider web, whose outlines are difficult to see but whose clean, silken strands hold tight."[11]

The inferior socioeconomic status of the Mexican-Americans may be greater than most Americans would like to admit. Although Mexican-Americans are found in all walks of life, an examination of the 1960 U. S. Census data shows that they occupy an overwhelmingly large position in the lower-ranking occupations. Almost 75 percent of the Mexican-Americans are employed as manual workers. This concentration in the unskilled occupations has had a severe effect upon their incomes. The 1960 Census data indicate that the Mexican-Americans in the Southwest earned between $1,000 and $2,000 less per year than did the Anglo unskilled workers. In all of the five Southwestern states, the average incomes of Mexican-Americans are far below that of the population in general.

The greatest barrier to the acculturation, assimilation, and achievement of the Mexican-Americans probably is culture conflict. Other immigrant groups to the U. S. have felt the blow of discrimination.[12] The Chinese, Jews, Italians, Irish, Polish, etc., are common examples. However, the faster the immigrant group moves toward adopting the customs and language of the dominant culture, the less discrimination they seem to experience.[13] Madsen believes that any ethnic group that fails to show a maximum faith in America, science, and progress will be subject to discrimination. It would be additionally difficult for the members of this group to assimilate if they are physically distinguishable, if they use a foreign language, and if they hold to cultural ways that are not compatible with the dominant culture.[14]

Unlike other immigrant groups, the Mexican-Americans have preferred to hold to their Mexican cultural ways and Spanish language. This may be attributed to their close proximity to Mexico.

The question then arises: Which of the Mexican-American cultural ways is in greatest conflict with the dominant Anglo culture? Extensive and careful review of numerous studies by Angell, Chilcott, Kluckhohn, Madsen, Simmons, Strodtbeck, Zintz, and others indicates that there are two Mexican cultural characteristics that are the mirror image of the Anglo culture. These are concerned with feelings of personal control (fatalism) and delay of gratification (future orientation). Could it be that even third- or fourth-generation Mexican-American students are actually more fatalistic and present-time oriented than their Anglo peers? What might this mean in terms of curriculum and cultural conflict?

To answer these questions, the writer set up an exploratory study at the College of Education, University of Arizona.[15] A total of 168 male, Mexican-American seniors and 209 male, Anglo seniors were selected randomly for testing at four urban Tucson high schools. A special questionnaire, adapted from a similar instrument developed by the Institute of Behavioral Science, University of Colorado, was revised, judged for content validity, tested for reliability, and then administered to the sample population.

The statistical analysis of the data pertaining to the two cultural characteristics of delayed gratification (future orientation) and feelings of personal control (fatalism) provided a number of significant differences when the means of the two sample populations were subjected to independent tests.

The Mexican-Americans showed a mean of 6.90 on the measurement of their feelings of personal control, while their Anglo peers had a mean of 8.51. Measurement of the tendency to delay gratification provided a mean of 3.99 for the Mexican-Americans and 4.63 for the Anglos. In each case, the differences between these means were significant at the .05 level.

Marked contrast, therefore, is seen between the Mexican-Americans and the Anglos. The Mexican-Americans are significantly lacking in feelings of personal control and concern with delayed gratification when compared to their Anglo peers. These findings indicate that, whatever culture change has taken place among the second-, third-, and fourth-generation Mexican-Americans, it has not been great with reference to these two characteristics. It also should be considered that the students selected for this study were second-semester seniors and were, therefore, a select group of achievers in relation to their many peers who already have dropped out of school. One may have good cause to wonder how great these differences would have been if the study had been done with junior high students. Even with these very conservative results, the Mexican-Americans are seen to be significantly different from their Anglo peers.

Assuming that most of our school curricula are constructed by Anglos who apparently have significantly different orientations to life, then what over-all effect does this have upon the Mexican-American youngsters? What conflicts may be built into the curriculum that could permeate the whole subculture of education? Kneller provides a word to the wise when he asserts that, before we can attain our educational goals, we must be aware of the internalized antagonisms of the culture that may thwart the efforts of teachers.[16] Could it be that our Anglo-dominated curricula inadvertently thwart the efforts of both the Mexican-American students and their teachers? There may be a good reason to consider the findings of this study. Perhaps, we should examine the appropriateness of our curricula as they apply to the Mexican-American student in particular.

REFERENCES

1. Department of Rural Education, NEA: The invisible minority, Report of the NEA—Tucson Survey on the teaching of Spanish to the Spanish speaking, Washington, NEA, 1966, p. 6.
2. Chilcott, John H.: Some perspectives for teaching first generation Mexican-Americans, in *Readings in the Socio-Cultural Foundations of Education,* Belmont, Wadsworth, 1968, p. 359.
3. ————: The invisible minority, in *Readings in the Socio-Cultural Foundations of Education,* Belmont, Wadsworth, 1968, p. 359.
4. Broom, Leonard, and Shevsky, Eshref: Mexicans in the United States . . . a problem in social differentiation, *Sociology & Social Research, 36:* 153, January-February, 1952.
5. Madsen, William: *The Mexicans of South Texas,* New York, Holt, Rinehart, Winston, 1965, p. 106.
6. Officer, James: Barriers of Mexican integration in Tucson, *The Kiva 17:* 7, May 1951.
7. Tyler, Leona Elizabeth: *The Psychology of Human Deficiencies,* New York, Appleton-Century-Crofts, 1956, p. 305.
8. Henderson, Ronald W.: *Environmental Stimulation & Intellectual Development of Mexican-American Children: An Exploratory Study,* unpublished Ph.D. dissertation, University of Arizona, 1966, p. 142.
9. Henderson, Ronald W.: *Environmental Stimulation & Intellectual Devel-*

opment of Mexican-American Children: An Exploratory Study, unpublished Ph.D. dissertation, University of Arizona, 1966, p. 144.

10. Burma, John H.: *Spanish-Speaking Groups in the United States,* Durham, Duke University, 1954, p. 107.

11. Tuch, Ruth: *Not with the Fist,* New York, Harcourt Brace, 1946, p. 168.

12. Mach, Raymond W.: *Race, Class and Power,* New York, American Book Company, 1963, p. 118.

13. Mach, Raymond W.: *Race, Class and Power,* New York, American Book Co., 1963, p. 118.

14. Madsen, William: *The Mexicans of South Texas,* New York, Holt, Rinehart & Winston, 1965, p. 1.

15. Justin, Neal: *The Relationships of Certain Socio-Cultural Factors to the Academic Achievement of Male Mexican-American High School Seniors,* unpublished Ed.D. dissertation, University of Arizona, 1969.

16. Kneller, George F.: *Educational Anthropology: An Introduction,* New York, Wiley, 1965, p. 14.

CHAPTER 26

MEXICAN-AMERICAN GROUP COHESIVENESS AND ACADEMIC ACHIEVEMENT

GUY J. MANASTER and MARK B. KING

THE PURPOSE OF THIS STUDY was to combine a macroscopic viewpoint, a popular assumption about an ethnic group, and a single, if crude, population statistic to test an hypothesis.

The assumption is that Mexican-Americans (adults also, but in this instance adolescents) stick together, are "clannish" and "cliquish" or, more properly, are highly cooperative so that strict adherence to group norms is usual.[1-3] If and when this is true, the population variance, in whatever criterion, would be less for Mexican-Americans than for comparison groups. The hypothesis under study is that Mexican-American students' cliquishness is related to their minority status and that this may be tested in schools by comparing variance in achievement (GPA).

The hypothesis is gross, and it is recognized that a variety of contextual and situational variables may weigh on the results. Nonetheless, the value of the study is its simplicity in using GPA as an almost unobtrusive measure. Do Mexican-American students stick together more when they have to—when they are the minority—or is it a general characteristic of their culture? GPA variance is used in this study as a measure of sticking together, clannishness, and adhering to a group norm.

Formally, the hypothesis is: when Mexican-American students are in the minority in a school, the variance of their GPA scores will be lower than the other groups in the school, whereas, when they are the majority, their population variance of GPA scores will not differ from the other groups in the school.

METHOD

Data were collected in the public schools of a medium-sized southwestern U. S. city at two levels; seventh and tenth grades.

Manaster, Guy J., and King, Mark B., "Mexican Group Cohesiveness and Academic Achievement," *Urban Education* *VII(3)*:235-40, October 1972.

TABLE 25-I

School	Percentage Mexican-American	Black	White	Number of Students
Junior High				
1	85	11	4	228
2	54	43	3	275
3	30	39	31	419
High School				
1	60	31	9	385
2	30	2	68	253
3	18	14	68	277
Total number of students				1,837

The sample consisted of all students in those grades whose records were complete, from the racially mixed schools as shown in Table 25-I.

With the assistance of school system personnel, the Director of Student Development, and the Director of Research, schools were selected for the sample according to the percentage of Mexican-American students recorded in attendance. The intention was to sample, at both grade levels, from

1. a school composed of a very clear Mexican-American majority;
2. a school with an even ratio of Mexican-Americans to others; and
3. a school composed of a very clear Mexican-American minority.

It was hoped that the category "other" students in all six schools could be of the same racial composition, but this was impossible. The schools were chosen from predominantly working-class areas. The sample obtained was the closest available.

Grades from academic courses (i.e. English, math, social science, science, foreign language) were used to compute GPA. The significant variability of Mexican-American GPA scores in relation to black-white (other) scores was determined by the F-test.

RESULTS

The variances of Mexican-American scores do not differ significantly at the .05 level from the black-white (other) scores in any school in the sample. In fact, with one exception, Junior High School 3 (see Table 25-II), the ratios of variance of Mexican-American scores to other scores are in the predicted directions.

In the school in which Mexican-Americans are in the largest majority, Junior High 1 (85% Mexican-American), the Mexican-Americans showed a greater variance of scores than did the others, although this is not statistically significant.

In the two schools in which Mexican-Americans were only slightly in the majority, High School 1 (60% Mexican-American) and Junior High 1 (54% Mexican-American), there was virtually *no* difference between the variance of Mexican-Americans and others.

In two of the three schools in which Mexican-Americans were in the minority, High School 2 (30% Mexican-American) and High School 3 (18% Mexican-American), the Mexican-American scores displayed a lesser degree of variance than did the others, albeit at approximately the .10 level of significance.

However, in Junior High 3 (30% Mexican-American), although the Mexican-Americans are in the minority, their GPA score variance was significantly (.10) greater than the variance of the others.

DISCUSSION

The Mexican-American students who attended Junior High 3 were found to be from families which differed in at least two respects from the Mexican-American families represented in the other schools. They were of higher socioeconomic status, and

TABLE 25-II

VARIANCE OF GPA SCORES

School	% Mex.-Am.	Mex.-Am. S^2	Other S^2	F	$p < .05$	$p < .10$
Junior High 1	85	.8724	.6889	1.2663	1.68	1.46
High School 1	60	.8604	.8341	1.0315	1.22	1.19
Junior High 2	54	.7165	.7451	1.0399	1.35	1.26
High School 2	30	.6887	.8675	1.2596	1.35	1.29
Junior High 3	30	.7735	.6438	1.2014	1.22	1.19
High School 3	18	.7455	.9765	1.3098	1.42	1.29

they had moved from a Spanish-speaking community to the primarily Anglo neighborhood surrounding Junior High School 3.

The data from Junior High School 3 may be interpreted in a number of ways. The Mexican-American students in Junior High School 3 may be more "middle class" in achievement and value patterns than the remaining Mexican-American and other students in the sample. This interpretation prompts conclusions which refer to working-class Mexican-American students and which differentiate between the applicability of the hypothesis to working-class and middle-class students.

It may also be, however, that differing integration patterns emerge as having effects on achievement variance. The Mexican-American students in Junior High School 3 are from upwardly mobile families and live in a more racially integrated, primarily working-class area. The other Mexican-American students live in predominantly working-class Mexican-American neighborhoods. There may be an artifact effect such that Mexican-American minority groups in schools or any group when a minority in a school, are restricted in their range of social status, thus limiting their variance. However, for the comparative purpose of this paper, the hypothesis about working-class Mexican-American students across schools is not affected by this phenomenon.

The hypothesis was not confirmed precisely, but the trends seem worth noting. First, the prediction was reversed for middle-class Mexican-American students: they do not seem to stick together, as expressed by their GPA variance, when they are a minority in a school. Second, working-class Mexican-American students, when a minority in a school, show more cliquishness and have a smaller population variance on GPA than the others, but when the racial ratios are fairly even, this difference does not exist, as was predicted. Third, when the Mexican-American students are a clear majority, their variance seems to be larger.

In answer to the major question of this study, the data tentatively may be interpreted as saying: Those Mexican-American students who most need to, for reasons such as security (and those who are most prevalent and most studied), the working-class students, stick together more than their peers (as shown by lesser variance in their GPA scores) when they are forced to by the pressure of being the minority in a school. They are not as clannish and their variance is not relatively smaller when they are equally represented in a school; they would seem to be less clannish and show greater variance when they are a clear majority.

These findings raise questions about the basic assumption concerning this ethnic group and force one to posit that possibly any group, when in the minority, societally or in a particular institution, will tend to stick together and show less variance. It may be that much of the thinking concerning Mexican-Americans has tapped communalities related to their minority-group status and not those basic to their culture.

Also, if grade variance is swayed by the majority/minority situation, as our exploratory study has shown, the implications regarding integration are glaring. Mexican-Americans will become the minority group in many schools and are likely to pursue their course in this "minority huddle," strangling their spread of scholastic achievement. Where integration is carried out with attention devoted to both social status and neighborhood, there may be a greater chance to spread and raise academic accomplishment among Mexican-Americans.

REFERENCES

1. Hayden, R. G.: Spanish-Americans of the Southwest. *Welfare in Rev, 4:* 14, 1966.
2. Kluckhohn, F. R., and Strodtbeck, F. L.: *Variations in Value Orientations.* Evanston, Ill., Row, Peterson, 1961.
3. Madsen, W.: *Mexican-Americans of South Texas.* New York, Holt, Rinehart & Winston, 1964.

CHAPTER 27

SPANISH BILINGUAL STUDENTS AND INTELLIGENCE TESTING

MINERVA MENDOZA-FRIEDMAN

THE PROBLEM

THE STUDENTS. Chicano students in this country usually are not proficient in English or Spanish. For this reason, it is no solution to simply translate standardized tests or instructional materials into Spanish. There are cultural differences which also invalidate any such simple approach. Furthermore, the majority of Spanish bilingual students in the United States live in impoverished homes which have little in common with the school environment or the world pictured in the schoolbooks. This is also true of other minorities and poor-white children, and, to that extent, most of this article can be generalized to those groups.

The impact of intelligence testing on the community of Spanish-speaking children is this: A disproportionately high number are wrongly classified as "mentally retarded" on the basis of a test, and placed in educable mentally retarded (EMR) classes. For all practical purposes, this marks the end of their education. The child who might have developed normally becomes an academic retardate. The vast majority of Chicano children bear the stigma of subnormal intelligence scores in their "cum-folders" all through the school years. Teachers who look at these scores for guidance have low expectations of the Chicano children, which often become self-fulfilling prophecies. The children fall farther and farther behind as they travel through the grades, frequently dropping out of high school. The Chicano dropout rate is one of the highest in this country. Thus, the educational

Minerva Mendoza-Friedman, a California classroom teacher, delivered this paper to the QuEST conference of the California Federation of Teachers in February, 1973.

Friedman, Minerva Mendoza, "Spanish Bilingual Students and Intelligence Testing," *Changing Education*, Spring, 1973.

system and testing helps to keep our people impoverished, unemployed, and ignorant.

THE TESTS. The standardized tests do not identify the actual intellectual capabilities and potentialities of our children. Although there is much rhetoric about discovering "hidden ability," the main effect of the most widely-used tests is to stamp a child with a rating based primarily on his mastery of academic-type skills, most of all, *verbal fluency.* As a group, Chicano children fall at the bottom end of the scale, with very few individual exceptions. Many children score as "mentally retarded" on the tests, despite the fact that in their day-to-day activity (as witnessed by experienced teachers) they display mental quickness, normal or above-normal abilities, and so on. This calls into question the overall validity of the tests as applied to Chicano children.

We have in mind individual and group tests such as the Stanford-Binet, WISC, Culture-Fair Intelligence Test, Peabody Picture Vocabulary Test (and the Lorge-Thorndike Intelligence Tests which are mandated by the state of California for all sixth- and 12th-graders). The defenders of these tests argue that they *predict* academic success or failure: this is how the publishers justify the value of their product. This "prediction argument" misses the point altogether. Of course, the student who fails the tests tends to fail in his or her classwork, and conversely.

Both the test and the classroom materials are inappropriate for the Chicano bilingual/bicultural child. But there is a certain "scientific sanctity" to the IQ tests, which pretend to measure innate abilities. Therefore, the low IQ scores become a justification—a rationalization—for the failure of the educational system to meet the needs of Chicano children. The blame is placed on the children: supposedly the test "proves" that the child is "not bright enough" to do the classwork. This is why any serious attempt to carry out educational reform runs head-on into the testing system at an early stage.

THE GOALS OF EDUCATION

The educational system should function as an equalizing institution—not to pull anybody down to a low common denominator, but to counteract the effects of poverty, racism, and ignorance by providing each child with a sound basic education regardless of that child's social background. This is not an act of charity, but a right of all citizens and a necessity for the welfare of our nation as a whole. Public education in the U. S. is *rhetorically* committed to that goal, but as teachers and trade-unionists, we should fight to make the rhetoric become a reality.

There is some social mobility in the U. S., but this only benefits a handful of Chicanos. In order to compete for decent jobs, one needs a good education. Our children are not getting a good education, and it is no defense of the system to point at a few minuscule experimental bilingual programs scattered around the country. The main problem is to improve and transform the instructional system to serve our children. This means special teaching methods and specially trained teachers, appropriate books and programs, and a thoroughly revamped curriculum. And it means tossing out the window a system of standardized tests that fail our students and rationalize their failure.

The pernicious thing about standardized testing is that it provides pseudoscientific "evidence" to justify elitist educational practices. The most important tests in use today give a gigantic advantage to the children of college-educated, "school-oriented" parents. They rest upon academic skills, while purporting to measure such intuitive concepts as "brightness." They attach a low number to a Chicano child and then theorize, at his expense, as to what part of that low number is due to innate stupidity rather than a nonacademic environment and cultural-language differences.

To sum it up: The defenders of the current system of standardized testing use elitist arguments which are realistic-sounding only to the extent that the educational system is actually elitist in practice. "The Chicano child is destined to fail in school. Therefore, it is only fair that he or she fail the tests also." In fact, this proves that the tests are valid. And in turn, the tests prove that the schools are not to blame for failing the child. "He or she just isn't bright enough." This is the circular argument, corresponding to the vicious circle of low-expectation and low-achievement in which the Chicano child is caught. It is tied up with other elitist approaches to education, such as the widely-used *tracking system* with its concomitant racial segregation within ostensibly integrated schools.

HISTORY OF THIS CONTROVERSY IN THE U. S.

The academic literature contains studies of bilingualism and intelligence since the early part of this century in the U. S. Typical of the earliest papers is a comparison of Anglo and Chicano children in a Texas school system, done by Adeline White Scott in 1926. Ignoring the gross inequities between the two groups (not only language problems, but racial segregation and class differences) the author concludes that the "Mexican" children are of inferior intellience. She cites earlier studies which established a ranging of races and nationalities by intelligence (e.g., intelligence is inversely proportional to the percentage of black blood).

During the 1930s and '40s, there was a gradual shift in the position of researchers, although the prevailing opinion remained that bilingualism was detrimental to intellectual development. The experiments which justified this conclusion seem very crude and error-ridden by today's standards. Socio-economic differences among the test subjects were not taken into account, and even the notion of what constitutes bilingualism was vague and primitive.

This is a clear case of American provincialism. In other parts of the world, e.g. Europe and Latin America, bilingualism is most commonly found among the educated classes. No one would dream of arguing, for example, that an educated European would suffer intellectually as a result of training in French, English, and German. Here, in the U. S., bilingualism is mostly found in foreign-language communities formed through immigration, usually impoverished and poorly educated. Certainly this is the case of Chicano people in the U. S. By ignoring this basic fact, early researchers were led to attach a stigma to bilingualism itself as a cause of academic-intellectual difficulties. This stigma became part of the pressure-toward-conformity which has tended to suppress the cultural individuality of minority groups in the U. S.

Following the civil-rights movement of the early 1960s, many traditional educational practices were called into question including not only segregation, but the tracking system and standardized testing. Thus, the issue has become a public and political controversy rather than merely an academic dispute.

In 1971 and 1972, court cases were raised by Chicano and black organizations to prevent the use of standardized test scores for labeling minority children or placing them in mentally-retarded classes. The Bay Area Association of Black Psychologists, and the California Rural Legal Assistance (representing Chicano children) have entered suits. Some cases are still pending, while partial victories have been won in others. In San Diego, where 20 student plaintiffs sued the public schools for $400,000 in damages for the years they had spent in EMR classes, a decision was handed down which granted to all misplaced students in the district a token $1 each. The district agreed to eliminate racial and cultural bias from its placement tests.

The California state legislature passed two bills in the last session which would have eliminated some testing, but the bills were vetoed by Gov. Ronald Reagan. The legislators were successful in passing rules prohibiting any child from being placed in a special program without his or her parent's consent, and if the child is to be placed in a special class he or she has to be examined by a person of the same ethnic and cultural background. This is an area for action in which the AFT and the labor movement could accomplish much.

An article by John Garcia in *Psychology Today* (September, 1972) analyzes IQ testing in general and the Stanford-Binet test in particular. He points out that the Binet measures only a narrow sliver of human abilities—academic skills—and that the narrow, artificial design of the questions makes the test invalid as a determiner of genuine human intelligence and potential. The result is a white-middle-class bias.

DIFFERENT QUESTIONS

Garcia notes that the Binet designers made a conscious decision in 1937 to equalize the IQ scores of men and women by including a balance of women-oriented and men-oriented questions. Why could this not be done for other groups, such as Chicanos?

Since the IQ test itself, and the very definition of IQ, is artificial to begin with, there would be nothing illegitimate about such a procedure. Test publishers might object: "This would destroy the predictive powers of the IQ score." But it was considered worth the "sacrifice" to avoid stigmatizing women as intellectually inferior. Garcia comments that if the child receives a fair break on the test, but not in his education, then indeed the test will be a poor predictor. The solution is not to retain unfair tests, but to transform the entire situation—teaching and assessment procedures alike.

An article by Jane Mercer describes a research project recently conducted in Riverside, Calif. The IQ scores of a large number of supposedly mentally retarded or subnormal children and adults were examined, and compared with other evidence about their "adaptive behavior." Adaptive behavior means the ability of the individual to function effectively on day-to-day tasks appropriate to that person's age group. Mercer found that most Chicanos and blacks whose test scores were subnormal were actually functioning as normal people in their day-to-day lives: e.g. holding jobs, taking care of a house, etc., without special assistance. Their low IQ scores may have corresponded to poor achievement in schools (i.e., IQ may have measured ability in the narrowest academic sense) but not to subnormal performance in most life-activities. But these people were stigmatized with the label of mentally retarded or subnormal. It is interesting to note that Anglos who tested below normal tended to function below normal in daily life—that is, for Anglo subjects, the IQ score was a better indicator of overall mental capacity. One of Mercer's conclusions was that no child should be assigned to a mentally-retarded class on the basis of a test score alone, especially minority children.

A follow-up experiment in the same city tried to determine the connection between socioeconomic and cultural background, and IQ scores. Thousands of children—white, black, and brown—were studied. It was found that a direct relation existed between the IQ scores of black and Chicano children, and the similarity of their home environment with that of the white-middle-class child. In fact, black and Chicano children whose homes were the most like the Anglo home scored, on the average, slightly above the Anglo IQ mean. Children at the lowest end of the socioeconomic spectrum, and with the most cultural differences, scored the lowest on the IQ test.

The mean IQ of the Anglo group was 93.8, while that of the Latino group was 83.4. These were 12th-graders taking a 10th-grade test, which means that the scores are actually inflated. The Latino group scored substantially *lower* (77.0) on a Spanish translation of the test. In fact, this low score of 77.0 does not include a large subgroup of the Latinos who could not take the Spanish test at all because they do not read Spanish.

I was a teacher at Mission High School for four years immediately prior to this experiment, teaching bilingual classes among others. Therefore, I knew many of the Latino students in the experiment, and can testify that most of them were normally bright, and some superior. It was a representative cross-section of the *nonretarded* Mission seniors—i.e., these were students enrolled in normal high school programs. Their mean IQ score of 83.4 would be considered subnormal by most of the people who interpret these tests, and, of course, many of the students scored below this mean, in the mentally-retarded range.

My own thesis experiment, which I hope will soon be published, studied the performance of low-income Latino and Anglo students at Mission High School in San Francisco, on the 10th-grade Lorge-Thorndike Intelligence Test (administered to all San Francisco 12th graders).

In this experiment, I analyzed some of the test questions, and found that they were unsuitable for anybody except perhaps students with college-educated parents. The vocabulary is literary and academic. Many of the questions that purport to measure reasoning ability do not really do that, because our students are sure to stumble on the meaning of the words. In short, the Lorge-Thorndike Intelligence Test is a glorified vocabulary test. Even the mathematical section is unnecessarily wordy. Of course, it's impossible to do a mathematical problem correctly if you don't understand the exact meaning of the question.

SOLUTIONS: WHAT SHOULD BE DONE

It is always easier to criticize the status quo than to come up with workable solutions. This is not a fault of the critics. The status quo *exists;* it can be studied and analyzed with great care. Our solutions are mostly *hypothetical.* We do not run the schools, and the occasional innovators that one finds in the educational establishment tend to be isolated and without the funds to introduce new programs. The established practices, on the other hand, have powerful backers and a long tradition behind them. Nevertheless, there are sound educational principles which we can apply to the problems of Chicano children. It is no small step to challenge the gross inequities which stand in the way of progress.

There are a number of experimental programs in various places, concerned with bilingual education. As of late 1971, there were 147 bilingual projects in the U. S. (mostly Spanish), with 44 of them in California. "Bilingual" means that the cultural background and language of the children is taken as a starting point, not as a handicap. Cultural variety is encouraged and used as an educational and motivating resource.

Bilingual-bicultural education is *democratic* education, as applied to a particular subgroup of the population. Many of the ideas in these programs could equally well be used with other groups of children, including even the white-middle-class Anglo children, who are far from being a homogeneous group in the U. S. Unfortunately, the existing bilingual programs are too small and isolated to explore the full range of innovative techniques or to serve as a visible model for the larger system. We are still in the stage of tokenism in the practice of bilingual education. The question is whether these methods will ever be used with the majority of Chicano children.

In this short paper, I must concentrate on the testing aspect of the problem. This has affected bilingual programs insofar as they seek ways of assessing their own achievements with the children. The traditional tests have proved to be invalid for measuring the accomplishments of the bilingual programs. A pamphlet, "Bilingual Testing and Assessment," put out by the Bay Area Bilingual Education League, contains a discussion of many widely used intelligence tests. This report concludes that some of the tests (but not all) can be used for the *diagnosis* of a child's learning difficulties, but not for placement or for determining the child's potential; that is, not as tests of *intelligence*.

The BABEL pamphlet recommends criterion-reference testing as the most effective way to assess a bilingual program. C-R is a form of achievement test, geared to the curricular goals of a specific school or program. It is applicable to those subject areas (e.g., mathematics or English/Spanish grammar) which are easily broken down into small bits of information or performance skills. In these areas, the C-R test can determine what the child has learned and what he/she has not learned, thus aiding both diagnosis and curriculum improvements. The C-R test does not compare a Chicano child with Anglo norms, nor does it produce a magic number—the IQ—which labels the child as "bright," "normal," or "dull."

This is no panacea. The C-R test may become another standardized joke, if the same test is administered for an entire school district. Teachers may be pressured to adapt their teaching to a C-R test imposed from above. Insofar as C-R testing or "performance objectives" are linked to teacher evaluation and accountability, they may make teachers the scapegoat for the failure of poorly-financed, understaffed schools. Another danger is that C-R testing may consume weeks of school time and endless months of teacher-committee meetings. There is no idea so good that it cannot be ruined by an incompetent administration.

I have one further suggestion which should be pushed by the AFT whenever possible. The teacher colleges, community colleges, and education departments of universities should set up and greatly expand training programs for bilingual specialists. These programs should include colloquial Spanish and the history and culture of La Raza, and the study of innovative bilingual/bicultural educational methods.

CHAPTER 28

SPANISH-SPEAKING STUDENTS AND STANDARDIZED TESTS

PERRY ALAN ZIRKEL

A SUBSTANTIAL SEGMENT of the estimated 10 million Spanish-speaking people in the United States (including some 6 million Mexican-Americans and 2 million Puerto Ricans), is of school age. The language abilities of these Spanish-speaking children vary all along the continuum of Spanish-English bilingualism and various specific cultural and subcultural backgrounds. Despite these differences, Spanish-speaking children have faced certain general difficulties in their search for equal educational opportunities. As Rodríguez pointed out:

> To consider the Spanish-speaking a homogeneous group with a given set of characteristics and qualities is to stereotype. In focusing on education in the United States, the term Spanish-speaking is more accurate than any other, including Spanish-surname, for the basic elements of educational difficulties are language and culture.

Recognition of these difficulties is reflected in the growing controversy over the standardized testing of Spanish-speaking children. A federal court decision recently ordered the retesting of over 22,000 Mexican-American children in California who had been previously classified as "mentally retarded" on the basis of English language IQ tests. A memorandum from the director of HEW's Office for Civil Rights declared such special class placement of non-English-speaking children to be legally prohibited. USOE's Office for Spanish-Speaking American Affairs has urged commercial firms to develop better testing instruments for such children.

Perry Alan Zirkel is assistant professor of education at the University of Hartford (Conn.), where he is in charge of Evaluation of Connecticut's Migratory Children's Program. Beginning July 1, he will direct a bilingual program for the Teachers Corps.

Zirkel, Perry Alan, "Spanish-Speaking Students and Standardized Tests," *The Urban Review*, 5/6:32-40, June 1972.

A review of the research reveals linguistic, cultural, and psychological difficulties for Spanish-speaking children on standardized tests of academic aptitude and achievement. It is hoped that such a review will provide a step toward clarifying and resolving the causes of this controversy.

INTELLIGENCE TESTING

The core of the controversy has been the IQ testing of Spanish-speaking children. Pintner and Sánchez were among the first to warn that the use of English-language intelligence instruments with such children is questionable. Several research studies since then have placed the effectiveness of standardized individual IQ tests, much less group IQ tests, for Spanish-speaking children in serious doubt. These studies fall into various categories in terms of language factors.

IQ Tests: Spanish v. English. Several studies, which revealed that the language of the IQ test significantly affects the results for Spanish-speaking children, found that Mexican-American elementary and junior high school children attained considerably higher results on the Wechsler Intelligence Scale for Children (WISC) in Spanish than in English. Manuel found that the average IQ of a sample of 98 Mexican-American pupils on the Spanish version of the Stanford-Binet Intelligence Test (S-B) surpassed that of the English version.[1] Keston and Jiménez, who found the opposite to be the case with a sample of Mexican-American 4th graders, admitted, however, that their results were probably attributable to the relatively low Spanish language development of their sample and to the use of a Spanish version of the S-B that was developed in Spain and that was not modified to take into account differences in dialect and culture.

Despite the higher scores generally obtained by translating existing standardized IQ tests into Spanish with appropriate cultural modifications, there is evidence that such procedure may not totally solve the problem of effectively testing Spanish-speaking children. As early as 1927, Pintner emphatically stated: "It is perfectly absurd to imagine that any real comparisons can be obtained by translating tests from one language to another." Roca described the efforts of the Department of Education in Puerto

Rico to adapt and determine the norms of the WISC, S-B, and Goodenough-Harris Draw-A-Man Test (G-H), making changes to allow for differences in vocabulary frequency, cultural conditions, and order of difficulty, yet the three adapted tests produced generally depressed IQ scores for Puerto Rican children relative to American norms. As Roca noted:

> There is no doubt that no matter how well an intelligence scale is adapted from one culture to another, there are cultural differences which will make the children from the second culture score lower than those from the first.

Cote similarly found generally depressed mean IQ scores for Mexican-American children on several nonverbal intelligence instruments administered with the directions in Spanish.

Watson and Goodenough and Morris concurred that the search for a culture-free intelligence test is futile. Stablein, for example, found the Davis-Eells Test, an attempt at a culture-free test of intelligence, to be as discriminatory as other standardized measures between Anglo- and Spanish-American students. Nevertheless, the construction of specific intelligence tests for different cultural groups seems both possible and worthwhile. As Ramirez pointed out, such tests must be based on awareness of differences in the cognitive and incentive-motivational styles as well as the communication style of such students.

IQ TESTS: VERBAL v. NONVERBAL. That Spanish-speaking children face a language barrier that is built into standardized intelligence tests is further revealed in studies comparing their results on verbal and nonverbal subtests. Several such studies found the average performance scale score of Mexican-American children on the WISC to surpass their average verbal scale score. Darcy had similar results when comparing the scores of Puerto Rican children on the nonlanguage and verbal sections of the Pintner General Ability Test.

Moreover, verbal and nonverbal IQ tests have been found to discriminate differentially between Anglo- and Spanish-American children. Altus noted that the average verbal WISC score of Anglo-American children significantly surpassed that of Mexican-American children, but that their respective nonverbal WISC scores did not differ significantly. Christiansen and Livermore recently replicated these results, in which, furthermore, the same pattern was reflected in the four related intellective factors of WISC described by Cohen. That is, they found Anglo-American students to significantly surpass Mexican-American students with respect to the two verbal factors (Verbal Comprehension and Relevance), but not with respect to the two nonverbal factors (Perceptual Organization and Freedom from Distractibility). A consistently significant factor in the WISC performance of both the Anglo- and Mexican-American pupils was socioeconomic status (SES).

Several studies confirmed Altus' results by employing other IQ instruments. For example, the same pattern emerged in B. E. Johnson's comparison of the results of Anglo- and Mexican-American students on the verbal and nonverbal sections of the California Test of Mental Maturity. G. B. Johnson's sample of Mexican-American boys in grades 4 to 6 scored significantly below Anglo norms on a verbal IQ test, but their scores on a nonverbal instrument were not significantly different from the Anglo norms. Rice reported that Corwin arrived at similar findings by comparing the results of Anglo- and Mexican-American children on various verbal and nonverbal intelligence tests.[2] After administering a verbal IQ test to a group of Spanish-speaking youngsters, Coindreau concluded that the instrument was actually a test of English vocabulary. Thus, verbal IQ tests obscure an adequate assessment of the mental ability of Spanish-speaking children.

Merely using a nonverbal IQ test, however, may be insufficient to assess accurately the mental ability of Spanish-speaking children. Some researchers have indicated that nonverbal and verbal IQ tests may measure different abilities. Further, other researchers have pointed out that so-called "nonverbal" tests contain a verbal factor. Finally, even the language of the directions of a nonverbal IQ test may make a difference.[3] Whether this difference is significant or not remains a question. Pintner's view was that "nonverbal tests with verbal directions are not adequate. We cannot be sure translated verbal directions are equally hard or equally easy." According to Mahakian and Mitchell, scores of Spanish-speaking children in the primary grades on the Otis

Group Intelligence Scale were significantly higher when administered with the directions in Spanish than with the directions in English. On the other hand, Anastasi and Cordova did not find the language of instructions to be a significant factor in their study of the use of the Cattell Culture Free Test with Spanish-speaking children. The Puerto Rican Study similarly revealed no significant difference with regard to the performance of Spanish-speaking students on the Lorge-Thorndike Nonverbal Intelligence Test (L-T) with Spanish v. English directions.

IQ Tests v. Achievement Criteria. Further indications of the questionable validity of IQ tests for Spanish-speaking children can be seen in studies exploring the relationship between their IQ scores and their results on measures of academic achievement.[4] Such studies reveal differential results between Anglo- and Spanish-American children. Morper, for example, found that both the WISC and the L-T were significantly related to the results on the Metropolitan Achievement Test (MAT) for Anglo-American 9th graders, but that neither of these IQ measures was significantly related to the MAT for their Spanish-American counterparts. He reported that "the greatest differences between the Spanish-American and Anglo ethnic groups were observed when reading ability and comprehension were most involved in the obtaining of measurement."[5] Carrow similarly found differential effects of IQ on language achievement tests between Anglo- and Spanish-speaking children. The importance of the language factor is even more evident in a study by Philippus which revealed that nonverbal IQ tests correlated higher with grade point average than did verbal IQ tests for Spanish-speaking students.[6]

Mental Ability Tasks v. Tests. Studies by Jensen and by Rapier provide a further indication of the ineffectiveness of standardized IQ tests in determining the mental ability of Spanish-speaking children. Jensen devised a more direct method of measuring mental ability in the form of simple learning tasks. After testing a group of 36 Anglo- and Mexican-American children equated on the basis of age, SES, and IQ, he found that Mexican-American children with low IQs performed not only significantly better than Anglo-American children with low IQs but also as well as both Anglo- and Mexican-American high IQ children. Rapier also conducted two experiments involving various learning tasks and found evidence of different learning difficulties for Anglo- and Mexican-American children who were matched on the basis of age, SES, and IQ, especially for those children in the lower range of IQ. She found a lack of verbal association to be one of the difficulties for Mexican-American children.[7]

Summary

A review of the research on the IQ testing of Spanish-speaking children reveals the linguistic and cultural handicaps standardized IQ tests present for such children. Such variables as the language, cultural construction, and extent of the verbal factor of such tests seem to significantly affect the performance of Spanish-speaking children. The validity of such tests is further called into question by experimenting with direct learning tasks and exploring the relationship to achievement criteria. Thus, there emerges the paramount need to modify the use of present IQ instruments and to develop new specialized instruments that utilize the language and cultural background of Spanish-speaking children to facilitate rather than obfuscate the assessment of their academic abilities.

ACHIEVEMENT TESTING

A number of studies reported that Spanish-speaking children scored generally below Anglo-American children on standardized tests of academic achievement. Still, there is evidence that at least some of this discrepancy is caused by language factors.

ACHIEVEMENT TESTS: VERBAL v. NONVERBAL. The discrepancy between Anglo- and Spanish-American students was much greater in verbal than in nonverbal areas of measured achievement. The Coleman Report, for example, revealed that scores of verbal ability were consistently lower than nonverbal ability scores for Mexican-American and Puerto Rican pupils in grades 1 to 12. Palomares and Cummins noted that arithmetic subtest scores surpassed reading subtest scores of Mexican-American pupils in the early grades. Palomares and Johnson found that all but four of 50 Mexican-American pupils referred to EMR classes scored higher on the arithmetic subtest than on the reading and spelling subtests of the Wide Range Achievement Test. It is interesting to note that seven of these students were at or above grade level in all three achievement subtests and that only six of them had scores on the G-H indicating eligibility for EMR classes.

B. E. Johnson's study is an example in itself. He administered two standardized achievement tests to a sample of 103 Anglo- and Mexican-American 6th graders. He found that the Anglo subjects consistently surpassed the Mexican-American subjects in those subtests involving English language skills, but that there were no significant differences between the scores of the two groups on those subtests involving arithmetic skills.

Cline stated that socioeconomic as well as cultural-linguistic factors should be considered in assessing the performance of Spanish-speaking students on standardized achievement tests. His sample of Anglo-American 7th graders appeared to outperform their Mexican-American counterparts on all subtests of the Stanford Achievement Test. However, with SES held constant at the lower level, these differences became insignificant except in the arithmetic subtest, which favored the Mexican-American subsample.

ACHIEVEMENT TESTS: SPANISH V. ENGLISH. Studies of standardized achievement tests which have been translated into Spanish offer more direct evidence of the language barrier that Spanish-speaking students face in such tests. When Mahakian, for example, administered a standardized reading test in both original and translated versions to 210 Spanish-speaking children in grades 1 through 7, 83 percent achieved higher total scores in Spanish, with decreasing differences found in ascending grades. Thonis similarly found that sixteen out of nineteen Mexican-American students scored higher when tested with a Spanish translation of the Peabody Picture Vocabulary Test than they did with the standardized English version. According to Davis and Personke, the differences between Spanish and English administrations of the MRT were mostly nonsignificant for a group of Mexican-American 1st graders. However, the mean scores on the subtest that most appropriately reflected their language background (Word

Meaning) revealed a significant difference favoring the Spanish version.

Despite repeated reminders of Gaarder's statement at the 1967 U. S. Senate hearings on bilingual education, most writers and researchers on the subject of the education of the Spanish-speaking seem to have forgotten or neglected the importance of a major study conducted in Puerto Rico in 1926 by the International Institute of Teachers College, Columbia University, which involved the administration of over 69,000 standardized achievement tests in English and Spanish. The results of that study indicated that although English had been imposed as the language of instruction since the United States took control of Puerto Rico in 1893, the Puerto Rican children's achievement in English showed them to be markedly below that of continental children. But as Gaarder emphasized, "the Puerto Rican children's achievement through Spanish was, by and large, markedly superior to that of continental children who were using their own mother tongue, English."

Translating standardized achievement tests points to, but does not provide, the way to more equitable opportunities for Spanish-speaking students. As Finch stated, "The development of tests appropriate to Spanish-speaking children is far, far more than simply translating existing tests." A glance at Eaton's cross-cultural frequency list indicates the varying difficulty levels of lexical items across languages. Differences in dialect and spoken language further confound the intended equivalence of translated tests. The cultural boundaries that restrict meaning within languages are reflected in Hernández' description of a commercially available Spanish translation of a standardized English achievement test.[8] One of the items in the English edition called for the identification of the word *pie* by means of choosing the appropriate illustration from a series of pictures. In the Spanish edition, the item was translated, in accord with a "standard" Spanish-English dictionary, as *pastel*. The difficulty, however, became compounded rather than alleviated for Puerto Rican pupils; for *pastel* is a culturally and visually distinct dish for them in comparison with *pie* which has retained its "Anglo" verbal and visual identity in Puerto Rico.

ACHIEVEMENT TESTS: ESSAY V. OBJECTIVE. Caldwell and Mowry provided further evidence of the importance of the language factor for Spanish-speaking children when they constructed objective and essay tests designed to be of the same content and difficulty in each. Despite the fact that the objective tests were given first, thereby causing any practice effects to accrue in favor of the essay tests, the Spanish-speaking students scored higher on the objective tests. L. W. Johnson similarly found that Spanish-speaking children scored significantly below their Anglo classmates on a test of English vocabulary, though the deficiency was less in subject matter vocabulary tests.

ACHIEVEMENT TESTS: RELIABILITY AND VALIDITY. Some researchers, particularly Fishman, have questioned the reliability and predictive validity of standardized achievement tests for minority group children in general. This question remains unsettled, although not unstudied, with specific reference to Spanish-speaking children. In their study of Spanish-speaking 1st graders, Mishra and Hurt found significantly lower levels of reliability and predictive validity for those subtests of the Metropolitan Readiness Tests (MRT) that were most dependent on English language ability. On the other hand, Mitchell considered the general level of predictive validity of the MRT for Spanish-speaking 1st graders to be comparable to that for other ethnic groups.[9] Despite different sample sizes, criterion achievement tests, and lengths of the periods between testing, the reasons for these contradictory results are not totally evident and their clarification awaits further research. In a related study by Arnold, the MAT was quite reliable when used with Spanish-speaking 3rd graders, with the important proviso that an appropriate difficulty level be administered.[10]

Where standardized readiness and achievement tests do prove to be reliable and valid predictors of later achievement test results, this may mean no more than confirming the consistency of language difficulties for Spanish-speaking children in school. Personke and Davis, for example, found the MRT to be a generally better predictor of reading ability for Spanish-speaking 1st graders when administered in English than when administered in Spanish. Their conclusion bears repeating:

. . . perhaps the readiness test was valid but the reading program was not. Before accepting the program, or the test as a valid predictor of success in that program, it might be pertinent to examine some of the alternatives.

Summary

A review of the research on the use of standardized achievement tests with Spanish-speaking children reveals that, as in the case of the IQ testing of Spanish-speaking children, a verbal factor appeared to militate against their optimal performance. Those subtests most dependent on English language skills generally resulted in poorest performance, indicating a handicap in language ability rather than in learning ability.

PSYCHOLOGICAL REACTIONS TO TESTING

Many researchers have noted, but few have scientifically studied, the psychological reactions of Spanish-speaking students to testing. Palomares and Cummins indicated that Spanish-speaking children seemed to appreciate the special attention given to them via testing. But Armstrong and Smith noted a lack of test motivation in their Spanish-speaking subjects.[11] Anastasi and Cordova described the characteristic reaction of their Spanish-speaking subjects to testing as "a mild confusion, followed by amusement and indifference." They attributed this reaction to "linguistic bifurcation" between a Spanish-speaking home and an English-immersed school which resulted in "psychological insulation" to what goes on in the latter. As they further explained:

> Not only test performance, but also the general intellectual development which tests are designed to gauge, are seriously handicapped by the attitudes and intellectual habits resulting from the child's early linguistic confusion.

EXAMINER VARIABLE. The importance of linguistic and cultural background to the Spanish-speaking child is expressed in his reaction to the language and culture of the examiner. In a review of the "sad state of the art" of language testing for linquistically different learners, Bordie noted the value of a test administrator's giving directions in line with the language background of the child.

The interplay of linguistic, cultural, and psychological factors is revealed in the examiner effects on the test performance of Spanish-speaking students. Anastasi and de Jesus described an enthusiastic response from their Spanish subjects to testing, which they attributed to the effect of an examiner of the same ethnic group as the students. Palomares and Johnson found indications of the effect of an examiner variable by comparing the referrals of Spanish-speaking children to EMR classes from Anglo- v. Mexican-American school psychologists. Anastasi and Cordova also uncovered evidence of an examiner variable along the intertwined lines of language and culture by administering a nonverbal intelligence test to Puerto Rican pupils with directions in Spanish v. English. They found that a testing order beginning with Spanish favored the girls, while one beginning with English favored the boys. They attributed this difference to the greater degree of acculturation of the boys and, thus, a greater rapport with the Anglo examiner.

The complexity of the linguistic, cultural, and psychological dynamics of the testing situation is further revealed in two recent studies involving examiner effects on the WISC performance of Spanish-speaking students. According to Swanson and DeBlaissie, the use of a bilingual interpreter as an adjunct to a monolingual Anglo examiner did not significantly affect the WISC scores of a group of Mexican-American 1st graders. However, any linguistic advantages for such a testing situation may have been counterbalanced by the possibly intimidating presence of two adults. Moreover, the second-class status of these pupils' native language may have been reinforced, rather than reversed, by the subservient position of the Spanish-speaking interpreter in relation to the Anglo examiner. A study by Thomas, *et al.* showed that significantly different performance levels can be obtained for Spanish-speaking students on the WISC, depending on differences in examiner styles. Their study involved the testing of a group of Puerto Rican pupils by two Puerto Rican examiners. Although both examiners were equal with respect to sex, ethnicity, fluency in Spanish and English, and clinical experience, consistently higher scores were obtained by the examiner who encouraged active participation, verbalization, and repeated effort on the part of the pupils. Their results suggest that such students may have more equitable opportunities on IQ and achievement tests if teaching and testing procedures are "optimized" rather than "standardized."

Conclusion

A review of the research reveals that standardized intelligence and achievement testing presents linguistic, cultural, and psychological difficulties for Spanish-speaking children in terms of such internal or intervening variables as the language of the administration of the test, the extent of the verbal factor in it, and the ethnic background of its administrator.

Researchers have indicated the inadequacy of such tests for Spanish-speaking children. Several of them (Hernández, Herr, Hughes and Sánchez, Rodríguez) pointed out that standardized tests do not take into consideration the nonstandardized background of Spanish-speaking students. In their "Guidelines for Testing Minority Group Children," Fishman, *et al.* underscored the need for developing different norms for specific minority groups (see also Rankin and Henderson). Because of such inadequacies, several writers (Dieppa, Flores, National Conference, Palomares and Cummins, Rice, Roca, Rodríguez, Willis) have decried the lack of appropriate tests and have called for the development of more effective instrumentation. Bordie noted an emerging trend to develop new, specialized tests rather than to depend on traditional, commercially available instruments.

Rodríguez termed testing "an educational roadblock," which cuts Spanish-speaking children off at an early age from equal educational opportunity. He added that tests reflect the monocultural nature of the schools, not the bicultural background of such students. The "disadvantaged" label that is pinned on Spanish-speaking children by this monocultural school system is often cemented on by tests constructed from what for these children is a second language and culture. The recent developments of bilingual-bicultural education and tests, which use the linguistic and cultural background of the child as an asset rather than a liability, show that the label can be switched to "advantaged" Spanish-speaking children.[12]

REFERENCES

1. Spence, *et al.* found that Mexican-American children from homes where both English and Spanish were spoken scored significantly higher in both the WISC and S-B than Mexican-American children from homes where only Spanish was spoken.

2. Kittell obtained similar findings by comparing the verbal and nonverbal IQ scores of monolingual v. bilingual third graders who were from 15 different language backgrounds. However, he found the bilingual children to have significantly higher verbal and nonverbal results than monolingual children in grade 5.

3. Whether the directions are in a language at all may also make a difference. In a study involving children from various language backgrounds, but not including Spanish-speaking children, Pintner found the results on a nonverbal test with nonverbal directions to be higher than those on a nonverbal test with verbal directions.

4. Bordie pointed out that research has indicated a general lack of predictability of IQ tests for disadvantaged children, causing school authorities in several cities to discontinue their use. For a discussion of the decision to discontinue IQ testing in New York City, for example, see "Test Ban" in *List of Studies.*

5. Moreover, he found that neither IQ test was significantly related to grade point average for both Anglo- and Spanish-American children.

6. Cooper found somewhat different results for bilingual children in Guam, whose native language was Chamorros. He found that verbal IQ tests generally correlated higher with the results of the California Achievement Test than did nonverbal IQ tests.

7. Lerea and Kohut, on the other hand, found evidence that an association factor may have been an advantage of bilingual children from Greek, Polish, and Norwegian backgrounds in performing a verbal learning task.

8. The author would like to thank Mr. José Luis Hernández of USOE's Bilingual Education Office for his invaluable insights and professional assistance in the development of this article.

9. Robinson similarly found the MRT to be comparably reliable for "advantaged," "average," and "disadvantaged" pupils, black and white.

10. G. F. Johnson questioned the content validity of the MAT for Title I pupils in general. "A middle-class oriented achievement test is validated by middle-class criteria. Thus, the middle-class culture bias is not eliminated from the tests."

11. Cebollero questioned the applicability of the findings of the Armstrong study.
12. See, e.g., Gates: "Two-way" bilingual education programs can also facilitate the advantage of speaking Spanish for Anglo children. For a description of such a program, see Zirkel.

SUGGESTED READINGS

Altus, G. J.: WISC patterns of a selective sample of bilingual school children. *Journal of Genetic Psychology, 83:*241-248, 1953.

Anastasi, A., and Cordova, F. A.: Some effects of bilingualism upon the intelligence test performance of Puerto Rican children in New York City. *Journal of Educational Psychology, 44:*1-19, 1953.

Anastasi, A., and de Jesus, C.: Language development and nonverbal IQ of Puerto Rican preschool children in New York City. *Journal of Abnormal and Social Psychology, 48:*357-366, 1953.

Armstrong, C. P., *et al.*: Reactions of Puerto Rican children in New York City to psychological tests. A report of the Special Commission on Immigration and Naturalization of the Chamber of Commerce of the State of New York, 1935.

Arnold, R. D.: Reliability of test scores for the young "bilingual" disadvantaged. *Reading Teacher, 13:*341-345, 1969.

Bordie, J. G.: Language tests and linguistically different learners: The sad state of the art. *Elementary English, 47:*814-828, 1970.

Bransford, L. A.: A comparative investigation of verbal and performance intelligence measures at different age levels with bilingual Spanish-speaking children in special classes for the mentally retarded. Unpublished doctoral dissertation, Colorado State College, 1966. (*Dissertation Abstracts, 27:*2267A, 1967.)

Cahn, P. L.: From the Editor. *American Education, 6:*i, 1970.

Caldwell, F. F., and Mowry, M. D.: The essay versus the objective examination as measures of the achievement of bilingual children. *Journal of Educational Psychology, 24:*696-702, 1933.

Carrow, M. A.: Linguistic functioning of bilingual and monolingual children. *Journal of Speech and Hearing Disorders, 22:*371-380, 1957.

Cebollero, P.: Reactions of Puerto Rican children in New York City to psychological tests. *Puerto Rico School Review,* 1936.

Chandler, J. T., and Plakos, J.: *Spanish-speaking pupils classified as educable mentally retarded.* Sacramento, California State Department of Education, 1969.

Christiansen, T., and Livermore, G.: A comparison of Anglo-American and Spanish-American children on the WISC. *Journal of Social Psychology, 81:*9-14, 1970.

Cline, M., Jr.: Achievement of bilinguals in seventh grade by socioeconomic levels. Unpublished doctoral dissertation, University of Southern California, 1961. (*Dissertation Abstracts, 22:*3113-3114, 1962.)

Cohen, J.: The factorial structure of the WISC at ages 7-6, 10-6, and 13-6. *Journal of Consulting Psychology, 23:*285-299, 1959.

Coindreau, J.: Teaching English to Spanish-speaking children. *National Elementary Principal, 25:*40-44, 1946.

Coleman, J., *et al.: Equality of educational opportunity.* Washington, D. C.: U. S. Government Printing Office, 1966.

Cook, J. M., and Arthur, G.: Intelligence ratings for 97 Mexican-American children in St. Paul, Minnesota. *Exceptional Children, 18:*14-15, 31, 1952.

Cooper, J. G.: Predicting school achievement for bilingual pupils. *Journal of Educational Psychology, 49:*31-36, 1958.

Darcy, N. T.: The performance of bilingual Puerto Rican children on verbal and nonlanguage test of intelligence. *Journal of Educational Research, 45:*499-506, 1952.

Darcy, N. T.: Bilingualism and the measurement of intelligence: Review of a decade of research. *Journal of Genetic Psychology, 103:*259-282, 1963.

Davis, O. L., Jr., and Personke, C. P., Jr.: Effects of administering the *Metropolitan Readiness Test* in English and Spanish to Spanish-speaking school entrants. *Journal of Educational Measurement, 5:*231-234, 1968.

Dieppa, J. J.: The evaluation of English skills of Puerto Rican high school students. Paper presented at the Conference on the Education of Puerto Rican Children on the Mainland. San Juan, Puerto Rico, October, 1970.

Eaton, H. S.: *An English, French, German, Spanish Word Frequency Dictionary.* New York, Dover Press, 1961.

Felder, D.: The education of Mexican-Americans: Fallacies of the monoculture approach. *Social Education, 34:*639-642, 1970.

Finch, F. L. Vamos: To develop a bilingual examinacion. *Paper presented to 5th annual TESOL Convention,* New Orleans, March 6, 1971.

Fishman, J. A., *et al.:* Guidelines for testing minority group children. *Journal of Social Issues, 20:*129-145, 1964.

Fitch, M. J.: Verbal and performance test scores of bilingual children. Unpublished doctoral dissertation, Colorado State College, 1966. (*Dissertation Abstracts, 27:*1654A-1655A, 1966.)

Flores, S. H.: The nature and effectiveness of bilingual education programs for the Spanish-speaking child in the United States. Unpublished doctoral dissertation, Ohio State University, 1969.

Gaarder, A. B.: Statement before the Special Subcommittee on Bilingual Education of the Committee on Labor and Public Welfare, U. S. Senate, May 18, 1967. *Florida Foreign Language Reporter, 7:*33-34, 171, 1969.

Galvan, R. R.: Bilingualism as it relates to intelligence test scores and school achievement among culturally deprived Spanish-American children. Unpublished doctoral dissertation, East Texas State University, 1967. (*Dissertation Abstracts, 28:*3021A-3022A, 1968.)

Gates, J. R.: The bilingually advantaged. *Today's Education, 59:*38-40, 56, 1970.

Goodenough, F. L., and Morris, D. B.: Studies in the psychology of children's drawings. *Psychology Bulletin, 47:*369-433, 1960.

Hernandez, J. L.: Testing, guidance, and culture: Their theoretical and practical interaction. Unpublished paper prepared at Interamerican University, San German, P. R., October, 1969.

Herr, S. E.: The effect of pre-first-grade training upon reading readiness and reading achievement among Spanish-American children. *Journal of Educational Psychology, 37:*87-102, 1946.

Holland, W. R.: Language barrier as an educational problem of Spanish-speaking children. *Exceptional Children, 27:*42-50, 1960.

Hughes, M. M., and Sanchez, G. I.: *Learning a new language.* Washington, D. C.: Association for Childhood Education International, 1958.

International Institute of Teachers College: *A survey of the public educational system of Puerto Rico.* New York, Columbia University Bureau of Publications, 1926.

Jensen, A. R.: Learning abilities in Mexican-American and Anglo-American children. *California Journal of Educational Research, 12:*147-159, 1961.

Johnson, B. E.: Ability, achievement and bilingualism: A comparative study involving Spanish-speaking and English-speaking children at the sixth grade level. Unpublished doctoral dissertation, University of Maryland, 1962. (*Dissertation Abstracts, 23:*2792, 1963.

Johnson, G. B.: Bilingualism as measured by a reaction-time technique and the relationship between a language and a non-language intelligence quotient. *Journal of Genetic Psychology, 82:*3-9, 1953.

Johnson, G. F.: Metropolitan tests: Inappropriate for ESEA pupils. *Integrated Education, 9:*22-26, 1971.

Johnson, L. W.: A comparison of the vocabularies of Anglo-American and Spanish-American high-school pupils. *Journal of Educational Psychology, 29:*135-144, 1938.

Keston, M. J., and Jimenez, C.: A study of the performance on English and Spanish editions of the Stanford-Binet Intelligence Test by Spanish-American children. *Journal of Genetic Psychology, 85:*263-269, 1954.

Kittell, J. E.: Bilingualism and language, nonlanguage intelligence scores of third-grade children. *Journal of Educational Research, 52:*263-268, 1959.

————: Intelligence test performances of children from bilingual environments. *Elementary School Journal, 64:*76-83, 1963.

Lerea, L., and Kohut, S. M.: A comparative study of monolinguals and bilinguals in verbal task performance. *Journal of Clinical Psychology, 17:*49-52, 1961.

Mahakian, C.: Measuring intelligence and reading capacity of Spanish-speaking children. *Elementary School Journal, 39*:760-768, 1939.

Manuel, H. T.: *Spanish and English editions of the Stanford-Binet in relation to the abilities of Mexican children.* Austin, University of Texas, 1935. Cited by L. S. Tireman, Bilingual children. *Review of Educational Research, 11*:340-352, 1941.

Mishra, S. P., and Hurt, M., Jr.: The use of Metropolitan Readiness Tests with Mexican-American Children. *California Journal of Educational Research, 21*:182-187, 1970.

Mitchell, A. J.: The effect of bilingualism in the measurement of intelligence. *Elementary School Journal, 38*:29-37, 1937.

Mitchell, B. C.: Predictive validity of the Metropolitan Readiness Tests and the Murphy-Durrell Reading Readiness Analysis for White and Negro Pupils. *Educational and Psychological Measurement, 27*:1047-1054, 1967.

Morper, J.: An investigation of the relationship of certain predictive variables and the academic achievement of Spanish-American and Anglo pupils in junior high school. Unpublished doctoral dissertation, Oklahoma State University, 1966. (*Dissertation Abstracts, 27*:4051A, 1967.)

Morrison, J. R.: Bilingualism: Some psychological aspects. *Advancement of Science, 14*:287-290, 1958.

National Conference on Bilingual Education: Washington, D. C., Educational Systems Corporation, 1969, ERIC:ED 033256.

National Education Association: *Las voces nuevas de Sudoeste: Symposium on the Spanish-speaking child in the schools of the Southwest.* Washington, D. C., NEA Department of Rural Education, 1966.

Palomares, U. H., and Cummins, E. J.: *Assessment of rural Mexican-American pupils preschool and grades one through six: San Ysidro, California.* Sacramento, California State Department of Ed., 1968 (a) .

————: *Assessment of rural Mexican-American pupils preschool and grades one through twelve: Wasco, California.* Sacramento, California State Department of Education, 1968 (b) .

Palomares, U. H., and Johnson, L. C.: Evaluation of Mexican-American pupils for EMR classes. *California Education, 3*:27-29, 1966.

Personke, C. L., Jr., and Davis, O. L., Jr.: Predictive validity of English and Spanish versions of a readiness test. *Elementary School Journal,* November, 1969, pp. 79-85.

Philippus, M. J.: Test prediction of school success of bilingual Hispano-American children. Colorado: Denver Department of Health and Hospitals, 1967, ERIC: ED 036577.

Pintner, R.: The influence of language background on intelligence tests. *Journal of Social Psychology, 3*:235-240, 1932.

————: Nonlanguage tests in foreign countries. *School and Society, 26*:374-376, 1927.

Puerto Rican Study Research Report: *Developing a program for testing Puerto Rican pupils in New York City public schools.* New York City, Board of Education, 1959.

Ramirez, Manuel, III: Social responsibilities and failure in psychology: The case of the Mexican-American. *Journal of Clinical Child Psychology, 1:* 5-8, 1972.

Rankin, C. J., and Henderson, R. W.: Standardized tests and the disadvantaged. Research report from Arizona Center for Early Childhood Education to National Lab on Early Childhood Education, November, 1969. ERIC: ED 034594.

Rapier, J.: Effects of verbal mediation upon learning of Mexican-American children. *California Journal of Educational Research, 18:*40-48, 1967.

Rice, J. P., Jr.: Education of subcultural groups. *School and Society, 92:*360-362, 1964.

Robinson, H. A.: Reliability of measures relating to reading success of average, disadvantaged, and advantaged kindergarten children. *Reading Teacher, 20:*203-210, 1966.

Roca, P.: Problems of adapting intelligence scales from one culture to another. *High School Journal, 38:*124-131, 1955.

Rodriguez, A.: The challenge for educators. *National Elementary Principal, 50:*18-19, 1970.

————: Education for the Spanish-speaking: Mañana in motion. *National Elementary Principal, 49:*52-56, 1970.

Sanchez, G. I.: Bilingualism and mental measures: A word of caution. *Journal of Applied Psychology, 18:*765-772, 1934.

Senate Hearings. *Center Forum, 4:*5-23, 1969.

Singer, H.: Bilingualism and elementary education. *Modern Language Journal, 40:*444-458, 1956.

Spence, A. G.; Mishra, S. P.; and Ghozeil, S.: Home language and performance on standardized tests. *Elementary School Journal, 71:*309-313, 1971.

Stablein, J. E.; Willey, D. S.; and Thomson, C. W.: An evaluation of the Davis Eells (Culture Fair) Test using Spanish and Anglo-American children. *Journal of Educational Sociology, 35:*73-78, 1961.

Swanson, E., and DeBlaissie, R.: Interpreter effects on the WISC performance of first grade Mexican-American children. *Measurement and Evaluation in Guidance, 4:*172-175, 1971.

The "test ban" in New York City Schools. *Phi Delta Kappan, 46:*105-110, 1964.

Thomas, A.; Hertzig, M. E.; Dryman, I.; and Fernandez, P.: Examiner effect in IQ testing of Puerto Rican working-class children. *Journal of American Orthopsychiatry, 41:*809-821, 1971.

Thonis, E.: *Bilingual education for Mexican-American children: A report of an experiment conducted at the Marysville Unified School district.* Sacramento, California State Department of Education, 1967.

————: *Bilingual education for Mexican-American children . . . an experiment: A report of the second year, September 1967-June 1968.* Marysville California, Marysville Unified School District, 1969.

Watson, G. B.: *Social Psychology: Issues and Insights.* New York, J. B. Lippincott Co., 1966.

Willis, R. M. An analysis of the adjustment and scholastic achievement of forty Puerto Rican boys who attended transition classes in New York City. Unpublished doctoral dissertation, New York University, 1961. (*Dissertation Abstracts, 22:*795-796, 1961.)

Zirkel, P. A.: Two languages spoken here. *Grade Teacher, 88:*36-40, 59, 1971.

PART VII

BILINGUAL-BICULTURAL EDUCATION: A NECESSITY

CHAPTER 29

THE MEANING OF BILINGUALISM TODAY

NELSON BROOKS

ABSTRACT: Bilingualism is the habitual use of two languages by one person; in its purest form the two are quite separate. Its attainment is not marked by the crossing of a boundary but by a gradual transition, the earliest stages of which can be valid within limits. On its inner side, bilingualism relates to preverbal thought, making available to the speaker two separate systems of expression. The best place for the development of bilingualism is the home. The next best place is the classroom, but only if it provides ample practice in face-to-face communication. An exclusively philological approach does not encourage the separation of the two language codes. An all important ingredient in helping the learner gain control of the new language as an entity separate from the mother tongue is the dyadic factor—the behavior of two individuals considered as one.

THREE QUESTIONS of prime importance stem from the above title: What *is* bilingualism? How is it attained? To what extent can it be developed in the classroom? In attempting to state what bilingualism "means," we may, on the one hand, consider its importance and, on the other, the actual phenomena referred to when we put the word to use in the context of the present.

Nelson Brooks (Ph.D., Yale University) is Associate Professor of French at Yale, Director of Summer Programs, and Director of the Summer Language Institute. He has taught French at school and college levels for the past forty years. Since 1957 he has been conducting courses in the Yale Graduate School for future teachers of foreign languages. He is the author of several language tests, of the book *Language and Language Learning,* and of numerous articles on pedagogical subjects. Since 1958 he has served from time to time as consultant to the language program of the U. S. Office of Education. From 1960 to 1964 he served as a member of the Board of Education in New Haven, Connecticut. He was director of the project that produced the *MLA Cooperative Foreign Language Tests.* In 1966 he published a brochure on teaching culture in the language class.

With minor changes, the text is that of a talk given 24 Aug. 1967, at the Conference on the Role of Canadian Universities in the Teaching of English and French as Second Languages, Laval University, Quebec, Canada. It was also published in the *Proceedings* of that meeting.

Brooks, Nelson, "The Meaning of Bilingualism Today," *Foreign Language Annals, 2(3):*304-309, March 1969.

311

There are a great many different languages, hundreds of them, although only a restricted number are spoken by vast populations. We know too that there are many areas of the world that are termed bilingual, where everybody speaks two languages, without seeming any the worse for it. We know also that there are vast areas of the planet that are unilingual, many of them only now beginning to realize the extent to which this circumstance may be a disadvantage.

We know further that contact between various countries and various cultural groups is increasing along a geometrical curve. This is clearly evident in the areas of travel, commerce, military deployment, and of academic study and research. In all these, the advantage, if not the necessity, of knowing a language other than one's own stands out in sharp relief.

Of course, bilingualism provides no assurance of positive and desired results; it only removes barriers that otherwise would exist. Knowing another man's language is by no means a guarantee that friendly relations will be established and maintained. But *not* knowing the other man's language is a sure guarantee that normal human relationships will be impossible.

There are, as well, other more subjective values that accompany bilingualism. Is not the bilingual individual in a better position to evaluate life's predicament because he can view it from two points of view rather than one? In one's inner life as well as in contact with others there may indeed be an enrichment due to the fact that thoughts may evolve in more than a single mode. This circumstance may be compared to that of the musician who can play not only the violin but a keyboard instrument in addition. Sometimes I think of life as a statute that can be seen by the unilingual from one position only, but it has an additional meaning for the bilingual who can observe it from two different vantage points. What I am suggesting does not automatically follow from bilingualism, but there are many advantages in having two languages at one's disposal.

I have been speaking about bilingualism as if it were a specific quality or condition that is well understood and agreed upon by all. The truth, of course, is far otherwise. I should like to trace some boundary lines that may result in increased understanding of what it is we are talking about.

In simplest terms bilingualism is the habitual use of two languages. In its ideal form it is the ability to speak a language other than one's mother tongue with approximately equal facility, so well, let us say, that no trace of language *A* appears when language *B* is being used. This ideal is frequently reached. We all know many people whose control of two languages corresponds to this description. Yet right away we note that there are many people who *almost* meet these requirements but not quite, usually because some trace of the mother tongue is apparent when the second language is being used. The inadequacy may appear in the sound system, although a letter written in the second language by the same person may show no trace of the mother tongue. On the other hand, all the details of the sound system may be in good order, while a letter may reveal inadequacies in syntax or in idiom. These facts suggest that there is no clearly marked coastline or frontier separating bilingualism from approaches to it. There is, rather, a continuum in which one thing shades off into another with no sharp line of demarcation. This is an important point, for it amounts to saying that bilingualism may be very modest and limited at the beginning, yet may be valid as far as it goes, even near the start of the experience with the second language.

I believe we shall be able to penetrate even more deeply into the nature of bilingualism if we are willing to accept an analysis of language behavior that corresponds to what I like to call the "Vygotsky Spectrum." In the early part of the present century, a Russian psychologist, Lev Vygotsky, wrote a book entitled *Thought and Language* that has only recently become available in an English translation. The author's conclusions are well summarized in the final chapter, in which we can discern a range of language activity beginning at a point deep within the mind of the individual and ending in a printed literary masterpiece. The successive phases of this spectrum or continuum are identified as follows: First, *Consciousness*, then, *Thought*, Thirdly, *Thought in Words*. Next, *Inner Speech*. At this point overt language behavior begins and we have *Spoken Monologue*. Then, *Dialogue*.

After this, *Normal Social Talk*. Then the many representations of spoken speech in *Writing*. Finally, the metamorphosis of mere language into *Fine Art*, such as we would find in the printed works of a poet or novelist or playwright.

If we accept this analysis as valid, at least for the moment, how does it apply in the case of our ideal bilinguist? There must be for him two separate systems of expression, and they must differ as soon as the encoding of language has begun. They can be identical only in the areas of consciousness and preverbal thought.

At what point does the bilingual choose the language in which his thought will be expressed? Overt language must of course be in one language or the other. It is as difficult to speak French and English simultaneously as it would be to play the violin and the oboe at the same time. At what point is the decision made? At what point do the paths diverge, ending up in one case in French and in the other in English for the ideal bilinguist? It seems clear that the choice is made before thought is encoded into language. If this were not true, the message would often be awkward and incomplete, if not incomprehensible.

By locating the basis of bilingualism deep within the mind we are reiterating what is often said: That to be bilingual is to be bicultural—for the locus of individual culture is precisely in the values, the allegiances, and the prejudices, positive and negative, of preverbal and postverbal thought.

When we are young, ideal bilingualism is well within the reach of everyone. As we grow older, if we have not habitually followed a dual path and encoded our thoughts in one language or the other, it becomes harder with each succeeding year to abandon the pathway of the mother tongue and to move easily and freely along the pathway of the second language.

If this analysis of bilingualism is valid, it has profound and far-reaching implications for our programs in foreign language and literature, none of them more important that the disengaging or suppression of the mother tongue while the second language is in use. This leads us directly to our second question: How is bilingualism attained?

It is, I think, already clear that the separation of the two languages and the frequency of use of each in its own terms remain critical. We may find a better answer to our question if we pause to recall how control over the mother tongue is attained. It is necessary to recognize that the mother tongue is not learned on an individual basis. There is now general agreement that the little human ape (that we all once were) is genetically programed to learn language. He does not learn it by himself, however. He learns it through association with others. I mention this because the dyadic factor in language behavior, so long overlooked by both linguist and psychologist, is of such vital importance in the learning of the mother tongue in the first few months and years of life. This dyadic factor is no less important in launching our learner on the path that leads to the full control of two languages.

If bilingualism is attained through language in use, the simplest form it can have is that in which a speaker and a hearer relate to each other and to a situation. The situation can be the physical reality in which the speakers are functioning, or it may be the image of that reality stored away in the cerebral cortex of each speaker's brain. Probably the most common circumstance in which ideal bilingualism is attained is the home, or the playground, or the succession of informal situations in which people come in contact and interact in the language that seems most appropriate. We are now very close to the formal situation of the educational system, and are thus led to an examination of our third question: To what extent can bilingualism be developed in the classroom?

If we admit that bilingualism is not a border to be crossed with one final step, but rather a height to be gained by a long and steady climb, we must also admit that the preparation for bilingualism and a significant advance toward its realization are indeed possible in the experience of the language classroom. The nub of the matter is the nature of that classroom experience and this, of course, is precisely our chief concern.

During the past decade, at least in the United States, we have seen in our classrooms the development of a contrast, an opposi-

tion—perhaps better a polarity—between what we have been calling the "traditional" approach to language learning and the
"new" or "modern" or "audiolingual" approach. Upon close examination we find that we have at bottom a polarity between
philology and communication. Let us examine these one at a
time.

In philology, interest is centered upon a text, first upon establishing the accuracy and authenticity of that text and, if there
are variants, upon collating these into a single and preferred
form. One then proceeds to analyze the text, to explicate its con-
tents from many different points of view, referring in particular
to the facts and the values of language, of culture, and of literature. The accepted notions of the importance of form in language and the traditional norms of grammar come to us
from philology. It is not difficult to understand why philology
has long been considered in the academic world the best, if not
the only port of entry to another language and its literature.

Having paid our respects to language in textual form (and I
would be the last to lessen this respect in any way) we are obliged
to recognize that there is far more to language than meets the
eye.

We cannot brush aside the elementary fact that language is, at
bottom, a phenomenon of sound. The human voice can make
and the human ear perceive intricate yet very systematic patterns
of sound waves to which stable meanings can be attached. During most of the history of the human race, possibly the better
part of two million years, it was a matter of sound waves and
sound waves only, until the invention of writing some five or six
thousand years ago. With sound waves pictured in writing, light
began to play a very important part in language. But the significant role of visibility in language should not blind us to the true
facts. Even today, for a great number of the people on this
planet, language is a matter of sound only. For every child the
world over, at least until he goes to school, language is a matter
of sound and sound only. Indeed, throughout our adult life,
most of the language we produce and receive is a matter of spoken speech that has no reference to a printed text.

In the total area we call language, therefore, ample room must be found for speech in spoken form. It is at this point that we turn from philology to communication. In contrast to philology, communication is a concept of another order. Every living organism possesses the basic ingredients of communication by the mere fact of being alive. To be able to receive and send a message is something that the simplest living things can do and that a stone cannot. Of course language has its roots in communication, but the latter covers a vastly greater territory. We can have communication without language—witness two people dancing on a ballroom floor. We can also have language without communication—witness inner speech or the less inspired moments at a cocktail party or a faculty tea. But when language and communication work together we have a factor in human relationships that has not yet been fully explored or even understood, essentially because we have not yet examined in depth its spoken aspects and its dyadic or teeter board character.

When we hear the word "communication," we are likely to allow its meaning to be bounded by the military, the economic, and the so-called "mass media." But communication is not only a factor in violence, power, and economic gain. Communication is also a dominant concern of the lover, of the poet, the musician, and the artist. Communication may indeed be drab and mundane in the extreme, but it also plays a part in the noblest efforts of the human spirit. He who sends a telegram or phones his wife communicates. But Dante, Shakespeare, Montaigne, Michelangelo, and Bach do so as well. With these two poles of philology and communication in mind, let us see how bilingualism relates to each one.

Whatever the rewards may be to the student of a philological approach to the learning of another language—and there are many—the sad fact is that anything resembling bilingualism is not one of them. If we have proved anything in our language courses in America over the past fifty years, we have proved this. On the other hand, in a language course that is based on communication, the student learns to do as best he can with the new language that which the native speakers of that language normally do with it—that is, to use it, not to take it apart; and in situations that temporarily invalidate the mother tongue of the learner.

The communication approach teaches the student slowly but surely to build up a control of the new language and quite clearly leads to a valid start toward bilingualism.

American psychologists have talked of late about two systems of handling two languages: a "compound" system and a "coordinate" system. In the light of the analysis we have made, the coordinate bilingual chooses one path or the other *before* he encodes his message. The compound bilingual (if we can call him a bilingual) first encodes his message in his mother tongue, then restates it—*tan! bien que mal*—in the second language. A limiting factor in the philological approach to language learning is that the compound system seems to be quite satisfactory. There is no need to abandon the language one is used to, in fact one never leaves home. The comfort and security of the mother tongue are ever present. But observe the implications of this in relation to the cognitive processes we are describing. The compound bilingual never experiences the intellectual freedom and satisfaction of expressing his thought directly in the second language. Not only is he impeded by the formulations of his mother tongue, he is also denied the privilege of fully exploiting the idiomatic potential of the second language. In fact, the compound system cheats the learner of some of the most valued rewards he might otherwise receive.

We must recognize that many people have feared courses based on communication because they felt they would deprive the learner of many of the undoubted values that result from a philological study of another language. Although such fears have been widespread and voiced quite vigorously, no tangible evidence has been produced to substantiate them. On the contrary, within the past year facts have come to light that prove that the success of a college senior who is majoring in a modern language and its literature is related in a very positive way to a foreign language experience in the elementary school, a time, of course, when only the communication aspects can be taught.

To be sure, this approach implies many things that are new and different. It implies new classroom techniques, new materials, new training programs for teachers, a new time sequence and beginning point for the individual learner, and a corps of teachers who are both native and non-native speakers of the target language.

This newness, however, should not be thought of as an orientation toward any new method. Those of us who work in the field of French need at times to be cautioned about the use of the word "method." We all know and respect the importance that this concept has come to have for those who speak French. But when we deal with language learning, there are some basic considerations we should not overlook. The search for *the* method of language learning is quite like the search for the Holy Grail. One is about as likely to succeed as the other. Those who are in hot pursuit of *the* method of language learning—indeed who claim at times to have found it—overlook individual differences and the fact that the learning of the mother tongue, which is universally so successful, proceeds without any method whatsoever.

It may seem to you that I am encouraging a turning away from the basic values of humanism and turning instead toward science. But this is not so. Grateful as I am to the scientists for their many valuable contributions to our understanding of language and how we use it, I have serious reservations about many of their recommendations because of the limitations that are inherent in the very philosophy of science. I find my views on this matter well sustained by one of the best of scientists, Noam Chomsky of the Massachusetts Institute of Technology.

> I am, frankly, rather skeptical about the significance, for the teaching of languages, of such insights and understandings as have been attained in linguistics and psychology. Surely the teacher of language would do well to keep informed of progress and discussion in these fields. . . . Still, it is difficult to believe that either linguistics or psychology has achieved a level of theoretical understanding that might enable it to support a "technology" of language teaching. It seems to me that there has been a significant decline, over the past ten or fifteen years, in the degree of confidence in the scope and security of foundations in both psychology and linguistics. I personally feel that this decline in confidence is both healthy and realistic. But it should serve as a warning to teachers that suggestions from the "fundamental disciplines" must be viewed with caution and skepticism (*1966 Northeast Conference Reports,* New York, 1966, p. 43).

Let me give you an example of why, as a language teacher, I welcome such words of caution from a scientist. One comes away from a review of linguistic literature on bilingualism with the impression that to the linguist bilingualism is essentially a matter of interference, the clash of two different language codes. One comes away from a review of psychological literature on bilingualism with the impression that to the psychologist bilingualism is essentially a matter of switching from one code to another. A language teacher, on the other hand, sees in bilingualism the *absence* of interference, of codes in collision, and the *absence* of nimble shifting from one code to another. Rather, he sees bilingualism as the ability to relate to one person in language *A* and to a different person in language *B,* with interference and shifting as far removed from the situation as possible.

What both groups of scientists appear to have overlooked is the extent to which language behavior is dyadic behavior, that is, two considered as one. Their researches bear every evidence of the naïve notion that language is individual behavior, pure and simple, and that communication through language is in terms of words. The blunt truth is that both these assumptions are wrong. Language is not individual behavior when it is first learned nor when it functions in communication. Language thoroughly permeates our inner lives, as we all know. But when language is used for communication between individuals it involves not one person alone but at least two. The best model for making this clear is the seesaw, in which everything that happens at one end is directly related to what happens in terms of the weight and movement at the other end. When the scientists eventually stumble upon this inescapable fact, and when they recognize that communication cannot take place in terms of isolated words (but only in terms of a context), they will be in a position to help us far more than they have up to now in understanding language and its use by human beings.

This circumstance is due, I suppose, to the scientists' overriding interest in analysis. All will agree that the abnormal and the accidental are often powerful agents in revealing what lies beneath the surface of complicated situations and reactions. But a teacher's work is not analysis, it is synthesis. For if learning is not synthesis it is nothing.

Clearly, the language teacher finds himself caught in a crossfire of conflicting recommendations coming from both humanists and scientists. I am not recommending that we cry "A plague on both your houses!" Rather, that we cry "Respect to both your houses—and will you please respect ours." It is time for language teachers to recognize that they have their own task to fulfill, and to seek the aid of all their helpful colleagues in so doing.

There is time for me to refer only briefly to what is implied in instruction in language as communication. But may I list some of the recurrent themes that are most important. There are three objectives that persist like a baroque ground bass or continue throughout any well-conceived language course. They are: language competence, cultural insight, and literary acquaintance. These objectives are very different from each other but they are closely interrelated and merit attention at every point. An early start and continuing progress imply extensive school-college collaboration, an assignment that often calls upon the college instructor for a new look at the role of translation and language analysis and for a reevaluation of speech in spoken form. Many new procedures in the measurement of progress, achievement, and proficiency are also implied.

To sum up, I have taken it as my assignment to explore the inner side of bilingualism and to show how this can be related to classroom instruction. I believe that by broadening and deepening our understanding of bilingualism and by modifying and improving classroom instruction we shall be able to bring the two into a more intimate and productive relationship than we have up to now. In accomplishing this, nothing needs to be sacrificed. We will have to start earlier, work more effectively, sequence matters in a different way, measure our learners' progress more carefully, and collaborate much more extensively than we have in the past. If bilingualism is not established in the home, the next best place is the language classroom in the schools. Yet the schools cannot do this by themselves. They must have the cooperation of colleges and universities in perfecting their programs, they must have the assurance that those in higher education will know about, and build upon, what has been accomplished in the schools. But matters can be arranged so that our student will end by having all that ever accrued to him through a philological approach and, in addition, will have through a sustained experience in communication in his second language the basis of bilingualism that is his goal and ours.

CHAPTER 30

ON BILINGUAL EDUCATION

JEROME R. REICH and MICHAEL S. REICH

PROGRAM CHECKS DROP-OUT RATE

THE TERMS "CULTURALLY DEPRIVED," "culturally disadvantaged," or "culturally different" are all too familiar to educators today. Often these terms are used to disguise or to excuse the failures of our educational system. One of the groups which has suffered from these failures is the Spanish-American group. This article will deal with the background of this problem in Chicago and the steps which are currently being taken to alleviate and overcome it.

Some Spanish-American children may be classified as culturally disadvantaged. Family income may be limited. The educational level of the parents may be low—at least as interpreted, or misinterpreted, by educators in this country. The family may have little or no experience with urban living. The home may be broken. The children may be neglected. The values, norms, and sanctions of the Spanish-American group may differ from those of the dominant "anglo" group. And, above all, language handicaps may discourage academic success.

The home and its surroundings may also hinder the Spanish-American child. Many Spanish-Americans live in the least desirable residential areas, either in slums or in low-cost, public housing projects. Living conditions may be noisy, crowded, poorly lighted, and lacking in educational materials, toys, and games. Spanish-American children like all children learn much in the street from peers. Fearlessness, bravery, and daring physical prowess are the norms learned by boys and fit into the general

Jerome R. Reich, Professor of History at Chicago State University, spent nineteen years working as an administrator for the Chicago Public Schools, including ten years as a principal. Michael S. Reich is a senior political science major at Northwestern University.

Reich, Jerome R., and Reich, Michael S., "On Bilingual Education," *Illinois Schools Journal*, 52(2):26-34. Summer 1972.

term "machismo," or masculinity, which is so valued in the Spanish-American culture. These children learn to be independent and tough, and to outsmart the representatives of middle-class authority.

The attitudes, values, and norms of the Spanish-American slum dweller—isolated from the wider community—are designed to strengthen and reinforce his own way of life. Unfortunately, because these values tend to contradict middle-class culture, they are seen as malicious, evil, deliberately nonconforming, and threatening by the middle-class teacher. Like other "culturally disadvantaged" groups, many Spanish-Americans are primarily concerned with the everyday problems of obtaining food and winning some measure of economic security. These problems leave them little time to explore the world around them.

It is also clear that the Spanish-American child is caught between two oftentimes contradictory cultures: his native one, to which he adheres at home, and the middle-class "anglo" culture, to which he is exposed at school. The diversity causes a high incidence of emotional problems for these children. For example, in school a young girl is taught to be active and responsive, to take the initiative in discussions, and to face new people and situations on her own. However, in her home environment, she is expected to be passive and sheltered. She is even forbidden to go out into the streets to play with other children. A child's expected behavior, sex role, and attitudes may be completely contradictory in two cultures.

This contradiction handicaps the school in its planning of meaningful programs for disadvantaged Spanish-American youth. The school attempts to stimulate individuality in pupils, encourage self-assertiveness, initiative, self-expression, and creativity. These tasks do not coincide with the concept many Spanish-American parents have concerning the role of the school. Spanish-American parents expect their children to be submissive and respectful.

The lack of relationship between the school curriculum and Spanish-American cultural patterns results in little motivation to succeed in school. For example, a lesson on "community helpers" is generally presented in a manner that bears only slight if any resemblance to the realities of the experiences of the children with these "helpers." At school the policeman is idealized as an individual who helps and protects those in need of his assistance. In reality, many policemen assigned to Spanish-American areas are not always sympathetic to residents, and in many instances the police have an image the opposite of the one presented in school.

The area of social studies is equally unrealistic. The United States is pictured as a land of opportunity, and text books exclude all references to the realities of poverty, discrimination, and hostility which many Spanish-Americans face. Not only is this type of curriculum unrealistic to the child, but he is also unable to present his views on the subject because of his limited knowledge of English and the generally held fatalistic attitude of many culturally disadvantaged groups that they probably could not change anything anyway.

But the major problem of the Spanish-American youth is the language barrier. The child simply must understand English if he is to enjoy any amount of success either in school or in a job. Many of these children speak Spanish at every opportunity. It is hard for them to realize that it is an absolute necessity to speak English. Often a youth does not realize this until he reaches adolescence, and by this time he may be far behind in his educational development.

Failure to understand English creates many problems for the school and the children. Because the school system and the child are so closely interrelated with each other, a misconception on the part of one party can have an adverse effect on the other. For example, English is the main vehicle for learning, and the Spanish-American lacks facility in it. He can only rely on nonverbal communication. However, here too gestures are influenced by a cultural background which he does not understand. As a result of this, the child begins to feel inadequate. He cannot solve the problems of adjusting to a new language and a new culture. He cannot seek support from his parents because they too are faced with similar problems. The child reasons that it is better not to try again if he fails. He becomes indifferent, uninvolved, and apathetic. This whole attitude he develops is the result of a culture shock, which is caused by the confusion he senses between his native culture and his new "anglo" culture.

The school cannot properly test the intelligence or achievement of Spanish-American children by the use of standardized tests. When these children are tested, they do poorly because of their language handicap. Therefore the children are not placed in the proper grade level. In the high school the student appears more inadequate than he really is and may not be counseled correctly. College is usually not recommended for him, and many Spanish-American students will virtually be encouraged to leave school as soon as it is legally possible for them to do so.

What then is the future of these Spanish-American children? As we have seen, they are handicapped by poor living conditions, mutual misunderstanding between the school and themselves, and a language barrier. Previously the school systems which faced the problems of culturally disadvantaged groups looked upon these problems in terms of behavioral and disciplinary difficulties and neglected to look at their social and economic causes. Today school administrations are beginning to look at these problems in cultural terms.

The culturally disadvantaged child, like any other child, values education. Many Spanish-Americans acknowledge poor home environments but believe that through proper education they can improve their condition. The crucial term here is proper education. By middle-class standards proper education consists of (1) humanistic education to "help the child comprehend his experiences and find meaning in life"; (2) citizenship education to develop "active, aware citizens who will work devotedly for society's improvement"; and (3) intellectual education "to have the child acquire the analytic ideas and problem solving tools that are developed by scholars." To these broad generalized goals are added the specific aims of acquiring the fundamentals of reading, writing, arithmetic, health, and science. This whole theory of education exhibits middle-class value patterns with emphasis and orientation toward careers and occupations, interest in enriching experience, recreation, and the desire for respectable civic responsibility.[1]

The culturally disadvantaged youth's attitude is more utilitarian. Education is usually not an opportunity for development of self-expression or self-realization but rather a means of acquiring a secure job. He wishes to see a clear correlation and transition between his schooling and his future occupation. Unfortunately this is usually not seen in our schools. The disadvantaged student does not see any correlation between knowledge of history or mathematics and driving a truck. He fails to realize that his future employer will wish to see a diploma and an account of his achievement in school before hiring him.

Therefore it is the school's responsibility to create programs which will alleviate or compensate for any deficiencies these culturally disadvantaged youth bring into the classroom. The school must provide the type of educational climate which will improve and develop the learning capabilities of these children. It is essential that the teacher who works with these disadvantaged groups recognize that these children lack the resources that are readily available to the middle-class groups but have other resources that can be even more valuable.

Teachers must give the child support and encouragement. They must give him instrumental aid and convince him that he is progressing in his day-to-day schoolwork and that he is reaching some agreed upon short-term and long-term goals. The teachers must also instruct the youth in cognitive skills and provide him with information, illustrations, and clarification. Teachers must encourage these children to show that they do in fact care about his progress. For Spanish-Americans an additional type of program—an intensive English language program—is essential for school success. The inability to communicate fully in English is the most serious handicap most of their children face in schools in the United States.

In the Chicago area several programs have been organized aiming at instructing Spanish-American youth in English. These programs initially faced several problems. A critical question was how much emphasis should be placed on the youth's native language. Many educators believed that Spanish should be de-emphasized or even ignored. They maintained that bilingualism was a handicap causing underachievement in school, mental confusion, and language difficulties. However, when programs for teaching English as a second language were instituted, a contrary view—that the speaking of the native Spanish language was not to be neglected—was accepted. The developers of these educational programs felt that bilingualism was not a detriment to education. It only appeared to be one because many times the school and the community considered children who did not speak English at all times to be ignorant. Because of this new view of bilingualism, Spanish language and culture gained real importance. In fact, one of the objectives of these programs is to help the child develop positive feelings about himself, his culture, his language, and his personal worth as an individual in addition to developing his skills and language arts, mathematics, science, and social studies.

Another problem which had to be resolved was whether the teachers in these programs should be monolingual in Spanish or English or have knowledge of both languages. And if the teacher knew both languages, which one should be emphasized? This difficulty was resolved by creating six types of models for teaching non-English speaking children the academic subjects; these models are based on material prepared by the Chicago Board of Education.

MODEL 1—BILINGUAL TEACHER. The bilingual teacher uses the children's native language to clarify concepts and meanings. He utilizes the multimedia and the audio-lingual approach to language learning.

MODEL 2—MONOLINGUAL TEACHER. Assisted by a bilingual teacher aide, the teacher utilizes the aide's knowledge of the children's native language to clarify meanings and concepts. Games and songs are taught in both languages.

MODEL 3—MONOLINGUAL TEACHER. The monolingual teacher utilizes background knowledge of the child's background culture and experience and uses the multimedia and the audio-lingual approach in teaching the academic subjects.

MODEL 4—SPANISH BILINGUAL TEACHER. The Spanish bilingual teacher introduces the non-English speaking child to his new culture and his new environment in the child's first language. Major objectives of this class are to build the child's self-image through stories of the contributions of his ethnic group to this country and to develop all the skills in his native language.

MODEL 5—BILINGUAL TEACHER OF SPANISH FOR NATIVE SPEAKERS OF SPANISH. The bilingual teacher of Spanish for native speakers of Spanish introduces the child to his new culture and his new environment and to the ethnicity of Chicago and the United States. The objective is to develop his self-image through a study of the contributions that his ethnic group has made to this country in the field of work, industry, and the arts and sciences.

MODEL 6—COOPERATING TEACHER. The cooperating teacher explains the program for teaching non-English speaking children to the administrators, the teachers, other special personnel, and to the community and he conducts workshops for the classroom teachers and others involved in teaching non-English speaking children.

One of these special educational programs which incorporates all of the above concepts—emphasis on bilingualism, development of pride in the Spanish heritage, and the varying models of teaching—is the TESL program or Teaching English as a Second Language. In addition, the TESL program recognizes the general difficulties which Spanish-Americans face in addition to language deficiencies. The TESL program is centered in several Chicago schools and is rapidly expanding throughout Spanish-speaking communities.

The TESL program is based upon more than thirty years of experience. The audio-lingual or aural-oral method was developed during World War II. It combines descriptions of the languages with intensive pattern practice. During the war English language materials were prepared for speakers of Italian, Spanish, Portuguese, and German, and in the 1950s similar programs were sponsored by the State Department for a variety of other languages. English language installations have been established in many foreign countires. TESL programs were encouraged by the passage of the Elementary and Secondary Education Act of 1965 and multiplied after the passage of the Bilingual Education

Act of 1968. Many of the early programs were located in the Southwest, but they have since spread to all parts of the United States.

One of the authors observed the TESL program located at Senn High School on the north side of Chicago. Senn High School was eligible for TESL facilities because of its significant percentage of Spanish-speaking and other foreign language-speaking students. The drop-out rate from Senn High School was also particularly high among Spanish-speaking students. Obviously a remedy in the form of the TESL program was desperately needed. The TESL program at Senn High School serves approximately three hundred and twenty students. Its staff consists of the director, eight teachers, clerical personnel, and teacher's aides. All of the TESL personnel are under the control of the principal of the school and must follow the standard forms of evaluation and grading as do the other teachers.

As in the rest of the city, the immediate goal of the Senn TESL program is the lowering of the drop-out rate among Spanish-speaking students by giving them a workable conversational knowledge of English. The Senn program adheres to the theory behind the TESL project, which teaches English along the line of a sequenced development of grammatical structures, particularly verbs. This style of instruction also stresses time, place, manner, and the teaching of phrases as they are needed in the context of a particular structure. Simple sentences are first demonstrated and are later developed into compound sentences with balancing conjunctions and finally extended to complex sentences with dependent clauses.

The TESL program de-emphasizes the need for vocabulary although it realizes many words and expressions are essential for adequate communication. When vocabulary is studied, the words are treated as they relate to the structure of the sentence and not to their content.

The Spanish-speaking student is not taught grammar, at least consciously. That is, he is not taught that in the sentence "The world is round," *the* is an article, *world* is a noun subject, *is* the verb, and *round* the predicate adjective. Instead the individual is repeatedly exposed to the sentence and hopefully comes to realize the significance of the position each word occupies. Later other words are substituted while the structure of the sentence remains the same. A lesson begins with a basic sentence: "John wakes up early every morning." The sentence is then extended to "He gets up at 5 o'clock every morning" and then altered to "He likes to get up early in the morning." The lesson continues by describing what John does when he gets up. One sentence states, "He washes his face and hands." Then "He shaves." Subsequent sentences are "After he got dressed, he ate breakfast." "He had eggs for breakfast" and then, "He always eats eggs for breakfast." One can clearly see the aim of this lesson. The student is now able to express in English fairly standard practices one follows upon getting up.

The Spanish-speaking student is also taught to answer and construct questions. The student is asked "What time do you get up?" The answer must be "I get up at 6 o'clock." When asked "Did John take a shower?" the student must reply "Yes, he took a shower," or "He takes a shower every morning." When asked "Did you see John's toothpaste?" the response must be, "Yes, I saw it in the bathroom" or "There it is on the sink." However, this highly structured pattern of response can be adapted by the teacher to a variety of classroom uses, according to the needs and abilities of the students. For example, when the lesson is concerned with time, the teacher may comment on a student's lateness. Any other instance in which the lesson and student behavior are related will also be utilized by the instructor.

The Spanish-speaking students are also instructed in the formation of negatives. These drills are more difficult than answering affirmatively because the individual must know where the negating word is placed. In the question "Does Mary speak English?" the response must be "Mary doesn't speak English." When the sentence is "Does John speak English?" the response required is "Mary doesn't speak English and John doesn't either."

Another aspect of the TESL program is its teaching of writing. It must be remembered that composition is not among the immediate objectives of the project. At the beginning levels most composition usually takes the form of copying exercises from the textbook (*Intensive Course in English,* Elementary Part I and Intermediate Part II, published by English Language Services); and it is only at the more advanced levels that composition assumes a less structured form. Most Spanish-speaking students found composition more difficult than conversation. The reason for this disparity in success between conversational and composition skills is that composition requires more linguistic skills than conversation, which basically requires only the ability to repeat correctly.

After examining the methods of the TESL program we should evaluate its success in educating Spanish-speaking students and its relation to general theories of instructing bilingual youths who come from culturally diverse backgrounds. First, let us consider the question of TESL's success at Senn High School. The initial goal of the TESL program at Senn was to reverse the increasing drop-out rate of Spanish-speaking youth because of language disabilities. Apparently the program has accomplished this goal. Although no statistics have as yet been published, the director was confident that the TESL program has been invaluable in keeping Spanish-speaking youths in school. Even allowing for possible bias on her part, it did seem that the enrollment in the program remained virtually constant during the course of several weeks during which observations were carried out.

Students in the TESL project were divided into five different levels with most of the students in the lower two levels. It was evident that the program has given most of its students an adequate background in English. On the first level the classes were repeating simple sentences and at the fifth level the class was engaged in a very involved discussion of poetry. Many of the students in the class participated, and technical terms such as imagery, rhyme, alliteration, and mode were discussed in great detail and used with facility.

A possible weakness of the program is that at present the teachers lack formal training in the methods of bilingual education. Most of the teachers in the Senn program happened to do their student teaching in the TESL program and later continued in it. Still other teachers were assigned randomly to the program and do not even have this limited preliminary experience with bilingual instruction. This lack of special training will eventually prove detrimental to the program because the TESL approach involves very highly planned and structured patterns of instruction which require, if they are to be successfully executed, thorough teacher preparation.

The TESL program would also benefit from teachers with a knowledge of and appreciation for Spanish culture. When a Spanish-speaking student enters a TESL class he must conduct all conversations with the teacher in English. On occasion a student would say to the teacher: "What is wrong with Spanish?" The teacher would usually reply that nothing is wrong with Spanish, but one must speak English to be successful in the United States. The conversation would cease after this and the usual lesson would continue. The actual merits of Spanish were never discussed with the students. However, if the TESL program is to be successful, it must not attempt to thrust the predominant culture of the United States on these youths or tell them even indirectly that their Spanish culture is inferior. Although no teachers have actually said this to a student, the atmosphere of the TESL program, given the total dominance of English and the almost complete disregard of Spanish language and culture in the classroom, seems to imply it.

Conflicts caused by "culture shock" manifested themselves on the individual and group level. On several occasions discipline problems resulted from differences in ability to speak English. The students who were involved in the TESL program ridiculed newcomers to the class who had absolutely no knowledge of English. Students who had some ability to speak English were not subject to this abuse. This very interesting phenomenon seemed to suggest that a higher status developed around the ability to speak English at the expense of the Spanish culture. However, among themselves or outside the classroom, the students spoke Spanish exclusively, no matter what their level of English was. It is clearly evident that these Spanish-speaking students are caught in a severe and possibly demoralizing conflict between their Spanish culture and the new one they meet in the United States.

In the handbook, *Human Relations, In-Service Training, and Communications for Programs for Non-English Speaking Children,* published by the Chicago Board of Education, it is explicitly stated that the culture of Spanish-speaking youth is a major factor in their attitude in life generally and school specifically. The handbook reminds teachers that they should be aware of the often conflicting demands of the two cultures—the one in which the Spanish-speaking student lives, the one of his home and neighborhood—and the other of the school. The teacher must realize that the cultural diversity of these Spanish-speaking children enables them to enrich the school program with their bicultural experiences. These experiences include folk arts, cooking, music, literature, and dances which can be utilized as a vehicle for cross-cultural education.

It is felt by the Board of Education that optimum success in attaining these aims will be achieved only by the utilization of bicultural, bilingual teachers. Therefore it turned to Chicago State University to conduct a summer program for Spanish-Americans with B.A. degrees. These students were to participate in an intensive six-week course of study to prepare them to be provisional teachers in the public schools of Chicago which had significant numbers of Spanish-American children. It was hoped that this project might serve as an incentive and model for educational programs which will produce a generation of Spanish-American citizens who will participate as equals in the main stream of American life while still retaining their own rich cultural traditions. A later article will deal with this summer program and its results during the following school year.

REFERENCE

1. Gottlieb, D., and Ramey, Charles E.: *Understanding Children of Poverty.* The Foundations of Education Series, 1967, p. 61.

CHAPTER 31

THE BILINGUAL EDUCATION MOVEMENT AT THE CROSSROADS

LAWRENCE WRIGHT

THE MOST CONSPICUOUS failure group in the American educational system is composed of children whose home language is not English. Most of these children are Spanish-speaking. Their progress through school is retarded by their inability to converse in the language of instruction, and consequently they drop out of school at an alarming rate. In the Southwest, 40 percent of the Mexican-American students do not finish high school; in Boston, 90 percent of the Puerto Rican students drop out before they get to high school. And yet the almost unbearable truth about the plight of non-English-speaking children in American schools is that most of them are given no help at all. The U. S. Commission on Civil Rights (in Report III, "The Excluded Student," Mexican-American Education Series, May, 1972) found that by the eighth grade 64 percent of the Mexican-American students in the Southwest are six months or more behind their expected grade level in reading, but only 10.7 percent are given remedial reading instruction, and only 5.5 percent are enrolled in English as a second language (ESL) classes. The same report found that, four years after passage of the Bilingual Education Act, only 2.7 percent of the Mexican-American students in the Southwest were enrolled in bilingual education programs. Thus it is important to temper any discussion of bilingual education with the understanding that so far the concept is largely academic.

Congress presumably wanted more than a token acknowledgement of the problems of non-English-speaking children when it passed the Bilingual Education Act of 1968, which amends Title

Lawrence Wright is a free-lance writer based in Nashville, Tenn., where he has been a staff writer for the *Race Relations Reporter*.

Wright, Lawrence, "Bilingual Education Movement at the Crossroads," *Phi Delta Kappan, LV(3):*187-189, November 1973.

VII of the Elementary and Secondary Education Act and is generally referred to as Title VII. The original authorization for the bill was $400 million, to be spent over a period of six years; however, only $117 million of that money has been spent, according to Dick Goulet, program director for bilingual education in the Title VII office. The authorization for fiscal year 1973, for instance, was $135 million, but after much haggling between the administration and Congress the actual expenditure will be $35 million, used to support 213 projects in 32 states and territories and involving 19 languages other than English. Of the estimated 100,222 students enrolled in Title VII projects, 91,138 are in Spanish/English bilingual programs. Most of the projects are five-year proposals.

Bilingual programs ideally include equal numbers of non-English-speaking children and children proficient in English; in fact, many projects have only token numbers of English-speakers at best. The children are supposed to be instructed by teachers who are themselves bilingual, but because of the paucity of qualified teachers fluent in a language other than English the programs frequently are characterized by English-speaking teachers and an assemblage of ethnic aides. Appropriate materials are still being formulated, and standardized tests to measure the progress of the children are a long way off, according to Goulet, because regulation tests such as the Metropolitan are unsuitable and tests geared directly for bilingual classrooms must endure years of norming. Consequently, too many bilingual programs are flying blind, supported only by the assumption that bilingual education must be the answer to the learning problems of non-English-speaking children—an assumption with much logic but little demonstrable success to back it up. "Right now achievement is not spectacular," Goulet conceded. "But we do know one thing: We're not hurting the child. And at least he's learning another language."

One of the major problems precipitated by the lack of funds in the Title VII office is that there are only eight staff members to monitor the 213 projects; consequently, site visits are rare and standards vary. And although Title VII subsists on minimum funding, there are dark rumors of bureaucratic waste—rumors that raise the hackles of Title VII officials. Goulet insists that at least $31 million of the total $35 million will be going directly to the classrooms. Recently a confidential audit of a bilingual television project in Berkeley, California, surfaced in Jack Anderson's column. The audit suggested that the television project, no longer under the direction of the Title VII office, was squandering large sums of money in excessive travel expenses, salaries, and consultant fees. Other bilingual projects have been questioned, and the General Accounting Office is investigating the matter.

The capacity for hyperbole in the Office of Education is well developed; unfortunately, the Title VII office is no exception. All of the articles, legislation, and litigation concerning bilingual education in recent years have been based on figures that were formulated by the Title VII staff in 1968—figures that were puffed up to begin with and have been embroidered and inflated since. The original study determined that there were five million school-age children (nearly one school-age child in 10) from non-English-speaking homes in the U. S., and of these nearly four million speak Spanish. Goulet estimates that the current figure must be closer to six million non-English-speaking school-age children, five million of them Spanish-speakers. All this comes as a surprise to the officials at the Bureau of the Census. According to the *Current Population Reports* (P-20, No. 250, "Persons of Spanish Origin in the United States: March 1972 and 1971"), there are 9,178,000 persons in the nation whose mother tongue is Spanish (not 15 million, as some education officials believe), but only six million speak Spanish in their homes. There are 3.4 million Spanish-American children between the ages of 5 and 19, of whom two million actually speak Spanish at home.

This year another major federal bilingual program begins operation. The Emergency School Aid Act of 1972 reserves 4 percent of the total appropriation for bilingual education, which makes $9 million available to fund 40 programs in 1973. Unlike the Title VII legislation, the ESAA program does not stipulate that the children involved come from impoverished backgrounds —a requirement Title VII officials would like to see eliminated. The thrust of ESAA is to facilitate desegregation, and communities seeking ESAA funds must be under a comprehensive desegregation plan acceptable to the Office for Civil Rights. Unlike Title VII, ESAA programs are approved and administered by the regional commissioners of the Office of Education, which places the programs under closer scrutiny. In fact, 1 percent of the total appropriation is reserved for evaluation of programs, and some communities actually returned their grants when they realized that the evaluation would be so much more stringent than the Title VII programs.

There are provisions for bilingual education in much of the recent legislation, especially in administration bills. The Education Professions Development Act (now incorporated into the National Center for Improvement of Educational Systems) will expend $2,852,000 for training bilingual teachers and counselors —funds that have been mishandled, according to several sources. Bilingual projects are authorized for migrant education (Title I —Migrant, ESEA) and Indian education (Indian Education Act of 1972), and other funds are available through the Ethnic Heritage Program (Title IX of ESEA), and through the Head Start and Follow Through programs (Economic Opportunity Act). However, officials cannot determine just how much is allotted to bilingual education under these acts, and the interpretation of what constitutes bilingual education varies from office to office.

TABLE 30-I

BILINGUAL PROJECTS FOR SCHOOL YEAR 1973-74

State	State Funding	ESEA Title VII Projects	ESAA Projects	Languages (Cultures)
Alaska	$ 200,000	1		Yupik (Eskimo)
Arizona		9	1	Navajo, Spanish (MA) *
California	$4,000,000	61	3	Spanish (MA), Portuguese, Chinese, Pomo Indian, Tagalog (Philippine)
Colorado		7		Spanish (MA), Ute, Navajo
Connecticut		3	1	Spanish (PR) †
District of Columbia	$ 175,000 (est.)		1	Spanish
Florida		3	2	Spanish, Eeleponkee (Miccosukee)

Idaho		1		Spanish (MA)
Illinois	$2,300,000	4		Spanish
Indiana		2		Spanish
Louisiana		4	4	French (Cajun), Spanish
Maine		3		Passamaquoddy (Algonquin) French
Massachusetts	$4,000,000	7		Spanish, Portuguese, Italian, Chinese, Greek, French (Haitian)
Michigan	$ 88,000	4		Spanish
Montana		3		Cheyenne, Crow, Cree (Chippewa)
New Hampshire		1		French
New Jersey		4		Spanish
New Mexico	$ 694,140	12	2	Spanish (MA) Navajo, Zuni, Keresan, Acoma
New York	$1,500,000	26	4	Chinese, Spanish, French (Haitian)
Ohio		1		Spanish
Oklahoma		3	1	Muskogean (Seminole), Choctaw, Cherokee
Oregon		1		Spanish (MA), Russian
Pennsylvania		2		Spanish (PR)
Rhode Island		2	1	Spanish, Portuguese
South Dakota		1		Lakota
Texas	$ 700,000	40	19	Spanish (MA)
Utah		1		Navajo
Washington	$ 500,000 (est.)	2	1	Spanish (MA), Chinese, Japanese
Wisconsin		1		Spanish
Guam		1		Chamorro
Mariana Islands		1		Palauan, Ponapaean
Puerto Rico		1		Spanish (PR)
Virgin Islands		1		Spanish (PR)
Total		213	40	

Note: States without bilingual projects for 1973-74 include Alabama, Arkansas, Georgia, Hawaii, Iowa, Kansas, Kentucky, Maryland, Minnesota, Mississippi, Missouri, Nebraska, Nevada, North Carolina, North Dakota, South Carolina, Tennessee, Vermont, Virginia, West Virginia, and Wyoming.

* MA—Mexican-American
† PR—Puerto Rican

The first state law governing bilingual education was the Massachusetts Transitional Bilingual Act of 1971. It is still the only state law that mandates bilingual instruction and at the same time provides substantial funds to implement local programs—$4 million this year. Other states may mandate bilingual education without providing the necessary funds, as in Pennsylvania, or may provide funds without compelling bilingual instruction, as in New Mexico, New York, and Washington. Texas has recently passed legislation that establishes bilingual education as state policy for non-English-speaking students, and has budgeted $700,000 this year and $2 million next year, after which the funding will come from general education funds. California appropriated $5 million last year for an experimental program funded for two years only. The California law stipulates that at least one-third of the class be proficient in English in order to ensure that the class is actually bilingual. Although Louisiana does not have a law governing bilingual education per se, it has embarked on an innovative program designed to preserve the French-speaking heritage of its Cajun population. This year the state has provided $1 million to augment French instruction at the primary level, and will bring 212 teachers from France, many of whom will be doing alternate service to their military obligation, to teach in the Louisiana schools. Altogether, there is over $14 million in state funds committed to bilingual education this year, much more than the year before and probably less than there will be next year.

The chances are that the laws governing bilingual education soon will be modified substantially. Senator Joseph Montoya and Senator Edward Kennedy each have bills that would revise current federal programs. Montoya wants to amend Title VII to provide matching federal funds to state and local funds in order to assure communities of continuing aid to bilingual education. Presently bilingual projects are funded for five years only. Under Montoya's bill the federal government would provide 75 percent of the funds for the programs. The bill also includes more restrictive language concerning how the programs will be administered. The senator is considering further legislation for the training of bilingual teachers. Kennedy's bill would draw all the various bilingual programs into a single administrative agency and would expand the focus of bilingual education to include preschool and vocational training. Kennedy also wants to enlarge the teacher preparatory training program and to establish a national advisory council on bilingual education.

Even if Congress makes some badly needed changes in bilingual education legislation, the effect on non-English-speaking children will be slight unless more money is appropriated. Thus the quiet progression of the *Lau v. Nichols* case to the Supreme Court may soon determine the shape of bilingual education in this country irrespective of congressional action.

There are four major suits concerning bilingual education currently in the federal courts. In New Mexico and Texas the district judges have ruled that schools in Portales, New Mexico, and San Felipe Del Rio, Texas, must institute bilingual programs to accommodate the needs of the Mexican-American students. In New York a suit brought by Aspira of New York, Inc., a Puerto Rican development agency, against the Board of Education of New York City is still tied up in district court. However, *Lau v. Nichols*, a class-action suit brought on the behalf of the non-English-speaking students of Chinese ancestry in San Francisco, has been appealed to the Supreme Court after going against the plaintiffs at the district and appeal levels. Originally the suit asked for bilingual education for the Chinese students represented by Lau, but that has been changed to merely compensatory English instruction following the *Rodriguez* decision earlier this year, in which the Court ruled that education is not a constitutional right. The *Lau* case is based on the due process and equal protection clauses of the Fourteenth Amendment, Title VI of the Civil Rights Act of 1964 (which says, in part: ". . . no person in the United States shall, on the grounds of . . . national origin . . . be denied the benefits of . . . any program or activity receiving federal assistance"), and the First Amendment guarantee of free speech—a right the *Lau* attorneys claim is vitiated by the lack of knowledge of the English language which effectively prohibits Chinese-speakers from participation in the political process. According to Edward H. Steinman, principal attorney for *Lau*, this case asks that the Court look deeper into the affairs of the classroom than it has done before—something the Court seems loath to do. "The Court never wanted to become a school board and choose between various methods," Steinman says. "However, *Lau* says we can't accept the surface quality of an educational program; we must go into the classroom and see what is actually taking place—we must pierce this veil of equality. . . . Obviously, if we lose, it could be very damaging."

So far the bilingual education movement has been so limited in effect that the impediments are not yet major obstacles and the fissures in philosophy have not yet widened into chasms. But in the distance one can see formidable problems looming and battle lines being drawn.

There have never been enough teachers fluent in languages other than English to implement even the most tentative bilingual programs. In New York, for instance, Puerto Ricans constitute 26 percent of the student population but only 1 percent of the teachers. Certainly the existence of bilingual programs provides incentive for the preparation of minority bilingual teachers; still, it will take years to bring the number of qualified minority teachers into balance with the student population, and even if this is done there is still some question as to the desirability of having the preponderance of Puerto Rican teachers in New York shunted into bilingual programs composed for the most part of Puerto Rican students. It's unlikely that bilingual programs will have much success in finding many Spanish-speaking Anglo or black teachers, and success may become more unlikely now that language requirements in high schools and colleges are being eliminated.

Monolingual teachers searching for jobs find that the employment situation, already bleak, is exacerbated further by the sudden demand for qualified bilinguals. The recent California legislation, in fact, excuses bilingual teachers from certification. Established teachers may feel threatened by the team-teaching bilingual education format, which, Goulet notes, "replaces the regular school program. It's not an add-on."

Which languages qualify for bilingual education? No one really knows. In San Francisco, for example, children entering school represent households in which 63 different languages are spoken. Already there are federal projects in Chinese and Spanish and a community-funded program in Philippine Tagalog. But what about Japanese and Korean? Or, for that matter, black English?

(The black community has begun to lobby for a bilingual program since it has become known that black reading scores are the lowest of any minority group in the city.) Then too, the new California law stipulates that one third of the bilingual class be proficient in English, which makes state-funded bilingual programs feasible in direct proportion to the popularity of the language among English-speakers. How many English-speaking children want to learn Tagalog, Korean, or Pomo Indian?

Underlying the bilingual movement is a widespread reaction against the melting pot theory of assimilation—a reaction that has become formalized with the introduction of the term "bicultural," now found everywhere in tandem with the word "bilingual." Bicultural education is not easily defined. What it means in effect is that students are taught to acknowledge ethnic differences and appreciate them—but it also cements the necessity for hiring minority teachers familiar with the cultures being taught.

The most vocal reaction so far against certain trends in bilingual education comes from Albert Shanker, president of the New York City local of the American Federation of Teachers and vice president of the New York State United Teachers. Shanker, himself a non-English-speaking child when he entered school, favors bilingual education in order to preserve the child's native language and provide a transition into ordinary classroom instruction; however, he has repeatedly objected to the bicultural component, calling "bicultural" a "code word." Shanker suspects that there is a quota system implicit in the demands for bicultural education. "What bicultural education means around here is that if you're Cuban you can't teach Puerto Ricans," says Shanker, who claims that there are a number of bilingual Cuban teachers who can't get appointments because they are not Puerto Rican. More to the point, however, is the threat some established teachers feel to their own positions, and Shanker believes that much of the bilingual movement has more to do with minority hiring than with education. "I don't cling to the idea that with every new wave of immigrants you have to throw out the teachers who represent the previous group of immigrants," Shanker said. "There are still too few Puerto Rican graduates to implement a bicultural program . . . and it would be a terrible mistake to drop the requirement for certification of bilingual teachers. It would be like saying drop the requirements for bilingual doctors or lawyers. It would automatically mark the bilingual program as inferior."

Shanker thinks more money should be made available for bilingual programs, but he opposes making such programs compulsory. Last year he proposed that bilingual education should emphasize instructing English-speaking teachers in another language—a proposal that is not highly regarded outside his own union. He contends that many of the current bilingual projects are not bilingual at all, that they are "run by nationalists who think students don't need English to succeed in the mainstream American culture." "I'll go further than that," he said. "I have grave doubts as to whether the majority of Spanish-speaking parents want bilingual education for their children at all. They are certainly much less anxious for it than a small number of fashionable nationalists or educators."

"Bilingual education is a hypothesis that presumes to ease a child's entry into school—but it's only a hypothesis," says Shanker. "It's like every educational movement—oversold in the beginning and evaluated before it has fully developed."

The National Education Association does not share Shanker's reservations about bilingual education. The NEA adopted a resolution in 1972 urging provision of the necessary funds and materials for non-English-speaking children, and has recently filed an amicus brief with the Supreme Court in connection with the *Lau* case, saying in part: "The practical exclusion of any large group of children from public education, because of factors for which the children themselves are not responsible, is a matter of the gravest concern to those who . . . are interested in the education of American children."

Nor does the NEA shy away from the issue of quotas. In an amicus brief filed in connection with *U.S. v. Georgia,* the NEA urged the judge to examine districts where there were serious discrepancies between the ratios of minority teachers and pupils to see whether discrimination had taken place. "That's not a quota system," says Sam Ethridge of the NEA, "but it's as close as you can come to it."

Just now proponents of bilingual education are trying to develop programs that will shore up the underpinnings of the bilingual movement. Resolutions are being proposed and adopted in state legislatures urging that colleges and universities assume greater responsibilities in training bilingual teachers. In Massachusetts, teacher training programs are expanding, and in California a bill is pending that would make over $400,000 available for grants in teacher preparatory programs. The California bill would establish a "career ladder" for ethnic aides to become qualified teachers. More money may soon be approved for materials and test development. Still, the problems are manifold and apparently destined to multiply.

And the results are meager. In Boston last year, out of a school-age Puerto Rican population of perhaps 10,000, a total of 63 graduated from high school. This is appalling—but it's better than before. Between 1965 and 1969 only four Puerto Ricans graduated in Boston. The true returns won't be in for several years. Meanwhile, bilingual education is marching, crabwise, ever onward.

CHAPTER 32

THE COMPELLING CASE FOR BILINGUAL EDUCATION

JEFFREY W. KOBRICK

IN 1968 A SPANISH-SPEAKING community worker named Sister Francis Georgia, observing certain children "visibly roaming the streets" of Boston, conducted a door-to-door survey in a Puerto Rican section of the city. Of the 350 Spanish-speaking school-aged children she found, 65 percent had never registered in school; many others rarely attended or had dropped out. Armed with these facts, Sister went to the Boston School Department to seek help in locating and providing meaningful programs for Spanish-speaking children who were out of school. Skeptical, Boston school officials told her to produce the "warm bodies"; if she did, they said, "seats" would then be found.

At about the same time, leaders from Boston's poverty communities formed a "Task Force on Children out of School" to investigate the way the school system dealt with poor children generally. Among other things, the task force found that as many as half of Boston's estimated 10,000 Spanish-speaking school children were not in school. Between 1965 and 1969 only four Puerto Rican students graduated from Boston high schools.

Three years later, through the efforts of Sister Francis Georgia, community leader Alex Rodriguez, the Boston task force, and two key legislators, Education Committee Chairman Michael Daly and House Speaker David Bartley, Massachusetts passed the nation's first comprehensive state bilingual education law.

The law declares that classes conducted exclusively in English are "inadequate" for the education of children whose native tongue is another language and that bilingual education programs are necessary "to ensure equal educational opportunity to

---

Jeffrey W. Kobrick is an attorney at the Harvard Center for Law and Education.

Kobrick, Jeffrey W., "The Compelling Case for Bilingual Education," *Saturday Review,* April 29, 1972, pp. 54-57.

every child." Massachusetts thus became the first state to *require* school districts to provide bilingual programs for children whose first language is not English. (Other states including New York, California, Illinois, and Texas have laws *permitting* local school districts to provide bilingual programs.) The law calls for the use of both a child's native language and English as mediums of instruction and for the teaching of history and culture associated with a child's native language. It authorizes state expenditures of up to $4 million a year to help districts meet any extra costs of bilingual programs.

The Massachusetts law is a carefully constructed and innovative piece of legislation that hopefully will stimulate legislative efforts elsewhere. Indeed, because the federal Bilingual Education Act has been so underfunded—"Congress has been appropriating drops," notes Senator Walter Mondale, "when showers or even downpours are needed"—there is a critical need for state legislation and funding in areas where there are substantial numbers of Puerto Rican, Chicano, Indian, and other non-English-speaking children. The U. S. Office of Education estimates that five million children attending public schools "speak a language other than English in their homes and neighborhoods." And increasing evidence reveals the almost total failure of our monolingual, monocultural school systems to provide for these children's educational needs.

In New York City alone, 250,000 Puerto Rican children attend the public schools. The estimated dropout (or "pushout") rate for these students has been put as high as 85 percent. Of those who survive to the eighth grade, 60 percent are three to five years below reading level. Nor is the plight of thousands of Puerto Rican children any better in the schools of Bridgeport, Chicago, Philadelphia, Newark, Hoboken, or Paterson. In "The Losers," a report on Puerto Rican education in those cities, Richard Margolis writes: "Relatively speaking, the longer a Puerto Rican child attends public school, the less he learns."

Between two and three million Spanish-speaking children attend school in five Southwestern states where, as Stan Steiner shows in *La Raza: The Mexican Americans,* the schools serve only to "de-educate" any child who happens not to be middle class. More than a third of the Spanish-speaking children in New

Mexico's schools are in the first grade, and over half of those in grades above the first are two years or more overage for their grade level. One Texas school board required "Spanish-surname" children to spend three years in the first grade until a federal court stopped the practice. Chicanos are still put into classes for the mentally retarded on the basis of intelligence tests administered only in English; again, federal courts are in the process of abolishing this form of discrimination. The average number of school years completed by the Chicano in the Southwest is 7.1 years.

Statistics relating to the education of the more than 200,000 Indian children in public or Bureau of Indian Affairs schools are equally dismal. In 1960, 60 percent of adult Indians had less than an eighth-grade education. Today the Indian dropout rate is more than twice the national average and in some school districts is 80 or 90 percent. In an all-Indian public elementary school near Ponca City, Oklahoma, 87 percent of the children have dropped out by the sixth grade. In Minneapolis, where some 10,-000 Indians live, the Indian dropout rate is more than 60 percent. In Washington, Muckleshoot children are automatically retained an extra year in first grade; and the Nook-Sack Indians automatically are placed in slow-learner classes.

One reason schools are failing in their responsibility to these children is that they offer only one curriculum, only one way of doing things, designed to meet the needs of only one group of children. If a child does not fit the mold, so much the worse for him. It is the child who is different, hence deficient; it is the child who must change to meet the needs of the school.

During the first four years of life, a child acquires the sounds, the grammar, and the basic vocabulary of whatever language he hears around him. For many children this language is Spanish or Cree or Chinese or Greek. Seventy-three percent of all Navajo children entering the first grade speak Navajo but little or no English. Yet when they arrive at school, they find not only that English is the language in which all subjects are taught but that English dominates the entire school life. Children cannot understand or make themselves understood even in the most basic situations. There are schools where a child cannot go to the bathroom without asking in English. One little boy, after being rebuffed repeatedly for failure to speak in English, finally said in Spanish: "If you don't let me go to the bathroom, maybe I piss on your feet."

The effects of this treatment on a child are immediate and deep. Language, and the culture it carries, is at the core of a youngster's concept of himself. For a young child especially, as Theodore Andersson and Mildred Boyer point out, "Language carries all the meanings and overtones of home, family, and love; it is the instrument of his thinking and feeling, his gateway to the world." We all love to be addressed, as George Sánchez says, *en la lengua que mamamos* ("in the language we suckled"). And so when a child enters a school that appears to reject the only words he can use, "He is adversely affected in every aspect of his being."

With English the sole medium of instruction, the child is asked to carry an impossible burden at a time when he can barely understand or speak, let alone read or write, the language. Children are immediately retarded in their schoolwork. For many the situation becomes hopeless, and they drop out of school. In other cases, believing the school system offers no meaningful program, parents may fail to send their children to school at all.

Schools seem unmoved by these results. At any rate, the possibility of hiring some teachers who share a child's culture and could teach him in a language he can understand does not occur to them. Since the curriculum is in English, the child must sink or swim in English.

The injustice goes further: Having insisted that a child learn English, schools make little or no constructive effort to help the child do so. Instead schools assume, or expect, that any child in America will "pick it up" without any help from the school. Alma Bagu tells this story about a little Puerto Rican girl's day in school in New York:

> Sitting in a classroom and staring at words on a blackboard that were to me as foreign as Egyptian hieroglyphics is one of my early recollections of school. The teacher had come up to my desk and bent over,

putting her face close to mine. "My name is Mrs. Newman," she said, as if the exaggerated mouthing of her words would make me understand their meaning. I nodded "yes" because I felt that was what she wanted me to do. But she just threw up her hands in despair and touched her fingers to her head to signify to the class I was dense. From that day on school became an ordeal I was forced to endure.

Like most of the people teaching Spanish-speaking or Indian children, Mrs. Newman presumably did not know the child's language. Yet she treated a five- or six-year-old as "dense" for the crime of not knowing hers.

The variety and perversity of the abuses committed against children are unending. In New York it is not unknown for teachers to lecture Puerto Rican students on how rude it is to speak a "strange" language in the presence of those who do not understand it. In the Southwest, where it is widely believed that a child's native language itself "holds him back," children are threatened, shamed, and punished for speaking the only language they know. Stan Steiner tells of children forced to kneel in the playground and beg forgiveness for speaking a Spanish word or having to write "I will not speak Spanish in school" 500 times on the blackboard. One teacher makes her children drop a penny in a bowl for every Spanish word they use. "It works!" she says. "They come from poor families, you know."

These are not the isolated acts of a few callous teachers. America's intolerance of diversity is reflected in an ethnocentric educational system designed to "Americanize" foreigners or those who are seen as culturally different. America is the great melting pot, and, as one writer recently stated it, "If you don't want to melt, you had better get out of the pot." The ill-disguised contempt for a child's language is part of a broader distaste for the child himself and the culture he represents. Children who are culturally different are said to be culturally "deprived." Their language and culture are seen as "disadvantages." The children must be "reoriented," "remodeled," "retooled" if they are to succeed in school.

Messages are sent home insisting that parents speak English in the home or warning of the perils of "all-starch diets" (which means rice and beans). Children are preached middle-class maxims about health and cleanliness. The master curriculum for California's migrant schools prescribes "English cultural games," "English culture, music, and song," "English concept of arithmetic"; nowhere is there mention of the Indo-Hispanic contributions to the history and culture of the Southwest. When Robert Kennedy visited an Indian school, the only book available on Indian history was about the rape of a white woman by Delawares. Even a child's *name* is not his own: Carlos becomes Charles; Maria, Mary.

THE MASSACHUSETTS STATUTE

Every school district is required to take an annual census of all school-aged children of "limited English-speaking ability" and to classify them according to their dominant language. Whenever there are twenty or more children who share the same native language, the district must provide a bilingual program. A separate program must be provided for each language group.

The statute calls for the teaching of academic subjects both in a child's native language and in English; for instruction in reading and writing the native language, and in understanding, speaking, reading, and writing English; and for inclusion of the history and culture associated with a child's native language as an integral part of the program.

Although the school district's obligation to provide a bilingual program is mandatory, participation by the children and their parents is voluntary. Any parent whose child has been enrolled in a program has a right to prompt notice of such enrollment (in two languages), a right to visit his child's classes and to confer with school officials, and, finally, a right to *withdraw* his child from the program.

Parent Involvement:

Parents are afforded the right to "maximum practical involvement" in the "planning, development, and evaluation" of the programs serving their children. Parents, along with bilingual teachers, bilingual teachers' aides, and representatives of community groups, also have the right to participate in policy-making and implementation of the law at the state level.

Bilingual Teachers:

The statute creates a new state certification procedure for bilingual teachers that softens some of the previous rigidities and repeals a former U. S. citizenship requirement (which still exists in thirty states). It also allows bilingual teachers who have met some, but not all, of the certification requirements for teachers to serve provisionally and to count two years of provisional service toward a three-year tenure requirement.

State Reimbursement:

The bilingual statute provides for state reimbursement to local school districts for that portion of the cost of a bilingual education program that "exceeds" the district's average per pupil cost. Additional costs not covered under the bilingual statute are eligible for reimbursement under the general aid to education statute. Although the program is "transitional"—a student's *right* to participate lasts only three years—any individual school district is allowed to go beyond this minimum, and programs that are "permitted" by the statute are reimbursed on the same basis as those that are "required." If a program gains support in a particular community, it is entirely possible that it could be extended into a full bilingual program.

The English-Speaking:

The major weakness of the statute is that it is *silent* on whether English-speaking children may be enrolled in bilingual programs and thus does not contain adequate safeguards against the isolation of minority children in such programs. Bilingual education can be of great benefit to English- as well as non-English-speaking children, and provision for the enrollment of English speakers should be made. The *Harvard Journal on Legislation* has recently published a revised version of this statute, which provides for the enrollment of English-speaking children in the bilingual program.

Humiliated for their language and values, forced to endure the teaching of a culture that is unrelated to the realities of their lives, it is no wonder that children withdraw mentally, then physically, from school. "School is the enemy," said a Ponca Indian testifying before Congress. "It strikes at the roots of existence of an Indian student."

Far from accomplishing its professed aim of integrating minorities into the "mainstream," the monolingual, monocultural school system has succeeded only in denying whole generations of children an education and condemning them to lives of poverty and despair. There is no more tragic example of the fruits of such policies than that of the Cherokees.

In the nineteenth century, before they were "detribalized," the Cherokees had their own highly regarded bilingual school system and bilingual newspaper. Ninety percent were literate in their own language, and Oklahoma Cherokees had a higher English literacy level than native English-speakers in either Texas or Arkansas. Today, after seventy years of white control, the Cherokee dropout rate in the public schools runs as high as 75 percent. The median number of school years completed by the adult Cherokee is 5.5. Ninety percent of the Cherokee families in Adair County, Oklahoma, are on welfare.

Obviously, no particular "program," not even a bilingual one, can be expected to cure all this. The remark of the 1928 Meriam Report on Indian education holds true today: "The most fundamental need in Indian education is a change in point of view."

Bilingual-bicultural education is perhaps the greatest educational priority today in bilingual communities. Its aim is to include children, not exclude them. It is neither a "remedial" program, nor does it seek to "compensate" children for their supposed "deficiencies." It views such children as *advantaged*, not disadvantaged, and seeks to develop bilingualism as a precious asset rather than to stigmatize it as a defect. The very fact of the adoption of a program recognizing a child's language and culture may help to change the way the school views the child. It may help to teach us that diversity is to be enjoyed and valued rather than feared or suspected.

There are also strong arguments supporting the pedagogical soundness of bilingual education. Experts the world over stress the importance of allowing a child to begin his schooling in the language he understands best. Such a policy makes it more likely that a child's first experience with school will be a positive rather than a negative one. Moreover, as John Dewey and others have said, language is one of the principal tools through which children learn problem-solving skills in crucial early years. Policies that frustrate a child's native language development can cause permanent harm by literally jamming the only intellectual channel available to him when he arrives at school. Those who would concentrate on teaching a child English overlook the fact that it takes time for a child unfamiliar with the language to achieve a proficiency in it even approaching that of a child raised in an English-speaking home. In the meantime, struggling to understand other academic subjects, children fall hopelessly behind. In a bilingual program, by contrast, two languages are used as mediums of instruction; a child is thus enabled to study academic subjects in his own language at the same time he is learning English. Bilingual programs teach children to read their own language and to understand, speak, read, and write English (in that order). Language is oral. It is *"speech* before it is reading or writing."* When a child enters school already speaking and understanding a language, he is ready to learn to read and write it. A program that prematurely forces English on a child can guarantee his eventual illiteracy in that language.

The "English-only" approach also misses the prime opportunity to teach a child to read his own language. Recent experience indicates that development of literacy in one's native language actually enhances the ability to learn English. When the Navajos evaluated their own bilingual school at Rough Rock, Arizona, they found that the children were more proficient in both languages than they would have been "if you tried to stuff English down the throat of a child who can't understand what you're talking about." Nancy Modiano reports similar results in a highly controlled experiment with Indian children in Chiapas, Mexico. The children who had read first in their native language showed greater proficiency in reading *Spanish* (the national language) than their control peers who had been instructed solely in Spanish. Modiano explains that the children were much more confident about learning to read in a language they already knew; having learned the mechanics of the reading act, they could apply their skill in learning to read another language.

In addition to facilitating the learning of English, bilingual education has other benefits. It helps to correct what Bruce Gaarder, former chief of the U. S. Office of Education's modern language section, has called "an absurdity which passeth understanding." More than $1 billion a year is spent on foreign language instruction. "Yet virtually no part of it, no cent, ever goes to maintain the native language competence which already exists in American children." Bilingual education also allows English-speakers to learn a second language far more effectively than they could in a foreign language program, because their classmates are native speakers. And it develops and enhances children's intellectual capabilities. Bertha Treviño found that in the Nye School, outside Laredo, Texas, both Spanish- and English-speaking children learned mathematics better bilingually than they did when taught in English alone. In Montreal, children who were educated bilingually scored higher on both verbal and nonverbal intelligence tests and "appeared to have a more diversified set of mental abilities" than their monolingual peers.

Despite the promise of bilingual education, however, only a handful of programs were in operation in the United States during the 1950s and 60s. In fact, prior to 1968, twenty-one states, including California, New York, Pennsylvania, and Texas, had laws requiring that all public school instruction be in English. In seven states, including Texas, a teacher risked criminal penalties or the revocation of his license if he taught bilingually.

In the late 1960s the Chicanos in the Southwest and other groups mounted a widespread campaign for bilingual, bicultural education. In 1967 Senator Ralph Yarborough of Texas introduced a bilingual education bill in Congress, which finally passed, in modified form, as an amendment to Title VII of the Elementary and Secondary Education Act of 1965.

The psychological impact of the federal Bilingual Education Act, a landmark in our history, cannot be overestimated. It reversed a fifty-year-old "one-language" policy and committed the moral force of the national government to meeting "the . . . educational needs of the large numbers of children of limited English-speaking ability in the United States." The act provided financial assistance to local educational agencies for, among other things: " (1) bilingual educational programs; (2) programs designed to impart to students a knowledge of the history and culture associated with their languages; (3) efforts to establish closer cooperation between the school and the home."

This commitment by the federal government has slowly influenced states and local communities. Since 1968 eleven states have passed laws permitting local school districts to provide bilingual instruction and, as stated earlier, one state, Massachusetts, has required school districts to provide bilingual education programs (although participation by the children is voluntary).

Nevertheless, even today very few children enjoy the "luxury" of bilingual education. Title VII has become a highly selective program presently serving only 88,000 of an estimated five million non-English-speaking children. The problem rests primarily with the funding structure of Title VII, which has proved singularly unable to stimulate comparable state and local efforts. The federal act, for example, pays the entire cost of the programs it supports. But since Title VII is grossly underfunded, the federal programs necessarily remain limited. If a local government wishes to institute additional bilingual programs, it must appropriate money from local funds. There is no provision for sharing costs across levels. Thus each level of government becomes reluctant to support a comprehensive bilingual program because it fears it alone will bear the possibly large costs of the program. If, however, costs were shared among the different levels of government—federal, state, and local—each agency might be willing to contribute more.

The Massachusetts legislation provides a needed innovation in this respect. The law requires school districts to offer bilingual programs but provides for state reimbursement of that portion of the cost that *exceeds* the district's average per pupil cost. For example, if a district's annual expenditure per child is $800 and the cost to offer bilingual education is $1,000, the district will be reimbursed $200. The philosophy of the Massachusetts law is that a local school district has an obligation to spend at least as much for the education of a bilingual child as it does for the education of any other child. The funding formula thus allows state money to go much further than if the state alone bore the cost. By redirecting money from the regular program to a program that better serves the needs of the non-English-speaking child, scarce resources are put to much more productive use.

The appeal here, however, is not to expediency. Many children in this affluent land are being denied their fundamental right to equal educational opportunity. To the needs of these children society must respond, and now.

CHAPTER 33

BILINGUAL EDUCATION—NO!
BICULTURAL EDUCATION—YES!

MARION L. DOBBERT

THE NATION IS BEGINNING to develop bilingual education programs for its Spanish-speaking migrant children. People involved in planning for these programs are fully aware of the fact that there are more differences between Spanish-speaking children and Anglo-English-speaking children than differences in language; and differences in cultural heritage and lifestyles are mentioned for consideration in planning programs.

I have participated in such a planning session and I would like to examine the issues of heritage and lifestyle, since very few school administrators and only a few teachers are trained to deal with the matters involved when we say that Mexican-American, Indian, or black children have a different cultural heritage and lifestyle. As a cultural anthropologist specializing in the study of complex cultures and education, my training has been aimed at the study of cultural differences.

From an anthropological point of view, any two groups of people with different histories will have a different way of life, a different culture, even though the two groups may live next door to each other. Because conditions will have been at least slightly different for each group, they will have developed slightly different ways of making a living, explaining the world, organizing society for living, making decisions, and raising children. This is why we Americans are not like our English, German, or other ancestors, nor even like a mixture of parts from all our ancestors. The conditions of frontier society, both physical (native plants, soils, climate) and social (the need to work together in

Marion Dobbert is presently doing research on the anthropology of education for the University of Wisconsin, Madison. She is also an instructor at Aurora College, Aurora, Illinois.

Dobbert, Marion L., "Bilingual Education—No! Bicultural Education—Yes!" *Illinois Journal of Education, 63(4):5-9*, September/October 1972.

new ways to survive), created a new culture. Even the North and South have somewhat different cultures because different physical and social conditions have prevailed in those regions since the foundation of this country and, thus, a person from the North or South who moves to the other region often finds himself uncomfortable. How much more uncomfortable a Spanish-speaking or Indian child must feel!

The culture concept provides us with a tool for seeing just where those uncomfortable differences lie. A good basic operational definition of culture for analytical purposes would look something like this:

> Culture is the term for a whole, unique way of life that consists of (1) an economic system for production, consumption, and distribution of goods, services, and satisfactions; (2) a social system which organizes people by families, by work groups, by economic groups, by religious groups, etc.; (3) a political system for making decisions on all levels; (4) a system for explaining the world and the forces in it that operate upon human beings; and (5) a system of passing on these systems to the next generation.

The culture concept illustrates clearly and forcefully the precise cultural differences between one group of Spanish-speaking Americans and the middle-class Anglo-Americans who have shaped our school system. I will use as an example the Mexican-American migrant workers of Hidalgo County, Texas, since much of the information can be generalized to other Mexican-Americans although, of course, the Mexican-Americans of anywhere are not exactly like those of Texas and individuals may be very different.[1] Also, Mexican-Americans in other socioeconomic niches differ greatly from the patterns described below.

It could be said that the Mexican-Americans of Hidalgo County belong to the same economic system as school teachers. Their jobs may be different, but they pick and pack the Del Monte vegetables and fruit that we all eat and they are paid in "good ol' greenbacks." While this is true, it does not say everything. A migrant's or day laborer's wages are so low that often his wife and children must work at least part of the year to meet basic expenses, and migrant and day labor jobs are not permanent. Thus, the labor and time of women and children may be an important economic asset, which is not generally true among middle-class Anglos. Secondly, many migrant workers maintain two seasonal households, a permanent one in Hidalgo County for winters and a summer household on the road.

In the area of economic consumption, the spending patterns of many Mexican-Americans, particularly those of recent migrants, are different than those of middle-class Anglos. The lower economic class in Hidalgo County do not believe in spending money to "get ahead." To "get ahead" and have more and better possessions than one's neighbors would shame them, and a good person would not thus insult other members of "La Raza." He may give his extra money to the Church or he and his wife might buy a religious picture with it. Satisfaction is derived from this pattern of life because working on the land is a "noble and natural labor." If a man's income provides the necessities—good food, beer, cigarettes, and an occasional movie—he sees his life as a fulfillment of his God-given role and feels no need for social mobility. This kind of economic satisfaction is hard for a middle-class Anglo to understand, yet it is a part of the Mexican-American economic system which must be understood since school education is closely connected with upward social mobility.

The social system of Mexican-Americans, too, varies from the Anglo social system. The migrant Mexican-Americans of Hidalgo County do not regard the social system as a ladder to climb, whereas Anglos of the Horatio Alger tradition do. If this difference is viewed with eyes of prejudice, Mexican-Americans look lazy to Anglos and Anglos look avaricious to Mexican-Americans. One works to climb and the other does not, and, of course, neither group would want to be like the other. But, if this matter can be seen in cultural context, perhaps it can be dealt with rationally.

Most Anglos are aware of the different family system of Mexican-Americans, the family system in which the father is the absolute head, given absolute respect and obedience from his wife and children. For a Mexican-American this tight family is his primary shelter from all the evils of the world. A person knows he does not stand alone. The whole family backs him, loves, guides, and guards him. In fact, a Mexican-American thinks of himself as a family member first, and as an individual second. In return, the individual is always a representative of his family and must do nothing to cast shame upon it. Thus, this strong family provides very important social control and where it functions well, children grow up to be respectable adults. It contrasts strongly with Anglo households which try to create independent individuals. In order to teach individualism, Anglo families often give up the closeness and warmth the Mexican-American families share.

Kluckholm and Strodbeck have identified three basic ways people make decisions and get things done.[2] Each of these is a basic political system and is founded on a different principle. Anglo-Americans make many decisions on an individual basis. In voting, each individual decides for himself and all the individual decisions are added up to make the group decision. This individual principle is also used in running family affairs to a great extent, particularly with older children who make their own plans subject to parental veto. In a collateral decision system, everyone in the group must agree before the decision can be made. Some American Indians have used this kind of a system. Mexican-Americans have traditionally used a lineal system. In this system, people are arranged in a hierarchy with respect to social rank, virtue, or age. The decision is made by the highest person and followed gladly by everyone else because it is felt that the highest person deserves that rank and ought to be followed. In Mexican-American communities, elders and males rank at the top of the group. Elderly males of good families make community decisions because they are wise and respected. Fathers make decisions in families, or failing a father, the eldest son, if he is old enough. The advantage of this kind of a political system is that people feel confident the decisions are the best because they are based on the experience and understanding acquired by a respected elder and upon the collective intelligence of the men.

All cultures have a system for explaining the world to man and pointing out his place in it. Again Kluckholm and Strodbeck have identified three possible ways of looking at the relation of man to Nature/God. Man may be considered as subject to Nature/God; he may consider himself in harmony with Nature/ God, as do many American Indians, or he may consider himself as superior to Nature/God. A Mexican-American believes that he is inferior to God the Creator. This is certainly a logical belief since man does not control wind, rain, floods, volcanoes, or even fires in his home. Similarly, he does not believe he can control the course of his life. Rather, he believes his course is controlled by fate, which is God's will. For this reason, a man does not try to change his station or plan for his distant future but tries to live today as he is, as God would have him. Anglo-Americans feel that they are superior to Nature and although we agree that we cannot control floods and volcanoes, we, unlike the Mexican-Americans, think that we will someday. We also think we control our own fates and, thus, we lay out our courses of life through college. We plan for our movement up the ladder in various companies or schools to become managers or deans; our retirement; etc. We expect to achieve the goals by our own personal strength, and because we do not have complete control, we pay the price in ulcers, heart attacks, and "nerves." This difference in viewpoint has also led to much prejudice on both sides between Anglos and Mexican-Americans.

The fifth system, passing on these social beliefs to one's children, also differs between Anglo- and Mexican-Americans. If we consider the very different economic, social, political, and belief systems that children from two cultures learn, it is evident that the socialization of the young children is very different. A very small Anglo child learns to "stand up for his rights" against other children, even to talk back to his parents, to compete in games, and to speak out his likes and dislikes. This is necessary for individualization in Anglo culture; it helps bring about his future success in school and business. A very young Mexican-American must, on the other hand, learn respect for male elders, learn to think of his family first, learn a strongly differentiated sex role and become an intelligent strong man or a weak dependent woman. Small children learn these things informally at home through parental discipline and, probably more important, through watching their parents who are models for them. This informal system has already done a great deal for a child by the time he is six years old. He has changed from a squalling bundle of potentialities into a cultured individual. The informality of the system does not mean that it works less well. Schools should not underestimate the power of this early education. In fact, Mexican-Americans think more highly of this home education, which lasts until a child marries, than of school education, since to them, "an 'educated' person is one who has been well trained as a social being . . . displays polish and courtesy in his social relationships . . . knows how to avoid offending others . . . knows all the rules of Latin etiquette . . . respects his elders and conducts himself so as to receive the respect due him."[3] A school education is often thought of only as useful for boys who have to work and get along in the Anglo-world. How different from Anglos who think school important enough to occupy six hours of a child's day, nine months a year for twelve to eighteen years or more and who dismiss home education as a mere matter of discipline.

This discussion does not begin to cover all the cultural differences between Anglos and Mexican-Americans even in the five categories listed, since culture as a way of life has infinite ramifications. I have mentioned nothing of Mexican-American history, Catholicism, or curanderos to mention three of the most important; but I do hope it makes explicit the kinds of factors that must be considered in planning bicultural education. This kind of cultural material must be considered in planning a bilingual/bicultural program. Certainly the needs, aims, and hopes of the non-English-speaking children who appear in our schools are formed of and are part and parcel of their whole cultural background; and because these children have been formed in a different culture, it is wrong to assume they have the same patterns for learning, can work in the same social classroom set-up, have the same motivations, and wish to learn the same things in school as Anglo-English-speaking children. Since Spanish-speaking children live in and learn economic, social, political, and belief systems that are greatly different from those learned by Anglo children, it would probably be wiser to assume that none of the classroom curricula, social set-ups, or teaching techniques would be useful to them.

That last statement puts forth a pessimistic image of educators burning books and tearing down buildings to begin again. We hardly need to go that far. After all, the children we are discussing do live in the United States and share many things with Anglos by virtue of that fact alone. Besides, burning and tearing is hardly a practical suggestion. Practical suggestions should begin from where we are.

A school that wants to develop a truly bicultural program for its Spanish-speaking Mexican-American migrant children would need to know two things in order to begin its planning. One, where to get data on the five aspects of Mexican-American culture, and two, how it could possibly use such overwhelming and complex data once obtained.

The very best information for the first purpose could be obtained by getting a grant to support a year's field study by an anthropologist in the community for which the program is being planned. The anthropologist could prepare the results of the study for distribution to school district personnel and could teach an in-service institute to prepare teachers to understand the children's cultural background. Such a study need not be expensive; it could be done for about $6,000 by a graduate student for his dissertation. Shorter field studies would also be useful. In desperation, a trained cultural anthropologist could probably provide a good in-service course based on book-knowledge, but because cross-cultural issues are so complex, it would be better to have a field study. There are many anthropologists in the Council on Anthropology and Education who are trained to help schools obtain and use cultural information.*

The bicultural program must be developed by and in conjunction with the people for whom it is planned. If the community whose children participate in the bicultural program do not have

---

* Write Harry Lindquist, Secretary-Treasurer, Council for Anthropology and Education, South Stadium Hall, University of Tennessee, Knoxville, Tennessee 37916.

a heavy hand in the planning and running of the program, it cannot possibly be bicultural, because no matter how much Anglo planners know about Mexican-Americans, they are still Anglo in culture. So the program, to be bicultural and to utilize the best of the two cultures involved, must be run by both cultures. This is the only possible way to take account of the deep differences in culture and to develop a program fitting those differences in culture.

At this point, also, the cooperating anthropologist of education can be of great use. Because the persons planning the bicultural program are from differing cultures they are very likely to fail to understand each other on many occasions. The anthropologist as a trained cross-cultural observer can "translate" for both sides. Also, if the two sides seem to find insoluable differences, the anthropologist out of his experience with many cultures should be able to help find a compromise based on true understanding. Thus, after much hard discussion and careful work based on real cross-cultural comprehension, a genuine bicultural program should emerge.

Bilingual programs, conceived as such, do not reach the heart of the problem. Bilingual programs treat a symptom of biculturalism, language difference. Bicultural programs, on the other hand, reach out to teach the whole child as he is and treat him as a whole human being, not as a deviant who speaks the wrong language.

REFERENCES

1. Madsen, William: *The Mexican-Americans of South Texas.* Chicago, Holt, Rinehart, and Winston, 1964. All information in this article on Mexican-Americans is taken from Madsen's book.
2. Kluckholm, Florence, and Strodbeck, Fred: *Variations in Value Orientations.* New York, 1961.
3. Madsen, p. 21.

PART VIII

RESHAPING TEACHER EDUCATION FOR THE SPANISH-SPEAKING CHILD

CHAPTER 34

NEW TEACHERS FOR NEW IMMIGRANTS

HARRY N. RIVLIN

B Y THIS TIME, virtually everyone knows that the schools in the big cities face major problems as they seek to educate their changing pupil population. The urban schools have an equally major opportunity to help their youngsters develop their potentialities and to continue the social climb they have begun. But the problems will not be solved and the opportunities will not be exploited unless the urban schools have an adequate supply of able and willing teachers.

At present, the problems are most acute in the big city, especially in the inner city. But our population is so mobile and social movements show so little respect for city limits that the problems now so prominent in the inner city will soon become the problems of almost all American education.

Many of the schools' problems arise from social changes and cannot be solved by the schools. The schools cannot wait until the community settles such issues as segregated housing and economic discrimination, for the schools must teach the children who are enrolled right now. Social change is no new phenomenon—undoubtedly Adam told Eve as they were leaving the Garden of Eden that "This is a period of great social change." And society's institutions have always lagged behind changes in that society.

The issues of urban education are analogous to those faced when great waves of immigration washed America's beaches at the turn of the century. Our current immigrants are in transition not from one nation to another, but from one subculture to a potentially more fulfilling one. To serve them in their quest, our schools must provide them first and foremost with better teachers. Dr. Rivlin, Dean of the Division of Teacher Education at CUNY, here suggests a plan for the preparation of these "new" teachers, calling vigorously, among other things, for a longer and more intimate collaboration between colleges and school systems.

Rivlin, Harry N., "New Teachers for New Immigrants," *Teacher College Record*, 66(8):707-18, May 1965.

Cultural Migrants

The children who present the great problem and challenge to today's schools may well be regarded as our new immigrants even though they are American citizens and may not be newcomers to their urban communities. The Southern Negro, the Puerto Rican, and the displaced rural family are immigrants because they have moved from a cultural setting with which they have been familiar to one that is markedly different. Even the Northern Negro and the Mexican-American present many of the social characteristics of the immigrant as they seek to escape from a population eddy in which they have been trapped for generations.

What makes the urban schools' problems so frustratingly difficult is that pressures are being exerted by opposing groups, each of which is right. Virtually all educators are agreed that schools must provide compensatory education when children are handicapped by the paucity of intellectual resources at home, the inadequacy of the schools previously attended, or the absence of a family academic tradition. No educator is against correcting educational and social conditions which interfere with learning.

The schools are under great pressure from groups that want not only Freedom *Now!* but Good Education *Now!* As American citizens, our new immigrants are unwilling to wait for an acculturation process that lasted generations for the older immigrants. They want their children to climb the social ladder with all other American citizens' children. Since all teachers agree that the demand for good education for the new immigrants is basically right, it is hard to resist the pressure for better schools and better teachers for the educationally handicapped.

The schools are also under pressure from another group, which is also right. In 1900, only some 4 or 5 percent of our college-age population went to college. Today, almost half of that group is enrolled in post-secondary school institutions, and the percentage is still increasing. If middle-class parents believe that the schools cater to the educationally handicapped at the expense of their own seemingly educationally talented youngsters, these parents may withdraw their children from the public schools and enroll them in private schools or leave the city—at least the inner city. As an unfortunate by-product of such transfers, the school system loses parents who have been most effective in supporting public education in the past. The stereotype of the big city schools as concerned only with the educationally disadvantaged does a great disservice, for it implies that the city schools have little interest in working with the educationally talented. How can we have integrated education if there are no middle-class children with whom to integrate?

Teachers in Extremis

Today's teacher must, therefore, be able to deal with both the handicapped learner and the talented one, and he needs great insight and ability to help a handicapped learner become a talented one. Teachers are expected to work with the slow readers and the nonreaders who, in earlier days, would have left school. Today, a wiser and a more concerned society no longer ignores the dropout, and teachers are expected to be educational and psychological experts who can keep the dropout in school and make schooling vital and useful for him.

Clearly, the pressures from both eager disadvantaged parents and anxious middle-class parents are legitimate. Adjusting the school to respond constructively to these pressures remains, nevertheless, a difficult undertaking that cannot be successful without capable teachers.

Today's teachers are better educated than were the teachers in the 1900s who had to teach the immigrants of those days. In 1900, for example, no state required a college degree of elementary school teachers and only two states required a baccalaureate degree for secondary school teaching. In 1964, however, 46 of the 52 state systems (including the fifty states, the District of Columbia, and Puerto Rico) required at least a baccalaureate degree for an elementary school certificate, and all 52 required at least a baccalaureate degree for secondary school teachers.

Now that our teachers are better educated, why aren't they better prepared to deal with our new immigrants? Why do so many of our young teachers experience a feeling of "cultural shock" when they are appointed to their first job? Why do so many teachers discard what they learned at college and become the kind of teachers their colleges refuse to accept as cooperating teachers to whom student teachers can be entrusted?

Before I am listed erroneously as having enrolled in the Society for Attacks on Teacher Education, let me state positively that the average young teacher today is better prepared to teach, in terms of both general education and professional training, than was his 1900 predecessor; and let me point out, too, that thousands of new teachers each year accept appointments to urban schools and stay. I know, moreover, that there are a great many thoroughly competent and interested teachers in our inner-city schools who are slandered unmercifully by those who speak of "slum schools staffed by inferior teachers." Yet, the persistent problems indicate that changes in the ways in which we prepare and assign teachers are in order.

One aspect of the problem is illustrated by a new college which started an education department with everything in its favor. The college had a great educator as president and a carefully chosen student body. Among these students were some who wanted to teach; and from this group, the education department selected those to be prepared for teaching. The department was free to appoint the ablest and most imaginative faculty it could find and to create the program it thought best. Relations with schools both in the suburbs and in the city system were so cordial that experiences with children and with varied schools were included as part of every major professional course. Student morale was high, and faculty morale was high. As one of the professors commented: "We have the best teacher education program in the country. If you don't think so, ask us."

Yet life was not perfect. Students returned from the schools with accounts of good teaching and bad. They related some horrible examples of teachers who violated every one of the principles discussed in seminars. At first, even these reports were encouraging because they indicated how much the schools needed the kind of new teachers this college was preparing. Then came a bombshell. Some of the teachers the students were describing were products of *their* program!

Crushed by Reality?

This incident is not unique, for every college has seen some of its graduates mature into superb teachers while others quickly slough off whatever they have gained while preparing to teach. Walter Cook found marked changes between the attitudes of beginning students in teacher education programs and those of seniors. Within a short time after graduation, however, the attitudes reverted to what they were at the beginning.

What happens to these young, enthusiastic, ambitious teachers after only a few years in the classroom? It is easy enough to blame the schools for crushing the new teacher. It is just as easy to blame the colleges for an unrealistic teacher education program. As educators, however, we have little interest in the grand jury's problem of whom to indict. What concerns us is the more constructive question of how best to correct the situation.

When educating for a profession, should we focus the preparation upon the first job that a recent graduate is likely to get or upon preparation for a lifetime professional career? Professional men and women must be prepared adequately for beginning their career, but they must also be prepared to keep growing. In teacher education, we have moved from the normal school's preoccupation with the first job to the college's emphasis upon preparation for a professional career. Is it possible that we are paying too little attention to the demands of the first job?

However greatly we may decry it, we cannot ignore the fact that many new teachers will have their first teaching appointment in an inner-city school with children who present serious educational and social problems. Educators may well envy other professions which reserve the most serious problems for the most experienced and the ablest practitioners; but the fact is that teachers are appointed to fill vacancies, and there are more vacancies in schools that have serious problems than there are in the so-called better schools.

Today's teachers need and get a liberal education far richer than that offered in any of yesteryear's normal schools. Yet these normal schools performed a function, albeit a narrow one, effectively. A normal school graduate could take charge of a class the first day after graduation and take charge competently. Granted that today's new teacher faces more complicated problems, he must nevertheless also be prepared thoroughly for the first year of teaching.

This is no plea for the restoration of the normal school, but our colleges must pay more attention to preparation for the first year of teaching. To be sure, teachers must be prepared as professional educators rather than trained narrowly as competent beginning teachers. It is also true, however, that a teacher who is prepared for a professional career, but who cannot survive his first year of teaching, does not stay long enough to become a professional teacher.

It is at this point that it becomes apparent that our concept of preservice education is outdated. At present, the preparation of the teacher up to the time of appointment is very largely the concern of the college, with the school system playing a minor role. Once the recent graduate is appointed, however, he becomes a full-fledged member of the school system, with the college playing, at best, only a secondary role and often none at all. Much will be gained if the schools and the colleges work together in the preparation of a prospective teacher and continue this cooperation up to the point of tenure.

Ideas into Practice

The colleges may be right in refusing to instruct future teachers in some of the outdated practices still used in the schools, but they may be underestimating the difficulties which young teachers experience in trying to change existing practices. The problem may not be that of realistic or unrealistic preparation, but rather of the difficulty of translating an idea into practice. If the teacher education program were to continue through the teacher's probationary period of appointment, the newly appointed teacher could be helped to find ways of dealing with his current difficulties without necessarily sacrificing all hope of changing current procedures. Similarly, if the new teacher has continued support and guidance in his period of transition from novice to professional, he may be helped to solve his difficulties without either feeling frustrated or having to sacrifice his idealism for a dreary surrender to "reality."

That some young teachers are able to solve their problems and maintain their faith in themselves, in education, and in their students may be attributable to their inventiveness, adjustability, and idealism. No system of mass education can rely on such unusual successes by unusual teachers. If the unusual is to become the usual, we have to see the first years of teaching as part of the process of learning become a teacher.

Many colleges and school systems now recognize the importance of preparing urban teachers more adequately for their responsibilities. According to the results of a survey conducted recently by AACTE, more than 200 institutions are either presently conducting programs specifically designed to prepare teachers for urban schools or are planning to introduce such programs. Given such an effort, how can we develop in our prospective teachers the skills, the insight, the sense of social need, and the self-confidence that are essential for successful teaching in urban schools? To a degree, these are the same qualities that are needed by any successful beginning teacher. They must be developed to a high degree, indeed, in a beginning urban teacher because the problems are overwhelming for those who are less than adequately prepared intellectually, professionally, and emotionally.

A Proposed Program

The pattern of teacher education proposed here is one answer to these questions. Taken as a whole, it is different from any now in use, but many of its elements have been tried by various institutions and schools. It is based on ten assumptions.

1. No teacher education program can be effective without close cooperation of schools and colleges. The school room and not the college is the place where teachers learn most about how to teach, but teaching is more than a craft to be mastered through an apprenticeship.

2. The education of a new teacher is not completed on Commencement Day, regardless of whether the degree is a bachelor's or a master's. The first years of teaching are of critical importance in influencing professional development and should be included in a program of pretenure teacher education. Schools and colleges should work together with the teacher during his first years of teaching so that he may not only become more competent and skillful but also develop the background and the attitudes necessary for a member of the teaching profession.

3. Teachers should be prepared for educational change, for participating in deciding which educational changes should occur, and in helping to effect them.

4. Individual differences in abilities, interests, and background are as important among prospective teachers and teachers as they are among elementary and secondary school students. The teacher education program and the requirements for certification should be sufficiently flexible to allow for such variations. Classroom teachers also vary in ability, and we should provide opportunities for advancement that keep superior teachers in the classroom.

5. Certification as a teacher should be granted only after completion of a full program of teacher education and not on the basis of the completion of specified courses or of a specified number of credits in teacher education. This program, in turn, should be sufficiently flexible to allow for varying rates of progress in completing the program, with students' being credited for what they have learned outside of class and outside of college, and with students' being advanced from one level of preparation to the next in terms of their ability and not in a lock-step based solely on the lapse of time.

6. Attending classes is only one of many ways of learning, and prospective teachers can learn a great deal from directed reading and independent study, from working with children and schools, and from their own past experiences. These should be recognized by the college and by the certifying authorities.

7. Teaching is so complex a skill that careful gradation of learning experiences is important. The responsibilities entrusted to prospective teachers and beginning teachers should, therefore, be proportionate to their ability to assume these responsibilities. Moreover, the prospective teacher's performance in the classroom as school aide, assistant teacher, and intern offers a valid basis for determining whether he should be permitted to continue his program in teacher education.

8. Supervisors of assistant teachers and interns should be selected in terms of their expertness as classroom teachers and their ability to help prospective teachers and beginning teachers rather

than on the basis of their graduate degrees and excellence as productive scholars. Teacher education programs should take advantage of the insight and skill of experienced classroom teachers.

9. Members of the college faculty who have a doctorate should carry the responsibility for those aspects of the teacher education program in which the advanced study leading to the doctorate is essential. It is wasteful to use such people to perform duties that can be discharged effectively by others.

10. Students who perform useful service in the schools as part of the teacher education program should be paid for their services, but no student should receive an honorarium solely for being a prospective teacher.

To Teach in Cities

If present trends continue, virtually all of our new teachers will be either undergraduate students at a liberal arts college or graduates of such institutions. Within this framework, how can we prepare better urban teachers?

The goal for the initial phases of teacher education should be the relatively modest one of preparing good beginning teachers who will know what to do, how to do it, and why.

The college program should include courses in urban sociology, cultural anthropology, and psychology, for learning is affected by both social and psychological factors.

Because teachers must be able to write and speak correctly and effectively, intensive courses in composition and in speech should be included when necessary.

Undergraduate students who wish to complete their college program within four years and yet be prepared to teach should be required to attend at least one summer session in order to fulfill the requirements for the degree.

The time which a student spends in the schools should be included in his college program so that he will not have to slight either his college or his school duties.

By serving in the schools, the student has a first-hand basis for deciding whether he really wants to prepare for teaching and should be permitted at the end of any semester to withdraw from the program without penalty. The college and the school, on the other hand, also have in the student's school service a sound basis for judging his competence as a teacher and for determining whether or not he should be permitted to continue in the teacher education program.

There need be no chance in the total number of credits assigned to education courses but major courses should be planned in large blocks of credits so that adjustments can be made within a course without the academic rituals that go with expanding or contracting any activity conducted by the department.

The first education course should deal with Urban Education: Its Problems, Practices, and Opportunities. Based on the student's background in urban sociology, cultural anthropology, and psychology, it should help him to see the fallacies of the common stereotypes of "the culturally deprived child" and the "slum school."

While enrolled in this course, the student should serve as a community service aide in a social agency and as a school aide, being paid for his school service at an appropriate rate.

College and School

The existing courses in psychological foundations and in curriculum and methods should be replaced by a two-semester course, taught if necessary by a team of college teachers, dealing with the applications of psychology to methods of teaching. For this course to deal adequately with all that students must know, greater reliance than is now customary will have to be placed upon guided reading and independent study.

While enrolled in this course, the student should be appointed by the school system as an assistant teacher, assigned to a specially selected classroom teacher for three hours a day and receiving one fourth of the salary of a beginning teacher. He should assist the teacher with the clerical and teaching responsibilities and should get experience in working with individuals, groups, and the class as a whole.

The teacher to whom the assistant teacher is assigned should be selected by the school and the college, receiving his regular salary from the school system and an additional fee from the college.

Members of the college faculty should work with these classroom teachers in order to help them be more effective in working with their assistant teachers.

Assistant teachers who are so competent that they are ready to become interns at the end of their first semester should be appointed as interns instead of being compelled to serve a full year as assistant teachers. Whether they take the second half of their combined psychology-methods course or be excused from it should depend upon their achievements and needs.

Upon completion of their service as assistant teachers, students should be appointed as interns and assigned full time to a school under the direction of a supervising classroom teacher who is selected and paid by both school and college. Interns should assume only half the teaching responsibilities of a regular teacher and receive half the salary of a beginning teacher.

All interns and all teachers in their first year of full-time teaching should take a college course concerned with such classroom problems as methods of teaching, class management, and discipline as they arise from direct experience. This course should be taught by a person in close touch with the schools who can deal constructively with the problems presented. The instructor may be a member of the college faculty or of the school staff.

Interns who demonstrate after only one semester that they are ready for the full responsibilities of teaching should be appointed as regular teachers instead of completing a year of internship.

When interns are appointed to a regular position, they should be paid at the second step of the salary schedule in recognition of their service as school aides, assistant teachers, and interns.

College graduates who have not been prepared to teach should be welcomed as a promising source of future teachers if they have the intellectual and personal qualities essential for teaching. Because they are such a heterogeneous group, they will need programs tailored to fit their varied abilities and needs. Some will come with great assets gained from service in the Peace Corps, from active participation in programs dealing with urban problems, or from teaching experience in a non-school setting. Some will need academic courses to bring their subject matter background up to date. But others may bring the negative attitudes of those who have failed in previous jobs and see teaching as a solution to their own problems rather than as a career for which they wish to prepare.

If the college graduate needs to take courses to improve his background for teaching, he should be appointed as a school aide and paid for his services.

As soon as the college graduate demonstrates that he is ready, he should be appointed and paid as an assistant teacher as described above and take the psychology-methods course along with the other assistant teachers.

Upon completion of his service as an assistant teacher, he should be appointed and paid as an intern, taking the classroom problems course.

College graduates who demonstrate such competence in the classroom as to indicate that they do not need a full year as an assistant teacher or as an intern should be permitted to meet each requirement in a semester.

Upon completion of the internship, college graduates should be appointed as regular teachers on the second step of the salary schedule.

Beyond Appointment

All newly appointed teachers should be enrolled in a program of graduate studies and in-service education planned jointly by the institution in which they have matriculated and by the school system that employs them. Their professional education should help them through the trying first years and bring them to eligibility for a tenure appointment as fully prepared teachers.

The master's degree program should be flexible enough to be adjusted to the individual teacher. It should enrich subject-matter mastery and include both advanced courses in his special field and more general courses needed to fill gaps in his academic background. It should deal with the problems faced by classroom teachers, but on a higher level of conceptualization than was possible in the course planned for interns and beginning teachers.

Graduate courses in education should broaden the teacher's point of view (e.g. comparative education), deepen the teacher's insight into the educational process (e.g. new curricular procedures), and improve the teacher's skill (e.g. teaching the non-reader).

Whether in-service courses offered by the school system or specifically requested by it should receive graduate credit should be determined by their level and scope and not by their sponsorship. To earn graduate credit, the course must go beyond the immediate situation, however serious that situation may be, and rise above the how-to-do-it-better level, regardless of how great the need for increasing teacher competence. These considerations should not stop the school system from conducting in-service activities, when necessary, without graduate course credit.

Because graduate study is demanding and teaching is demanding, full-time teachers should not be permitted to enroll in more than one course in any semester. Teachers should be encouraged to spend either a semester or two summer sessions as full-time resident students at their university.

The school system and the college should jointly establish Teacher Education Centers in the public schools in a cooperative experiment in the improvement of elementary and secondary education.

These centers should be operated as regular elementary and secondary schools and should be staffed by administrators and teachers jointly selected by the school and the university because of their professional ability and their demonstrated interest in working with prospective teachers and beginning teachers.

The staff of the Teacher Education Center should be appointed adjunct members of the university faculty. They should have the opportunity to broaden their professional background by visiting other schools and by participating in some of the professional meetings and other activities of a college faculty.

Members of the university faculty, from other departments as well as teacher education, should be actively involved in the Teacher Education Centers in order to help them see what colleges can do in both liberal arts and professional courses to prepare the teacher for meeting his responsibilities. They may be assigned to a teaching responsibility or to working with the school faculty on a major project like the reorganization of the school's mathematics program.

Payment as Service

While it is possible to adopt the proposed pattern of service as school aide, assistant teacher, and intern as preparation for teaching without paying for such service, there are reasons for such remuneration in addition to the principle that people should be paid for professional services rendered.

For undergraduates, the program entails a considerable financial loss. Not only will they have to spend at least one summer and possibly two summers at college if they are to get their degrees within four years—and forego the possibility of earning money during these summer sessions—but the additional time spent in school service during the junior and senior years will make it impossible for them to have any part-time employment during that period. While they are serving as interns, moreover, they will receive only half-pay rather than the full salary which other new teachers get when they are appointed. Since the school service rendered by these prospective teachers not only prepares them to be more effective teachers in urban schools but also improves the quality of the education which children receive, it is unfair to expect the student to subsidize this service personally.

We take too little advantage of the educational opportunities presented by students' part-time employment. Why not use their part-time jobs as a way of helping the student to sample a career before spending years preparing for it? Why not use these jobs as a way of preparing for a career? Why not take advantage of part-time employment as a means of recruiting the teachers we need?

We have not recruited enough college graduates for teaching. We have research evidence that college graduates who are in the thirties or forties and who are adequately prepared for teaching have a better rate of retention in the schools than have undergraduates with equal preparation for teaching. It is difficult to recruit adults for teaching, however, if they have to undergo a time-consuming period of preparation without remuneration and then have only the modest salaries of teachers to which to look forward. Adults are likely to be eager to get into the classroom and start working and earning a salary, and are just as likely to be impatient with a required series of college courses that stand between them and the job they think they are ready to accept.

There is also a possibility that preparation for teaching may become increasingly a post-baccalaureate program. Recruiting students for such programs will be difficult because we shall not be able to offer our graduates as great a proportion of assistantships, fellowships, and scholarships as is available to those going into other graduate programs. Why should a college graduate enroll in a program leading to the teaching of science when he is more likely to be aided financially if he takes his graduate work in science and then goes into industry rather than to the high schools? Payment for subprofessional services in the schools may be a feasible substitute for the scholarship grants that would otherwise be needed in large numbers.

The very rate of payment underlines its being remuneration for services rather than a scholarship grant. It is assumed that both assistant teachers and interns will be learning half the time and serving the schools half the time. Since assistant teachers are in schools for half a day, they are paid for only half their time, or at the rate of one-fourth of the beginning teacher's salary ($\frac{1}{2}$ of $\frac{1}{2}$ or $\frac{1}{4}$). Similarly, interns who are in school for a full day receive only half the salary of a newly appointed teacher.

To Know the Setting

There are other values, too, in having the students paid for their services. City superintendents complain that the reason they do not get enough new teachers is that the colleges present the city schools in a poor light. What better way is there of correcting a false image, if it is a false image, than by letting the students work in the schools as paid members of the staff? Having the school system responsible for these payments will also impress upon the school officials their stake in the selection and preparation of prospective teachers.

All in all, there is so much to be said in favor of paying school aides, assistant teachers, and interns that funds must be found to make such payment possible. To be sure, urban schools face serious financial difficulties and cannot be expected to look kindly at any proposal that increases operating costs. But good education is expensive, and there are no cheap ways either of educating children or of preparing their teachers.

The only reason for not paying students for service as community service aides is the difficulty of finding legal ways of financing. Clearly, the colleges cannot pay students for aiding community agencies, and schools cannot pay people for service in outside agencies. Since most philanthropic organizations operate on a narrow margin, it is unlikely that they can employ additional student assistants. Of course, the arguments that apply for payment for school services are equally valid for the agency work that students do. Unfortunately, realism compels one to admit that these services will probably continue to be rendered on a voluntary, unpaid basis for some years to come.

Aside from financial problems, a major weakness of the general proposal is that it does not go far enough. It seems to stop when tenure is granted as though that were the end of teacher education. Clearly, teachers on tenure must continue to grow if they are to survive as professional people. What such a program of in-service education should be, which activities it should include, and what the roles of the college and the school system should be in planning and conducting it are questions that deserve as full a discussion as does the preparation of the teacher up to the point of tenure. These questions have not been dealt with here, but they are too important to be ignored.

Neither has enough been said about the liberal arts background of the teacher, even though the teacher obviously needs to be both broadly educated and educated in depth in his area of specialization. Inasmuch as the proposed professional program could be adopted in colleges which have widely different liberal arts programs, it would be unnecessarily restrictive to base it upon a single pattern of liberal arts education. Of course, my failure to deal with needed changes in the liberal arts programs may reflect timidity. But it will be difficult enough to change the professional part of the teacher education program without trying to revolutionize the entire college at the same time.

Certainly the conditions in the schools play an important part in determining whether thoroughly prepared teachers will stay or whether they will either resign or seek appointment elsewhere. Rather than yield to the temptation of telling the superintendent how the schools should be run, we shall have to leave to the superintendents and the other school administrators the responsibility for seeing that their schools offer teachers sufficient stimulation and satisfaction. With so many schools looking for good teachers, a thoroughly competent teacher will not stay in a school that is unsatisfying.

In some ways, this program is bound to make teaching in an urban school more attractive. Teachers who are better prepared for urban teaching should find it more satisfying and less frustrating. The program provides for the appointment of school aides who can relieve the teacher of many chores that do not require the services of a professional teacher. It includes the use of assistant teachers who can help the classroom teacher in teaching individual pupils and in providing the supplemental instructional services for which the classroom teacher now has neither the time nor the energy. By offering classroom teachers an avenue of recognition and reward without leaving the classroom, it helps retain able and experienced classroom teachers. More, however, needs to be done, and it is the superintendent and the rest of the school personnel who must decide what to do and how to do it.

Sharing Responsibility

It is to be expected that colleges will be reluctant to assign to classroom teachers so large a share of the responsibility for working with their students. In a sense, the colleges really have no choice. With the increased numbers of students going to college and the shortage of people with the doctorate who can be appointed to college faculties, the colleges will find themselves under increasing pressure to raid the schools in the search for college faculty. Does it not make more sense to use college professors primarily for those responsibilities which demand the doctorate? Thus, college professors, with their broader background, are more likely to know about new developments in education and about promising practices used in schools in various parts of the nation and abroad than is a classroom teacher in a specific elementary or secondary school. But the college professor, who is necessarily limited in the number of times he can observe each student, cannot be as helpful in aiding the novice teacher in his immediate problems as is a competent classroom teacher who is there all day every day.

The proposal does not abandon college students to the schools and it does not eliminate the influence of the college professor, for new teachers need his help. Even a good classroom teacher may overemphasize the importance of imitating his own procedures, for he is often unable to analyze his own teaching style, let alone that of another person. We need the college person to keep service as an assistant teacher or intern from becoming merely a trade apprenticeship.

The Judicious Test

In this proposed pattern,* college faculty will work closely with the master teachers. An important by-product of this relationship is that the classroom teacher who is associated with the college in working with student aides, assistant teachers, and interns has a stimulating avenue of in-service education open to him. These contacts should help the classroom teacher to broaden his own outlook on teaching as he profits from the wider experience of the college faculty member with whom he works. Moreover, the recognition that the classroom teacher receives when he is invited to participate in such a program of teacher education is important psychic income that has significant morale-building value.

While debates serve many useful purposes, they should not be the basis for determining whether we should change our pro-

---

* Some facets of this pattern were first presented at a Task Force meeting of the Great Cities School-University Teacher Education Project funded by the Co-operative Research Branch of the United States Office of Education (Developmental Grant #OE-05-10-131) .

grams for preparing teachers. No program should be accepted because it is presented persuasively, and none should be rejected because of inexpert presentation. If the problem is as serious as that of finding better ways of preparing the teachers we need for our new immigrants, any promising proposal should be tried out and evaluated. We have sufficient research sophistication to know how to evaluate a program that has been tried out experimentally.

Such an experimental try-out is not without its dangers. This is an era of crash programs and pilot projects. Unfortunately, however, many crash programs are not followed through after the publicity has worn off. And many pilot programs lead only to a publication and not to the extension of innovative work that has proved to be successful.

Because our new immigrants need good teachers so desperately, I hope we shall find the means of testing the proposed program. Then we shall know whether to reject it, modify it, or make it our new pattern for enabling urban schools to serve our new immigrants and their longer established fellow citizens.

CHAPTER 35

PREPARING TEACHERS FOR MEXICAN-AMERICAN CHILDREN

THOMAS P. CARTER

. . . education is a mirror held against the face of a people; nations may put on blustering shows of strength to conceal political weakness, erect grand facades to conceal shabby backyards, and profess peace while secretly arming for conquest, but how they take care of their children tells unerringly who they are.[1]

THE MOST PERSONALLY DISTURBING part of this introductory quotation by George Bereday is the last phrase. The serious undereducation of Mexican-Americans implies numerous unpleasant things about present and past Anglo society. We have not taken very good care of some of our children. In spite of our "professations" and grandiose statements concerning the goals of democratic education, the facts glare in our collective face. Innumerable social forces have belatedly brought the grievous conditions of this major sector of our population to society's serious attention. Governing elements of that society are slowly but surely directing the agencies and institutions under their control to take steps to improve the minority's status. The school is the only primary social institution directly under the authority of the community and as such is being directed to assume a major role in these efforts. Specifically, educational institutions must radically improve the academic achievement and school attainment of children of Mexican descent, thus providing them with

Published jointly by ERIC Clearinghouse on Rural Education and Small Schools. New Mexico State University, Las Cruces, New Mexico 88001 and ERIC Clearinghouse on Teacher Education, 1156-15th Street, N.W., Washington, D. C. 20005. This monograph was prepared pursuant to a contract with the Office of Education, U. S. Department of Health, Education and Welfare. Contractors undertaking such projects under Government sponsorship are encouraged to express freely their judgment in professional and technical matters. Points of view or opinions do not, therefore, necessarily represent official Office of Education position or policy.

the skills and credentials essential to climb the social ladder. Educators willingly accept this role—however, problems exist. Schoolmen often do not know how best to accomplish this goal, they do not comprehend the complexity of the problem, and they often assume too great a share of the responsibility for creating it. Educators tend to give too much credence to the exaggerated statements of both vocal minority group spokesmen and members of the "establishment." The school may be becoming the scapegoat of Southwestern society. Too many see the school as principally or solely responsible for the disadvantaged status of the minority. Unfortunately, very few educators or laymen recognize that the school reflects and is a microcosm of the society it serves. Indeed, the backyards of Southwestern communities are shabby, to paraphrase Professor Bereday. However, the total society, including formal educational institutions, created and perpetuated the shabbiness—the subordinate Mexican-American "caste." While the school has accepted its role in remedying the situation, it must not be assumed that it can accomplish the task alone. As the total community created the problem, it must cooperate to resolve it; the school unsupported by other agencies and institutions can accomplish little.

School board members and administrators faced with community pressure to accept the "guilt" for the minority's socioeconomic plight often "pass the buck." They merely transfer the responsibility for the Mexican-Americans' "school failure" to a single institutional ingredient—the teacher. It is regularly argued that the qualities and capabilities of Southwestern teachers are at fault. The villain within the institution is the teacher; re-educate the teacher, and the Mexican-American will succeed. While all agree that teachers must be better equipped in the skill area and must better understand minority children, it is not true that this alone will radically improve the school performance of the ethnic group. As is the case in general society, numerous forces are at play within the school. To improve the teacher without modifying other institutional elements is of little avail. Quality teachers plus other institutional changes can create the quality of schooling essential to contribute to other forces leading to raised Mexican-American group status. A multitude of socioeconomic and cultural conditions hold the minority subordinate; these same forces must help raise him to parity with other ethnic or racial groups. Regardless of the complexity of the situation, programs to improve the capabilities of the teacher are at least steps in the right direction.

Approaches to Solve the Problem

The type of approach or orientation taken by schools is crucial in determining the kind of teachers required and the nature of programs to prepare them. Educators have three major alternative approaches theoretically open to accomplish the goal of a better-educated Mexican-American. The three avenues for action correspond to an equal number of "causes" of low school and societal achievement. The first orientation perceives the Mexican-American culture and the socialization it provides its children as being principally responsible. This is the very prevalent "cultural deprivation" or "disadvantagement" position. The logical action by the school in this case would seem to be "change the child"—make him as much like average middle-class children as possible. A second position argues that conditions existing within the school itself produce the undereducated population. The remedy becomes "change the institution." Finally, there are those that see the nature of the rather distinctive Southwestern social systems as being responsible, the contention being that the agricultural economy and caste-like communities provide only limited opportunity for the minority. If this is the case, the school conceivably could encourage changes in the community. This threefold division of "causes" of Mexican-American low achievement in school and society is oversimplified, as are the three "solutions." In actuality we are not dealing with distinct causes or cures. Suffice it to say, for the purpose of this paper, that causal relationships exist among: diverse Mexican-American subcultures and subsocieties; school systems and the social climates they foster; and community socioeconomic systems. All are interrelated and mutually supportive. The qualities and capabilities required of teachers for minority children are dependent on which orientation is taken by the public schools. It may well require one kind of teacher to "change the child," another to "change the institution," and still another to lead in changing the local society.

To those schoolmen who subscribe to the interpretation that the Mexican-American home provides little of the experience deemed essential for school success, the solution appears clear. The "culturally deficient" Mexican-American child must be artificially provided with those experiences that the middle class enjoys naturally. This is the very common, almost omnipresent, approach of compensatory education. These programs imply as objectives the reorientation and remodeling of the culturally different child in order to adjust him to the regular school—into standard school programs and curriculums. Indeed, the measure of success of these efforts is the degree the "disadvantaged" become like the middle class. These objectives are to be accomplished by exposing the children to middle-class experiences and by providing remedial services when they fail to live up to the school (middle-class) norms. If this is possible the Mexican-American can be expected to be as successful (or unsuccessful) in school as are present majority group children. Such programs entail few major institutional changes and only slight modifications in the quality or quantity of teachers. There is no clear evidence that the school can remake the ethnically distinct child into a facsimile of the "standard American child." Nor is there objective data that clearly establish that any specific compensatory or remedial program reaches its long-term objectives of sustained higher academic achievement or higher rates of participation in secondary or higher levels of schooling. Perhaps only time is lacking, and future longitudinal studies will clearly demonstrate that ESL, Head Start, remedial reading, "cultural enrichment," or what have you will produce the kind of Mexican-American who will succeed in school and society.

The *training* of teachers for compensatory and remedial programs presents far fewer problems and necessitates much less curricular reorganization at the college level than would the *education* of individuals for other and more comprehensive approaches. Many of the skills necessary for a capable compensatory or remedial teacher are essentially technical. In-depth understanding of the total teacher-learner and school-community situation would be ideal; however, it is not absolutely essential for such tasks as being an acceptable remedial teacher, using a language lab, conducting a "Culturally enriching" field trip, or using the most modern overhead projector. While the distinction between *training* (how to do something—perform some skill) and the broader concept *educating* is terribly oversimplified, it is made here to stress a crucial consideration. The minimum preparation of teachers to mesh with the overwhelming majority of existing school programs entails little more than technique acquisition; colleges and universities could with relative ease provide this training. In spite of this, observations in the field support the notion that very few teachers of Mexican-Americans in regular, compensatory, or remedial classes have acquired even minimal quantities of the essential skills. Either the colleges have not provided the training, the teachers have not attended the programs, or if they did, the teachers have not learned what was taught. Something is amiss.

The second orientation or approach implies that conditions within schools inhibit academic achievement and encourage early dropout by Mexican-Americans. Steps to remedy this situation require teaching personnel possessing comprehensive understandings not required in schools operating under the simpler compensatory education approach. It is extremely difficult to find programs that involve a conscious desire to substantially modify the school. This "adjust the school to fit the culturally different population" position finds even fewer practitioners than adherents. Quite a few educators agree that standard middle-class schools have failed many Mexican-Americans. Regardless, few are able to institute programs to substantially modify curriculums, teacher attitudes, school social climates, home-school relationships, or other crucial areas. Unfortunately, most present school practices and programs are approaching the stage of self-justification and self-perpetuation. Very few schools are flexible enough to realistically adjust to local situations. Only a very limited number have objectively investigated negative school social climates[2] sustained by such common conditions as cultural exclusion, fostering too rapid Americanization, rigid tracking, curricular rigidity, rote teaching, overly rigid behavioral standards, ethnic cleavage, *de facto* segregation, and biased and pessimistic staffs. The limited number of educators who recognize the causative relationship between such conditions, low achievement, and early mental and physical dropout is hard pressed to substantially improve the situation. It is far simpler and much less threatening to concentrate school efforts on "phasing in" the "out of phase" Mexican-Americans than it is to seriously study and change institutional factors.

However, if a school system takes this more radical avenue, it requires teachers educated to a rather sophisticated level. These teachers must be able to comprehend and grapple with the often intangible, but multitudinous, aspects of their own and others' society, culture, language, learning styles, personality, and behavior. Additionally, such teachers must understand the role and function of the school as a social institution, especially as it relates to ethnic minorities. The problems created by cross-cultural schooling and possible remedies must be understood. In the course of the last five years, I have conducted hundreds of interviews with teachers of Mexican-Americans and observed countless classrooms. Very few teachers with the comprehensive insights necessary to cope with culturally diverse students were encountered. Most manifested extremely shallow and biased appraisals of the situation—few recognized the importance of institutional factors. Of the exceptions, the majority were impotent, powerless to change institutional practices and conditions.

The education of teachers as described in the previous paragraph is a big order. Their preparation would demand substantial modifications in institutions of higher learning, a task perhaps even more difficult than that of changing lower level schools. Regardless, if educational leadership is essentially satisfied with present school conditions, practices, and curriculums, as well as with the compensatory education orientation, there is little need to educate such individuals. They would have few places to go—few school districts would employ such teachers. The teacher who is prepared to contribute to institutional self-analysis and change, if hired by districts with little desire to do either, would probably be seen as a troublemaker and a disruptive influence. He would not last long.

A third possible avenue to improve Mexican-American school and societal achievement is that of using the school as an agent of directed or nondirected social change. Here the school would attempt by numerous means to change conditions in society. The present socioeconomic systems in much of the Southwest provide only limited numbers of social slots and roles for their subordinate Mexican-American populations. The very common caste-like social structures inhibit upward mobility and the high aspirations of most minority members. School and community leaders profess that job, residential, social, and political discrimination do not exist and that the ideals of America are practiced locally. Regardless, Mexican-Americans learn early that the inverse is often the case. With this recognition, many correctly perceive that "Mexicans" have little chance in local society and that school perseverance and high school graduation do not guarantee them the higher social and economic status they desire. Local school boards and educators might lead the way to change these community conditions and belief patterns; however, it is very doubtful that they will, as educational leaders are too intermeshed with conservative community power elements. Further, it is doubtful that the school could accomplish much by acting independently of other institutions or counter to the mores of local society. If the teacher prepared to contribute to institutional change would find few schools desirous of his services, what of the teacher who actively attempts to change society? Very few districts would knowingly employ teachers who actively campaign for or promote the elimination of job discrimination, *de facto* school or residential segregation, or "five o'clock social segregation."

Needed: A New Breed of Teachers

Without a clear understanding of the interrelated causes and the possible solutions of Mexican-American low achievement and attainment by both educators in the field and in the college, there is little hope of establishing realistic programs to prepare teachers. Both understanding of the problem by the two groups and cooperation between them are essential. Heedless of these two necessities, teacher preparation institutions blithely continue to certify teachers who will have life-long contact with the minority, but do little or nothing to specially prepare them. I know of few special courses, sequences, or tracks intended to provide future elementary or secondary teachers with either essential skills or understandings. While there are specific courses in some colleges that concern the disadvantaged, the poor, and the urban school crisis, few are required in the regular credential sequence —very few specifically treat of the Mexican-American. Little is done by the institutions legally charged with the pre-service preparation of teachers; nevertheless, many of these same institutions sponsor in-service programs. Most are in the form of federally assisted summer institutes. Programs on the teaching of Mexican Americans are among these. The majority stress specialized, almost technical, aspects of teaching the minority. Understandably, the bulk are based on the compensatory approach so prevalent in public schools.

Teacher preparation institutions have done, and continue to do, little to aid their students in coping with the problems associated with cross-cultural schooling and the teaching of the ethnically different Mexican-American. Public schools are attempting much more. Colleges and universities are not only failing to lead the way toward improved school opportunity for the minority, they also are failing to follow the lead of lower level institutions. The average teacher preparation program is as adequate for teachers in upstate New York in 1940 as it is for teachers of Mexican-Americans in the lower Rio Grande Valley of Texas in 1969. This condition prevails in spite of the fact that most Southwestern education faculties are well aware that: the vast majority of their students will teach some Mexican-Americans; a large percentage will teach in classes or schools with a majority of Mexican-Americans; most future teachers of Mexican descent will teach in schools where their own group predominates; both minority group spokesmen and public school educators advocate special programs for teachers; and the Federal Government promotes and could in numerous ways support such programs. Yet little or nothing is done. My institution serves as a good example. The University of Texas at El Paso graduates about 450 students a year who are granted elementary, secondary, or "all-levels" credentials. Of these about 75 percent will teach in the immediate geographic area—an area composed of over 50 percent Mexican-Americans. If our graduate is of Mexican descent, and about 35 percent are, he is almost inevitably assigned to *de facto* segregated minority schools by local school districts. In spite of this, there is no required course or course sequence within Education to acquaint our students with any aspect of the so-called "Mexican problem." However, as a stop-gap measure, student teachers are exposed to from three to six lectures on the subject—the only time in their entire college education sequence that such content is introduced. What makes the situation even worse is that the required teacher preparation omits those courses in which content might logically apply to minorities, culture, or values. No sociology, history, or philosophy of education is required. The dean and the faculty know something should be done; we know it could be done; little is. Our situation is bad; however, we have made a token gesture toward teacher understanding. How different are other Southwestern teacher preparation institutions?

Changes in Teacher Preparation

The "state of the art" of teaching the culturally different Mexican-American is at a low ebb. Improvements in the quality of teachers, as well as in all segments of the institution and general society, will hopefully enhance the minority's socioeconomic chances. Improvements in the teacher must be recognized as only an easy place to begin the needed chain of changes. However, the teacher is the one element in this chain over which control can be easily asserted. The present or future teacher can be helped to do a better job with minority children. Before any program to accomplish this is proposed, some further exposition of present teacher weaknesses is necessary. Regardless of the orientation taken by a school, two aggregates of teacher inadequacies are evident. One is the lack of technical skill in the "science of teaching" area; the other is a severe personal limitation in understanding culture, personality, and behavior.

Teacher inadequacies in the skill area should be obvious to any well-informed and careful observer. Administrators are usually quite vocal in describing teacher shortcomings of a more-or-less technical nature. Too many teachers are ill-prepared to effectively use the more modern approaches to teaching English as a second language. While most "direct methods," including the audio-lingual, are simple to use—few know how to use them. The technical equipment connected with these foreign language teaching techniques is rarely utilized to its full potential or even close to it. I have observed the most traditional sort of formal grammar being "taught" with a most sophisticated and expensive electronic language laboratory. Numbers of audio-visual aids likewise are not utilized maximally. This failure to best use such expensive equipment, and therefore waste the taxpayers' money, is legend. Teachers of remedial subjects usually are ill-prepared to measure, diagnose, or "treat" learning problems. The crucial need for well-trained remedial teachers was mentioned by almost every administrator I interviewed. The more modern techniques for the teaching of reading seemed to have missed most teachers—"projective techniques" are rarely employed in many schools. The inability to validly interpret the measurements of achievement and IQ of ethnically different children is widespread. However, perhaps the biggest skill failing among teachers of Mexican-Americans is their almost universal inability to communicate in Spanish. All factions seem to concur that this skill is essential for teachers of the minority. There is no valid reason, except institutional ineptitude and rigidity, why teachers cannot become relatively proficient in the language spoken by so many of their pupils. I could go on; however, I'm sure that at least in regard to skill deficiency among teachers, many would concur.

The severest weakness of teachers is their failure to understand a number of concepts concerning culture, society, personality, and behavior. Teachers almost universally have little understanding of the effects of the first two on the latter two, or of interrelationships among the four concepts. Specifically, three areas of teacher deficiency are evident; the great majority: (1) fail to recognize the overwhelming influence of culture on personality and behavior; (2) have extremely limited knowledge of, or contact with, Mexican-Americans; and (3) do not grasp the role and function of the American school in general society, nor recognize its influence on the ethnically different child. Very briefly, the following common teacher behaviors, and many others, encourage the belief that most fail to fully comprehend the concepts mentioned above or their importance to learning. Teachers regularly are pessimistic concerning the minority's ability to learn, equate race (national origin) and intelligence, prohibit Spanish speaking, act negatively toward ethnic peer groups, misinterpret Mexican-American behavior in school, stereotype the group, maintain extreme social distance with minority members, and take absolute ethical and moral stances. They obviously fail to recognize how all these affect the child growing up in two cultures.

The two preceding paragraphs have touched upon teacher inadequacies. Any program to specially prepare teachers for Mexican-Americans must have as its prime objective the overcoming of the inadequacies described. Teachers must acquire both skill and knowledge. As no one can really know what someone else knows, changed teacher behavior must be the principal criterion of success or failure of programs. The existence of concepts and theories in the mind of the teacher can only be demonstrated by action. The appropriateness of this action is *the* important test. The teacher well-prepared to teach minority children must be able to constructively synthesize skills and knowledge into appropriate school practices and curriculums.

In order to better prepare teachers of Mexican-American children, I suggest that some rather radical surgery be done upon present programs.* What is proposed is a clean removal of existing formats of teacher preparation. From the static colleges of education constantly receive from all their publics, one would suppose radical reorganizations were an everyday occurrence. As you know, they are not. Regardless, for teachers of the minority, three major changes are suggested. First, the content taught must be reorganized and presently slighted areas strengthened. Second, vastly increased student involvement with the minority must be arranged. Students must be forced to interact with the real world

---

* It always concerns me at this point as to whether the proposed changes would not be equally appropriate for teachers of *any* category of children.

within the school, with the minority community, and in activities such as **P.T.A.** that bridge the two. The field experiences should, as much as possible, be coordinated with the content presented in the classroom. Third, small group seminars, modeled after "T-group" or "sensitivity sessions," must become an integral part of the program. These seminars are catalysts; without adding any new ingredient, they should hasten the process of interaction between what is presented in class as reality (and the theories to explain it), and what is observed and coped with in the field. These seminars must force a reconciliation, or at least a constructive encounter, between content taught by more formal methods and content "taught" through experience. Content, seminars, and field experience are all essential to the preparation of quality teachers. One of the components without the others strikes me as little improvement over present emphasis on content. It is impossible to propose specific arrangements of these proposed program components. Whether they are utilized in a special track for teachers of Mexican-Americans, a special course or two, an institute, or an in-service program depends on innumerable conditions. The three components can be modified to fit specific requirements as to time, money, faculty, and the nature of students. Even a one-day "pre-first-day-of-school" teacher institute could be organized along the recommended lines.

Much of the present content of teacher certification programs is applicable for our specially prepared teachers and should be retained. However, all should be carefully scrutinized and reorganized to eliminate repetition. It seems to me that the "knowledge," theory, and skills might be better arranged into three cores: (1) the sociocultural; (2) the psycho-personal; and (3) the professional-technical. However, other descriptive terms might be applied—what matters is that content be somehow interrelated. The psycho-personal core should stress psycho-linguistics, the effect of cultural marginality and value conflict on personality, and areas related to adolescent ethnic behavior. The professional-technical core includes those skills usually taught in methods courses: the how to teach, how to organize, and how to test areas of instruction. Teachers of the minority need additional skills.

Four major aggregates of skills must be stressed. These include the skills associated with remedial teaching, the ability to use psychometric instruments and to correctly interpret them vis-à-vis the culturally different, the crucial ability to communicate in Spanish, and the techniques of modern foreign language teaching. Perhaps an ideal way to accomplish the last two would be to use the audio-lingual technique in teaching the future teacher Spanish. Thus the English speaker would gain the essential new language while learning techniques usable in teaching English. The student's ongoing experience in the school and community must provide ample opportunity to practice and demonstrate competence in these skills.

The so-called sociocultural content core is the most crucial for teachers of Mexican-Americans and is also the area that is most slighted in regular teacher preparation sequences. Indeed, it is appalling how few teachers are objective in their views of society and culture or have any real grasp of culture's influence on themselves or their students. This core must bear the burden of providing an objective understanding of: (1) the concept of culture and society; (2) cultural evolution, social change, and the individual problems in coping with them; (3) the profound and perhaps all pervading influence of culture in determining human personality and behavior; (4) the concepts of caste and subculture as they exist in the modern world, especially the Southwest; (5) the nature and history of the diverse Mexican-American groups and their cultures; (6) the role played by the school in transmitting the "general national culture"; and (7) the theoretical and practical aspects of problems related to cross-cultural schooling, especially vis-à-vis language difference and normative conflict. The objective presentation of theories and concepts relative to the preceding may well induce a sense of shock in many, especially since the concurrent field experience forces the student to confront social reality. This real world so different, yet so similar, to the one in which he lives may produce "culture shock." It is intended to. No teacher can succeed with the culturally different and/or poverty community unless some rather personal things occur. The student's basic assumptions about himself, the world he lives in, and his explanations of both must be subjected to reappraisal. The "folk myth" explanations of such items as race, achievement, or poverty must be destroyed. Too often such unsound explanations deter an individual's ability to cope with the very real problems associated with such ideas. The sensitivity session experiences in the seminars must provide the emotional support essential to the individual as he reconstructs himself and his beliefs. This core hopes to demonstrate that culture, society, and human behavior are understandable, and that to understand them fully, one's own values, beliefs, and attitudes must be examined objectively.

Specific attention should be focused on the influence of culture on personality and behavior. Man's views of himself, others, and the world are all influenced by the social environment in which he is nurtured. Inherent in this is the idea that truth, beauty, and morality are socioculturally determined. Claremont Graduate School conducted a teacher "reeducation" project with content and objectives similar to most proposed here. This graduate level project dealt with the:

> . . . educator's great difficulties with pupils, parents, and communities of heterogeneous social or ethnic natures and high mobility by showing some of the social and cultural aspects in the relationships of all parties and in the abilities of pupils to learn at school. This meant showing educators what culture is, its particular manifestations in different traditions (whether the manifestations be different languages and religions or different modes of treating a mother), how one recognizes specific cultural factors influencing individual and group conduct, how families pass on their ancestral cultures, even when they seem assimilated to another, how a pupil might manifest his special heritage in the classroom, and how a teacher might unwittingly do the same.[3]

In this project participants were encouraged or "forced" to understand culture's influence on their own individual perceptions, attitudes, and behavior—to see culture as manifest within themselves. Teachers were aided in this process by participating in small group seminars not unlike those suggested here.

Teachers must become aware of the Mexican-American culture characteristics. The world view, value orientations, family relationships, and roles of the group must be well known. However, major problems exist that must discourage the teaching of any set list of distinctive characteristics. One problem is that we have very little objective information concerning Mexican-American culture in general. Inversely, we have too much subjective information. Let me illustrate. No contemporary widespread empirical study indicates that a monolithic or static Mexican-American culture exists. Every indication is that minority culture varies by geographic area, that even within the same geographic area differing kinds and rates of acculturation are evident, as well as that distinct adaptations to the dominant Anglo societies have been and are being made. Only two cultural items appear even close to universal—Mexican-Americans *tend* to speak Spanish and to be Roman Catholics. The cultural diversity of the group is extreme; however, most of the literature describes one uniform and rather static culture.[4] Mexican-Americans are usually pictured as being, among other things: fatalistic, present-time oriented, patriarchal, superstitious, personalistic, and generally carriers of a "folk culture." While such may describe certain isolated groups or be valid appraisals of older conditions, there is no reason to believe it characterizes present Mexican-American culture in general. What we are constantly told about the culture does not appear to correspond with reality.

There are other reasons for not teaching the specifics of Mexican-American culture. The characteristics ascribed to minority culture in most descriptions mesh all too perfectly with the almost universal Anglo stereotype of "Mexicans" in general.[5] To teach these might lend a certain measure of scientific validation to presently held but unsound overgeneralizations. It is also doubtful that descriptive statements foster the in-depth awareness of cultural differences teachers must acquire. Dr. Fred Romero's recent research on teacher knowledge of the influence of culture on school behavior points up the dangers of the casual treatment of culture. He found a:

> . . . general teacher sensitivity to, and awareness of, socio-cultural differences of the . . . Spanish-American and Anglo. This teacher awareness . . . could very well be superficial and not based on real knowledge

of what constitutes a culture value system. In addition, cultural sensitivity may result from attitudes formed from operating stereotypes. Under these conditions a lack of real sensitivity could, in fact, exist.[6]

Too detailed, but superficial, descriptions of cultural characteristics of Anglo-Mexican cultural differences probably discourages in-depth understanding. For example, if teachers are taught that minority families teach their sons to be *macho*, this one characteristic (whether valid or not) may be used to describe or interpret wildly diverse male behavior. Such treatment of culture is entirely too simplistic. The objective of this core is not to describe Mexican-American culture in general, but to provide teachers with the skills and insights necessary to determine the cultural characteristics of the group with which they are in contact. The teacher's knowledge of local cultural variations is essential to the ability to incorporate cultural items into the curriculum, and to the teacher's skill in coping with children's difficulties in "learning" two sets of norms. The combination of theory of culture and society, and the continual field experience plus the seminars, should help the student to objectively describe and interpret any culture he encounters. No teacher should be told about Mexican-American culture; instead, programs must be established to force him to "see and feel it."

I recently came across a statement in an education text that is the very antithesis of the kind of knowledge teachers must acquire. To illustrate the general lack of information rampant, let me quote the only paragraph in the book concerning America's second largest minority:

In the Southwest, the Mexican-Americans continue to live in the slum atmospheres they have known for so long. The work they undertake is seasonal and they are finding that greater mobility is necessary. These migrants are working their way toward the East, and as they do they discover that both their skin color and their language are handicaps.[7]

This sort of misinformation must be countered. Teachers must understand the present socioeconomic status of this group as well as recognize the forces that led to the present situation. An objective history of this minority in the Southwest and the group's hispanic roots must be presented. Glorification and idealization of this tradition must be avoided. A "glorified heritage" is just another "folk myth" to be destroyed prior to gaining real understanding.

In summation, let me stress a number of points. Two major considerations are evident in planning teacher preparation programs or projects. What kind of teachers do the public schools want? This must be determined by a careful analysis of the orientation of a school and the nature of programs it undertakes to enhance Mexican-American school performance. After arriving at the answers to these riddles, it is essential to cooperate with teacher preparation institutions to establish the kinds of programs necessary. Schools of education, it must be remembered, may be just as inflexible and rigid as the public schools. Thus, it may be necessary to prod them a little or to aid the "young turks" inside to do so. Both schools and teacher preparation institutions must change before any real benefit will trickle down to our ultimate clients—children. Perhaps steps to specially prepare teachers for minority children will encourage the needed changes.

Hopefully, some of the items suggested to specially equip teachers for minority children will be useful. The specific items in any program must be determined "on the spot." However, every program should include the crucial components—content and field experience and some arena where students can reconcile the two. What has been suggested is far from a perfect outline—it was not intended to be. I have omitted many considerations and slighted others. Regardless, let me emphasize in conclusion that teachers must be prepared to cope with the problems associated with cross-cultural schooling. To do so involves teacher awareness and understanding of social reality. Any program must *force* teachers to comprehend and deal with the real world of children, minorities, and poverty. As the function of all teachers is some sort of action, it behooves any program to destroy "folk myths," stereotypes, and idealized pictures of reality. If programs fail in this regard, we can expect teacher behavior to be less than adequate, since it would be based on false premises. The school is charged with helping to solve grievous social problems. To do so requires a new breed of educator—one equipped to make objective appraisals of problems, and to take rational and appropriate steps to encourage their elimination. It's a big order—we must get on with it.

REFERENCES

1. Bereday, George Z. F.: *Comparative Method in Education*. New York, Holt, Rinehart and Winston, 1963, p. 5.
2. For additional information on conditions and practices in schools that promote negative social climates see:

    Carter, Thomas P.: *The Mexican American in School*. Published in 1969 by the College Entrance Examination Board, New York.

    Gordon, C. Wayne, *et al.*: *Educational Achievement and Aspirations of Mexican-American Youth in a Metropolitan Context*. Mexican-American Study Project Educational Sub-Study, Center for the Evaluation of Instructional Programs, Graduate School of Education, University of California at Los Angeles, March, 1968. (Mimeographed.)

    Parsons, Theodore W., Jr.: *Ethnic Cleavage in a California School*. Unpublished Ph.D. dissertation, Stanford University, 1965.

    Coleman, James S., *et al.*: *Equality of Educational Opportunity*. U. S. Department of Health, Education and Welfare, Office of Education. Washington, U. S. Government Printing Office, 1966. See also the unofficial analysis of the Coleman document by George W. Mayeske, "Educational Achievement Among Mexican-Americans: A Special Report from the Educational Opportunity Survey," National Center for Educational Statistics, U. S. Office of Education. Technical Note 22, Washington, January 9, 1967.

    Michael, John A.: High school climates and plans for entering college. *The Public Opinion Quarterly, XXV*, Winter, 1961, pp. 585-594.

    Wilson, Alan B.: Residential segregation of social classes and the aspirations of high school boys. *American Sociological Review, XXIV*, December, 1959, pp. 836-845.
3. Landes, Ruth: *Culture in American Education*. New York, John Wiley and Sons, 1965, p. 15.
4. For detailed contemporary description of these assumed characteristics see:

    Johnson, Kenneth R.: *Teaching the Culturally Disadvantaged*, Unit 1. Chicago, Science Research Associates, Inc., 1966.

    Zintz, Miles V.: *Education Across Cultures*. Dubuque, William C. Brown, 1963.

    Hayden, Robert G.: Spanish-Americans of the Southwest: life style patterns and their implications. *Welfare in Review*, April, 1966.

5. See:

Simmons, Ozzie G.: The mutual images and expectations of Anglo-Americans and Mexican-Americans. *Daedalus,* Vol. 90, No. 2, 1961.

Parsons, Theodore W., Jr.: *Ethnic Cleavage in a California School.* Unpublished Ph.D. dissertation, Stanford University, August, 1965.

6. Romero, Fred E.: A study of Anglo-American and Spanish-American culture value concepts and their significance in secondary education. *A Research Contribution for Education in Colorado,* Denver, Colorado State Department of Education, September, 1966, III, No. 2, p. 7.

7. Rees, Helen E.: *Deprivation and Compensatory Education: A Consideration.* Boston, Houghton-Mifflin, 1968, p. 13.

CHAPTER 36

MINORITIES: AN INSTITUTE FOR PREPARING TEACHERS OF PUERTO RICAN STUDENTS

FRANCESCO CORDASCO and EUGENE BUCCHIONI

E LEMENTARY AND SECONDARY SCHOOL Puerto Rican students are
confronted by the usual array of educational difficulties and
emotional and social problems related to poverty or low-income
status. In addition, Puerto Rican students demonstrate the life
styles, values, and normative understandings and responses characteristic of Puerto Rican culture. The lack of specially trained
teachers prepared to work specifically with Puerto Rican students
is a major factor affecting the quality of the educational program offered to Puerto Rican students. Furthermore, teachers
who are not specially trained contribute significantly to conflict
in schools with large Puerto Rican enrollments. The lack of professional skills in areas such as remedial reading for Puerto
Rican students, conversational Spanish, the teaching of English
as a foreign language, and guidance of Puerto Rican students,
as well as the general lack of knowledge of Puerto Rican culture
and of the Puerto Rican experience on the mainland, are additional factors contributing to unsuccessful school achievement
and widespread academic retardation common among Puerto
Rican students.[1]

The writers propose a Staff Development Institute for Elementary and Secondary School Teachers of Puerto Rican Students,
which will be concerned, consequently, with the development of
knowledge of, and insight into, Puerto Rican culture and the
Puerto Rican experience in the U. S.; specific professional skills,
such as remedial reading for Puerto Rican students, methods and
materials for the teaching of English as a second language, and

The authors are, respectively, professor of education, Montclair State College,
Upper Montclair, N. J., and associate professor of education, Lehman College, The
City University of New York.

Cordasco, Francesco, and Bucchioni, Eugene, "An Institute for Preparing
Teachers of Puerto Rican Students," *School & Society*, Summer 1972, pp. 108-9.

specific guidance procedures to be used with Puerto Rican students; conversational Spanish as spoken within the Puerto Rican community to enable teachers to relate to, and communicate more effectively with, both parents and children whose knowledge of English is very limited; and bilingual education—its philosophy, structure, objectives, curriculum, and methods and materials of instruction. Teachers, together with other school personnel, will participate in the program, forming teams of about four teachers from schools with high percentages of Puerto Rican students in attendance. The function of the team structure will be to provide a nucleus of individuals in selected schools so that a variety and diversification of professional skills will be available.

Each participant in the institute will take seminars entitled, "Puerto Rican Students in American Schools" and "Aspects of Puerto Rican Culture and History." Each member of a school team will choose from the following offerings: philosophy, structure and curriculum, and methods and materials of instruction in bilingual education; remedial reading for Puerto Rican students; teaching of English as a second language; conversational Spanish; and guidance of Puerto Rican students. Finally, a synthesizing seminar will be offered to each participant on the basis of level of teaching: elementary teachers will take "Elementary Education for Puerto Rican Children," and high school teachers will be expected to complete "Secondary Education for Puerto Rican Students."

The institute should be implemented through lectures, discussions, films, readings, field trips, and with extensive contact with members of the Puerto Rican community. An important feature of the institute should be the inclusion of many Puerto Rican professionals and other members of the Puerto Rican community in the various offerings and activities of the program.

Some attention should be given to the selection of participants in terms of the following criteria: reasonable competency and satisfactory service in a school; general social and emotional maturity; and commitment to the education of Puerto Rican students and to teaching in the Puerto Rican community.

Through interviews, letters of recommendation, and the examination of the professional history of the applicants, an attempt should be made to select only those teachers who have a firm commitment to the education of Puerto Rican students, and who demonstrate the characteristics required for success in the institute and for implementation of learnings, skills, and knowledge derived from the institute in their respective schools. In addition, each participant selected should possess the leadership potential necessary for developing required changes as part of the team returning to each school. In this way, the impact of the institute will go beyond that of the participants alone, and will be extended to other members of the school staff, who will be encouraged to use the members of the team completing the institute as leaders or resource people in the education of Puerto Rican students.

Costs for the institute may be defrayed in part by Federal or by local funds, depending upon budgetary exigencies. Title I (Elementary and Secondary Education Act) funds may be budgeted appropriately within existing guidelines, and, where districts have applied for Title VII (ESEA) funds, the institute may be part of the program (within Title VII guidelines) for the education of non-English-speaking children.

REFERENCE

1. Cordasco, Francesco, and Buccioni, Eugene: *Puerto Rican Children in Mainland Schools: A Sourcebook for Teachers.* New York, Scarecrow/ Grolier, 1972.

CHAPTER 37

ORGANIZATION OF THE
BILINGUAL SCHOOL

A. BRUCE GAARDER

A BILINGUAL SCHOOL is a school which uses, concurrently, two languages as mediums of instruction in any portion of the curriculum except the languages themselves. Thus, for example, arithmetic taught in both English and Irish, or arithmetic in English and history in Irish, or all subjects (except Irish and English) in both tongues would constitute bilingual schooling. English through English and all other subjects in Irish would not. The teaching of a vernacular solely as a bridge to another, the official language, is not bilingual education in the sense of this paper, nor is ordinary foreign language teaching.

Bilingual schools of several kinds and varied purpose are now and have long been in operation worldwide. This paper assumes that there are at present sound reasons, which will become increasingly more compelling, for establishing many more such schools and seeks to set forth some guidelines for their organizers. These reasons, briefly stated,

for *adding the mother tongue* as a teaching medium are

    a. to avoid or lessen scholastic retardation in children whose mother tongue is not the principal school language

    b. to strengthen the bonds between home and school

    c. to avoid the alienation from family and linguistic community that is commonly the price of rejection of one's mother tongue and of complete assimilation into the dominant linguistic group

    d. to develop strong literacy in the mother tongue in order to make it a strong asset in the adult's life

for *adding a second tongue* as a teaching medium are

This article was written by the author in his private capacity. No official support or endorsement by the U. S. Office of Education is intended or should be inferred.

Gaarder, A. Bruce, "Organization of the Bilingual School," *Journal of Social Issues,* Vol. XXIII, No. 2, 1967.

a. to engage the child's capacity for natural, unconscious language learning[1, 10, 11]

b. to avoid the problems of *method, aptitude,* etc., which beset the usual teaching of second languages

c. to make the second language a means to an end rather than an end in itself[11]

d. to increase second language experience without crowding the curriculum

e. plus other well-known reasons which do not concern us here: to teach the national language, to provide a lingua franca or a *world status* language, for cultural enrichment, and economic gain.

The literature on bilingualism gives virtually no information on the organization of bilingual schools. Furthermore it generally omits consideration of the teaching-learning process itself: what happens in the classroom—the interaction of teacher, pupils, methods and materials—and the theories of language and language learning underlying those happenings. This paper gives central importance to what happens in the classroom, and it is largely based on such a body of theory.[8] The position taken here is that however desirable—or undesirable—bilingual schooling may be, its effectiveness can neither be assessed nor assured without full consideration of school organization and classroom practices.

The following chart shows some basic features that differentiate bilingual schools:[11]

	Mother tongue added	Equal time and treatment	(no example known)
One-way school: one group learning in two languages		Unequal time and treatment	Hiligayon in the Philippines; Welsh in Wales, in some schools.
	Second tongue added	Equal time and treatment	In some Welsh-English schools, one language alone on alternate days.
		Unequal time and treatment	Irish in southern Ireland; Russian in non-Russian USSR; most bilingual schools in Latin America; English in Nigeria; French in Madagascar; English in Wales in some schools; French or Spanish in grade 12 in nine Virginia high schools.

Two-way	⌠ Segregated	⌠ Equal time and treatment	Spanish-English, Miami, Florida (mixed classes in grades 4-6)
school:	classes	Unequal time and treatment	(no example known)
two groups, each learning			
in its own		⌠ Unequal time	Spanish-English, Laredo, Texas;
and the		and treatment	English-Sweedish, Viggbyholmssko-
other's	Mixed		lan, Sweden; German-American
language	classes		Community School, Berlin-Dahlem.
		Equal time	English-French, Ecole Active
		and treatment	Bilingue—Ecole Internationale de Paris; L'Ecole Internationale SHAPE, St. Germain; the European School, Luxembourg.

The dynamics and pedagogy are not at all the same in a school which adds the mother tongue as in one which adds a second tongue. In the *two-way* model both the mother tongue and the second tongue are added.

Organization is here viewed as process and product. That is to say, organization is taken as (a) the process or course of action followed in bringing a bilingual school into existence and (b) as the educational structure which follows upon and is to some extent determined by (a). The view taken here is that the most important factors entering into the structure of bilingual schools are the time allowed for each of the languages, the treatment and use of each language and whether the language which is added to the previously existing system is the mother tongue or not. Other factors, too, can make a great deal of difference to the school's effectiveness, e.g. whether individual teachers teach in one or in both languages, whether one or two languages are employed within an individual class period, the relative socio-economic status of native speakers of each of the languages and the relative prestige of each.[2, 4]

Organization as Product

Coral Way Elementary School

A bilingual school which can be used to illustrate the major organizational patterns and the problems of bilingual schooling is the Coral Way Elementary School in Miami, Florida.* In opera-

---

* The Coral Way project was established with Ford Foundation support. The director of the Ford Foundation Project was Dr. Pauline M. Rojas.

tion since 1963, in a neighborhood broadly representative of all economic levels but mostly lower middle class, it is a six grade school with normally four classes at each grade level and a total of approximately 720 pupils. Half of the pupils enter the school as monolingual speakers of English; half are native speakers of Spanish (Cubans), some of whom know bits and pieces of English. Coral Way Elementary is a *two-way* bilingual school, since each group learns through its own and the other's tongue. Since Coral Way has segregated classes (the language groups are not mixed in grades 1 to 3 and only a limited extent in grades 4 to 6), it is in effect two *one-way* schools. For the Cubans (in this United States setting) Coral Way adds the mother tongue; for the Anglos[†] it adds Spanish, a second tongue. It gives as nearly as possible *equal time and treatment* to the two mediums. Finally, since either of the two halves, the Anglo or the Cuban, could function alone as a *one-way* school with complete effectiveness, Coral Way exemplifies all the organizational possibilities except that of *unequal time and treatment*.

Equal Time, Equal Treatment

Equal time, equal treatment means curriculum-wide (except for the languages themselves) use of both languages as mediums. Coral Way presents all subjects in grades 1 to 3 through the mother tongue for approximately half the day, and all are taught again through the other tongue during the following half. These are segregated classes. There is, however, free interchange of both languages for physical education, art, music and supervised play, during which periods the groups are mixed.

There are two sets of teachers, native English and native Spanish (four teachers in all, one for each of the four classes at each grade level), plus four bilingual teaching aides. The aides perform two kinds of teaching task: they are responsible for the physical education, art, music and supervised play; and they give special help to slow learners and transfer students. Even more importantly, they allow the regular teachers free time every day

---

† A term widely used to differentiate native English speakers from native speakers of Spanish.

for consultation and planning for the purpose of coordinating the two halves of each child's program.

The Coral Way bilingual school program was initiated in grades 1 to 3 simultaneously, work in the second language being increased by stages until by approximately mid-year each child was receiving half of his instruction through each of the languages. After the initial year this procedure was followed in the first grade only. As noted above, in grades 1 to 3 new concepts and skills are learned first through the vernacular and then reinforced by being taught again through the second tongue. This is not slavish imitation of the first teacher by the second one, but rather the presentation of the same content and concepts in a fresh, somewhat different way by a teacher with the varied perspective of another country‡ and another language. In the fourth and fifth grades (the third year of operation of the school) it was found that the pupils' command of the second language was such that they could learn through it alone without need of a duplicate class in the vernacular.

Despite the carefully coordinated dual-perspective double teaching of each subject, the basic methodological principle is that of expecting the instructors in each language to act in the classroom as if that were the only language in the world and the children's entire education depended on it. This means that work in one language is not presented in terms of or with reference to the other one.

One of the most difficult problems at Coral Way arose from the need to provide the same curricular time allotments as in other Miami schools. Although the reinforcing procedure gives maximum second language experience with minimum crowding of the curriculum, some time inevitably goes to the second language per se. This reduces the amount of extracurricular activities during school hours.

The most crucial teaching problem is the proper initiation of pupils (in grades 1 to 3 during the first year of the school and in grade one thereafter) to the second language. The same problem occurs with latecomers and with transfer pupils who enroll initially above grade one. The Coral Way solution has two special

---

‡ The Spanish medium teachers at Coral Way were born and educated in Cuba.

features: (a) close coordination of each day's second language experience with the preceding experience in the vernacular, and (b) careful structuring of the second language experience so that although the teacher-class interaction gives the impression of complete spontaneity, the teacher's portion is in fact worked out in advance to introduce and review constantly a specified corpus from the form and order systems and from the lexicon of the new tongue. Detailed linguistic sequences for English and Spanish *as second languages* were developed in order to meet the needs of the several content areas of the curriculum. The oral lesson material is supplemented by a great many pictures of objects and activities. As an additional precaution to assure a good second language beginning without detracting from the other curricular areas, the school day is lengthened one hour during the last twelve weeks in grade one, and one hour throughout the year in grade two. In grade one the second language is taught by the regular second medium teacher. Transfer pupils get special help with their second language from the aides. These pupils sit with their grade-mates all day except during the regular class in the second language, when they receive semi-private instruction from the aides. This special help, 30 to 45 minutes daily, may be required for only a few weeks or it may go on for an entire year.§

Indications of Success

There are several indications that the Coral Way bilingual school has been successful. The introduction at the fourth and fifth grade levels of mixed classes in each language without re-teaching in the other was based on the teachers' judgment that learning had become equally effective through either language alone.‖ Those Anglo pupils who entered Coral Way in the first

---

§ Similar concern for developing readiness for second language work in the newly-enrolled pupil is reported from the Ecole Active Bilingue (Ecole Internationale de Paris), L'Ecole Internationale SHAPE St. Germain, and the German-American Community School, Berlin-Dahlem. See Stern, *op. cit.,* 58, 59, 61.

‖ Preliminary findings of a three-year doctoral study of pupil achievement at Coral Way, scheduled for completion in 1967, show that on successive administrations of the Cooperative Inter-American Tests (H. Manuel, University of Texas), which have equated forms in English and Spanish, the learning curves for each group in its two languages are coming very close together. (Communicated by the researcher, Mrs. Mabel Richardson.)

grade in September 1963 (and who therefore have been exposed for the longest time to the possibly harmful effects of receiving half of their schooling through a foreign tongue) have been the object of close attention. On the Stanford achievement tests, administered in the spring of 1966, their median percentile ranking was as follows: paragraph meaning, 85; word meaning, 93; spelling, 99; arithmetic reasoning, 93; and arithmetic computation, 60. Their median score on the Otis Alpha test of mental maturity was 89. These pupils are not a selected group. Thus far the scores of the Cubans on these tests (all given in English) are generally lower than those of the Anglos, despite the fact that fluency in English is a prerequisite for taking them. Expert observers have noted that the Anglo children acquire excellent pronunciation of Spanish, while the English of some of the Cuban children shows interference from Spanish. This is attributed to the fact that the former group hears nothing but native Spanish, while in the homes of the latter one hears a good deal of heavily-accented English spoken by adult immigrants.#

It is scarcely surprising that the Cubans' scores on tests of achievement given through the medium of their second language are lower than those of the Anglos. A fair comparison could be made only if both groups were tested through both languages. Extensive testing of Puerto Rican children by the International Institute of Teachers College, Columbia University, using comparable Spanish and English forms of the Stanford achievement tests showed this to be true.[5]

Unequal Time, Unequal Treatment

Unequal time, unequal treatment for each of the languages characterizes most bilingual schooling throughout the world. Typically, the added language (i.e. taught in addition to the na-

---

These data and much of the other description of Coral Way school were furnished by Mr. Lee Logan, the school principal. His help is here gratefully acknowledged. An incidental fact of interest is that the annual cost at Coral Way attributable to its being a bilingual school is about $17,000 in excess of what it would cost as a monolingual school. This is a four per cent increase of the school's annual budget. The extra money goes to pay the teaching aides and to buy Spanish language teaching materials.

tional, official or regular school language), whether it is the mother or the other tongue, is kept in a subordinate position. This is commonly true of the mother tongue, as when rising nationalism forces the introduction of history through Spanish in Mexican French-language schools, or when African vernaculars are introduced in the early primary grades as a mere bridge to the eventual exclusive use of English. It is true of the other tongue, as in the USSR where several hundred high schools were to teach some academic or scientific subjects—especially physics and mathematics—through English, French or German[9] or in the United States, where there is a movement currently under way in a few high schools and colleges to teach such courses as history and geography through the medium of the second language to advanced students of that language.

One of the most promising unequal time and treatment programs in the United States is for schools where some of the students at each grade level have in common a mother tongue other than English. The program is simple. Instead of ignoring or deploring the children's home language the school provides regular instruction in and through it for something like a period a day in all grades. The course material may be, for example, Spanish language arts and literature** or it may be a sampling of all areas of the regular school curriculum. The latter seems better, for it takes virtually no time away from the regular curriculum and has the added advantage of employing the language as a means to ends other than achievement in the language itself. The latter system also contributes more to curriculum-wide literacy in the mother tongue.

The question of time and treatment, equal or unequal, is central to the larger question of the alleged handicap of bilingualism most often reported in the literature in school situations where the mother tongue is the subordinate language, given markedly unequal time and treatment, ignored completely or

---

** Such a program, *Spanish-S,* is established in Dade County, Florida. Course of study bulletins may be secured from the Superintendent, Dade County Public Schools in Miami.

even made the object of official censure. There is increasing awareness that the cause of any handicap may not be the existence of bilingualism per se, but school policy regarding the teaching of both languages and sociological factors extrinsic to the school itself.[6, 7]

Organization as Process

Wherever bilingual education is to be an innovation great care should be exercised to inform and orient all sectors of the community—particularly parents, pupils and all persons officially concerned with the school—to the rationale, procedures and goals of the program. In addition to general meetings of all parents, separate grade-level meetings have been found desirable.

The teachers should have native-like command of the language taught, with academic preparation and experience through that medium. In order to maximize the dual perspective pupils can get from bilingual schooling, the teachers should be native speakers educated in the country where the language is native. A special feature of the Coral Way program commends itself to this writer. During the summer preceding the opening of the school and the two following summers a six-weeks workshop on teaching methods and materials and for program planning was conducted for the Coral Way teachers. The first summer there was a required course in descriptive linguistics and another in the structure of the English language, for all teachers. As noted above, the use of teacher aides frees time every day for the regular teachers to coordinate work in the two languages.[††]

Regarding teaching materials little can be said in the brief space of this essay. In some vernaculars books and other materials are inadequate or nonexistent. As for the added second language, if suitable texts are available from the language's home country a healthful biculturism can result from the chance to use them in addition to texts prepared for use in the country where the school is situated, but overemphasis or exclusive use of books

---

[††] In the opinion of the Coral Way principal, Mr. Lee Logan, the first requisite for success is that the school principal have the privilege of selecting every member of the staff. The second requisite is that aides be employed as noted above.

based on a foreign environment can divorce the school from the reality of the child's home and community.

The course of action to be followed to bring a bilingual school into existence should be set with full awareness of the essential differences between teaching the mother tongue and teaching a second language.

Deep Grammar

The native speaker of a language (including the native speaker-teacher) usually has no awareness of the *deep grammar*[12] of his own language, i.e. the interdependent systems of phonology, morphology and syntax which comprise it, and the extent to which the native speaker-child brings virtually complete, thoughtless mastery of the systems to school with him at the age of six. As with his own regional accent and the complex body motion which accompanies his own speech, he doesn't know or knows only vaguely that the deep grammar is there and is concerned in the classroom with the niceties of usage (Say "as a cigarette should," not "like a cigarette should."), with grammatical nomenclature (This is a verb, and this is its direct object.) and with orthography (*i* before *e* except after *c*). Usage, nomenclature and orthography, whatever their importance, are of the surface alone; they are applied on top of the deep, thoughtless mastery which the native speaker-child acquired at home.

Grammatical nomenclature and the niceties of usage are at best a sort of polish on the surface of the deep grammar, the language itself. This polish can be applied quite effectively when the pupils speak an acceptable variant of the subject language, especially if theirs is the same variant as the teacher's. The polish is largely ineffective with the speaker of an unacceptable variant; the configuration of his deep grammar is so different that the polish, applied in the traditional ways, doesn't even touch the surface. Finally, there is the situation of the child who is not a speaker of the language to which the teaching is applied. In the sense of the figure used here, he has no deep grammar in the new language, hence no surface to be polished.

The point is that for pupils who speak unacceptable variants of their school language (e.g., English-based Jamaican Creole or Liberian Pidgin English) just as for pupils who are learning a second or foreign language, the normal materials and methods and orientation of the mother tongue class are not very effective.

Another common weakness in the teaching of a second language derives from the assumption that language is composed of words and that teaching is therefore teaching words. The grain of truth in this assumption gives the child no clue to any of the structural or paralinguistic differences among, for example, these utterances (which would be enormously more complex if presented orally, as they must be to the neophyte):

1. I haven't seen him for five years.
2. Hace cinco años que no lo veo.
   (It makes five years that not him I see.)
3. Seit fünf Jahren habe ich ihn nicht mehr gesehen.
   (Since five years have I him not more seen.)

Yet visits to the classrooms reveal teachers who, irrespective of the materials that are being used, are concerned largely with the *names of things* and word-correspondence from language to language.

Next, there is the teacher who is overly aware of the traps described above, particularly the importance of developing in the child a sense and command of the stuff of language itself, what we are calling deep grammar. Here the most serious weakness lies in over-structuring the course materials at too early an age, i.e., too early and overt dependence upon pattern drills based on contrastive analysis of the two languages, or upon the strict sequencing of the order of presentation of the features of the new language. Such drills and sequencing are not in themselves bad. The harm seems to come when their use requires that children 3 to 7 years old focus their attention on the language itself rather than beyond language, on their involvement in events or situations. The way out of the dilemma is suggested above in the description of Coral Way. If the child is to acquire the intuitive sense of deep grammar which he lacks, the teacher must know how to give it to him in ways which, however structured and systematized they may be, have the appearance and effect of complete spontaneity. For as Penfield says, speaking of the child's learning of a second tongue, ". . . language is not a subject to be studied nor an object to be grasped. It is a means to other ends, a vehicle, and a way of life."[10]

Finally, there is the question of whether or not to allow teacher and pupils to use both of the languages of a bilingual school during a given class period (as opposed to confining each to its own class periods or its own part of the day). In the United Nations Nursery School in Paris children three to five years old are mixed without regard to mother tongue and the teachers use both languages, a sentence in one then the same sentence in the other, especially at the beginning of the year with three-year-olds. This practice is implicitly justified on the grounds that two thirds of the school population is transient and that the children need above all security and understanding. Four- and five-year-olds are allowed to hear each language alone for increasingly longer periods of time.[3] But the weight of opinion seems to favor the one language-one person principle.

Unquestionably a young child learns a second language quickly and effectively if it is the unavoidable means to his full-time involvement in all the affairs of his life. Much less than full-time involvement will suffice for him to learn the new language. The minimum time, the optimum kind of involvement, and the affairs most conducive to this learning process *in a school* are still largely unknowns. Water falling drop by drop into a bucket will fill it, unless, of course, the conditions are such that each drop evaporates before the next one strikes.

REFERENCES

1. Anderson, Theodore: The optimum age for beginning the study of modern languages. *International Review of Education, 6*:298-306, 1960.
2. Carroll, John B.: Research problems concerning the teaching of foreign or second languages to younger children. In *Foreign languages in primary education: the teaching of foreign or second languages to younger children.* (Report on an International Meeting of Experts 9-14 April, 1962, International Studies in Education), H. H. Stern, Ed. Hamburg: UNESCO Institute of Education, 72-80, 1963.
3. Dartigue, Esther: Bilingualism in the nursery school. *French Review, 4,* 1966.

4. Fishman, Joshua: Bilingual sequences at the societal level. In Carol J. Kreidler (Ed.), *On teaching English to speakers of other languages, Series II.* Champaign, Illinois, National Council of Teachers of English, 139-144, 1966.

5. (The) International Institute of Teachers College. *A survey of the public educational system of Porto Rico.* New York, Bureau of Publications, Teachers College, Columbia University, 93-149, 1926.

6. Jensen, J. Vernon: *Bilingualism—effects of childhood bilingualism.* (Reprinted from *Elementary English,* Feb. 1962, 132-143; April 1962, 358-366) Champaign, Illinois, National Council of Teachers of English, 1962.

7. Lambert, Wallace and Peal, Elizabeth: The relation of bilingualism to intelligence. In Washington, D. C., American Psychological Association, *Psychological Monographs: General and Applied,* 1962, No. 546, 76, No. 27.

8. Moulton, William G.: *Linguistics and language teaching in the United States, 1940-1960,* Utrecht, Netherlands, Spectrum. (Also available from Superintendent of Documents, U. S. Government Printing Office, Washington D. C. 20402, 1963.)

9. *New York Times,* October 11, 1964.

10. Penfield, Wilder, and Roberts, L.: *Speech and brain mechanisms.* Princeton: Princeton University Press, 1956, chapter 9.

11. Stern, H. H. (Ed.): *Foreign languages in primary education: the teaching of foreign or second languages to younger children.* (Report on an International Meeting of Experts 9-14 April, 1962, International Studies in Education), Hamburg, UNESCO Institute of Education, 1963.

12. Twaddell, W. Freeman: Does the FL teacher have to teach English grammar? *PMLA, 57(2):*20, 1962.

13. UNESCO: *The use of vernacular languages in education.* (Monographs on Fundamental Education-VIII), Paris, UNESCO, 1953.

PART IX

EDUCATIONAL AND SOCIAL ISSUES

CHAPTER 38

THE STRUGGLE FOR LA CAUSA

PETER BORN

The keys to success for the Latin emmigrant in the United States are education and employment. The older person needs a job to take care of his family, and the younger one needs an education so he can compete for a better job later.

U. S. Rep. Herman Badillo
of New York, the only
Puerto Rican in the House
of Representatives.

THROUGHOUT HISTORY, the Spanish-speaking have found it difficult to fit into Anglo society. Early American writers, particularly those in New England, glorified Anglo-Saxon traits as most noble. This tended to create prejudices against anyone who was even slightly different.

The creators of the melting pot theory rationalized that the foreigners could become acceptable if they were forced out of their little colonies, made to give up their foreign tongues, and be more or less coerced into "doing things our way." So every attempt was made to break up the "Little Italys," "Little Polands," and "Little Irelands."

But not every group found this process easy and not every foreigner wanted to be "melted." Some felt their cultural background was something worth saving.

The values of Puerto Rico and old Mexico, for example, contrast sharply with technological, material-minded America. Because Latin countries have traditionally had a two class society— the rich and the poor—there was little upward mobility. Instead of prizing outward symbols of success such as a car or a house the Latins stressed the inner human qualities of self respect, a man's honor, his dignity, and amount of responsibility in caring for his family.

Born, Peter, "The Struggle for La Causa," *The Latins,* A background report prepared by the Chicago Tribune Educational Services Department, 1972, pp. 9-16.

A sheepherder was imprisoned in his station of birth, so he was judged on how he tended his flock and provided for his relatives. Many Latins could not comprehend the American system of dispensing wealth only on the basis of merit, nor could they understand why people would take welfare from indifferent strangers.

Life south of Miami and Los Angeles is a matter of interconnecting personal relationships. Men depend on relatives and friends rather than impersonal systems, as is done in industrial America.

Even religion was viewed in highly personalized terms. The Spanish tended not to identify with church hierarchy or ideology. The Catholic saints were worshipped as deities who were also warm benefactors and friends. It has been said that during the Spanish Civil War of 1936 to 1939, men would risk their lives to rescue their "santos" from the burning Catholic churches they had just set fire to.

The lack of upward mobility in Spanish society also was responsible for an ingrained sense of fatalism that many Anglos mistook for lack of ambition. If a project fails, some Latins may simply shrug and say that it wasn't meant to succeed. Or others may throw up their hands and say, "You are Mexican, you have to pick cotton." They ponder the spirit and soul of life rather than try to conquer the world physically. Those of lower station cherish what they have rather than concentrate on what they could get.

Preoccupation with a man's intrinsic worth is seen strongly in male-female relationships where the man's masculinity, or machismo, is strongly emphasized. If the man has macho, it means he exercises firm authority over his family, receives respect from younger persons, demonstrates fidelity to family loyalties, values relatives above others, and masters the tasks that men are responsible for—be it cutting wood or practicing law.

Machismo had been attacked as a domination of women, but that has not been necessarily true, even though there is a glaring double standard in sexual behavior. Women, however, often serve in public office. In 1962, of the seventy-six municipios surrounding San Juan, Puerto Rico, ten had women mayors. Dona Felisa Rincon de Gautier ruled San Juan itself for twenty years.

The Latin personality has suffered greatly in the American melting pot. When a daughter wants to be "an American girl" and go on dates unchaperoned, the father may see himself as a moral failure. If the wife finds work while the husband cannot the man may say he is "castrated." If the son becomes involved with a street gang or turns to drugs the father may blame himself for losing control of the family.

To Latins, the most difficult aspect of American thought is the prejudice tied to skin color. Due to racial intermarriage, a single Puerto Rican family might offer every color variant from black to white. Some sociologists have said that "whiteness" in Puerto Rico depends on a person's social standing rather than his skin color.

In the U. S., the Puerto Ricans were regarded as near-black, but they identified themselves with the Italian or Jewish situation of forty years ago. Few of them settled in the South.

The Mexicans, however, were forced to live with racism, especially in Texas and southern California, where movie theaters and restaurants were split into "Mexican" and "white" sections up until the late 1940s. Discrimination still exists.

A Mexican-American lawyer, James de Anda, surveyed the compositions of courtroom juries sitting on civil cases in 1967. He reported that even though 45 percent of the residents of Nueces County around Corpus Christi, Texas, had Spanish surnames, only 5 percent of the jurors were of Latin extraction. According to De Anda, discriminatory practices were ended the following year, there was a 40 percent increase in Mexican-American jurors, and the trial verdicts changed radically.

He charged that Chicanos are kept off juries in other places, especially when the plaintiff has a Spanish name. One civil suit ended with a hung (undecided) jury when one of the jurors reportedly held out because "no Mexican is worth $10,000."

Another illustration arose from the 1967 killing of a San Antonio resident in an altercation with a law officer. After investigating charges of wrong-doing, the Justice Department closed the file with the notation that "prosecution of a white police officer for killing a Mexican would have little chance of success in the southern district of Texas."

Indeed, lack of rapport with police is one of the most critical problems of the Latins. In extreme moments, Chicano militants have accused law officers of genocide.

Like school administrators, police officers are authority figures in a system that has often been viewed as oppressive. To compound problems, there are few policemen of Latin origin.

In many cases, therefore, Latins and police confront each other without even the advantage of speaking the same language.

A federal study issued in 1970 reported that in the 243 police departments in five southwestern states only 5.7 percent of police personnel were Latins, while the Spanish-speaking population of those states was 11.8 percent. Even more disproportionate is the percentage of Latin policemen in Chicago. A government study released in September of 1972 said Latins represent 7 percent of the city's population but only 1 percent of the police force.

The obstacle appears to be in meeting police requirements rather than the lack of recruits. According to the report, 353 took police examinations, which is a number more than double the size of the Latin segment of the Chicago force.

The multiple-choice test given candidates, "disqualifies about 70 percent of the black and Spanish-American candidates, but only about 35 to 40 percent of other candidates," the report said.

But it was the physical examinations that shoved Latins aside "at almost twice the rate" of other candidates. Although the height requirements have been dropped to 5 feet 7 inches, the study concluded that "the main cause of rejection of Spanish-Americans [50%] continues to be height."

This rejection rate poses serious problems for police because the need for bilingual officers in Spanish neighborhoods far exceeds the number of suitable recruits.

Lieutenant Steven Flaherty of the Chicago police personnel headquarters said: "I think we're one generation too soon. Those who speak Spanish can't speak English. We tried to run a special course, but they didn't even seem able to learn how to fill out the right form."

The language problem poses not only an obstacle but the strongest point of disagreement between the Latin population and the public schools. In 1969, 80 percent of the Mexican-

American students dropped out of Texas high schools. The figure was 73.5 percent in California, 76 percent in Illinois, and 57 percent in New York City. And 86 percent of those who remained in the New York schools lagged behind in reading levels for their age and grade.

Many Mexican-Americans, living in the border regions of the Southwest, and Puerto Ricans, who only recently emigrated, stick to their mother language because they have not had an opportunity to master English or they remain tied to their former culture while living in isolated colonies.

A 1965 study made in San Antonio revealed that 71 percent of the husbands and wives interviewed spoke only Spanish to each other; 94 percent of the grandparents communicated with their children in that language; and 89 percent talked to their grandchildren in Spanish only.

School officials previously tried to break down the language barrier by outlawing the use of Spanish in every phase of school life, despite the fact that in some districts enrollments were 80 to 90 percent Mexican-American. In a south Texas school, children who were caught speaking Spanish were forced to kneel on the playground and beg forgiveness. Unable to speak either language, thousands of children become prisoners of the educational system.

Occasionally educators have tested the intelligence level of Spanish-speaking children in English and then placed them in classes for the mentally retarded on the basis of the inaccurate scores.

Ysidro Ramon Macias, editor of the Chicano magazine *El Pocho Che,* published in Oakland, California, claimed that two thirds of the students in classes for the mentally handicapped in one southern California district in 1970 were Mexican-Americans. Most were not handicapped at all—except in their ability to read and understand test questions written in what was, to them, a foreign language, English.

The rural legal Assistance Foundation sued the board of education in California Monterey County for damages done to a group of Mexican-American pupils, ranging in age from eight to thirteen, who were placed in classes for the Educably Mentally Handicapped on the basis of IQ tests written in English. After being retested in Spanish, the suit charged, the average score of the pupils improved by fifteen points, but school officials refused to accept the second test results or to retest the children themselves. A court settlement was reached in a different case in San Diego in September, 1972. Attorneys representing twenty Mexican-American and black students argued that the city's Unified School System had no right to place their clients in special classes on the basis of standard IQ tests designed for white, middle-class students. The school district did not admit fault, but it did agree to a settlement, approved by the United States District Court, under which 2,500 improperly placed students will receive a token payment of $1 each. Moreover, the district promised to eliminate "racial, cultural, environmental or linguistic bias" from all future testing.

These students represent extreme cases where children are condemned to a future with little opportunity, but even those who escape the stigma of low educational status may develop psychological problems. Some Latin educators have argued that a child can develop an inferiority complex because of cultural prejudice. A thirteen-year-old Mexican-American girl wrote an essay entitled "Me" as an English assignment in her Southwestern school. She was an honor student, a member of the band, outstanding in girls' athletics, popular with fellow students, and admired by teachers. Instructors thought she was free of problems until they read her essay:

> To begin with I am Mexican. That sentence has a scent of bitterness as it is written. I feel that if it weren't for my nationality, I would accomplish more. My being a Mexican has brought about my lack of initiative. No matter what I attempt to do, my dark skin always makes me feel that I will fail. Another thing that gripes me is that I am such a coward. I absolutely will not fight for something even when I know I am right. I do not have the vocabulary that it would take to express myself strongly enough. Many people, including most of my teachers, have tried to tell me I'm a leader. Well, I know better! Just because I get better grades than most of my fellow Mexicans doesn't mean a thing.

Recognizing the need to cut through the walls of silence encasing Latin children, the federal government began promoting bilingual language teaching in the late 1960's. Congress provided $15 million for school programs using Spanish to teach English. And school districts around the nation began experimenting with bicultural as well as bilingual programs.

In 1968, the San Antonio schools concentrated on upgrading a child's fluency in Spanish so that the transition to English would be easier. The initial program ended in 4th grade, but some children had achieved a 5th grade reading level instead of the usual lagging of at least one year behind.

San Diego devised a program of teaching English as a second language. The program has been used as a demonstration project for other school districts to use as a model. The first completely bilingual grade school was opened in New Jersey in 1969.

The need for more bilingualism was underlined by Senator Adlai Stevenson of Illinois who has pledged to fight for more money from Congress. "They cannot become part of society without their birthright—an education," he said. "And they cannot receive an education in a tongue they do not understand."

However, the bilingual effort has lagged behind expectations. Despite increases in the numbers of Spanish-speaking teachers and counselors, there is a persistent shortage. Only 800 of New York City's 57,000 teachers are bilingual, enabling them to reach about 4,200 of the school system's 100,000 Puerto Rican students.

In Chicago, only 1.2 percent of the city's 25,733 teachers were listed as Spanish-speaking in April of 1972, while 12 percent of the student population is Latin.

The Spanish-speaking, unlike other immigrant groups in the past, have time working against them. The Greeks, Italians, and Poles were able to wait a generation or two for the public schools to catch up to their needs. Today's Puerto Ricans and culturally isolated Mexican-Americans must compete within the modern education explosion that has made high school and college degrees mandatory for entrance into the job market. The Latin youngsters are caught between an increased pressure in job competition and the indifference of some school officials who simply do not expect them to survive the educational process.

"Only a small percentage will go on [to college]," said the

Reverend Jose Burgos of Chicago in 1968. "High schools are crippling places for our young people. They don't drop out, they're pushed out. These schools are forty years behind—they think the community is still all white and middle class."

A Puerto Rican self-help group, Aspira, began helping high school graduates enter college in 1961. First organized in New York and then in Chicago, the organization motivated 800 Latin youngsters to attend universities in 1972. In 1971, however, less than 2 percent of the students in Chicago-area colleges were Latin.

Also, the employment situation has grown grimmer as the nation suffers through unemployment, and inflation eats away what little the poor do earn. The 1970 census placed 35.1 percent of New York City's Puerto Rican families below the poverty line of $3,743 for a family of four. The figure was 24 percent for black families and 8.9 percent for whites.

Unemployment estimates ranged up to 50 percent in the large Spanish-speaking community of Bridgeport, Connecticut, even though Latins make up only 15 percent of the population.

The median income of Mexican-Americans in November, 1969, was $5,488—70 percent of the national median. Chicano unemployment almost doubles the national figure, and the Mexican-American middle class is small when compared to whites and blacks. Chicanos owned 1 percent of United States businesses and only three of its 13,500 commercial banks in 1971.

The Equal Employment Opportunity Commission issued a report in May, 1970, saying that the lack of job opportunities for Latins amounted to an outright caste system. "There is evidence of a job caste that walls off white-collar jobs from minority workers," the report stated. "When we speak of poverty, too often we hear of Birmingham [Ala.]—blacks—the South. But the poorest city in the nation is San Antonio, followed by El Paso and Corpus Christi."

One of the commission members, Vincent T. Ximenes, recommended that stronger legal steps be taken to cut off the flow of cheap labor from Mexico, forcing industry to employ more Spanish-speaking Americans.

The Chicano way of life in the cities mentioned by the commission is pitiful at best. A Citizens Board of Inquiry into Hunger and Malnutrition estimated in 1965 that 150,000 San Antonio residents went hungry. Sixteen people starved to death that year. Some mothers were so anemic that they were automatically given blood transfusions before giving birth. Mothers on return visits to postnatal clinics brought in infants weighing less than they did at birth.

The national unemployment rate in November of 1966 was 3.7 percent. It was 4.2 percent for all of San Antonio and 8 percent in that city's Mexican barrio. A staggering 47.4 percent of the Mexican-Americans were employed in jobs below their capabilities and needs, and another 15 percent of the Chicano jobless were not even officially listed.

The average family income in San Antonio's Mexican barrios was $2,876 in 1966 compared with the national level of $6,300.

Economic self-development has proven so difficult that the concept has been bitterly characterized as one Chicano selling tacos to another.

Latin problems are lumped together with those of the blacks by government agencies, so the two groups must compete for poverty dollars. The black civil rights movement has inspired many of the Latin militants, but it has also left them slightly back in the shadows.

The situations of the two groups is one of contrast rather than similarity. "We didn't come here [to America], we started here," says Ricardo Romero, leader of the Denver-based Crusade for Justice, a militant Chicano group. "Our roots are deep and we won't relinquish them."

A member of the Colorado Economic Development Association, Edward Lucero, said, "We're two different cultures with different philosophies, but we both have stomachs and we get hungry. We don't have the color problem. We have an economic problem. Any Chicano with money can move anywhere in town. We're a little more pacified. But the younger people, they're turning toward militancy."

The presence of poverty in the midst of plenty has led to pressures that have created identity crises within the Latin population. Following the lead of black militancy, Chicano youths of the Brown Berets in the West and the Puerto Rican Young Lords in the East have startled their pacified parents by confrontation with the Anglo. The Latins tended to be conservative in the past, thinking of authority figures such as judges and school principals as honorable men of the community rather than faceless targets of protest. Now the tactics of the young upset the older generation.

The restlessness of the young, however, has played a large part in making "brown power" a reality.

Jose Angel Gutierrez, 27, developed the Mexican-American Youth Organization (MAYO) in the late 1960's in south Texas. MAYO led a 1,700-student boycott against the Crystal City, Texas, school system in 1967. The rebellious Chicano students demanded more bilingual courses, the introduction of brown studies, and an end to discriminatory methods of picking cheerleaders, homecoming queen candidates, and baton twirlers.

The walkout served as a prelude to a massive voter registration campaign conducted by another group Gutierrez helped found, La Raza Unida (United Race), which later developed into the main Chicano political party.

La Raza Unida and MAYO succeeded in a quiet revolution in the 1968 Crystal City elections, winning not only school board presidency and two school board posts, but three city council seats and the positions of county clerk, county treasurer, two justices of the peace, and a county judgeship.

The Chicano youth movement gained a national outlook the following year in Denver when Rodolfo (Corkey) Gonzales, founder of the Crusade for Justice in 1966, organized a nationwide youth conference. Youths came from as far away as Alaska and Florida, but a week before the conference convened a confrontation developed in the city's rotting westside Mexican barrio.

A teacher had allegedly told his students that "Mexicans are dumb because they eat beans. If you eat Mexican food, you'll become stupid like Mexicans."

A massive walkout by Mexican-American students was followed by a riot when the students tried to reenter the school to present demands for the employment of more Chicano teachers.

Not only were additional teachers hired, but the school board found $150,000 in improvement funds for the school that local officials had previously claimed did not exist.

Flushed with victory, the young people opened their liberation conference and proclaimed the "Spiritual Plan of Aztlan," a manifesto that denounces "gringo" domination and calls for a rebirth of the "bronze people."

Gonzales himself is a symbol of brown revolt. A former prize fighter and rising Democratic politician, he had swiftly risen above the ghetto's miseries, but he rejected the Anglo's form of success and all its entrapments.

Leading the Crusade, Gonzales has preached autonomy for Latins in the barrios of Denver. His organization runs its own bilingual school, operates several small businesses, and harbors grand plans for several Chicano farms that will supply a Chicano market.

The organization calls attention to the plight of the Mexican-American with a variety of methods. In 1967, Gonzales chose the mayoral election as a stage for protest. He ran for office with the sole purpose of suing the victor for violating the election funding law. The maneuver enabled Gonzales to subpoena 50 of Denver's leading citizens, who were forced to sit in the courthouse until the judge ruled the law to be out of date.

"Let them know what it feels like when we sit around waiting in welfare offices," Gonzales said.

Another Chicano leader using the courts as a weapon was Reies Lopez Tijerina, who has led a land restoration fight in New Mexico. His cause is to reclaim huge parcels of land guaranteed to defeated Mexicans after the Mexican-American War of 1846 to 1848. At present, 2 percent of the 100 million acres protected by the 1848 treaty of Guadalupe-Hidalgo is actually in the hands of legal Mexican heirs. The rest is in the form of private developments and state parks that function as the backbone of New Mexico's chief industry—tourism.

There is little question that the treaty was ignored and the land stolen, but 120 years of Anglo ownership is hard to undo and observers believe the government will spend millions to repay the heirs.

The grass roots efforts of Gonzales, Tijerina, and Cesar Chavez among the migrant workers was paralleled by the quieter work of more establishment-oriented groups such as the Political Association of Spanish-Speaking Organizations, the League of Latin American Citizens, the Mexican-American Political Organization, and the American GI Forum.

The foundation for Latin political activism was laid during World War II when thousands of Mexican-Americans and Puerto Ricans advanced to leadership positions in the armed services and then obtained college educations under the GI Bill.

For the first time in their lives many Latins were treated as equals. The acquisition of leadership skills, combined with advanced learning, taught them how to walk down the corridors of power.

The Chicanos, who have traditionally voted Democratic, organized an overwhelming "Viva Kennedy" campaign in 1960 that later earned them government posts in California and the nation's capital.

An ingrained distrust of government and lack of fluency in English had previously diminished Latin voting power; but the Voting Rights Act of 1965 removed language requirements, paving the way for Chicano and Puerto Rican political independence.

The Latins discovered that they could act as a swing bloc, influencing elections in districts they heavily populate such as Texas, southern California, and New York City.

Chicano leaders claim credit for the election of Senator John G. Tower of Texas, a Republican who broke the Democratic Party's firm hold on state politics. This potential of brown power on election day was not lost on other politicians, including President Richard Nixon who ordered his staff in 1971 to raise the percentage of Latin job holders in the federal bureaucracy from 2.8 to 7 percent.

The President announced the creation of 35 high-level posts, paying $25,000 a year, for Latins and appointed Phillip Sanchez to the powerful position as director of the Office of Economic Opportunity. Another Mexican-American, Mrs. Romana Banuelos, became the United States Treasurer, a position of honor if not power.

The Latins could be a potent political force by 1976, or sooner, because 18-year-olds can now vote and the Latins are the nation's youngest minority.

Senator George McGovern was mindful of this during a Presidential campaign sweep through New Mexico in 1972 when he told 10,000 Chicanos and Indians that "there is a better day coming" for them. But there is some doubt among the Latins that that they can arrive at that day on the Democratic bandwagon.

McGovern's Chicano organizer, Natividad Chavira, quit the campaign staff in September of 1972 reportedly because he thought the senator was not making enough effort to capture the brown vote.

The Mexican-Americans, in particular, have shown signs of abandoning their traditionally Democratic allegiance. Many delegates of the La Raza Unida conference held in September of 1972 wanted to endorse McGovern's candidacy, but the party leaders convinced them that the group must separate from the Democrats and Republicans.

Rodolfo Gonzales, who lost the party chairmanship to Jose Angel Gutierrez, described the two parties as "a monster with two heads that eats from the same trough."

"The only results from the Chicano have come from our movement, our marches, and our martyrs," he said.

By 1976, the party hopes to have its own Presidential candidate. Gutierrez said a Presidential campaign could provide the leverage needed to make the established parties heed demands listed in this year's La Raza Unida platform.

The availability in Spanish of any subject taught in schools.

National health insurance and free medical clinics.

A guaranteed annual minimum income, higher minimum wages, and a sharing in government farm subsidies by farm laborers.

The appointment of Mexican-Americans as judges, and the extension of free legal aid to Mexican-Americans.

A redistribution of the nation's wealth and a break-up of monopolies.

The honoring of original Spanish and Mexican land grants in the Southwest.

An end to real estate taxes.

And the most important demand of all was the call for complete Chicano self-determination. As Gonzales later said: "The Democratic machine can be broken. It is not working for us. We must break it down and build one that will work for us."

CHAPTER 39

SUCCESS—WITH A SPANISH ACCENT

THE GREAT AMERICAN success story—retold with a Spanish accent—is alive and well in the sprawling Florida city of Miami.

Another chapter in the rags-to-riches tale is being written by Cuban immigrants, who fled penniless from Fidel Castro's Communist island over the last decade, settled in Miami and today are a large part of the city's middle class.

The great mass of refugees have achieved economic success in a time span and to a degree that is just short of spectacular. And what makes the story even more cheering is that the Cuban's swift climb from refugee to prosperous businessman is due primarily to his own talents, adaptability and industriousness.

Today there are colonies of Cubans scattered around the country through the resettlement efforts of the Cuban Refugee Program, a part of the United States Department of Health, Education and Welfare. New York, New Jersey, California and Illinois have some of the largest Cuban populations.

But nowhere is the Cuban success story as visible as it is in Dade County, Florida, and its principal city.

The Cuban influx has virtually "Latinized" Miami, making it bilingual, and giving it a flavor many old-timers think it lacked.

Although Cubans live in almost every section of the city and in the suburbs, the focal point of the colony is centered along Eighth and Flagler Streets, in southwest Miami, "Little Havana."

The street conversations are in the rapid staccato of Spanish; the food, coffee and businesses are Cuban; the shop signs are in Spanish; the people read Spanish-language newspapers and listen to Spanish-language radio stations and watch Spanish-language television.

Si, Yellow Pages

Cubans account for about 87 percent of the estimated 350,000 Latin Americans in a county that has a population of 1.3 million.

"Success With an Accent," *Nation's Business*, March 1972, pp. 78-82.

In all, roughly 650,000 Cubans have left their country for the United States since Castro came to power in 1959.

Wherever the visitor to Miami turns, the Cubans' presence can be felt. They operate about 60 percent of all the service stations in the city. Companies they own are putting up about 35 percent of all construction, including a 40-story office building that will be the tallest in Florida when completed.

There are four bank presidents of Cuban origin in Miami, 36 vice presidents and about 125 other Cubans serving at other bank officer levels. At last count, Cubans operated 20 cigar manufacturing plants, 45 bakeries, 30 furniture factories, over 200 restaurants, a dozen private schools, 10 garment plants and three radio stations. There is even a Latin American phone directory for the city, published by a Cuban immigrant and his wife and daughter. It has 167 yellow pages of advertising for some 500 firms, many of them Cuban owned.

Other statistics point to the potent economic force Cubans have become in the local economy.

Total annual income of Cubans in Dade County was nearly $600 million in 1971 and since 1967, the median income of Cuban families has risen from $5,244 to $7,200. Ninety percent of Cuban families own autos; 39 percent own their own homes and there is television and radio in virtually every home.

Local businessmen and bankers agree the Cuban influx that began in the early 1960s did much to boost the economy of south Florida. The area was in a recession at the time. Earlier strong population growth had flattened. Commercial development slowed, and overbuilding by eager developers left hundreds of homes empty.

But the arrival of the Cubans helped spark new growth. Dade County's economy became one of the most vibrant in a state which was among the fastest growing in the country during the 1960s.

Major portions of downtown Miami look a lot better today then they did 10 years ago, thanks to "Cuban renewal." As in other American cities, downtown Miami was going to seed as suburbia beckoned many. The Cubans moved in and did much to rehabilitate the area.

One department store executive credits the survival of his downtown store to newly arrived Cuban clientele. "Economically," says Dade County Mayor Stephen Clark, "the Cuban community is the best thing that ever happened to Miami."

Bilingual Talent

Another facet of the Cuban immigration to south Florida has been a surge in the location of Latin American headquarters of big, blue chip firms in Dade County. A major reason is the pool of bilingual talent in the area. Thirty-three companies have set up shop in suburban Coral Gables alone.

Companies with trade headquarters located in greater Miami include Dow Chemical, Eastman Kodak, Pfizer, International Harvester, Johns-Manville, Coca-Cola and Goodyear. Many of the divisions are directed by Cubans.

Indeed, in the words of Carlos J. Arboleya, president of Fidelity National Bank and himself a former refugee, the area "is one of the fastest growing international trade centers in the world." Local air and port facilities are expanding at a fast pace to accommodate a 15 percent rate of growth in exports and a 12 to 13 percent growth rate in imports, he notes.

He cites estimates that a quarter of all firms doing business in Latin America will have offices in Dade County by 1975.

The successful Cuban transplant to U. S. shores is explained partly by the immigrants' backgrounds. They were the cream of their country's upper and middle classes—professionals, businessmen, teachers and craftsmen. Even in recent years, with the arrival of refugees such as farmers and semiskilled workers, the educational level of the Cuban has on average been exceptionally high. About 59 percent of the immigrants graduated from high school; some 33 percent have college educations.

Still, the barriers were formidable. Most refugees escaped with little or no money. Language was a major problem. Many Cuban businessmen, lawyers and other professionals worked as waiters, drove cabs or scraped by at other such jobs at first.

A classic example of the successful readjustment is Carlos Arboleya, who in eight years moved from refugee to president of a bank.

A Havana banker and former all-Cuban halfback at the University of Havana, Mr. Arboleya left Cuba in October, 1960, following Castro's nationalization of the banks. Arriving in Miami with his wife, Marta, a 2-year-old son and $40, he sought a job in banking but was told he was "over-qualified."

A bus strike was on and after hitchhiking around for several days, he got a $45-a-week job as a clerk in a shoe factory. In 18 months, he became comptroller of the shoe company. From there, he was able to return to banking. And in 1969 he was named the president of Fidelity—at 40, the youngest bank president in the city. On the same day, he became an American citizen.

High on Americanism

While Mr. Arboleya credits hard work with much of the success in the Cuban immigration story, he is lavish in his praise of the opportunities he found. "Only in America," he says earnestly in his plaque-lined office, "could this happen. The opportunity is here if you want it." Like many of the successful Cubans in Miami, he is active in numerous civic projects and is politically conservative.

"I am very strong on Americanism," he says. On a nearby table are stickers for visitors with the slogans "America—Stand Up for It" and "America—Love It or Leave It."

One of the most spectacular rags-to-riches stories is that of David Egozi and Eugene Ramos who fled to this country in late 1960 with $40,000 after the Castro government confiscated their shoe business.

They started a small shoemaking operation in Miami with 16 employees who turned out about 120 pairs of shoes a day. A loan of $35,000 helped them along.

They saw a vast potential for leisure footwear in the United States and strove to introduce new production and marketing techniques to be able to undersell imports. Earnings were reinvested to purchase newer and more efficient machines.

Today, Suave Shoe Corp. employs 1,900; 99 percent of them Cuban, who work in a modern 300,000-square-foot plant in an industrial park north of Miami. Daily output is 300,000 pairs of shoes. From sales of 9 million and earnings of $405,000 in 1965, the company rang up sales of 55 million and earnings of $2.6 million in fiscal 1971.

Mr. Egozi, 39, and Mr. Ramos, 46, are millionaires several times over.

Such stories—though few are on as grand a scale—abound in Miami. Time and again, refugees saw the need for a service or product, set up shop, worked hard and today have thriving businesses.

As middle class entrepreneurs, many of the newcomers had a talent for commerce, industry or a skilled trade, and a desire to achieve and succeed in their new country. The Cubans' collective success contains many tales of individual triumphs.

Isidoro Rodriquez lost his $3 million trucking company to Castro and came to the U. S. in early 1961. In Miami he began a catering service to sell Cuban fare to his countrymen who were streaming into the area. It led to the foundation of National Foods, which today has annual sales of $500,000. The big seller: banana chips, a snack food similar to potato chips.

Anthony C. Rivas, 38, was a salesman in Cuba and worked as a waiter in a Miami Beach hotel after he came to the United States. He took a course in income tax preparation and recruited customers by trudging door to door. Later he took a course in real estate, and got a license. Today he operates a $1-million-a-month real estate business, employing 30 salesmen. Active in civic affairs, he says: "We just try to help people and they come back."

Rogelio Barrios left Cuba in 1961 because he "didn't like the Communists." He set up a small, used car business in Miami and perceived an opportunity for quality, custom-made auto seat covers. He and another employee labored from 6 A.M. to midnight. He recalls competitors said, "You won't last six months." Today he employs 10 and his seat cover business is thriving.

Miguel Herrero was a well-known entertainer in Cuba and has built his supper club, "Los Bocheros," into one of the prime attractions in Little Havana night life. Mr. Herrero and his wife and son serve up flamenco dancing and Spanish songs along with Cuban cuisine that attracts American as well as Cuban-born patrons.

Terner's is a family firm, like so many of the Cuban businesses. Father Benjamin and sons Moni and Luis run a company that produces handbags and provides airline stewardess accessories, such as gloves, scarves, belts and handbags, to United States domestic airlines. The company is benefiting from the trend toward career apparel in business and has a large piece of producing the accessories for American Telephone and Telegraph's shift to uniforms for its 600,000 female employees. "We saw the possibilities 10 years ago. We started to get the airlines. We got referrals," explains Luis Terner.

They Repay Debt

Traditionally strong family ties have played an important part in the Cuban community's ability to take root in the United States. Many of the 6,000 Cuban businesses in Miami are staffed with the sons, brothers, uncles, sisters and wives of the owner. And on a wider scale, later-arriving Cubans find homes, advice and jobs with the help of countrymen who preceded them to the United States shores.

Another helping hand was the United States government. Through the efforts of the Cuban Refugee Program, no other immigrant group has been accorded a more helpful welcome to our shores. Since its beginning in early 1961 through fiscal 1971 the program, which includes flights from Cuba, food and health assistance, a separate welfare system and a job-oriented resettlement project, cost the United States taxpayer $584 million.

But federal officials are quick to point out the Cubans have more than repaid the debt. "They have paid millions of dollars in local, state and federal taxes," says Howard H. Palmatier, director of the refugee program. "Their presence and efforts have created, directly or indirectly, literally thousands of jobs throughout the United States—which generate even more tax revenues."

In 1963, about 45 percent of Cuban immigrants to the United States were receiving governmental assistance. Now, only about 10 percent, or 50,000 Cubans, receive government help, with about 80 percent of those over 60 years of age. Close family ties probably help keep some older or job-seeking Cubans from needing government aid.

Miami police report the Cubans are law-abiding citizens, laying to rest an early fear in the United States government that overcrowded and low-income neighborhoods would produce a high crime rate.

Inevitably, in a movement as large as the Cuban immigration, some frictions have developed.

Carlos Arboleya notes there is some resentment because of the rapid rise of the Cubans. "The large majority of people in Miami used to look upon us as the 'poor Cuban refugee,'" he says. "Now, almost overnight, they don't see us as poor anymore."

One major complaint against the refugees is that they moved into jobs that would have gone to Americans, particularly blacks.

Robert Sims, Dade County's community relations director, is one who believes Cubans moved into many clerk, sales and personnel type positions that would have gone to blacks. He also thinks the demand for bilingual workers in the area is another handicap for blacks.

There have also been problems in the areas of housing and education due to the Cuban immigration, Mr. Sims says. The problems of integration in the schools have been "compounded," he says, and adds: "Neither the Latin nor the black benefits from the other in integrated schools."

Cling to Tradition

But overt friction between blacks and Latins has not been high, Mr. Sims says. "The conflict is not towards the Latins," he says, "but towards the white power structure."

Many native Americans think the Cubans are too clannish. Undoubtedly, they do tend to cluster. But many Americans don't understand how much the Cubans value inherited ways of doing things. And as banker Carlos Arboleya points out, the Cubans are increasingly becoming more a part of the community—joining business groups, civic associations and school PTAs.

Many Cubans, in fact, fret about the "Americanization" of their children.

Language continues to be one of the problems in better communication. But the Cubans are learning English. And the Berlitz School of Language in Miami reports a lot of Americans are studying Spanish, about 80 percent of them businessmen.

Cubans, Mr. Arboleya maintains, cannot be expected to expunge all traces of their past. "I can't be a good American if I'm ashamed of the country of my birth," he says. It's not an unreasonable sentiment, an American businessman points out, if you consider how other ethnic groups in the United States cling to some of their traditions.

"Both sides have to be diligent in understanding the needs of each other to make the final blending," says Mr. Arboleya.

CHAPTER 40

ANGLO-AMERICAN TEACHERS, MEXICAN-AMERICAN STUDENTS, AND DISSONANCE IN OUR SCHOOLS

DIANA MACK DRAKE

José IS AN ALERT Chicano child, happy about entering first grade because he knows that his parents value an education for him. He is ready to respond to his teacher's requests because he has learned to respect persons who are in positions of authority. He is eager to learn. But his first encounters with school bring shocks that he is not prepared to cope with.

He discovers that he is not allowed to speak Spanish, although it is the language he can best communicate in and the language of those who mean the most to him—his parents and friends. His teachers indicate that Spanish is not so "good" as English. He must try to learn through an alien tongue (English) that he does not speak or understand very well, if at all. And he must try to learn to read in English, even though he cannot yet easily speak it. He finds that he does not learn so well or so quickly as the Anglo children (who are fluent in the language of instruction) and that he has been placed in a group for "slow learners" and has been labeled "mentally retarded."

José is surprised to find that in his school books, and in the pictures of "important people" that he sees on the walls and in the halls of his school, none of the people look like him or his friends. They are all Anglos.

José also discovers that while he has been taught at home that it is not proper to call too much attention to oneself, his teachers frequently make statements such as, "Let's see who can get this done first," or "Let's see whose paper (or project) is the very best!"

Drake, Diana Mack, "Anglo-American Teachers, Mexican-American Students, and Dissonance in Our Schools," *Elementary School Journal*, 73:207-12, January 1973.

He discovers that his appearance is different from that of his Anglo classmates and that this difference is judged to be "inferior" by his teacher, whose own frame of reference is the Anglo middle class. He remembers how his older brother was forced to wear a different style of shirt and to shave off his sideburns in order to be allowed to attend junior high school.[1-5]

The school environment, in the demands it makes on José, has not taken into account who he is in a positive sense—the characteristics, capabilities, and skills that he brings with him in his attempts to deal with the world. The school requires of him tasks and performances in which success depends on skills and attitudes that are unfamiliar to him. At the same time, the school has failed to encourage him to use and build on the strengths he does have. In short, José's encounter with school is full of dissonance.

Dissonance "emphasizes a poorness of fit . . . between an environmental demand and the child's capacities or characteristics."[6] Thomas, Chess, and Birch[6] note that if a child is confronted with a task or demand so dissonant with his own behavioral style and ability that mastery is not possible, the outcome for the child may be excessive stress. If the dissonance persists, it can lead to maladaptive functioning and behavioral disturbance. One type of dissonance is that "between values and behaviors developed in the home and behavioral expectancies at school."[6] It is this sort of dissonance, with its accompanying excessive stress, that José faces in school. What can he do?

There are at least three responses to dissonance that we often see among minority children in our classrooms. All are ways of attempting to resolve the stress generated by dissonance between what has been learned at home and what is expected at school. These responses are typical of what any of us might do when confronted with dissonance. If the Chicano child shows these reactions more often than the Anglo child, it may be because our schools create more dissonance for the Chicano than for the Anglo.

First, José could try to become increasingly like the sort of child the school is asking him to be. He could stop speaking Spanish and speak only English. He could start competing with other children and more often be the "first" or "best" in his group. He could stop wearing hair styles and clothes styles appreciated by other Chicanos and dress more like middle-class Anglo children. He could leave behind his former Chicano friends—who are now increasingly unlike him and increasingly "unacceptable"— and associate primarily with Anglos. Perhaps at long last the school would recognize him and applaud his "progress." But at what price would José have bought acceptance? Do we want to put a child—any child—in a situation where he must give up his own unique identity, his ties with family and friends, and his own cultural heritage in order to be respected as a human being? Is José's background "inferior" and "disadvantaged," or are we so culturally deprived that we do not appreciate the strengths and the beauties of his culture and the contributions that his people have made to our country and to the world?

A second way of resolving the dissonance would be to take the opposite stand. José could reject not himself and his home, but the school. Let us suppose that José takes this path. What happens? José now continues to speak Spanish to his friends in school, even though he is punished for it. He persists in his preferred manner of behavior and dress, despite frequent visits to the principal's office for lectures and reprimands. He increasingly shows a lack of motivation to succeed, "laziness" in going about school tasks, apathy, hostility, and absenteeism. Eventually he simply "drops out." José has managed to salvage and defend some sense of self-respect and identity. But again, at what cost? The school has forced him to choose between identity and a sense of self-worth on the one hand and the acquisition of vital skills and knowledge on the other. This is a choice that does not need to be made, and we must stop forcing our children to make it. We have pushed children out of our schools by inflicting this decision on them; and we have thereby not only tragically and artificially limited the lives of those children, but we have also deprived ourselves of the ideas, the ideals, and the contributions that many more of these children might otherwise have given to our society and to mankind.

Third, we might find José simply accepting the school's judgment of him and stopping at that. If José takes this course he rejects neither his home nor his school, but simply concludes that those in authority at school are right. He is inferior, he is stupid, he will never learn much, he will never get very far. He has, after all, never quite understood why he did not seem to do so well as the Anglo children, given all the effort he put into his work (in the English that he was trying to master by himself). If his teachers have low expectations for him, he concludes that this must be because there is nothing to expect. He might as well stop trying. José stays in the "slow learner" group throughout his years in school, and he adopts his teachers' low evaluation of him as a person, thus having little self-esteem. He easily fits into those places at the lower end of the socioeconomic scale that the society seems always to have ready for Chicanos.[1] José concludes that perhaps that really is where Mexican-Americans belong.

None of these three ways of resolving stress forces the majority culture to reconsider its assumptions and attitudes. If José becomes Anglicized and succeeds in school, we can happily say that he is an "exception" and that he did well in school because he was "like us." We have not been forced to acknowledge the fact that persons different from ourselves can also learn, be intelligent, be creative, make competent decisions, act responsibly, and contribute to society. Neither have we been forced to acknowledge that our ways of relating to children and of educating them can be destructive. When we encourage children to identify with persons who think ill of them, we are requiring them to develop in ways that are self-defeating, productive of intrapsychic conflict, and tending toward ill health. If José becomes apathetic, defeated, or hostile, lags behind Anglo children in reading and other subject areas, and eventually drops out, then we feel we have evidence that confirms our belief that Chicanos are either too innately inferior or too "culturally deprived" to benefit from schooling and to "succeed" in our society. We have not been forced to see how our attitudes and expectations and our behaviors and educational practices have powerfully contributed to these outcomes.

There is, however, a fourth way of dealing with dissonance, a way that is appearing more often among Chicano youth. It is to recognize the dissonance, to point it out to others, and to attempt to affect it at its source in the external world. Consider some of the educational demands[7] that Chicano high school students made in East Los Angeles in March, 1968:

> Compulsory bilingual and bicultural education in all East Los Angeles schools, with teachers and administrators to receive training in speaking Spanish and Mexican cultural heritage.
>
> Textbooks and curriculum should be revised to show Mexican contributions to society, to show injustices they have suffered and to concentrate on Mexican folklore.
>
> Students must not be grouped into slow, average, and rapid ability groups and classes based on the poor tests currently in use which often mistake a language problem with lack of intelligence. A more effective testing system for determining IQ must be developed.
>
> New high schools in the area must be immediately built with renaming of existing schools after Mexican heroes to establish community identity.
>
> Cafeteria menus should have more Mexican dishes, and mothers should be allowed to help prepare the food.

The students are telling us—in perceptive, creative, and intelligent terms—that they do want to learn and do well in school, but that they also want to be recognized as human beings who are proud of having a cultural heritage that is worthy of the respect of others. They want to be recognized as individuals who can contribute meaningfully to society as Mexican-Americans. They are asking us to re-examine our tendency to equate "different" with "inferior," and to confront and acknowledge the devastating and unnecessary conflict that we have forced on Chicano children in our schools. They are asking us to be cognizant of the different characteristics that different pupils bring to our classrooms, and to plan a school environment that will ensure growth by providing opportunities that are consonant with those differences.

As educators, how can we respond constructively to these demands? We can begin by seeking out information on school programs that encourage all children to be proud of who they are as individuals and as members of a particular cultural group. We can search for programs that foster in children a respect for and an appreciation of persons who come from different cultural backgrounds. We can learn about the theory and the practice of bilingual, bicultural educational programs for Spanish- and English-speaking children, programs that have been encouraged under the Bilingual Education Act (now Title VII of the Elementary and Secondary Education Act of 1965). A bilingual school is one "which uses, concurrently, two languages as mediums of instruction in any portion of the curriculum except the languages themselves."[8] For instance, science will be taught in both Spanish and English, or arithmetic in Spanish and social studies in English, or all subjects will be taught in both tongues. Bilingual education does not mean offering a course in Spanish or English as a second language, while teaching all other content in English.[8]

For the Spanish-speaking child, "bilingual education means the opportunity to teach the child educational concepts in all phases of the curriculum in his mother tongue while he is learning English. This means we are preventing his educational retardation while reinforcing his language and his culture."[4] Bilingual education strengthens the relation between school and home through a common bond; and it places the child in an atmosphere that fosters personal identification, self-worth, and achievement.[9] Bilingual education develops a strong literacy in the mother tongue to make it an asset in the adult's life,[8] and it develops strong literacy in English. For the English-speaking child, bilingual education engages the child's capacity for natural, unconscious language learning; it facilitates the learning of a second language without crowding the curriculum; and it provides cultural enrichment.[8] It also lets the child experience a second language as a meaningful tool for interpersonal interaction and thinking, rather than as a purely academic, nonfunctional subject.

A bicultural school is one whose curriculum is drawn from two cultures. An implicit objective is to foster the belief that every culture is good and beautiful within itself.[10] Bicultural schooling means, first of all, that the academic content of the curriculum will reflect two cultural perspectives. When nutrition is discussed, examples of a well-balanced meal will include not only food commonly eaten by anglos, but also food commonly eaten by Mexican-Americans. We will accurately convey the idea that a well-balanced diet can be put together from the food of any culture, not just Anglo-American. Similarly, the reading materials, discussions, and examples that we use for any topic will have a bicultural rather than a monocultural viewpoint.

Bicultural schooling, however, means more than simply a concern for the "culture loading" of the academic content that we teach. Ideally, it means providing a classroom atmosphere in which different cultural values and styles of learning and being are provided for and valued. Each child will have the opportunity to learn in ways that are congruent with the behavior that he has been taught to value and with which he feels comfortable. He will experience that his way of being as a person is respected and is compatible with learning. Bicultural schooling also means that each child will learn to respect actions, beliefs, styles of learning, and values that are different from his own.

Having gathered information about programs such as these, we can be of help by sharing what we have learned with other parents, teachers, administrators, and members of the community who are concerned about the healthy growth of our children. We can then explore how such a program could be carried out in the school in which we work.

We can help by looking—now—at our own teaching, our own curriculum. Which of our reading materials, classroom decorations, discussions, and examples on any topic are monocultural in nature? How can we expand each of these aspects of school to produce bicultural learning? Do we interact with our pupils in ways that encourage each child to feel of value in and of himself, and to grow in respect for and appreciation of individuals from cultures different from his own? We will need to change our curriculums and our ways of interacting with others if we are to eliminate or reduce the dissonance that we have often created for Chicano children in our schools. As we make these changes, we will be fostering personal and intellectual growth for ourselves as well as for our pupils; we will be fostering the development of a society that is composed of healthy rather than damaged human beings;[11] and we will be standing for a society in which cultural differences are respected and cherished as valuable human resources in a multilingual, multicultural world.

REFERENCES

1. Carter, T. P.: *Mexican Americans in School: A History of Educational Neglect.* New York, College Entrance Examination Board, 1970.
2. Hernandez, L. F.: *A Forgotten American: A Resource Unit for Teachers on the Mexican-American.* New York, Anti-Defamation League of B'nai B'rith, 1970.
3. Nava, J.: *Cultural Backgrounds and Barriers That Affect Learning by Spanish-speaking Children.* Unpublished manuscript, Los Angeles Board of Education, 1966.
4. Rodriguez, A.: *Bilingual Education—Now!* Paper presented at the State Conference on Compensatory Education, San Francisco, May 7, 1968.
5. Rosen, C. L., and Ortego, P. D.: *Problems and Strategies in Teaching the Language Arts to Spanish-speaking Mexican-American Children.* Unpublished monograph. Las Cruces, New Mexico, ERIC Clearinghouse on Rural Education and Small Schools, New Mexico State University, February, 1969.
6. Thomas, A., Chess, S., and Birch, H. G.: *Temperament and Behavior Disorders in Children.* New York, New York University Press, 1968.
7. McCurdy, J.: East Side High School Students List Demands, *The Los Angeles Times,* March 17, 1968, Section A, page 1.
8. Gaarder, A. B.: Organization of the bilingual school. *Journal of Social Issues, 23:*110-21, April, 1967.
9. Rodriguez, A.: *Bilingual Education.* Paper presented at the National Conference on Educational Opportunities for the Mexican-American, Austin, Texas, April 25-26, 1968.
10. Carter, T. P.: Way beyond bilingual education. In *Mañana Is Now!* Albuquerque, Southwestern Cooperative Educational Laboratory, 1970.
11. Aragon, J.: Talk presented at meeting of the Employment Security Commission, Salt Lake City, Utah, September 24, 1970.

CHAPTER 41

TRUTHFUL TEXTBOOKS AND MEXICAN-AMERICANS

KAY GURULE

THE TEXTBOOK TASK FORCE of the Mexican-American Education Commission unequivocally rejects all the basic texts in the Social Sciences which were submitted for examination. Not only did the Commission find that none of the basic texts met the legal criteria, but it also found basic contradiction between the state law and the current state adoption policy.

The delay which takes place between the adoption and the actual placement of the textbooks, together with the amount of time the textbook will remain in use (a total of seven years), ensures that the student will never deal with current issues.

Even more important is the fact that the state policy denies the rights of local schools and communities to select and prepare books or other materials relevant to the students and precludes the use of current, viable materials by maintaining the adoption policy.

The adoption of these books also limits the scope of selection sources for the students and is contrary to the free inquiry method which is basic to the Social Science disciplines.

We cannot accept the validity of a policy whereby the authority mandating the textbook each student must read is placed in the hands of the politically-appointed State Board of Education. Are these the people who should be determining what our children should read? What qualifications do they have other than the diplomacy of politics?

The writer is Chairwoman, Textbook Task Force, Mexican American Education Commission, Los Angeles, California. Her article is based on the Task Force response to the submission by publishers of social science textbooks for adoption by the California State Curriculum Commission. The Mexican American Education Commission was created by the Los Angeles Board of Education in response to community demands.

Gurule, Kay, "Truthful Textbooks and Mexican-Americans," *Integrated Education,* March-April 1973, pp. 35-42.

Under the present policy of institutionalized selection from book company lists, teachers are rigidified to the point where they simply become authoritarian transmittal belts of inferior texts in expensive covers. The fancy packaging cannot conceal the serious deficiencies.

The Mexican-American Education Commission cannot subscribe to this entrenched textbook policy selection. We recognize that within this kind of climate, the opinions of Commissions such as ours are often ignored. Therefore, if texts such as have been submitted are accepted for use in the Social Sciences, we can only conclude that the State Board of Education is using the evaluators as window dressing.

PUBLISHERS: THE TEXTBOOK INDUSTRY

In 1970 the national sales of textbooks totaled a staggering $800,000,000, a sum larger than some countries' entire treasury. Out of this amount, $415,500,000 went for the purchase of programmed textbooks for the elementary and high school classes. Interestingly, the book projection figures for 1980 (made in 1968) were $400,000,000. (Source: Predicast Corp., Cleveland, Ohio)

This incredible leap in sales is defined with painful clarity by Robert W. Lock, Executive Vice President, McGraw-Hill Book Company, in an article that appeared in the *Saturday Review,* January 16, 1971. He wrote: ". . . the most important assets offered by textbook publishers . . . may well be their large and experienced staffs of school and college salesmen, who at the very least know how to find the decision makers."

This in-group of well-dressed hucksters who have access to the "decision makers" (State Board of Education) thus form the golden circle of the publishing education industry. What emerges is a chain reaction of ever-increasing profits, and miseducation becomes the by-product of a successful business transaction.

Ivan Illich states the problem very well in his article, "Schooling: The Ritual of Progress," *New York Review,* December 3, 1970:

Each subject comes packaged with instruction to go on consuming one offering after another, and last year's wrapping is always obsolete for this year's consumer. The textbook racket builds on this demand. Educational reformers promise each new generation the latest and the best and the public is schooled into demanding what they offer.

What has this to do with meaningful teaching methods and learning materials in a Social Science class attended by Chicano students? The expensively bound and designed books reveal several things. First, they reveal the publisher's resistance to our needs because their primary concern is to sell the product to the State Board of Education . . . which means publishing books that reaffirm entrenched cultural attitudes at the expense of truth. Second, and even more important, they reveal the fact that the concept of "the textbook" for a specific subject is obsolete, irrelevant, and a misuse of taxpayers' money.

Further, the Commission feels that minority communities such as ours have received the "band-aid treatment" from these publishers. Are the pictures of Congressman Roybal, the Aztec calendar, and the Olmec rain god enough to cover the totality of Chicano life in an Anglo-American culture? The Mexican-American culture has dominated the entire Southwest history, language, life-style, art, economics . . . we see no discussion of this in the texts our children read.

We can no longer allow the "decision makers" on the State Board of Education to knowingly accept the lists of available texts from publishers, who conveniently use each other as self-validating references, without making them accountable to the historical facts.

The end result of the present policy is a majority of children coming out of the classroom with a negative self-image, stifled critical thinking processes, and a deep disillusionment with schooling. The Mexican-American Education Commission cannot support the continuation of this destructive policy.

THE MYTHMAKERS OF AMERICAN HISTORY

The question we must address ourselves to is that most of the history in Social Sciences taught in our public schools is composed of myths that social science teachers, writers of texts and school administrators have been weened on. Necessarily, it follows that American children are indoctrinated with these myths from infancy. Because of this indoctrination, students have no way of separating legend from truth.

Dr. Thomas A. Bailey's presidential address to the Organizations of American Historians, Dallas, Texas, April 18, 1968 (*Journal of American History*) points up the problems in this regard.

> But even today our history texts suffer from being too American-centered, as though we were the hub of the universe and all other nations were barbarians dwelling in outer darkness! . . . Textbook writers from McGuffey on up have been among the most active preservers of hoary myths. (If they do not know any better, they are beyond their depth.) But if they deliberately falsify the record to secure lucrative state adoptions, they are prostitutes. Publishers have been more guilty than the authors, for they have different critical standards. But we can only look with shame on numerous textbooks dealing with the Negro and Civil War that have been published in two editions: one for the North and one for the South, as though there could be a northern and southern truth, on a take-your-pick basis.
>
> Perhaps the most fruitful contributor to historical mythology is sheer ignorance. . . . We Americans continue to believe that we are a mighty nation . . . because there is something in our genes that enabled us to become great. This superiority complex has strengthened the conviction that we can impose our democracy on illiterate peasants in faraway rice paddies, including those of Vietnam. The myth that we won all our wars in spite of being unready for them, has repeatedly caused us to skate to the brink of disaster.

Regarding what is to the Commission the biggest stumbling block to historical honesty, Dr. Bailey says:

> The myth of American righteousness has resulted in some glaring inconsistencies. Our nationalistic textbooks tend to stress the view that there are two sides to every international dispute: Our side and the wrong side. (Note the textbook perspective on the Mexican-American War.) We excuse our sins, if we excuse them we must, by pointing the accusing finger at other nations. . . .

It is our contention that racist attitudes are learned as a manifestation of our super-nationalistic posture.

We place much of the responsibility on the social science

teachers who seem to be willing to accept the "best" of the worst textbooks available for Chicano children rather than seek out other materials and teaching aides.

It is fortunate for us that some students are becoming aware of the discrepancies between the textbook history/historical fact and textbook political science/present-day reality.

Today, all Americans in our rapidly moving society are in crisis, because we have come full circle. Our myths are coming face to face with our reality and the students find us wanting.

We offer our recommendations.

A CHICANO APPROACH TO THE SOCIAL SCIENCES

We realize that because most teachers do not live in the Chicano community, and few speak the Spanish language, they are literally entering a foreign country each day. The only element lacking is a passport. Because of the language barrier, the differing cultural patterns, the different people, teachers move insecurely through their daily working hours under tension relating to the unknown. We also recognize that that which is unknown is often misunderstood and is usually feared. Unfortunately, children can feel this reaction, but interpret it as dislike which seriously affects what happens in the classroom and erodes the valuable cultural heritage of the Chicano child.

In an effort to encourage a more honest approach to subject matter, we suggest these four basic guidelines:

1. No material should be demeaning from the Mexican-American child's point of view. His identity as a worthwhile human being must be affirmed.
2. The community in which the child lives must be viewed in positive terms and should be included as an integral part of the Social Sciences curriculum.
3. The teacher must understand the Chicano community in which he teaches, and understand his own cultural biases.
4. The treatment of the Mexican-American should *not* be isolated, but an integral part of the United States in general and Southwestern United States in particular.

In an effort to implement these guidelines the following areas of educational development need to be explored: ATTITUDE RETRAINING, TEACHING STRATEGIES, MATERIALS AND RESOURCES.

Attitude Retraining

1. The teacher's primary teaching responsibility is to aim at helping the child discover himself first, and not the materials that promote the "get-ahead" syndrome.
2. There must be a form of training developed, free of defensive attitudes, to psychologically release teachers to become aware of their own feelings and prejudices. This will enable them to become more sensitive to the feelings of their students.
3. The teacher should evaluate for himself the positive and extensive native Mexican and native American (Indian) heritage in the American history and culture. This can be implemented by a more reasonable understanding of European contributions to the United States and the Southwest in particular. (Columbus did not discover America.)
4. Each school should make serious efforts to develop a team from Social Science disciplines and active leaders in the local community to retrain educators.

Teaching Strategies

1. Visit the homes of students; listen to how the families feel.
2. Participate in community-action groups.
3. Learn to speak Spanish.
4. Encourage students to explore the human resources of the community.
5. Teachers should plan activities with their students, encouraging students to express their observations of the teacher and of the classroom situation.
6. Students should be encouraged to explore story-telling traditions.
7. The teacher should reevaluate the learning process and how to recognize it. The self-inquiry method vs. lecture-one-correct-answer approach; authors such as Dennison, Holt, Kohl, Kozol, Postman and Weingartner should be explored.

Materials and Resources

1. Members of the community are the most relevant teaching resources in the life of the child.
2. Utilization of expendable materials such as newspapers, periodicals, paperbacks, sheets of paper, comic books.
3. Materials that are available to children at neighborhood sources (parks, gas stations, stores) open at hours that children can visit.
4. Information presented through multi-media such as films, filmstrips, tapes and/or records.
5. Pictures and photos of people and places in the community, not just judges, educators, politicians, sports figures or tourist sights.
6. Other related materials, not ordinarily recognized as "educational materials."

The textbooks and teaching methods offered in today's schools are not relevant to the Mexican-American community. We need materials and attitudes that are consistent with truth, how learning really takes place, and the needs of our children.

Our recommendations are meant to revitalize and revolutionize the failing educational system. Our present situation is one of crisis. The educational system, textbook industry and Boards of Education must take positive action in order to become relevant in a situation of rapidly expanding Chicano self-awareness.

A Brief Outline of the Events that Led to a Class Action Suit Against the California State Board of Education for Adopting Racist Textbooks

In the State of California, all textbooks supplied for use in grades K through 8 are adopted by the State Board of Education and printed by the State Printing Office. Royalties of approximately $16 million (1971) were awarded to private publishers. The Social Science adoption for grades 5 through 8 are the textbooks under discussion. The State Board of Education is advised by its Curriculum Commission, which is in turn advised by its Evaluation Committees. This has been standard procedure since the 1880's.

None of the members of the Los Angeles City Board of Education were involved in any way with the research and all were actively *opposed* to any delay in adoptions which might be caused by our findings.

November, December 1970

As newly-appointed evaluators of the State Curriculum Commission, Raquel Galan-Gutierrez and Kay Gurule of the Mexican-American Education Commission and Margurite Archie of the Black Education Commission, initiated a team of community people to survey the more than 500 textbooks submitted for adoption by the State Board of Education.

February 1971

As a result of these textbook evaluations the MAEC Textbook Task Force, joined by the Black Education Commission, presented a formal report to the Evaluation Committee of the Curriculum Commission, and urged its members (representing a large number of Southern California Counties) go on record in support of State Education Codes pertaining to fair treatment of minorities in Social Science Textbooks.

One thousand copies of the report were published and distributed to everyone thought to have an interest in the matter (ethnic organizations, state departments, agencies, legislators, teachers, school districts, parents, students, etc.).

July 1971

At the legally-mandated public hearing before the State Board of Education in San Francisco, a large number of interested people testified against adoption of these textbooks on the grounds that they violated sections 9002, 9305, 8553 and 8576 of the California State Education Codes. This testimony was based on the allegations that the textbooks demean and misrepresent the role and contributions of Asian Americans, Blacks, Jews, Mexican Americans, Native Americans, and Women in the history of the United States. The Education Codes state:

> The board shall . . . (adopt) . . . only such textbooks which correctly portray the role and contribution of the American Negro and mem-

bers of other ethnic groups . . . in the total development of the United States and of the State of California. (9305/1969)

No textbook . . . shall be adopted . . . which contains any matter reflecting adversely upon persons because of their race, color, creed, national origin or ancestry. (9002)

. . . shall include the early history of California and a study of the role and contributions of American Negroes, American Indians, Mexicans, persons of oriental extraction and other ethnic groups to the economic, political, and social development of California. (8553, K through 4 and 8576, 5 through 8/1970)

The opposition expressed by this group was augmented in a report by a few of the members of the State Curriculum Commission which concomitantly recommended adoption of these textbooks.

August, September 1971

The Textbook Task Force maintained communications with the groups which testified at the San Francisco meeting and began a community organizing effort to halt adoptions of the illegal texts.

Because this was the first time the proposed textbooks had been opposed by such a large number, the State Board scheduled additional testimony at their Sacramento meeting.

This time, a larger group from all ethnic minorities voiced their opposition to the adoption on the same grounds.

October 1971

At the State Board meeting, which was "not open to public testimony" in San Diego, the Curriculum Commission was confronted by an even larger group demonstrating their opposition to the adoption of illegal textbooks. Many students from MECHA and BSU met with us.

At the suggestion of the MAECA, BEC and the Asian Commission (all community advisory Commissions to the Los Angeles Board of Education) and because of the public outcry against illegal adoptions, the State Board was persuaded to appoint a task force of 12 ethnic scholars to re-evaluate the textbooks.

November 1971

Ethnic Scholars were named by the State Board of Education to review 15 basic and 35 supplemental texts which were submitted by publishers. The 12 members of the Ethnic Task Force appointed are experts in the field of Social Science and came from a variety of ethnic backgrounds: Asian American—Mr. Lowell Chun-Hoon, Dr. Franklin Odo; Black—Ms. Mary Cleaves, Dr. James Banks, Dr. George Roberts; Mexican-American—Mr. Ignacio Aguilar, Dr. Carlos Cortez, Dr. Porfirio Sanchez; Native American—Dr. Forbes; Anglo—Dr. Walter Payne (Latin Studies), Dr. Alice Rotzel (Asian Studies), Dr. Lowell Bean (Native American Studies). The chairman of the Ethnic Task Force was the Assistant Superintendent of the State Department of Education. Ethnic Task Force members served without monetary compensation for their time.

The Ethnic Task Force reviewed all of the proposed textbooks over a period of five consecutive three-day weekend workshops at alternate locations in Northern and Southern California.

December 1971

The Ethnic Task Force report (Task Force to Re-Evaluate Social Science Textbooks Grades Five through Eight Report and Recommendations Bureau of Textbooks, Division of Administration and Finance, California State Department of Education, Sacramento, December 1971), was completed and presented to the State Board. This report found that of the 15 basic and 35 supplemental textbooks, 15 and 21, respectively, were found NOT in compliance with the law and cited several blatant examples of racism and sloppy scholarship to illustrate the fact that the conceptual basis of the textbooks could not be changed without major re-writing.

The Board formed a departmental staff committee to advise the publishers concerning the revisions of the texts. All of the members of the Ethnic Task Force were dismissed from their committee obligations except one and he was assigned to the Departmental Review Committee.

January 1972

The State Department of Education's Departmental Review Committee (four employees of the Department and two members of the old Curriculum Commission—all of whom had previously approved the textbooks) met with eight publishers to discuss the revisions.

Upon reviewing the proposed revisions eleven members of the Ethnic Task Force filed their complaint with the State Board because they felt that although the examples that they had cited had in some cases been corrected, those examples were by no means exhaustive and that *the underlying racism of the books was intact and the damaging effect on children had not been diminished.* They also challenged the composition of the Departmental Review Committee for its *lack of ethnic balance and expertise.*

March 1972

Thirteen of the 15 basic and 19 of the 35 supplemental Social Science textbooks were recommended by the Departmental Review Committee for adoption with minor changes. The Board adopted as recommended. Within a few days after the adoption, a temporary restraining order was sought on the grounds that these textbooks presented an imminent danger to children. (*Gutierrez, Gurule, Hirano and Salinas* vs. *State Board of Education,* filed by attorneys Joe Ortega of Mexican-American Legal Defense and Education Fund and Peter Roos of Western Center on Law and Poverty, both in Los Angeles.)

A temporary restraining order was granted by Superior Court Judge Gallagher in Sacramento, halting the signing of contracts until a full hearing could be scheduled.

Three continuations were granted, at the request of the State Attorney General, extending the temporary restraining order for two months. The State was successful in having the case assigned to another judge for a ruling on the points of law (no testimony taken on textbooks at this time, only points of law) where Judge

De Cristoforo ruled that the State Board of Education should have jurisdiction in the matter.

A Writ of Mandate was then filed in the State Supreme Court. Should this effort fail to get the case into the courts for a full hearing, another petition will be filed in the Supreme Court of the State of California.

INDEX

Date Due

JUL 2 1977		
CIRC JUL 1 77	MAR 16 '81	
APR 1 1978		
CIRC MAR 25 78	APR 4 1981	
MAR 25 1979		
APR 8 1979		
	APR 17 1981	
APR 24 1979		
	MAY 1 '81	
Circ APR 25 1979	Circ APR 26 1981	
	MAY 22 1982	
AUG 15 1980 2 1982		
Circ AUG 4 1980		Circ
2 1981		
	JUL 14 1982	

JUL 24 1982